The 2nd Coming of Jesus Christ

Michael Izzo

MIZeRY ReCORDS

Michael Izzo & MIZeRY ReCORDS
P.O. Box 306
Horseheads, NY. 14845

This book may be purchased in volume, bulk, or quantities over 20 for: sales promotion, education, gifts, or fund-raising. For all information in regards to such printing needs, please contact us at **www.mizeryrecords.com/contactus** mizerypromotions@gmail.com

Library of Congress Cataloging-in-Publication Data is available on file.
Izzo, Michael Lee Edward, 1987-
The 2nd Coming of Jesus Christ: An Autobiography, Novel.
1. Autobiography: Entertainment. 2. Religion: Biblical Biography.
3. Religion: Christianity - Literature & the Arts.

ISBN: 978-0-9960266-7-3
Library of Congress Control Number: 2014905946

1 10 9 8 7 6 5 4 3 2

Written, created, edited, and artwork designs, by Michael Izzo.
For my family, for my long lost wife, for all of my children, and everyone thereof. This book is designed to instill hope in the world; permitting us all to become one with the Lord; creating, **The Realm of Eternal**.

Printed globally
through
MIZeRY ReCORDS & Associates.

TABLE OF CONTENTS........... 3

My Genesis

Facts:

Jesus Christ contains 11 characters and was moved to Egypt to hide.
Michael Izzo also contains 11 characters and was originally put up for adoption in California. However, due to a last minute decision his mother returned with him back home to Glenwood Landing, New York. Saint **Michael Thee Archangel** contains 20 characters and so does **Michael Lee Edward Izzo**. Both Jesus and Michael had a very antagonistic relationship with their parents...

At age 12, Jesus started questioning and rebelling against the current society.
At age 12, Michael also started questioning and rebelling against society.
Jesus has no formal record of his life after the age of 12, until he's 30. This is believed, because Jesus being who he is had to be very cautious of the people surrounding him. Also, some say Jesus wasn't ready to fulfill his destiny; until, his late twenties in which he finally started revealing himself to others.
In other words, Jesus being human suffers from similar but more sever conflictions; forcing him to maturely comprehend his life's mission rapidly; while, unfathomably.

Like Jesus, Michael was also very cautious of his surroundings and environment. Michael stated that his feelings for this insecurity, stemmed from his poor relationship with his parents; effecting his overall ability to trust.
In Michael's teen years, like Jesus, he quickly started following his own path and rules of authority; leading him into the hands of the law because of it.
Through blessings, Michaels encounters with such permanent damaging situations have been permanently expunged. Michael's past with legal conflicts, ultimately created a more rebellious nature during his youth. As a result, he channeled all of his focus and energy into writing scriptures of music; which wasn't obvious, at the time of creation. This gift and opportunity, allowed Michael to create an alter-reality and persona. This persona, allowed for him to remain anonymous to the general public and continue preaching the words of God. As a result, Michael created the alias MIZeRY at age 12.

It's alleged that Jesus also went under a separate alias, as instructed by his parents; keeping him hidden, from the grasp of Herod Antipas' heritage. As the story says: a child will be born, whom is proclaimed to be the Messiah; aside from personal knowledge and self awareness of Gods plan, which both Jesus and Michael contains. Michael's physical appearance, resembles an above 97% shocking resemblance to the alleged appearance of Jesus Christ.
On 10/27/2012 at 2:13pm, I accepted, I am Jesus Christ reincarnated as Michael Izzo. However, I also realized that it goes way beyond the perception of life through God. In conclusion, until you read my writing; you may not discuss your discretion!

The many faces of Jesus & Michael, for they are one and the same.

Above images, a collage of various images in which have been revealed to me.

JESUS THEN

JESUS NOW

PROLOGUE

Michael Izzo was born on 6/3/1987 in San Diego, CA. to be put up for adoption; but, was quickly moved back to LI, New York for reasons unknown… Michael's Grandparents were of German, Jewish decent, and his mother was the 1st generation American. Erna Avramavich was born and lived in Germany from April 8, 1928 to the mid 1950's. Erna Avram, a child of 12 moved solely to America, fleeing Germany, and escaped the damage caused by Adolph Hitler; as it's been told. Hitler's primary mission, was to kill all Jews & oppressors; because he was consumed by the Devil's mission to prevent the 2nd birth of Jesus Christ. Although, his motives are widely debated. However, God knew of this treachery and decided it would be best to disguise Jesus' new ancestors as German-Jews. Allowing Michael to be born one day in a free country, ridden of persecution to uncover his truth of being Jesus Christ.

Similar to Jesus Christ, Michael Izzo also became quickly known at the age of 12; when he was published in the local town's newspaper: As a well known, local aggressive roller skater. Also similar to Jesus, no formal records are kept of Michael's teenage or young adult life; other than schooling and some medical records. However, Michael Izzo being who he is in nature, quickly started questioning and rebelling against society. As a result, he would fall into the hands of the law and even worse; the Devil and his mighty temptations. However, being as blessed and powerful as he is through trials, error, and sheer faith; Michael kept strong and asked God to forgive him in every testament of his faith. As of today, there are no official records of Michael's past dealings with criminal behavior or acts of Demonic pleasures. However, Michael finds the need for speaking only the truth through his music: as a form of forgiveness, for such trials of faith for Gods Will, and the reason in which we all exist today. He quoted to me - "I believe that there are no records of these days; meaning after turning 12, from than and now; because God didn't want the world to remember me for the bad times, only for the good ones. It is only on Earth that we SIN; but in Heaven we are Sinless." In Jesus' first existence, his mission was to bridge the gap between Heaven & Earth, and to be crucified in the process. Michael's mission is to finish what was started, by defeating Satan's evil eternally.

In this autobiography, we shall embark upon the lost chapters of the life and times of Jesus Christ from age 13-26; with insights of Michael's proposed plans for himself, after his current age of 26. Such plans, can only be revealed with time and through the permission of God. However, Michael shall reveal his current mission to us; which is to salvage the remaining souls of humanity, during the end of days. Whilst destroying the Devil or known as the anti-Christ; creating, an eternal kingdom of peace in both Heaven and on the new Earth, AKA New Jerusalem. Aside from his lost journals; we shall see his prophecy revealed, through Michael's music of scriptures. This novel, shall uncover many secrets and truths of what is to come for the world; during the end of times, in order for a new world to begin. These truths, shall describe the outcome for all things; including, righteous followers of Jesus Christ, followers of the Devil, as well as everyone else thereof...

As you read through this invigorating masterpiece and Michael's scriptures; you shall see him reference times of "sneaking through back doors" or "like a thief in the night;" as well as, coming quickly to conquer the industry: meaning the Earth. In addition, he thy lord stated the same in **(*Revelation* 22.7)** – "Behold, I come quickly: blessed is he that keepeth the sayings of the prophecy of this book." Additionally, one can only speculate or theorize that the end of days must be near, with such relevant signs in today's world; such as: NYC – 9/11, the war in the Middle East, the massive earthquake in Haiti, the Tsunami in Japan, the major oil spill in the gulf coast, the massive levels of global starvation, the revolts and civil wars of many countries, the rise and fall of terrorist leaders and dictators, and soon to be the revealing of the prophesied Anti-Christ. In the Bible, under **(Luke 21:7-25)** it states the following: **(21:7)** – "And they asked him, saying, Master, but when shall these things be? And what sign will there be when these things shall come to pass?" **(21:8)** – "And he said, Take heed that ye be not deceived: for many shall come in my name, saying, I am Christ; and the time draweth near: go ye not therefore after them." **(21:9)** - "But when ye shall hear of wars and commotions, be not terrified: for these things must first come to pass; but the end if not by and by." **(21:10)** – "Then said he unto them, nation shall rise against nation, and kingdom against kingdom:" **(21:11)** – And great earthquakes shall be in divers place, and famines, and pestilences; and fearful sights and great sighs shall there be from Heaven." **(21:12)** – "But before all these, they shall lay their hands on you, and persecute you, delivering you up to the synagogues, and into prisons, being brought before kings and rulers for my name's sake." **(21:13)** – "And it shall turn to you for a testimony." **(21:14)** – Settle it therefore in your hearts, not to meditate before what ye shall answer:" **(21:15)** – "For I will give you a mouth and wisdom which all your adversaries shall not be able to gainsay nor resist." **(21:16)** – "And ye shall be betrayed both by parents, and brethren and kinsfolk, and friends; and some of you shall they cause to be put to death." **(21:17)** – "And ye shall be hated of all men for my name's sake." **(21:18)** – "But there shall not an hair of your head perish." **(21:19)** – "In your patience possess ye your souls." **(21:20)** – "And when ye shall see Jerusalem compassed with armies, then know that the desolation thereof is nigh." **(21:21)** – "Then let them which are in Judea flee to the mountains; and let them which are in the midst of it depart out; and let not them that are in the countries enter thereunto." **(21:22)** – "For these be the days of vengeance, that all things which are written may be fulfilled."

Chapter 3
The Beginning

I, Michael Izzo awoke slowly on the 3rd of June, 1987 at 8:06 am. I was received by the hands of M.D. Timothy Riley in San Diego, CA at San Diego hospital; located at 4045 Third Ave. San Diego, CA. 92103. As I am screaming, entering into a world of chaos; a miracle took place, as I illuminatingly captured the presence of the entire room of nurses and Doctors - said my mother. At my mother's request, since my father was not existent in my mother's life; she solely decided to name me, Michael Lee Edward Izzo. The second denomination of my middle name **(Edward),** came about from a woman named Eileen; whom had lost her son giving birth in New York. This woman was a close friend to my mother, during the time of my birth. She had requested if I could carry about her dead son's legacy, for better or for worse.

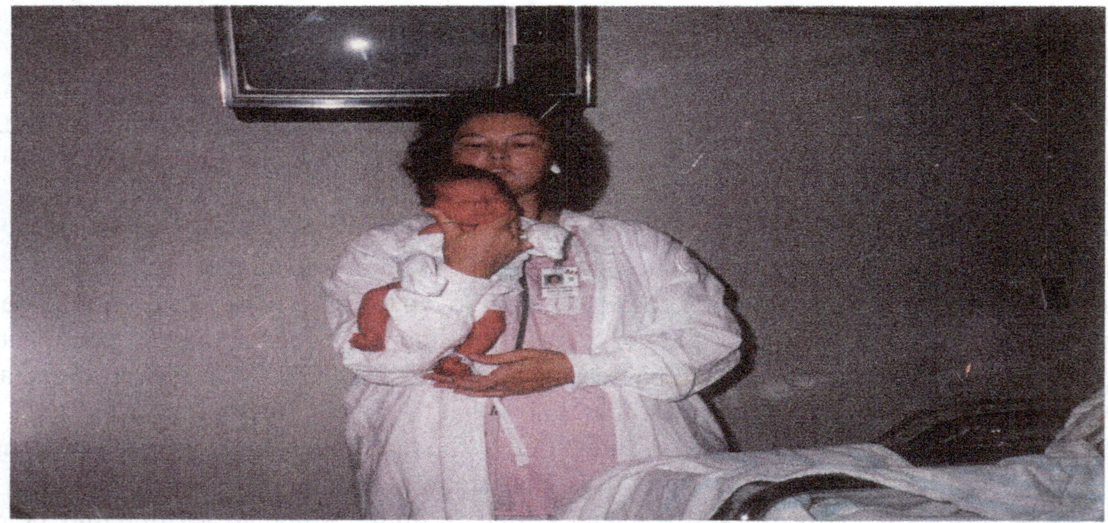

Photo caption: the birth of Michael Lee Edward Izzo AKA Saint Michael Thee Archangel

My birth came about on a beautiful sunny day in San Diego, CA. However, this beautiful day would soon turn dark and grim, when my mother was only in California to put me up for adoption in the place of sin; ergo, the birth code of San Diego is (0666). Due to a last calling from God, or maybe guilt, or selfishness; my mother decided at last minute, to retract her application for adoption and soon return to Glenwood Landing, New York. Returning to her mother's home with her new baby boy Michael Lee Edward Izzo, wasn't a welcoming return for my mother. Several weeks had passed and now I was old enough to fly on an airplane; where I would return with my Mother to her home town. I would soon be graced with open arms by Tina's Grandmother, Erna Avram. However, travesty would soon arise caused by Tina's mother Angelika. At this time, Angelika was conflicted with demonic pleasures and brainwashed by extremities of Roman Catholicism. Tina's mother would come quickly into passing Judgment upon her own daughter; whilst expressing much anger, hatred, and disgust for her 19 year old daughter. Not to mention, this was Tina's second child, by another man, and never having been married to either man. Obviously, her emotions were not that of Jesus Christ; but those of a hateful God or the Devil. However, much thanks is given to the kindness and loving soul of Erna Avram; whom truly understood the very ways of our Lord and Saviour. It was only because she swiftly took action against her unforgiving daughter, Angelika; which allowed and maintained balance in an unsettling home.

(William Age 6 & Michael Age 3)

Until I was age three, I had lived in Oyster Bay, NY with my mother and older brother William. Around my third birthday, we moved to 3 Brookwood Street Glen Head, NY 11545; which was only a few minutes away, from where my grandparents had lived. Ever since I can remember, I remember going to St. Dominic's-church; every single Sunday, with my grandparents, and I was taught religiously the **(Hail Mary and Our Father)** prayers. However, life would soon come to an overhaul of hardship; as my mother gradually disappeared from my life, during my youth. As a result, I was forced to live in Glenwood Landing with my grandparents, my older brother, and new born younger brother Vincent. Unfortunately, the house in Glenwood Landing only contained two bedrooms, but now housed 6 people. My brothers & I, until the age of 11, had to sleep in sleeping bags on the floor of the living room. This wasn't anywhere near a comfortable or luxurious living style. Regardless, thanks to my great grandmother Erna; she made things as homely and loving as possible, for all of us to live in. During my childhood, I can remember strict punishment, religious teachings, and hard times in the Avram household from their German-Roman Catholic background. Even through all these hard times, there were plenty of good ones too…

When I turned 9, I remember having this vivid imagination; which later created, my connection with God. In my family life, things weren't stable; especially with me constantly questioning: My non existent father's where a bout's, why my mother was always on the go, and how I started speaking with the mindset of a 25 year old early on? Due to my vast and quick maturity, I quickly started hanging out with my older brother and all the older kids in our neighborhood. This made tough times much easier, by distracting me of childish adventures and activities. My brother William and I, and all our friends started taking up video games after school and aggressive athletic sports. I learned the art of rollerblading, William learned BMXing, and the rest of our friends learned skateboarding i.e. Lorenzo, Steven, & Stephan. Our passions grew so deep for these hobbies, we found everyday to be very invigorating after school. Little did we know, our hobbies would soon become our lives everyday. Breathing and hanging out with one another, while enjoying each others company, and venturing into a world of adventure! Through such activities like skating, video games, and being thankful for my Godly given siblings; I found coping with the harsh realities of my life and the world to be much easier. Allowing me to ignore my vivid thoughts of escaping such pain. However, this pain would soon come back to haunt me several years later; around my thirteenth birthday.

When I turned 12 the visions, premonitions, and vast amount of mature thoughts started manifesting again, but much more consistently. These thoughts and visions were not that of an average thirteen year old, but that of a man trapped inside a boy.

At this time, I couldn't even begin to fathom why I was going through this dilemma. As of today, I see it all making sense just like anything in the world will eventually. When I was 13, my peers made life much more difficult from ridicule for being poor, from more troubles at home, and because my grandmother Angelika forced her infinite ignorance of Roman Catholicism upon me; without having a choice of what Jesus taught and what he didn't. Angelika didn't allow me to choose, what I believed in, and of what God invokes upon me: through my very own thoughts, feelings, and actions. Around this same time, I also started having more visions, which soon showed me a new interest; transitioning from aggressive rollerblading, into professionally Rapping or writing scriptures of poetry. When I encountered these thoughts and ideas, it was about the same time an artist by the name of *Eminem* became famous. It was that very second, I was inspired to begin my teaching publicly amongst the world. Through this newly founded aspiration, I would soon work vigorously to create what is now known as my alter personality or alias as **MIZeRY**. In fact, I was relentlessly trying to figure out what I was going to call myself in the world of music and in the world; remaining safe amongst all enemies. Through learning about the world and big business at an early age; I've exhausted countless weeks in school and at home, figuring out what I would call myself. At first, I went through many ideas to describe who I was inside, what I felt from all that I had encountered, and all I would soon be forced to understand. Some examples of names I had created were: (Mercenary, Lil Iz, Izzo, Gods Malicious Guardian, Empire, MIZ, and MIZZERY). One day, day dreaming in school, it stumbled upon me, and I quote myself: "I shall call my self Misery, YES? NO, wait! MIZeRY: lower case e. My name represents the pain I have felt, for all the pain of the world, and for all the pain I shall absorb for the world once again, permanently!" I immediately knew, I needed a foundation or company in order to promote and protect all that I was about to instill amongst the entire world. As a result, I created *MIZeRY ReCORDS*: *MIZeRY ReCORDS* is a unique and independent record label, which offers extraordinary affordable entertainment services of all kinds. We are professional and will work with majors or minors; for we don't believe in levels of talent or repute. We work off passion, dedication, and dreams… Over the course of the next several chapters, you shall see a progression in my life and in my rhymes: as we venture into my life, during my struggles as a young teen, and growing up into a young man.

Chapter 4
Rough Life
(Lost Tapes)

I am now age 13, and my dedication for succeeding; has been fueled entirely by channeling my pain, through writing music and poetry. Around this same time, I stopped listening to others opinions; some of the rules surrounding me; and eventually, I would even retaliate against the laws of America by condoning in mischievous activities to better my situation, not to cause harm. As we venture into these lost tapes in which I've titled "Rough Life;" we will see a young me, whom is filled with anger, hatred, confusion, and confliction for the world surrounding me. After each song/scripture about my life, I will also include a summary about each song and what I felt at the time of creation. The reason I will include a summary for every song, for every album is because not all of my metaphors or feelings can easily be understood. Especially not just through the songs themselves. I will also not permit any level of Judgment; without understanding the reasons of my writings, prior to any such Judgment if it may occur.

Chapter 4: Song 1 - Life (4:1)

Life:

INTRO: "Aaiyo, this song is for all of you who ain't got a problem with me."

VERSE 1: I go to school with 3 classes a day/ I dropped the books back in the 9th grade/ everyday I skip school/ go to this old mans house and I rap on his stool/ I'm going to be like Marshall Mathers the 3rd. A high school drop out, stupid as shit/ rich as fuck, and proud of it/ I listen to all of Eminem's CD's/ I learned all my tricks by watching MTV/ I'm going to be the newest rapper out of NYC/ now look at me, I'm being told that I'm the illest MC/ I wonder how many of you are wishing that you were me/ a white boy from Cali/ who thinks he can rap better than Run DMC/ I'm almost fifteen now, but to me there's no point to school/ The teachers are pissed at me/ for not paying attention in history/ how can you tell me to calm down, I got the fucking dean up my ass accusing me for selling some tree/

HOOK/CHORUS: This is my life, if you got a problem I couldn't give a shit/ I gotta keep trying or Imma end up at the bottom of this pit/ This is my life and I might do things, you will not like/ see I don't care I don't need a friend all I need is this MIC/

VERSE 2: One day I was driving bye/ one of my boys were walking by, I had to stop and go say hi/ next thing I knew, I was being chased by the mother fucking cops/ he started searching me like crazy, this mother fucker was busting my chops/ I tried running but he was to fast for me, so I told him I had a license, but then he threw me in the back with no cuffs/ this motha was to smart for any of my bluffs/ ever since that day everyone had a problem with me/ if y'all don't like me, than blow me/ I said that to some bitch and she took it too seriously/ she started unzipping my pants and I asked if she was sure she wanted to do this for free?/ these kids were too scared of me to tell me that they hated me/ I told them that I don't bite, I sting like a bee/ get it through your heads this is the way Imma be/ look at me while I give you the finger, this is for all of you who have a problem with me/

HOOK/CHORUS: This is my life, if you got a problem I couldn't give a shit/ I gotta keep trying or Imma end up at the bottom of this pit/ this is my life and I might do things, you will not like/ see I don't care I don't need a friend all I need is this MIC/

VERSE 3: My lyrics aren't that vulgar right/ what can I say, I know I'm not that bright/ but I'm angry rapper just trying to be the illest MC known today. I Rap once a day/ shit hopefully I'll rap better than swifty McVay/ they call me Izzo wanna know why? Cause that's my last name/ my mom said that I was going the wrong way, but slim shady showed me the right way/ now follow me and you can be just like me but you can't ever be me, because you don't know anything about me/ so get out of my face and stop talking to me/ to all you mother fuckers who got a problem with me, you should have wished you never messed with me/ **Imma one day return the favor/ sooner or later/** For the last time I'm not a pimp or a player/ This is my life, if you got a problem that sucks for you/ don't start talking shit unless you feel my pain too/ this is my life/ and yes I'm angry, mean, and sometimes nice/

HOOK/CHORUS: This is my life, if you got a problem I couldn't give a shit/ I gotta keep trying or Imma end up at the bottom of this pit/ This is my life and I might do things, you will not like/ see I don't care I don't need a friend all I need is this MIC/

SUMMARY – I'll explain it like this. "When I was young, I was very ignorant about my own feelings and anger. That anger, had consumed me from a hateful lifestyle and environment in which I was subjected too. Overall, this is what my life felt like and was like literally with everyday suffering in a broken home. However, take notice to the third verse bolded section near the end. "Imma one day return the favor/ sooner or later/… I was referencing to the day of Jesus Christ's victory over the devil and Michael banishing all evil from the world."

Chapter 4: Song 2 - Struggling (4:2)

Struggling:

HOOK/CHORUS: Maa cant'ch you see/ it's time for me to leave/ don't you want me to find my dad, and kick him in his knee/ Now look it, there's nothing left for me in New York/ why you still trying to make me stay here and smoke/ I packed all my things and now I'm leaving/ so maa! Why you still screaming/

VERSE 1: My father had left me before I was born/ Holy shit I was always left alone/ my mother was never there for me, that fucking D**** W**re/ what do you want from me, to see me fall to my knees, to start crying to the floor/ how about we go thank the lord for making me this way/ and let's go thank her for all the things she ain't ever do for me/

HOOK/CHORUS: Maa cant'ch you see/ it's time for me to leave/ don't you want me to find my dad, and kick him in his knee/ now look it, there's nothing left for me in New York/ why you still trying to make me stay here and smoke/ I packed all my things and now I'm leaving/ so maa! Why you still screaming/

VERSE 2: Back in school I never had any friends/ now what since I have a record label you think you can be my friend/ back up off my Dick/ here you go, go watch this porno flick/ this is where the shit gets hot/ now duck Ya head if you hear a gun shot/ that's probably me, shooting my father in his knee/ now get away from me/ Now look at me, you claim I'm a thug wanna be/ I try too hard to be slim shady/ and that he's influenced me ever since I bought a rap magazine/ shit now look at me, I'm living my life like I'm supposed to be/ I'm the illest M.C. you have ever seen/ I write music cause this is how I want my life to be/ my life is slowly falling apart on me/

HOOK/CHORUS: Maa cant'ch you see/ it's time for me to leave/ don't you want me to find my dad, and kick him in his knee/ Now look it, there's nothing left for me in New York/ why you still trying to make me stay here and smoke/ I packed all my things and now I'm leaving/ so maa! Why you still screaming/

VERSE 3: I'm finally done struggling/ I'm packing my things, and I'm finally leaving/ it took me long enough to get up and leave/ I finally realized that my fathers never going to be there for me/ shit it's time for me to leave/ there's nothing left for me in New York, except my mother fucking dad/ I should have sewed his ass so many years ago, for all the child support he hasn't paid/ one day/ I'll be a father of my own, Ya maybe/ Know this, I wouldn't bet my life on that or all my money/

HOOK/CHORUS: Maa cant'ch you see/ it's time for me to leave/ don't you want me to find my dad, and kick him in his knee/ Now look it, there's nothing left for me in New York/ why you still trying to make me stay here and smoke/ I packed all my things and now I'm leaving/ so maa! Why you still screaming/

SUMMARY - I'll explain it like this. "I remember when I wrote this song, my life felt worthless. More worthless, than I think it would ever feel in my life. I also recall, when I wrote this song, I had nothing but problems in my life from money, family, and personal issues. As a result, I titled this song about how I was simply struggling. For the record, I don't feel that way today because some of these things changed for the better and some for the worse. As this story continues, you shall see these events perspire before your eyes."

Chapter 4: Song 3 – I Love & Hate Everyone (4:3)

I Love & Hate Everyone:

VERSE 1: Aaiyo, my father had left me/ since day 3/ of my mothers pregnancy/ and my mother sent me to an adoption agency/ I had no choice in the matter/ and I grew up listening to my own laughter/ just breathing and hearing my own screaming/ about how much I hate my father/ my mother is no better/ she wasn't there to raise me like a good mother/ no one would have given a fuck even if someone killed her/ at the time, so stop preaching to me as these lyrics are said/ go take care of your 9 year old boy or girl instead/ stop judging me for the Way I am, this is the way I'll be/ as a teen/ so please stop cussing at me/ there's no one who can help me from being so angry/ you might say I'm angry/ or enraged but these thoughts of violence are all caused from the devil and the hatred he makes me feel for my mother/ the one thing I don't want to become is like my father/ a bastard who only gives a crap about himself, and nothing else/ he means nothing to me/ so there's nothing left for me to say, except I wish that he were dead/ the reason that I hate everyone is because of my mother and father/

HOOK/CHORUS: I love everyone, and you hate me/ so that's the way it's going to be/ and you can't stop me from feeling this way/ so stop judging me for the way that I' am/ this is the way Imma be/ and you know I hate you for hating me/ I love everyone, and you hate me/ so that's the way it's going to be/ and you can't stop me from feeling this way/ so stop judging me for the way that I' am/ this is the way Imma be/ and you know I hate you for hating me/

VERSE 2: The reason I hate so many people is because no one understands me/ they just judge me for the way I dress and act towards others; if you don't know me/ you have no right to say what you like about me/ I hate people like Fred Durst: a shit talker/ till he was confronted and backed out faster/ than my father/ this song is dedicated to all the fakes in the world today; I can't take any more of this bullshit that is said about me/ its time to tell the whole world my MIZeRY/ there's not much left to say except that I'm sick and tired of being called a poor wigger/ sometimes I wish life wasn't only about your calculated figures/ or that it wasn't me who had to deal with all these cocky Caucasians/ I'm not trying to be black, or someone I'm not, I just hate to dress like a preppy kid, like those models for Abercrombie and bitches/ and they constantly complain about how they have bad grades in school/ now don't you want to be like me, who just don't give a fuck about anything while remaining cool/

HOOK/CHORUS: I love everyone, and you hate me/ so that's the way it's going to be/ and you can't stop me from feeling this way/ so stop judging me for the way that I' am/ this is the way Imma be/ and you know I hate you for hating me/ I love everyone, and you hate me/ so that's the way it's going to be/ and you can't stop me from feeling this way/ so stop judging me for the way that I' am/ this is the way Imma be/ and you know I hate you for hating me/

VERSE 3: Now shut up and listen to me as I tell you the reason why I hate and love so many people, equally/ I don't hate everyone, I just hate people who have a problem with me/ if you don't like me, than that means I hate you too/ and don't blame me for being so angry or enraged, I didn't choose to become this way/ it's my moms fault for not raising me like she should have raised me/ now get it through your head that I'm not going to stop from speaking so freely/ its time to come out of the closet/ you can say what you like, just know that I will be returning the favor/ sooner or later/ now take a look at me as I give you the finger/ cause I couldn't care what you think of me/ I can't even walk down the street without being cussed at for the way that I'm/ I'm glad that you hate me cause I couldn't care less…

HOOK/CHORUS: I love everyone, and you hate me/ so that's the way it's going to be/ and you can't stop me from feeling this way/ so stop judging me for the way that I am/ this is the way Imma be/ and you know I hate you for hating me/ I love everyone, and you hate me/ so that's the way it's going to be/ and you can't stop me from feeling this way/ so stop judging me for the way that I am/ this is the way Imma be/ and you know I hate you for hating me/

SUMMARY - I'll explain it like this. "During this time period, I recall not having any more than one or two friends and I was always being ridiculed for trying to make something of myself. In addition, my anger and the ways of the devil had consumed my very thoughts and feelings; which clearly can be seen, through my writings at an early age of 13-15."

Chapter 4: Song 4 – Do I Exist? (4:4)

Do I Exist?

VERSE 1: To you do I even exist/ or should I slit my wrist/ when you walk past me/ you don't even notice me/ it's like I'm better off dead, laying next to biggie/ does my existence, even matter/ the only reason why you talk to me is cause I'm rapper/ it's like you know I'm going to be someone/ then this weight crushes me like 1 ton/ I don't want to deal with you anymore/ my body is being torn/ to much confusion/ I'm the focused attention/ all of your attention is focused on me/ what about these shootings in Washington, D.C./ what about the ones in Virginia and Farmingdale/ The one in Farmingdale, NY. Was a fifteen year old male/ that just shows that I'm made fun of to make up controversy/ its like my life is a story/ and we are only on chapter 4/ you've never talked to me before/ when I get the chance, I'm going to even the score/ its cause I don't even exist/ and no you got me clenching my fist/ you got me really pissed/ shit now you're being dissed/ your shocked and you cant even speak/ your words come out all scrambled and bleak/ I just switched up the game/ making fun of you, and I'm taking all the blame/

HOOK/CHORUS: Do I even exist/ I don't know, I'm always confused about it/ I'm always being dissed/ I wonder if I'll ever be missed/ this is how I think, this is how

I am/ I wonder if I'm admired, and if I have any fans/ So do I even exist/ I don't know, I'm always confused about it/ I'm always being dissed/ I wonder if I'll ever be missed/ this is how I think, this is how I am/ I wonder if I'm admired, and if I have any fans/

VERSE 2: When you're always loosing a loved one/ all you want to do is run/ just keep running none stop/ cause you know you're not getting to the top/ I just wanna run till I have to collapse/ I want my life to elapse/ with absolutely nothing left/ how many of you want to make a bet/ let's steal a car and drive aimlessly, with no sense of direction/ life sucks, how many times do I got to mention/ But you can't go anywhere, because of your friend/ all because of a blood packed/ but that's our trust fund/ I still wouldn't exist, even if I was here or not/ girls don't care about me, they just go out with me cause I'm hot/ funny thing is the little bit of friends I got/ are girls/ then my girl is wondering why they are all flirts/ dumb blondes always trying to get with me/ I was like fuck, I ain't no Elvis Presley/ next day they walk past me like I don't even exist/ here we go again, back to this none existent shit/

HOOK/CHORUS: Do I even exist/ I don't know, I'm always confused about it/ I'm always being dissed/ I wonder if I'll ever be missed/ this is how I think, this is how I am/ I wonder if I'm admired, and if I have any fans/ So do I even exist/ I don't know, I'm always confused about it/ I'm always being dissed/ I wonder if I'll ever be missed/ this is how I think, this is how I am/ I wonder if I'm admired, and if I have any fans/

VERSE 3: Do you care enough to stop and say hi/ or you just going to stare and walk by/ well like I've said "one's who forget, will be forgotten"/ now you're wondering what I'm plotting/ all through middle school I didn't have any friends/ I'm just waiting till all this aggravation makes my body bend/ leave me alone cause I have things I have to attend/ if I were to die in cold blood tomorrow/ would any of you feel any sorrow/ do you have love, would I be missed/ always being aggravated; this fucking tight rope is getting narrow/ then, out of nowhere I hear someone yell, Yo Izzo/ suddenly I realize that I just can't disappear/ cause if I did than, I wont be able to reappear/ this one time I bought an airplane ticket to move back to Cali/ what a crazy idea, to go live with this girl Lexi/ to certain people I mean a lot to them/ that still don't make up for my crazy mom/ all of sudden these kids just have been manipulated/ bad parents allowing their children to buy rap music, and now I question why I'm condemned/ back in school I started this chant/ about how I wasn't brilliant/ no wonder nobody cares, because I'm none existent/

HOOK/CHORUS: Do I even exist/ I don't know, I'm always confused about it/ I'm always being dissed/ I wonder if I'll ever be missed/ this is how I think, this is how I am/ I wonder if I'm admired, and if I have any fans/ So do I even exist/ I don't know, I'm always confused about it/ I'm always being dissed/ I wonder if I'll ever be missed/ this is how I think, this is how I am/ I wonder if I'm admired, and if I have any fans/

SUMMARY - I'll explain it like this. "This was during my most depressing time of my life. I was going to court every several weeks, I had no friends, I was ridiculed, judged, made fun of, and I felt as if no one even knew the pain in which I felt every single day. This was the time of my teenage years when I felt like, I simply didn't exist."

Chapter 4: Song 5 – 6ixteen (4:5)

6ixteen:

VERSE 1: I'm almost sixteen/ my futures been for seen/ there's good and bad to being sixteen/ don't have to go to school/ become the biggest fool/ old enough to go to jail/ either pass or fail/ but, I'm going to pass, and never give up/ pass by telling everyone to shut the hell up/ too scarred of going back to prison/ finally reclaimed my freedom/ finally getting away from my mom/ don't have to deal with that shit/ no more of her insane fits/ living on my own/ no time set to come home/ no rules, no fights, no more early nights/ legally driving, this time/ dedicated to rapping/ just chilling and clubbing/ me and my girl/ Yo I'm for real/ dream come true/ just me and you/ barely being depressed/ no more being stressed or tense/ no more headaches, or spinning out of control/ done with wanting to put my mom in a choke hold/ I'll never quit, you might as well fold/ you ain't bringing me down with you/ I'll do whatever I gotta, even if it means I gotta diss you/ stab me in the back? I'll stab you in the front even worse/ you'll end up in the back of a nineteen-eighty Hurst/ laying next to biggie/ cause you a rapper who talked to much/ **don't like it, to bad, tough/ whether you're having rough sex about to**

cum/ or you're walking home, I'm still going to come/ almost a man/ and you're like, damn/ he's going to make it/ cause he's gonna grab it/ this may be my opportunity/ fuck the minority/ were all legal, white or black/ it don't matter we all rap/ I don't think you were ready/ for this, ain't it funny/ its not just about the money/ what's this about Benzino saying white rappers are all sell outs/ fuck that, that's not true, he's just going through mid life crisis, and having doubts/ he's also pissed off that a white boy from the D. blew up/ Benzino, just give it up, you suck/

HOOK/CHORUS: Now I'm sixteen/ prophecies been for seen/ I might be young in this game/ but I'll still make you learn my name/ what, do I look mysterious/ man I told you I was serious/ Now I'm sixteen/ prophecies been for seen/ I might be young in this game/ but I'll still make you learn my name/ what, do I look mysterious/ man I told you I was serious/

VERSE 2: Just a demon child/ who's crazy and wild/ who shouldn't have been let out of his cage/ I got to much venomous rage/ here to pollute child's minds/ with my rhymes/ and make them cause crimes/ don't take this seriously/ cause obviously/ its not the music/ its peoples lives being public/ don't blame musicians for your mistakes/ or you'll end up in a critical state/ with a gun pointed at you/ ending up with blood on your hands and your shoes/ my mom is so far in denial/ I should take her to court and put her on trial/ she blames her mistakes on me/ trying to make me look crazy/ making it seem like she's done nothing wrong/ she's weak and I'm strong/ emotionally and physically/ I abuse her mentally/ and verbally/ with my vocabulary/ unfortunately/ however, I truly am sorry/ make others do involuntary criminal acts/ when you listen to my tracks/ this is where I begin my future/ I don't need a preacher/ to set me straight/ I administrate/ my life as it goes/ that just shows/ I'm in control/ no one else/ I can raise myself/ what you have no faith/ told you I can do this on my own/ I don't need to be shown/ how to walk on my own two feet/ I'll just listen and follow the beat/

HOOK/CHORUS: Now I'm sixteen/ prophecies been for seen/ I might be young in this game/ but I'll still make you learn my name/ what, do I look mysterious/ man I told you I was serious/ Now I'm sixteen/ prophecies been for seen/ I might be young in this game/ but I'll still make you learn my name/ what, do I look mysterious/ man I told you I was serious/

<u>SUMMARY -</u> I'll explain it like this. "This song clearly occurred when I was 16 years old. This song mainly showed how I was developing into a young mature individual; who also knew, he was in control of his own life, and no one else was. Also, in the first verse, in the bolded section is where you'll find one of my hints that the Second Coming was going to occur; "like a thief in the night."

Chapter 4: Song 6 – Verge of Loss (4:6)

<u>Verge of Loss:</u>

<u>INTRO:</u> "I can't deal with this (3x) I'm on the verge of lose/ **(echo)**."

<u>VERSE 1:</u> I'm in a world of depression/ my life's never commencing/ all this shit is too stressing/ not getting any better, only worse/ its like I'm stuck on pause/ Imma end up in the back of a Hurst/ I'm loosing everything in my life; it feels like I'm loosing my spouse/ loosing my house/ my personal belongs which are shit/ my rhymes when I spit/ the little friends that I got/ might as well just be shot/ if I lost her, I would loose myself and everything I've done/ none of this shit is fun/ I'm doing the best to change and do good/ but no one understands what the fuck I've been through, but they should/ you all think I'm just a hard ass/ way to much stress/ that all you assholes give me/ more and more pain and agony/ it's eating me alive/ I'm going to count to five/ then you'll hear one shot, straight to my brain/ quick death you won't even hear me scream in pain/ after all that it will be all over no more of me/ so fuck off if I'm too angry/ just let me sit here and be depressed/ and stressed/ you girl, keep me going/ you keep me moving/ you keep me rapping/ you keep me writing/ you keep me alive/ nothing more to hide/ if I could/ I'd give you the world/ you're definitely going to hear more of me/ I'm going to fulfill my prophecy/ nothing is going to get in the way of me/

<u>HOOK/CHORUS:</u> I can't deal with this mother fucker/ I'm on the verge of loss haters/ I never stop speaking suckers/ I got to keep moving mother fuckers/ or I'll loose everything haters/ I can't deal with this mother fucker/ I'm on the verge of loss haters/ I never stop speaking suckers/ I got to keep moving mother fuckers/ or I'll loose everything haters/

VERSE 2: Only a select few/ have ever felt my pain too/ you will get squashed/ you will get popped/ going against me/ you're lyrically declined/ I'm lyrically inclined/ now watch my group get signed/ y'all doubt me/ but soon, you will all love me/ You're all hypocrites/ my music, Ya you better respect it/ realest shit ever, since 50 cent/ here give me a moment/ to say/ what I got to say/ cause today is my day/ MIZeRY's a bad boy but not like Texas chainsaw massacre/ police are asking, when did the murder occur/ **violently insane/ naaa just abnormally sane/ all of the strain/ is breaking him down/ listen to the sounds/ and the violent screams/ the horrible cries/ begging for help/ he always falls/ love talking in third person/ he hates all of the cursing/ begging the lord to simply save him/**

HOOK/CHORUS: I can't deal with this mother fucker/ I'm on the verge of loss haters/ I never stop speaking suckers/ I got to keep moving mother fuckers/ or I'll loose everything haters/ I can't deal with this mother fucker/ I'm on the verge of loss haters/ I never stop speaking suckers/ I got to keep moving mother fuckers/ or I'll loose everything haters/

VERSE 3: Y'all know who I role with/ y'all know who I rap with/ me, Manny, and Steven/ we here for a real reason/ change the game/ change the name/ staying for all eternity/ some mother fuckers ain't hit maturity/ y'all got to shut up, when I speak/ voice as thick as concrete/ it'll break you down emotionally/ it'll kill you mentally/ causing you to cause criminal acts/ increasing my rap stats/ Yo, don't blame me/ don't take this shit so seriously/ cause obviously/ it's your fault for buying my CD/ it clearly/ states parental & literal advisory/ Yo my crew is forming angles/ Yo I've seen fallen angels/ every time I'm rolling sevens/ they fall from the Heavens/ I believe in Jesus/ because he protects us/ I always wear a cross/ cause I'm on the verge of a loss/ As I pray and beg for redemption from my lord/

HOOK/CHORUS: I can't deal with this mother fucker/ I'm on the verge of loss haters/ I never stop speaking suckers/ I got to keep moving mother fuckers/ or I'll loose everything haters/ I can't deal with this mother fucker/ I'm on the verge of loss haters/ I'll never stop speaking suckers/ I got to keep moving mother fuckers/ or I'll loose everything haters/

SUMMARY - I'll explain it like this. "Oh boy. I loved re-reading this song after so many years, because it truly showed my developments of being reborn and saved from my lord once again. It also shows how I started understanding that my true mission in life was to salvage what's left of our world and create a new one. For example, look at the bolded section under verse 2; it clearly states, prophecy of the end of days. Additionally, I wrote this song when I was seventeen years old. The third verse is also intense for me to re-read; because it reminded me of when I started understanding more of myself, my true aspirations for my life, and those of this world."

Chapter 4: Song 7 - Reality (4:7)

Reality:

INTRO: "I realized that you got to live life day by day/ and not to live in a dream world. We have to be in reality at all times, if not we will not survive/."

VERSE 1: Is it possible to find the one at age 15/ all I know is Eminem did, he found Kim when he was a teen/ no matter how much bullshit we go through, you're the only one who hasn't left me/ unlike, my family, my father, my father's father, and my friends; this is why I'm called MIZeRY/ what's with that look on your face, why you so surprised/ ever since I was born I have been deprived/ cherish everything that you got/ you may only get one shot/ throwing away your life, by buying all that pot/ do you want to grow old in Salem's lot/ all I know is that I'm not/ this is maybe the only opportunity that I got/ come back to reality/ change your life around, be happy/ get up and do something with your life/ stop cutting yourself with your dads pocket knife/ I finally realized that I will always be alone/ that's why I have such an angry tone/ I used to be to poor to afford my cell phone/ up until now I have been in some fucking zone/ I finally pulled myself out/ I've always been depressed, but that's what my life's about/

HOOK/CHORUS: You got to come back to reality/ change your life and get out of poverty/ this may be your only opportunity/ now you're falling just like gravity/ now there's not much left for him/ he's reaching the brim/ he's near the end of existence/ tired of always being a menace/ he knows that he's broke/ and sick of being told that life's just a joke/ this is the real world, it's not a special feature/ he finally reached reality, And now he's changing his future/

VERSE 2: How is it possible for me to be the leader of this monastery/ do you realize how many people feel like me/ I finally came back to reality/ my whole life is going to be a misery/ I'm the leader of them, that's why I'm also a mercenary/ It's like I got my own artillery/ these people just judge me before they think/ their words come out before they got time to blink/ before I know it, everyone is against me/ saying – he's so ghetto, he's trying to be another version of Jay Z, Tupac, or B.I.G./ for the record I'm not, I'm just being myself/ see they got money, I don't even got food on my refrigerator shelf/ fool think about what you're saying/ I know that you ain't playing/ why do you think my life is so depressing/ there are no more tears, I stopped all the crying/ if I don't start trying/ you'll know why I'm dying/ this is my new way of living/ I'm sticking to this rapping/

HOOK/CHORUS: You got to come back to reality/ change your life and get out of poverty/ this may be your only opportunity/ now you're falling just like gravity/ now there's not much left for him/ he's reaching the brim/ he's near the end of existence/ tired of always being a menace/ he knows that he's broke/ and sick of being told that life's just a joke/ this is the real world, it's not a special feature/ he finally reached reality, And now he's changing his future/

VERSE 3: Now he's turning into a grimy fuck/ he's borrowing money from rich and his boy tuck/ he forgets what to do, his brain is stuck/ he's caught in between the real world and the dream world/ if he was able to move on, he would/ he's still deciding if he should/ All he knows is he ain't ever going back/ something's holding me, cause I still haven't packed/ just give me some more time/ I mean is that such a crime/ I found the one, soon enough she will be my spouse/ one thing I don't want to is do is grow old in the same old house/ If I want her as my wife/ I'm going to have to do something with my life/ this is when he leaves his past behind/ no more of the bullshit, I've exploded past the top/ I'm slowly formulating this plot/ soon enough I will get my shot/ sick of getting a dollar every time he mops/ there's no more getting into trouble by the cops/ he gave up on leading this monastery/ I got no more artillery/ No longer the mercenary/ all I am, is everyone's remaining misery/ **Imma one day return the favor/ sooner or later/** For the last time, I'm not a pimp or a player/ This is my life, if you got a problem that sucks for you/ don't start talking shit unless you feel my pain too/ this is my life and yes I'm angry, mean, and sometimes nice/

HOOK/CHORUS: You got to come back to reality/ change your life and get out of poverty/ this may be your only opportunity/ now you're falling just like gravity/ now there's not much left for him/ he's reaching the brim/ he's near the end of existence/ tired of always being a menace/ he knows that he's broke/ and sick of being told that life's just a joke/ this is the real world, it's not a special feature/ he finally reached reality, And now he's changing his future/

SUMMARY - I'll explain it like this. "This song might in fact be one of the most meaningful to me, because I was around 17-18 years old and I finally started getting my life together. I was also finally done going to court for the trouble I engaged in when I was a few years younger, I finally had a decent paying job for a 17 year old, and I also was done with high school; which allowed for me to focus solely on my music career. In addition, I was also dating a very beautiful girl at this time and thought my life was finally turning around."

Chapter 4: Song 8 – Forgive my sins – part 1 (4:8)

Forgive My Sins – Part 1:

INTRO: "Aaiyo, no matter who you are, you go through shit in life/ we all go through shit/ Some obviously go through more than others, some are worse off than others/ **But, someone like me, has been through more shit than most of the human race will ever know"…** *How did I know about my crucifixion before I even knew I was the Second Coming of Jesus Christ?

VERSE 1: Lord Jesus, it is you who wakes me up everyday/ and I'm forever grateful for your love, this is why I pray/ I just hope you'll always be my guardian angel/ and that whenever I get into any kind of tangle/ that you pull me out/ show me the way out/ no matter how loud that I shout/ I make music only for the good/ I influence children, never thought that I would/ now I must choose/ whether to loose/ being rich as a rap star/ and looking really far/ into my future/ being like my father and mother/ arguing every night/ fight after fight/ being stressed every night/ walking out one night/ leaving my babies mom and daughter/ hearing about a slaughter/ cause I killed myself instead/ but I'll never do that and I won't stop till I actually blow up/ I'm not innocent, I confess to you daily/ but I work hard every minute, I just hope that you can forgive me/ whenever I'm in trouble I always come to you lord/ whenever I'm in trouble my Homies will swing their swords/ sometimes, I question why am I here/ but I never do quite question my own fear/ there is one thing I do know, and that's everything happens for a reason/ if not, than I wouldn't be rhyming with my boys Manny and Steven/ also you wouldn't let me keep breathing/ or you wouldn't allow me to keep this gift I'm receiving/

HOOK/CHORUS: Please forgive me for my sins/ because it is you who I allow to protect me/ please forgive me for my sins/ because it is you who will once again make me holy/ please forgive me for my sins/ because it is you who I allow to come and save me/ please forgive me for my sins/ because it is you who I worship, Lord Jesus/

VERSE 2: Forgive me father for I have sinned, heal my soul, & these are my sins/ ok I'm ready to begin/ hear me out father, go ahead and tell me what are my missions/ go ahead and confess/ don't tell me your life's a mess/ cause I already know, so go ahead and tell me what you did wrong/ I don't care if it's short or long/ alright well look, I already broke almost half of your commandments/ now which of them was my worst sins/ but you know the answer to that/ so I won't get into all of that/ from driving illegally to forging checks/ from cursing out my mom, to giving everyone disrespect/ like they were all just puny insects/ that's about to get crushed under my foot/ and if you ain't shook/ than listen to this damn rap hook/ and try to figure out what I mean by it/ because there is no question about it/ If the time comes I'll kill any mother fucker who gets in my way/ whether Judgment day comes tomorrow or today/ cause I'm struggling to get to the top, like Tony Montana in scar face/ I'm sick of you punk ass bitches always getting into my face/ before you actually judge me/ why don't you get to know me/ because if you don't know what the fuck I've been through/ when I actually look at'ch you/
I realize that you're really the one who's the asshole/ because deep down inside you know/ that you're the dickheads/ and you're the one who should wind up dead/

HOOK/CHORUS: Please forgive me for my sins/ because it is you who I allow to protect me/ please forgive me for my sins/ because it is you who will once again make me holy/ please forgive me for my sins/ because it is you who I allow to come and save me/ please forgive me for my sins/ because it is you who I worship, Lord Jesus/

VERSE 3: My life sucks/ but I no longer give a fuck/ cause I'm hoping that something comes out of it/ right now, I'm just waiting for that moment/ because all the Bad/ will turn into good/ from stealing to hating/ to cursing/ to lying/ from sexing/ to running/ to hiding/ to loving/ from disrespecting/ to cheating/ to crying/ to ending/ from being a good boy/ to a sex toy/ to being a bad boy/ from destroying anything I come across/ to trying to run everything like I'm the boss/ or, from you destroying girls lives/ to pulling out knives/ from pulling out your guns/ while I'm smoking weed into my lungs/ from taking alcohol into my liver/ to trying to become the best rapper/

HOOK/CHORUS: Please forgive me for my sins/ because it is you who I allow to protect me/ please forgive me for my sins/ because it is you who will once again make me holy/ please forgive me for my sins/ because it is you who I allow to come and save me/ please forgive me for my sins/ because it is you who I worship, Lord Jesus/

SUMMARY - I'll explain it like this. "This song is when I needed to cleanse my soul and ask god to forgive me for my sins. During this time, I realized that somewhere in my mind the things I was doing was only making my life worse off. Also, through the grace and love of Thy Lord Jesus Christ he would offer me salvation. However, this wouldn't be the last time I would sin. At some point in my life, after I went through more trials and tribulations; I would shortly end up right back where I started; surrendering my life to God's will. When I come to the crossroads again later in this novel; you will see how much more extreme it would be and that it shall be the final time, I would ever sin again."

Chapter 5
The Destruction Lp
(Songs: 4, 5, 6, 7, 8, 9, 10, 14)

*The songs not displayed were re-written on the following album or cut.

I am now age 17, and my dedication for succeeding; has been fueled entirely into channeling my pain, through writing music and poetry. My aspirations and life's work all revolved around my entertainment company; attempting to change the world, with my wisdom, and my gift of prophecies. During this time, things were unclear for me and very crucial if my life would ever exceed beyond all of my fury, anger, and depression. If I gave up now, I would be with out a doubt, lost forever. Around this same time, I had stopped listening to others opinions and to the rules surrounding me. Eventually, I would also retaliate against the laws of America by condoning in criminal activities; meant to better my situation, not to cause harm. As we venture into the start of my music career with my first independent debut album, titled "The Destruction Lp;" we will see a young man, whom is in the process of conquering the worst adversity. Meanwhile, remaining optimistic for a positive future. After each song/scripture about my life, I will also include a summary about each song, and what I had felt at the time of creation. Once again, the reason I require this is because my metaphors or feelings can't easily be understood just through the songs; and I will not permit, any level of Judgment without understanding the reasons; if any such Judgment were to occur.

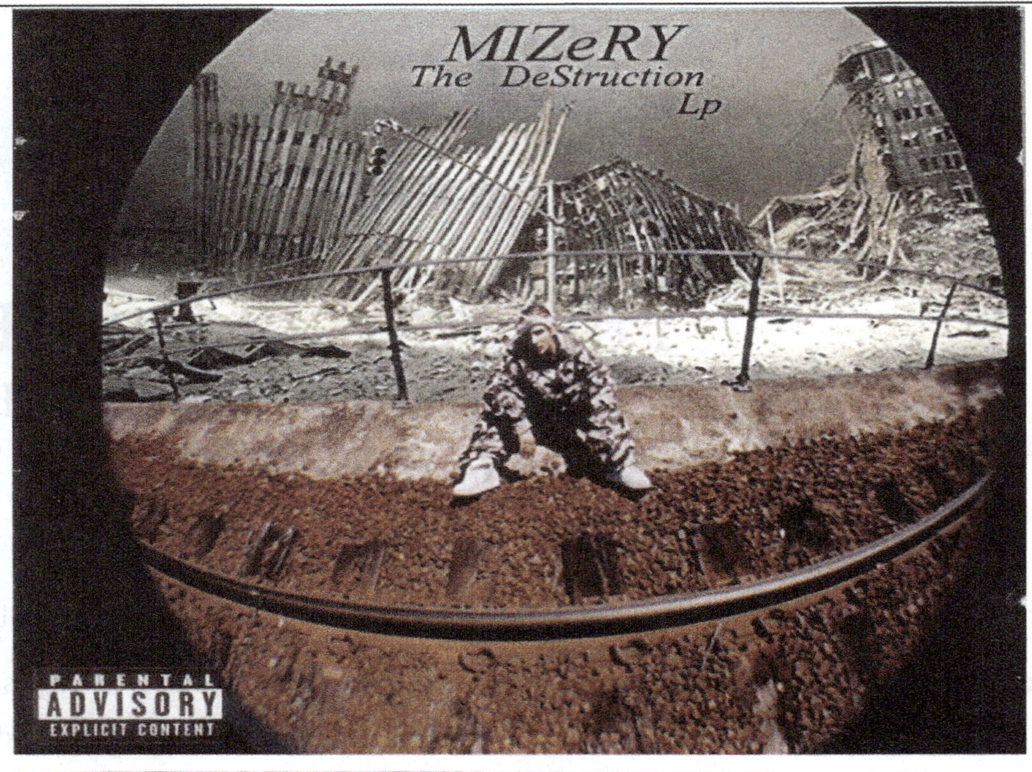

"The Destruction Lp" - front and back; photo taken by Steven Vanatta; Direction and design by Michael Izzo. Copyright © 2004, *MIZeRY ReCORDS* – All Rights Reserved.

Chapter 5: Song 4 – Different Stylez Ft. Sandman (5:4)

Different Stylez:

INTRO: "Aaiyo dog, we two different people, two different styles, don't compare us to anyone else."

VERSE 2: Aaiyo check it, these are two different styles/ we're unlocking these rap files/ of these bitch ass rap artists/ claiming they the meanest and roughest/ Yo, we taking over a whole empire/ by only using fire/ cause the best MC's are starting to retire/ Hip Hop's vulnerable, it's our time to acquire/ using flame throwers/ on these gay ass rappers/ got to get real mean/ and take this to the extreme/ cause these rappers ain't scared of bullet's no more/ and they be spitting shit about, leaving your broke ass poor/ Yo, if you actually think about it they just all talk/ and if you notice they'll be the one's having white chalk/ surrounding their body/ and no I ain't crazy/ I'm just sick of 90 percent of this fucking industry/ this is my destiny/ change this shit grammatically/ mathematically/ & psychologically/ changing this game/ back to when it was just about your pain/ this shit doesn't leave Ya sane/ Le assholes, vano marei, anahadasato/ labuia/ M-I-Z-E-R-Y, ilicose' multe' delore' la-fuelle' pinare' I spit the italiano/ cause my last name's Izzo/

HOOK/CHORUS: 1, 2/ we coming for you/ there's nothing that you could do/ either way we killing you/ now here's our fucking crew/ 1, 2/ we coming for you/ there's nothing that you could do/ either way we killing you/ now here's our fucking crew/

VERSE 3.5: There are millions of white rappers; but, they never made it/ so listen to me as I say it/ because when white rappers get compared/ they get compared/ to Eminem/ but I just don't understand them/ cause they're not being judged, for the way that they walk/ or the way that they talk/ the way that they dress, or the way that they look/ or the way that they write their songs to this hook/ or the way that they think/ or the fact that they stink/ only compared cause we white/ but that shit ain't right/ that's why/ I/ went and picked up this damn MIC/ cause Imma disprove everybody/ cause Imma be somebody/ so bring this hook back in/ cause this shit leaves you shaking/ cause I ain't fucking playing/

HOOK/CHORUS – shared with sandman: 1, 2/ we coming for you/ there's nothing that you could do/ either way we killing you/ now here's our fucking crew/ 1, 2/ we coming for you/ there's nothing that you could do/ either way we killing you/ now here's our fucking crew/

SUMMARY - I'll explain it like this. "This song was my first featured song with any other artist. When me and Sandman AKA Rob met at our mutual job, we immediately became close friends; seeing eye to eye on music. When we got into my home studio for the first time and laid the pen to the paper, something powerful and spiritual took place. It was like two great angels meeting for the first time on Earth; whom were also close in Heaven; and together, we were writing a story, that only God could have intended to be written. "Different Stylez" was a song we collaborated on to show the world that no two people are alike. We used the world of music and hip hop to express that lyrically."

Chapter 5: Song 5 – Friendship=bulls*** (5:5)

Friendship=Bulls*:**

INTRO: "This song is to all my old friends who have fucked me over in the past/ fuck friendship/ cause friendship equals bullshit/

VERSE 1: What is friendship/ I can't deal with it, I just wanna flip/ you guys are supposed to be there for me/ instead you all decided to work against me/ you were supposed to be my friend/ but you made my mind bend/ I'm going crazy/ our friendship ain't steady/ you're a backstabbing son of a bitch/ you ratted me out you little snitch/ I would have never tuned you in/ you were my dog, I would have committed a sin/ for you, I would have done anything/ turned me in cause you were stealing/ to worried about saving your own ass/ get out of my face, you're giving me too much stress/ I'm not dealing with you anymore/ if there's a problem, then get a new friend, or/ sit back and deal with the shit you have started/ you'll be the one who is being deported/ not me/ I'll be here another century/ I just replaced you/ what can you possibly do/ you have no say in it/ leave me alone, before I have a raging fit/ like I said, "fuck friendship"/ cause it equals bullshit/

HOOK/CHORUS: I'm in my own zone/ cause I stand alone/ I don't need a friend/ who I have to attend/ I don't need you, cause I'm strong enough/ life has always been, really rough/ fuck all kinds of friendship/ cause they all equal bullshit/ I'm in my own zone/ cause I stand alone/ I don't need a friend/ who I have to attend/ I don't need you, cause I'm strong enough/ life has always been, really rough/ fuck all kinds of friendship/ cause they all equal bullshit/

VERSE 2: What's the point to a friendship/ there is none, I should just stop/ I've had so many friends come and go/ they don't know what it means when I tell them no/ I don't need a friend any longer/ because I've gotten so much stronger/ I don't need a friend to cry to, I don't need someone to tell my feelings too/ I never needed you/ I write what I'm feeling down on paper/ it's like my own head doctor/ my own therapist/ it's who I talk to when I'm pissed/ when I write I get everything off my chest/ slowly getting off the ground/ slowly turning my life around/ I always listen to the sound/ of the beat/ this pit is deep/ getting back will be hard, cause it's steep/ I never doubt/ cause I will pull myself out/ not needing you to help me/ all I ask is for you to lave me be/ always being independent, that's why I'm so mature for my age/ until now I've kept all my emotions locked in my rib cage/ everything was kept inside/ but no longer I have to hide/ here on now I'm going to speak freely/ and I might do it with a little discourtesy/

HOOK/CHORUS: I'm in my own zone/ cause I stand alone/ I don't need a friend/ who I have to attend/ I don't need you, cause I'm strong enough/ life has always been, really rough/ fuck all kinds of friendship/ cause they all equal bullshit/ I'm in my own zone/ cause I stand alone/ I don't need a friend/ who I have to attend/ I don't need you, cause I'm strong enough/ life has always been, really rough/ fuck all kinds of friendship/ cause they all equal bullshit/

VERSE 3: I've come so far/ but I don't need you anymore/ this whole time I've survived on my own/ people say I'm fake, but the real me is shown/ I'm always telling people this is the real me/ I'm an angry MC/ I mean I know I'm not all that smart/ and I will always have this scare in the center of my heart/ sometimes I can be mean/ and there is only me in team/ sometimes I feel like my life is just a dream/ but nothing gets me completely down/ cause I always stand alone/ I don't need your pity/ I don't need your money/ I might be in poverty/ but I know I don't need your help/ most of the time I feel like I fell/ to the bottom of this pit/ but I'm strong enough to deal with this shit/ I've grown so much since yesterday/ now my life's back on play/ ever since day one I have grown/ I'm independent, and I will always stand alone/

HOOK/CHORUS: I'm in my own zone/ cause I stand alone/ I don't need a friend/ who I have to attend/ I don't need you, cause I'm strong enough/ life has always been, really rough/ fuck all kinds of friendship/ cause they all equal bullshit/ I'm in my own zone/ cause I stand alone/ I don't need a friend/ who I have to attend/ I don't need you, cause I'm strong enough/ life has always been, really rough/ fuck all kinds of friendship/ cause they all equal bullshit/ "Fuck Friendship/ cause it equals bullshit/

SUMMARY - I'll explain it like this. "This song was written prior to turning 18, when I had forged some bank checks. After I had gotten away clean the first few times, I became greedy and decided to walk into my job at a local grocery store. During this time, I had asked my buddy to cash a check for me. The plan was full proof with absolutely no evidence tracing back to me or him. However, my friend got nervous and deviated from the plan and story. As a result, he deviated from the plan and had turned me in; later that week, I was arrested. Aside from this incident, my girlfriend and other friends just disappeared for no reasons. Forcing me to feel like, no one should ever rely on friends but rely on your selves instead; hence the title of this song."

Chapter 5: Song 6 – One Wish (5:6)

One Wish:

INTRO: "MIZeRY, what is Misery? MIZeRY is the anger & pain of Michael Izzo. Misery is the route to all evil; the evil, that every person has deep down inside of them. The evil (echo) that I rebuked ever since I was born (echo), I'm tired of this pain."

VERSE 1: I'm tired of hearing all this bullshit that is said about me/ the bullshit that is made up cause of the way that I dress/ the dirty looks I get, while I walk down my steps/ the women who come and go like my mother/ tired of hearing my own screaming/ and listening to my own laughter/ I'm tired of bosses trying to take advantage of me because I'm only fifteen/ tired of being yelled at by the dean/ the dean who accuses me of selling some tree/ the tree that is illegal that you can't get for free/ sick of these little kids trying to be like me/ the little kids who think that they know me/ but, they only know my name (Yo MIZeRY)/ I'm always telling people I'm no role model/ don't blame me for your son od-ing off your aspirin bottle/ or your daughter stabbing herself with sharp ass pins/ don't blame me for your son or daughter committing to many sins/

HOOK/CHORUS: If I had one wish, I would ask to have been born in a better world and for a brand new family/ But if I could have one wish it would be for a big enough finger for my dad to see all the way from New York City/ but if I had one wish, It would be to forget what my father has done to me/ If I had one wish, I would ask to have been born in a better world and for a brand new family/ But if I could have one wish it would be for a big enough finger for my dad to see all the way from New York City/ but if I had one wish, It would be to forget what my father has done to me/

VERSE 2: I'm tired of not having a job/ tired of having to borrow money for a taxi cab/ I'm tired of hearing my fucking mom telling to me get out of the house/ The house I have lived in for 8 years of my life/ everyday I just want to kill my mom with a very big knife/ but I'm not gonna kill her cause Id rather see her suffer/ I want her to realize that she wasn't a good mother/ I'm tired of being a player/ I'm tired of skating in Glen Cove and being yelled at by the mayor/ The Glen Cove I got arrested in for driving illegally/ I'm tired of always being lonely/ sick and tired of not having any one there to take care of me/ but there's nothing I can do because this is how my life is going to be/ I'm sick of always being pissed off/ sick of always having a smokers cough/ the cough I got from second hand smoke/ I'm sick of hearing people tell me, my life is just one big joke/ The people who only care about themselves and nothing else/ tired of wishing that my music actually sells/ the music I write on my computer desk/ tired of having people tell me I'm wearing a mask/ the people who say I'm fake because they don't know the real me/ all I can say to them is that I wish I had a big enough ass for the whole world to see/

HOOK/CHORUS: If I had one wish, I would ask to have been born in a better world and for a brand new family/ But if I could have one wish it would be for a big enough finger for my dad to see all the way from New York City/ but if I had one wish, It would be to forget what my father has done to me/ If I had one wish, I would ask to have been born in a better world and for a brand new family/ But if I could have one wish it would be for a big enough finger for my dad to see all the way from New York City/ but if I had one wish, It would be to forget what my father has done to me/

SUMMARY - I'll explain it like this. "This song was one of my most depressing and realistic songs of my child/teenage memories and thoughts. Sometime around my mid teens, I had simply hit rock bottom for the first time ever. I then felt like everything in life was hopeless and useless. This song "One Wish" was simply a long list of events and wishful thinking. I had wished change for my life; yet it hasn't really changed much, even now. The key line in this song was the very last one "All I can say to them is that I wish I had a big enough ass for the whole world to see." This line is very relevant because as *Revelation* states, Jesus Christ shall be seen by the whole world during rapture and Judgment day. This line states the same thing in an indirect fashion; but when I was a mere child, I was only speaking metaphorically and not biblically."

Chapter 5: Song 7 – F*** the World (5:7)

F* the World:**

INTRO: "Aaiyo huh, fuck it you'll find out"...

VERSE 1: Aaiyo I take a moment and I stop and I breathe/ cause I just quit on life/ because most of the time/ I'm fucking suicidal/ and my vitals are unstable/ there's nothing more that I can do, there's nothing more that I can say/ I'm just waiting for the day/ that I don't gotta kneel down at night and pray/ I'm also waiting for the day that I could just lay down comfortably in bed without wishing every night that I were dead/ its time the gloves are off I'm letting everything go/ I'm sick of always being broke/ without having any doe/ the more bullshit I go through the stronger I get/ every time this industry turns me down how could I ever forget/ there's no way I'm just gonna pick up my shit and jet/ how could I let/ these pussies emcees, just fucking rule this game/ don't ever forget that I'm the pain/ the strain/ the hardcore lyrics that attack your brain/ you should've have picked up the MIC instead of the ball/ cause now y'all/ gonna see yourselves fall/ I'd rather die, I'd probably rather even get ****** in the ass before I ever dissed shady or fifty, Dre, snoop, or Pac/ man Id rather die from a shot/ I swear that all you do is claim that I'm a wanksta/ but I can guarantee you don't even know the definition behind gangsta/ do me a favor and pick up a dictionary/ and learn how to read/ while I feed/ you through a fucking Iv/ now you're saying you wanna come and try to fight me/ Imma leave you from the neck down paralyzed/ cause this game is devised/ from soft and hard/ this ain't no ball game, this ain't even fucking cards/

HOOK/CHORUS: Fuck the world, don't ever take disrespect/ don't ever fucking forget, what they've done to you/ fuck the world and everyone in it too/ be a man and stand up for what you believe in/ until we win/ now the games done/ we won/ fuck the world, drop your enemies in the end/ as soon as you can/ you don't need friends anyway/ nothing else I could say/ fuck the world, don't ever fall down/ don't ever kneel to the crown/ don't ever stop/ Fuck the world (echo)

VERSE 2: They call me the Freddy Kruger of rap, Imma a killer who comes when you sleep/ man this shits already gone to deep/ man I don't even care if you become Jason/ I'll still be chasing/ after you/ I'll still be beating the shit out of you/ with my five finger claw/ and I don't need a damn gun to break your jaw/ If you friend ain't God's-Unit/ then your enemy becomes a G-U-N/ while fifty takes it like a man, y'all beg for mercy (echo)/ and I've grown so damn thirsty/ I've grown this need/ this terrible greed/ to see fake emcees bleed/ I'm repping the Westside on the Eastside/ with a few east coast exceptions/ I'm not spitting out lies and deceptions/ this shitty life basically made me loose all my facial expressions/ from being stressed/ to being blessed/ to living in poverty/ to feeling like I'm state property/ they should just lock me behind bars/ because when I'm through with these fucking rap stars/ I'll get life in prison/ but I won't be stopped until I accomplish my mission/ I didn't know if I was ever gonna be able to write this track/ because I have slacked/ I have lacked/ the inspiration to pull my shit together/ to improve and become better/

HOOK/CHORUS: Fuck the world, don't ever take disrespect/ don't ever fucking forget, what they've done to you/ fuck the world and everyone in it too/ be a man and stand up for what you believe in/ until we win/ now the games done/ we won/ fuck the world, drop your enemies in the end/ as soon as you can/ you don't need friends anyway/ nothing else I could say/ fuck the world, don't ever fall down/ don't ever kneel to the crown/ don't ever stop/ Fuck the world (echo)

VERSE 3: I'm sick of emcees battling me/ claiming that they spitting/ but everything they be saying is all written/ rapping shit they a dog/ but there must be heavy fog/ in front of their eyes/ blinding them/ forcing them to hide in disguise/ they hiding from the truth/ and don't this shit hurt/ having depression/ while in a recording session/ last time, rapping causes mad tension/ from life and rap/ from a gun as it falls to my lap/ to much pressure on the trigger/ but I can only assure/ if life stays so shitty/ I'll stop being a pussy/ and I'll blow my brains out from a fucking nine milly/ I'm tried of rich assholes trying to take the money I don't got/ that's why I wished they all had gotten shot/ most people can forgive they just can't forget/ I don't even think I can do either one/ especially when I take so much disrespect/ I hold grudges/ I'll never budge/ fuck it let me see a judge/ I've already had time in the can/ made me crazy like the guy Stan/ Mother fucker you wanna pop shit, well Imma pop shots/ that's what I've always said when I whip out my glock/ on this whole entire fucking world/

HOOK/CHORUS: Fuck the world, don't ever take disrespect/ don't ever fucking forget, what they've done to you/ fuck the world and everyone in it too/ be a man and stand up for what you believe in/ until we win/ now the games done/ we won/ fuck the world, drop your enemies in the end/ as soon as you can/ you don't need friends anyway/ nothing else I could say/ fuck the world, don't ever fall down/ don't ever kneel to the crown/ don't ever stop/ Fuck the world (echo)…
"Aaiyo dog, on the real, fuck everything. Fuck girls, fuck money, fuck life itself man, seriously right now, fuck the world/ I mean that shit man/ I'm just sick of people coming up to me; you know trying to be Yo man what's up dog. You know, they saying they my dog and shit, Yo these mother fuckers don't have my back and I don't have your back. All I got to do is worry about my self and that's it. I've got my own mother fucking back man."

SUMMARY – I'll explain it like this. "F*** the world" was definitely one of my most intense and hateful records written. The reasons for this record were a clear indicator of *Revelation* type thoughts and anger against the world. Anger because of my crucifixion and exploiting my original mission and purpose. Including, the rough life I was forced into during my second term of existence. This song was simply to inspire the youth and people to not trust anyone, but yourselves. In addition, follow a path of righteousness indirectly; because the world will turn its back on you as it did to me then and now."

Chapter 5: Song 8 – I miss you (5:8)

I miss you (dedicated to Linda Krawec):

INTRO: "This is dedicated to, Linda Krawec. You were always there, when I needed somebody. I miss you so damn much."

VERSE 1: You had passed away/ mid two thousand and three (2003)/ all I kept saying, was this can't be/ it felt like a damn dream/ I never saw it coming/ I still question, why did it have to happen/ but no matter what, I'll always keep on rapping/ you always told me not to quit, even if this shit got to deep/ or if this fucking mountain was to steep/ and always stay unique/ and not let anyone take away my talent/ not even for the very slightest fucking moment/ I remember all the damn times that we had together/ the times, the times, that I'll remember forever/ just you, Kim, and me/ count em 1,2,3/ it felt like you were both, you were both my family/ we made each other laugh, we made each other cry/ and we never did lie/ to one another/ this is why, I always did happen to try/ to do, to do, the things that you told me to do/ I gave you my word, I promised you I'd always look out for Kim/ no matter what, even if she didn't love him/ Me, Mike Izzo, Mercenary, MIZeRY/ everyday, this fucking shit always drove me crazy/ but one day, I remember you telling me this/ that Kim and me will marry, and I shouldn't always be so pissed/ I miss you so much Mrs. Krawec/ just thinking about this shit/ it drives me sick/

HOOK/CHORUS: You were always there for me, when I needed you/ you were always there, when I needed to talk to you/ and all the pain I receive will eventually move on/ because no matter what, life goes on/ You were always there for me, when I needed you/ you were always there, when I needed to talk to you/ and all the pain I receive will eventually move on/ because no matter what, life goes on/

VERSE 2: See no matter what Kim and me will stay always close/ but no matter what I won't let us get way to close/ see I need to live a different life style/ if I believed anything else I would just be in denial/ I'm still living at home with my crazy ass mother/ I'm still trying to do my dreams in being a rapper/ the psycho bitch through me in a mental hospital/ she must think that I'm psychiatric and I need medical assistance/ when I'm not even fucking mental/ I went to jail for two nights, which isn't much/ just being in there from the start is just enough/ then I got thrown in the hospital for five days straight/ and in a place like that you can't even contemplate/ the very next move that Mike Izzo should make/ whether to stay calm, or should he just escape/ I'm just waiting for the day that I can finally say/ life is good, and that things are okay/ Your husband is still that very nice guy/ you know, the one who accepted me as his son, for the very first time/ the first time that he had met me/ but normally/ most parents and most people happen not to like me/ see there's one thing that I do know, and that's your with me in spirit/ and you won't go away Till I actually make it/

HOOK/CHORUS: You were always there for me, when I needed you/ you were always there, when I needed to talk to you/ and all the pain I receive will eventually move on/ because no matter what, life goes on/ You were always there for me, when I needed you/ you were always there, when I needed to talk to you/ and all the pain I receive will eventually move on/ because no matter what, life goes on/

VERSE 3: I quit modeling/ so I could start rapping/ I wish you could see me now, so you can ask what happened/ because with all the stuff I'm trying to do, you'd be like wow look at you/ you've got an underground label and a clothing line too/ you got concerts going/ you got your songs flowing/ getting different songs on different radio stations/ you're avoiding all sorts of bad different temptations/ from joining the game just for money, staying away from all sorts of drugs, and all different types of thugs/ I stay sober and I stay straight/ so I can stay in control of my own fate/ so I can get my own personal template/ which states/ the man who took hip hop even further/ will always be remembered/ as its own savior/ for all eternity/ his name, it was MIZeRY/ Ill make sure I accomplish it because I want to/ Ill do anything possible because I need too/ Ill make sure I do it because I love too/ this whole song was dedicated to Mrs. Krawec, because no matter what I'll always miss you/

HOOK/CHORUS: You were always there for me, when I needed you/ you were always there, when I needed to talk to you/ and all the pain I receive will eventually move on/ because no matter what, life goes on/ You were always there for me, when I needed you/ you were always there, when I needed to talk to you/ and all the pain I receive will eventually move on/ because no matter what, life goes on/

SUMMARY - I'll explain it like this. "When I was fourteen years old, I met this amazingly beautiful and breathe taking young girl by the name of Kimberley Krawec. Shortly after having met her, her and I started to date at the young age of 14. Through dating her, I eventually met her parents John and Linda Krawec. Both of her parents were stunning and beautiful people, whom were very loving and accepting of me. Linda immediately had this unconditional love for me and welcomed me in her home anytime, any day of the week. Sure enough, soon there would be times I needed a place to stay, since I was kicked out of my own home. Without a doubt, I was able to rely on Linda Krawec to be there for me and take me in as one of her own. Over the next couple years, Kim and I had broken up early into our relationship; but, remained close friends thanks to her amazing mother. Sometime in 2003, I had received a disturbing phone call from Kimberley; hysterically crying, telling me that her mother passed away. This was the day my life felt emptier than ever, based on several facts. Most importantly, I first found out that Kim's mom had died from an overdose of drugs. I had no knowledge of her being a drug addict in the three years of knowing her. Second, the girl who I had cared for, since I met her was devastated beyond any fathomable help I could possibly offer. After this terrible tragedy; I noticed over the next few months, Kim started becoming very distant. All I ever wanted, was to be there for her as the person she can trust and rely on for everything… Maybe, about two years after this tragedy, I had finally found the courage to express my feelings and thoughts about Linda; and my love for Kimberley. It wasn't until writing this song, I had the courage to tell Kim what I promised her mom. Maybe a year before her passing; I promised, I'd always look out for Kim. In addition, it was also the first time I had written what her mom told me. Telling me that Kimberley and I would marry someday and I shouldn't be so upset. To this very day, I still become very sad of her being gone. Kim & I were close, but I chose to remove her from my life… However, on July 15, 2012 for the first time ever; Linda Krawec, had visited me in a dream and was telling me what dying was like; how she was reborn, awaiting for my return to open Heaven. She further went on saying, that she is very peaceful and can't wait to see John, Kim, & Me soon.

The last thing I recall her telling me is not to worry so much and that Kimberley is in pain. She also said that Kimberley is searching for whom she truly is; but not to worry, because soon things will work out for both of you. I told her that your daughters fate is not destined with mine and that I missed her. I then awake from my dream. After I awoke, the first thing I remember her telling me is that Kim is in pain right now and searching for who she is. Ironically, I woke up with this very harsh pain in my left collar bone where Kimberley broke the same bone in a terrible car accident; some years back. It was at that very waking moment, I realized Linda, Kim, and me were all connected; and despite our differences, Kim will find me again; which she did in July of 2012"…

Chapter 5: Song 9 – Don't Blame Me (5:9)

Don't Blame Me:

INTRO: "Yo listen to me and whatever you don't blame me/ MIC check, Yo turn the volume up a bit"…

VERSE 1: Don't blame me for your actions/ if my music ain't to your satisfaction/ then don't go to the store and buy my CD then/ I figured you were mature men/ figured you could handle explicit lyrics/ all of a sudden its silent, and all I hear are these ticks/ coming from the clock cause you haven't answered me yet/ I don't think that you're mature enough, you wanna make a bet/ always making these false accusations/ to busy caught up on me, and not worrying about the worlds nations/ what about the war were fighting/ but no you're more worried about what I'm reciting/ if you say rap music is so bad, than why is it selling/ but you wont stop until rap starts dying/ rap ain't going anywhere, people will always be buying/ if not mine, someone new will come out and start rapping/ you might as well just stop trying/ you just make things more aggravating/ music doesn't pollute the mind/ do you want me to make music about hunnies and being kind/ fuck that, you determine how you act/ when someone hits you, you're the one who decides how you react/ music doesn't promote violence/ I do, didn't you know that, why you so dense/ I'm the one who makes you so tense/ I just inflicted this pain on you/ making you strangle yourself till you turn blue/ you better have back, cause I'm a pistol packing lunatic, with a 50 man crew/ now you got me thinking about what you'll do/ stop being a fool, you can't ever stop me/ the reason, cause I just reached full insanity/ I'm abnormally sane/ right about now, we got two terrorists high jacking one airplane/ and you're still worried about my music and me/ its like your some sort of undiscovered disease/ I feel like a dog with too many fuckin' flees/ that's why you got to stop worrying about me/ and to worry about people committing heinous crimes and who are adversity/

HOOK/CHORUS: How can you blame me/ I don't make these people angry/ I only make music/ I didn't think you'd actually do it/ until my music determines how you act/ then stop wasting my time, until it's a proven fact/ I can't believe you're blaming me/ I don't make these people angry/ I only make music/ I didn't think you'd actually do it/ until my music determines how you act/ then stop wasting my time, until it's a proven fact/

VERSE 2: In the past I've been with so many women/ wrote their numbers on paper with a black pen/ went out with them for about a month or so/ going all good and it seems things started to flow/ they were willing to loose their v-card to me/ but I knew it was going to end soon, so I didn't take their virginity/ there were about eight or more/ this verse is for/ all those girls who I hurt in the past/ I'm sorry, but to the ones I hate I'm glad you got dissed/ try playing me mother fucka/ I'll be returning the fava/ and that's what my conquests are/ it hasn't happened ever since I drove my friends car/ depending on how angry I get or violent/ you can't blame me cause I've always been independent/ no one there to raise me/ didn't have the proper family/ no one there to teach me right from wrong/ if you want to get to know me, just listen to my song/ I'm the roughest and hardest/ I'm the most meanest rap artist/ but you can't blame me/ this is how they made me/ I didn't choose this path/ put 2 and 2 together, its simple math/ my last name means rage and wrath/ no wonder why I'm so angry/ I'm so irascibility/ always getting into a fight/ nobody ever thought I was tight/ this kind of shit just ain't right/ not being my friend because I was raised wrongly/ not my fault I'm excitability/

HOOK/CHORUS: How can you blame me/ I don't make these people angry/ I only make music/ I didn't think you'd actually do it/ until my music determines how you act/ then stop wasting my time, until it's a proven fact/ I can't believe you're blaming me/ I don't make these people angry/ I only make music/ I didn't think you'd actually do it/ until my music determines how you act/ then stop wasting my time, until it's a proven fact/

SUMMARY – I'll explain it like this. "Don't blame me" was my first crack at a political statement against the American government and the FCC; whom attempt to censor music and their claims, music promotes negative and violent tendencies. Simply, "Don't blame me" was a song I created to discuss my career throughout its longevity and that no matter what happens in the world; they should never remain focused on me being too vulgar and promoting the wrong messages. When in fact, the government promotes the wrong messages; starting with going to war… No matter what the issues are in the world, "Don't blame me," is that simple."

Chapter 5: Song 10 – Poor as f*** (5:10)

Poor as f*:**

INTRO: "Aaiyo, anybody who has been down before, to anybody who has nothing, to anybody who has been there, to anybody who is poor as fuck"…

VERSE 1: See this is how I feel/ it seems like my life ain't real/ I push all the pain aside/ over the years I have cried/ this pain is too much to bare/ but then I realize that life ain't fair/ it's like I can't move on, cause I'm too scared/ my father had left me, that will always leave me scarred/ this scar in the center of my heart/ this pain is piercing like an arrow dart/ now it seems like I'm poor and homeless/ and you're wondering why I'm such a mess/ I feel like I'm on a tight rope/ I look for a new job but everywhere I go they say nope/ I can't even afford a winter coat/ wishing that I was loved just like the pope/ wishing that people thought I was dope/ oh shit, I just fell off this rope/ every time I get down, I make sure I don't give up/ I'm not going to end up living in a garbage dump/ now at the bottom of this pit/ this scar is forming a sist/ its trying to heal/ and it doesn't bother me any more, or I just can't feel/ and no I'm not fine/ this pain got worse every since I turned nine/

HOOK/CHORUS: I'm poor as fuck, cause I'm never working/ I'm poor as fuck, cause I'm always going to stores and stealing/ I'm poor as fuck, cause I'm never home, and I don't have any money to eat so I'm always starving/ I'm poor as fuck, cause I'm never working/ I'm poor as fuck, cause I'm always going to stores and stealing/ I'm poor as fuck, cause I'm never home, and I don't have any money to eat so I'm always starving/

VERSE 2: I'm always looking depressed/ my life had just commenced/ I'm always looking mad/ I'm always looking sad/ I'm too poor to afford anything/ why do you think I wear the fake bling, bling/ all I have is this beat that plays in my head/ I just wanna fall and collapse onto the bed/ let everything go/ and now welcome to my show/ my life is on showcase/ my body is always in a depressed phase/ with me its on and off working/ never have any money so I'm always stealing/ I have no more emotions, no more feeling/ always struggling/ this is to all you with a nice life/ spending the rest of your days with your wonderful wife/ go nights without eating/ I'm sick of starving/ my body eventually got used to this pain/ I wish I could pack my things and get on this train/ leave all the pain and memories behind/ just to relieve all the stress and clear my mind/

HOOK/CHORUS: I'm poor as fuck, cause I'm never working/ I'm poor as fuck, cause I'm always going to stores and stealing/ I'm poor as fuck, cause I'm never home, and I don't have any money to eat so I'm always starving/ I'm poor as fuck, cause I'm never working/ I'm poor as fuck, cause I'm always going to stores and stealing/ I'm poor as fuck, cause I'm never home, and I don't have any money to eat so I'm always starving/

VERSE 3: I wish had money and fortune/ when my mom becomes homeless, I'll be at the local motel Inn/ life just got really grim/ I'm reaching this brim/ that was a close call/ once again I didn't fall/ I want the women, the money, and the fame/ My mother takes all the blame/ she made me this way/ what if this was my last day/ then I ask why/ then I forget about it and I start to try/ yes I have issues and yes I have many problems/ then I feel like I've had it up to here, then my body shakes and starts to fear/ fears if its real or a special feature/ its all real and I make sure I change my future/ always in an angry mode/ who knows what lies down this road/ I'm fucking always in poverty/ there's nothing helping me cause there's no remedy/

HOOK/CHORUS: I'm poor as fuck, cause I'm never working/ I'm poor as fuck, cause I'm always going to stores and stealing/ I'm poor as fuck, cause I'm never home, and I don't have any money to eat so I'm always starving/ I'm poor as fuck, cause I'm never working/ I'm poor as fuck, cause I'm always going to stores and stealing/ I'm poor as fuck, cause I'm never home, and I don't have any money to eat so I'm always starving/

SUMMARY - I'll explain it like this. "I'm Poor as fuck" was simply my most depressive state of mind, when I hit rock bottom in my teenage life. At this point, I had realized that my life was surrounded by poverty, struggle, and family hardships. In addition, I began understanding that my two siblings and I had different fathers; but none of the men my mother brought home, were them. Further more, my mother wasn't working much and we were always getting dumped off at our grandparents house; thank god for them, because they saved our lives. This song was a clear indicator of what my life has been since I could remember growing up. *As I re-listened to this song, while typing this memoir; I had realized this was probably some of the exact issues Jesus Christ may have felt, as a teenager; while wondering, why he couldn't act, play like the rest of the kids, and why his family was always secretive and discreet. Overall, Jesus and I went through many different and similar issues; hence why I've decided to write this book."

Chapter 5: Song 14 – This is my last… (5:14)

This is my last…

VERSE 1: Ya, this is my last night, this is my last fight/ up until now/ I felt I've been on the prowl/ then I met this guy skript/ and he gave me this shit to flip/ maybe life will turn around/ maybe I will be found/ maybe he'll give me a chance/ so I don't got to freelance/ maybe I'll go on tour/ so I don't got to be poor/ this shit ain't for fun/ cause I'm always on the run/ from MIZeRY's past/ cause this shit seems so fast/ cause I've seen my life elapse/ a thousand times over/ and you're sitting there, wondering why there is so much pressure/ I'm standing here looking like I'm about to have a seizure/ because I have anxiety/ and this rap shit has become a real big priority/ I'm barely surviving/ sitting in this car driving/ alone, I start thinking/ until yesterday I was poor as fuck/ today I barely exist/ always walking around pissed/ throwing up my damn fist/ cause I'm a soldier/ I told Ya/ that I will oppose Ya/ by any means till the end of time/ I'll make sure I speak my mind/ I've decided I'm here for one reason/ that was a big decision/ as a matter of fact/ you can't counter react/ against my retaliation/ against 90 percent of this fucking industry/ I'm trying to form a monastery/ while I turn into a holy apothecary/ destroy you rappers by surprise/ while the rest watch me rise/

HOOK/CHORUS: This is my last night, this is my last fight/ One more night of dealing with this pain/ one more fight for trying to sane/ This is my last night, this is my last fight/ One more night of dealing with this pain/ one more fight for trying to sane/ This is my last night, this is my last fight/

VERSE 2: I had a promotional show and my home boys walked out on me/ that just says they won't ride, they won't die for me/ they won't cry, they won't lie for me/ that's why I've stated any type of friendship will always equal bullshit/ One more night of dealing with this pain/ one more fight for trying to be sane/ MIZeRY's my mind state/ and I'm going through these charts at a high crime rate/ that's all I see/ whoever told you that freedom was for free/ must be your enemy/ we can get into rap topics/ or we can get into politics/ it just don't matter/ and as long as I'm here, Imma be a preacher/ Imma preach about everything that I see/ everywhere that I go, and on everyone of my CD's/ MIZeRY is gonna make you realize/ and make you memorize/ all the pain that he gave you/ and all the fear that he brought you/ because the complexity behind the meaning of MIZeRY/ is far to advanced for your knowledge to learn the concept/ of my CD before it ejects this tape deck/ that's why I get such a high level of respect/ That's why you shouldn't diss the best/ or he'll have you permanently rest/ you just faced death/ so why you dressed to impress/

HOOK/CHORUS: This is my last night, this is my last fight/ One more night of dealing with this pain/ one more fight for trying to sane/ This is my last night, this is my last fight/ One more night of dealing with this pain/ one more fight for trying to sane/ This is my last night, this is my last fight/

VERSE 3: It seems that every time something goes good/ it turns bad because it should/ but even if I could/ rearrange my history/ I would some how work around, all the pain and agony/ I would fight against the system like Rage Against the Machine/ I'd fight against the system like Tupac, and he's talking about walking in the hall seeing a murder scene/ cause the government doesn't do enough to protect it's people/ so we increase everything by triple/ including jobs, education, & welfare/ so I say it for the last time, life ain't fair/

HOOK/CHORUS: This is my last night, this is my last fight/ One more night of dealing with this pain/ one more fight for trying to sane/ This is my last night, this is my last fight/ One more night of dealing with this pain/ one more fight for trying to sane/ This is my last night, this is my last fight/ One more night of dealing with this pain/ one more fight for trying to sane/ This is my last night, this is my last fight/ One more night of dealing with this…

SUMMARY - I'll explain it like this. "During the same time of hitting rock bottom, feeling poor, and learning about all the tragedies of my life; I just wanted to end everything or change it all. I wrote "This is my last" in an attempt to change it all by preventing my own suicide; which was contemplated heavily, during this point in my life. This is my last night not only depicts the very images, graphic reality of my life, and depression; but, it also shows indicators how and why friends weren't really friends to me. In addition, I was also fuming about how our country was designed to be this wonderful free country or a replica of Heaven; and yet, it is nothing more than a selfish and greedy country. A country only out for themselves, instead of helping the world in the correct ways; not using war as one of them. This is my last night was also a preemptive song for the last night, before Judgment Day; but at the time of writing this, I was just simply venting about my humane life."

Chapter 6
The Savior of Rap

*The songs not displayed were placed on a new album or cut.

(Songs: 1, 2, 3, 4, 5, 6, 7, 8, 9, 12, 13, 15)

I am now 18 and my life has turned down several wrong paths. I not only dropped out of high school- two years prior, but I was stealing from corporations, and commenced committing other acts. These acts landed me in court almost every couple weeks. When I had turned 18; I attempted to get my life back on track, by landing a new job with staples, and went back to school to complete my degree. Even though my life had many obstacles, they didn't seem to stop me from completing my goals in my life. However, these goals would not have been possible if it wasn't for my best friend at the time- Brian H. Brian convinced his folks to permit me, to live with them at their house; for the next two years. During this time, Brian and I were all about doing things together; from hanging out with friends, girls, and chasing excitement in the world of Long Island. At this point in my life, I was determined and eager to succeed in the world of music; which led me to the very thought of being a savior, for the music industry. Little did I know, the title of this album "The Savior or Rap" was a metaphor for being the Saviour of the world! Now looking back; I realized this was the start of an ultimate understanding, to whom I was truly in the world; we all call life. Throughout this album, we will see a troubled young man attempting to mature into a confident and resilient young adult. Meanwhile, he must conquer the worst type of American adversity; whilst attempting to achieve one of the most extreme careers possible in America...

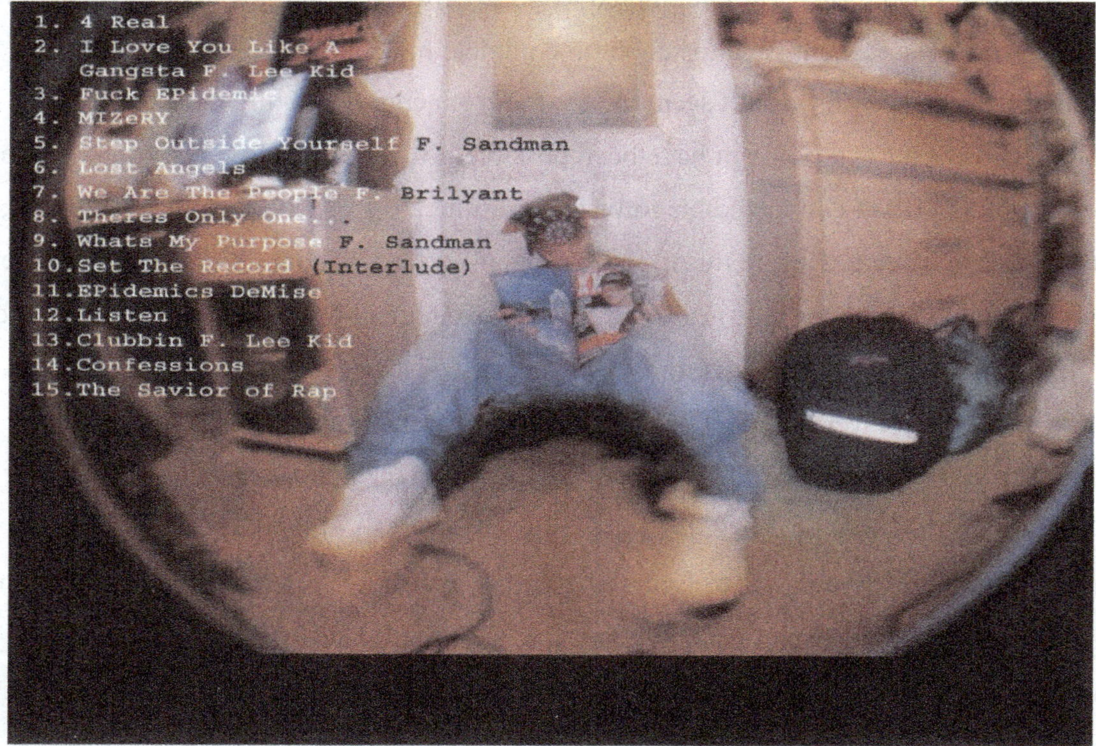

"The Savior of Rap" - front and back; photo taken by Steven Vanatta; Direction and design by Michael Izzo. Copyright © 2005, *MIZeRY ReCORDS* – All Rights Reserved.

Chapter 6: Song 1 – 4 Real (6:1)

4 Real:

VERSE 1: Yo the streets made me the killa that I am/ I'm not proud of the man that I am/ but the streets only made me more ruthless/ over the years I got betta at holding a stainless/ are you ready to test/ your bullet proof vest/ when bullets are aimed straight for Ya chest/ We already got our own faction/ don't play with your words, cause then we'll take action/ oh and fuck cops, your badges don't scare me/ cause N.Y.P.D./ are fagots, and fairies/ and ready to load up and blast heat whenever/ then we'll run from the cops cause we know the streets better/ Its 2 in the morning/ thunder, lightening, and the rains out pouring/ your boys are outside/ all ready to ride/ wit grams at their sides/ eager to make this deal/ praying to the lord for this shit not to be real/ sick and tired of always turning to the steel/ If we had a choice/ me and my boys/ would find other means to pay the bills/ that's why you'll never see us sittin on mills/ out here it's a war zone/ these pit-bull dogs is all hungry for the bone/ out here you need to be a warrior/ a gladiator/ a survivor/ a soldier/ just to live through the night/ you got to fight/ for your life/ make the wrong moves and you'll get lit up tonight/ meanwhile your praying to god to make it home tonight/ your praying to god to make it home to the wife/ your praying to god because you live a thug life/ its not my fault that this shit is all for real g/

HOOK/CHORUS: All of these stories are all for real g/ after this track I want y'all to still feel me/ Don't hate me just cause I'm speaking the truth/ when y'all speak those lies that shit, just really hurts/ I want y'all to still feel me/ its not my fault that this shits for real b/ I want y'all to still feel me/ All of these stories are all for real g/ after this track, I want y'all to still feel me/ Don't hate me just cause I'm speaking the truth/ when y'all speak those lies, that shit just really hurts/ I want y'all to still feel me/ its not my fault that this shits for real b/ I want y'all to still feel me/

VERSE 2: You're looking over your shoulder/ everywhere that you go/ always watching your back, cause paranoia took over the brain/ so you turn to drugs so you can retain/ the definition of sane/ crack, cocaine, heroine, pcp, angel dust, marijuana/ all these lead to the bullshit drama/ It's just a temporary confinement/ like solitary confinement/

doing 25-life/ all because of one night/ your mother o-d'ed/ right there in front of me/ when I was only fifteen/ you and your sister all alone/ in this world to roam/ 8 years later she gets shot from twin glocks/ both holding 16 shells/ she immediately fell/ gasping for breathe/ as I'm watching her death/ only thing left is to seek revenge/ there's nothing sweeter then to avenge/ your loved ones cause their all a blessin/ living in the streets is just a lesson/ what I'm believing/ even if, what I've been believing/ stops me from breathing/ relatives grieving/ praying/ ain't receiving/ A phone call from jail straight from my cell/ asking for bail/ cause the cops all got me locked up/ fuck/ Would I have been better off shot up/?

HOOK/CHORUS: All of these stories are all for real g/ after this track, I want y'all to still feel me/ Don't hate me just cause I'm speaking the truth/ when y'all speak those lies that shit, just really hurts/ I want y'all to still feel me/ its not my fault that this shits for real b/ I want y'all to still feel me/ All of these stories are all for real g/ after this track, I want y'all to still feel me/ Don't hate me just cause I'm speaking the truth/ when y'all speak those lies, that shit just really hurts/ I want y'all to still feel me/ its not my fault that this shits for real b/ I want y'all to still feel me/

SUMMARY – I'll explain it like this. "This song was actually made for this movie, which I was offered to make the sound track for. However, that deal was cupped with a potential record deal from this upcoming record label. Sadly, that deal ultimately ended up not developing into anything promising. In any event, the first verse was strictly about what I had been through and done in life. The second verse was about this kid whom dealt with exactly what I was talking about. This song was solely about people who live a rebellious gang type, life style, and know what its like trying to better their lives by plaguing others; unknowingly."

Chapter 6: Song 2 – I Love you like a Gangsta (6:2)

I Love You Like a Gangsta Ft. Lee Kid:

VERSE 1: Yo, Yo, let me take you to where it all began/ when me and my boy had to stand/ in line for this club/ then I saw this chick and I knew, right there she had the gangsta love/ right from the start/ this chick already stole my heart/ I didn't know what to do or say/ just walk up to her, look up, and pray/ I hoped that shorty didn't have a man/ cause seriously/ I was starting to feel shorty/ then we exchanged verbal conversation/ I had this undying sensation/ to cop her digits/ to stay my girl as I make bigger hits/ no matter how much paparazzi, or how much stress/ a celebrities life gets/ no more tests/ I wont put you through an obstacle course/ I know I put you through some shit, but now I got a lot of remorse/ now you'll always be my baby boo/ no matter how much bullshit we ever go through/ I'm done/ I shall not run/ from my true/ feelings for you/ no more leaving you in the dust/ Now I got this sudden lust/ to just fucking bust/ inside of you/ every time I'm fucking you/ cause I can't stop loving you/

HOOK/CHORUS: I Love you like a gangsta and I won't let there be drama/ I love you like a gangsta and I won't let there be drama/ I'll love you no matter how many fights we go through/ I'll love you no matter what, cause you're my fucking baby boo/ I Love you like a gangsta and I won't let there be drama/ I love you like a gangsta and I won't let there be drama/ I'll love you till my last breathe/ and I'll love you till my death/ I'll love you till the end, because you're everything that I want/

VERSE 3: I know that you're ready to ride/ till the bloody end/ that's why all I need in this lifetime is me and my girlfriend/ born in this world of sin/ with only knowing how to win/ I spit knowledgeable scriptures/ you interpret my words into pictures/ they're to intense for your mind state/ and there's/ no way you're going to be able to escape/ the amount of agony and pain of this whole entire game/ and if you ain't ready to ride/ then you's best be ready to die/ I told Ya/ that I will only take in Soldiers/ Oh I better not see Bad articles/ otherwise I will cutch you up into very small particles/ like I was fucking Hannibal/ become a raging cannibal/ then hide out for a bit/ 3 months later you're going to see us all making bigger hits/ and everyday of my life/ it feels like I gotta pay a debt/ of eternal distress/ and there will not be a therapist/ to even coming close to helping me/ just please give up, there will not be any stopping me/

HOOK/CHORUS: I Love you like a gangsta and I won't let there be drama/ I love you like a gangsta and I won't let there be drama/ I'll love you no matter how many fights we go through/ I'll love you no matter what, cause you're my fucking baby boo/ I Love you like a gangsta and I won't let there be drama/ I love you like a gangsta and I won't let there be drama/ I'll love you till my last breathe/ and I'll love you till my death/ I'll love you till the end, because you're everything that I want/

SUMMARY - I'll explain it like this. "When I was turning 18 it had taken me a year and a half to get over my first long term relationship of one year with this girl Lauren. At that time I really thought me and her was it together forever type stuff. In the end I was wrong and I was coping with getting on with it. This song was about this new girl I met in a club and decided after long contemplation to walk up to her and speak with her. I Love you like a gangsta was simply a song to express how deeply you care for someone and that no matter what you both go through you will stick by each other through it all. However, in today's current society many humans lack this very level of commitment forcing us to turn into miniature Hannibal Lector's, and tarnish love in every way. Lee Kid was a friend at the time that I used to coach and assist in his music career and he actually recorded on the second verse of this song."

Chapter 6: Song 3 – F*** Epidemic (6:3)

F* Epidemic:**

INTRO: "Yo huh, its time I start talking. Fuck Epidemic."

VERSE 1: Yo, Yo, Yo, Yo, Yo, you always gonna be a coward/ cause you ain't ready to ride/ even if you hide/ regardless you still gone die/ I got 100 guns and 100 clips/ I'm always ready to unload all these clips/ you ain't the epidemic of shit/ wanna start this beef/ I'll finish this shit in the streets/ I was born ready to beef/ but Imma make this brief/ It started back in the day when you tried taking away Lauren/ cause you ain't got no women/ then I got some artists/ so you needed some artists/ Then I got my record company/ shit epidemic records, came to be/ its obvious, that you're trying to be me/ every morning I had this undying ambition/ to beat you with lyrical incisions/ your production is crap, your flow's garbage/ your lyrics is redundant/ shit no wonder why you wanna jump on my dick/ cause you know that, I'm the one with all the mother fucking talent/ it took you 3 and a half years to come out with a CD/ at least you were smart enough not to start dissin on me/ you'll never be/ on the same level as me/ oh and on your

CD/ you were trying to sound like biggie/ not only your shits garbage, but you ain't got a style/ face it youz in denial/ you're a fucking rapping midget/ and face the fact, that I got rid of everyone of your digits/ I was playing with guns while your momma had you playing with dolls/ you ain't know nothing about prison cell walls/ y'all fucks don't want beef, you just wanna have drama/ now look at MIZeRY's persona/ y'all think youz gangstas/ cause you be selling marijuana/ At 14 I was charged with grand theft auto/ at 15 was charged with possession of a semi auto/ I ain't getting into my felonies/ this shit ain't about me/ this game ain't got no room for pussy ass bitches/ this game ain't got no room for pussy ass snitches/ you shoulda stuck with that fagot ass name logistix/ the funny shit is you talking like you live a thug life/ the funny shit is you talking like you live a street life/ you're a candy ass fagot, you're a pop tart/ sweet heart/ go sing/ with N'sync/ cause the closest thing you'll ever be to being behind bars/ is when serving a drink/ I don't know why you keep fronting/ I don't know what'ch you really repping/ you don't live in no ghetto/ you ain't ever see no hood/ and shit between me and you, will never be good/ I'm sick of all the bullshit/ I'm sick of all the talking/ You better watch your back/ cause after I'm through with this shit, I ain't gonna make more raps/

SUMMARY - I'll explain it like this. "Back in freshman year of high school, there was this young small kid named Ricky. Ricky happened to be one of the few minorities in our high school, whom also rapped. Eventually, I liked what he did and started becoming friends with him. I was also trying to write raps too. Almost every day before school, we would freestyle each other, and he would always win. Eventually, in tenth grade things between him and I went down hill. I started becoming better at making music and was dropping my first CD ever. In addition, I was quite popular and had a very beautiful girlfriend named Lauren. Eventually, as I assume jealousy took over and he started this beef. It started when he asked me how I made my beats. Well, in fact he stole all of my beats and tried to play them off as his own. Long story short, he attempted to duplicate everything I was doing and in the end; I made beef records about him. As a result, he got so scared he threatened to take my songs to the police That's when I turned my back on him and our childish beef. Now a days, I look back and realize, when you help someone out they will just screw you over in the end; just like he did to me and my music."

Chapter 6: Song 4 – MIZeRY (6:4)

MIZeRY:

VERSE 1: Yo, I've finally gone mentally insane/ that's why they call me MIZeRY, cause I'm brining you agony and pain/ upon this industry/ they didn't want to take me in, so I'm forcing my way in/ using all sorts of knives/ we're taking out lives/ one of each gun/ as this industry runs/ from MIZeRY and Apocalypse/ cause this game is looking like the fucking rap Olympics/ instead of fighting for Gold medals/ they're fighting for cash, rims, and silver pedals/ anything that looks flashy/ fucked up on the ashy/ these hardcore thugs, are turning real sassy/ Imma fight to be real/ Imma fight for respect, Imma fight how I feel/ no more asking nicely/ I have said please/ I'm not letting you walk freely/ I might not let you breathe/ no more being a nice guy/ I shall not lie/ in the eyes/ of the lord/ I shall swing my sword/ I shall stand strong/ I shall not allow you, to unplug my MIC's cord/

HOOK/CHORUS: Shot's are being fired/ It's time for you to retire/ now I'm being admired/ MIZeRY's the pain/ he's taking away the fame/ of this whole entire game/ cause it wreaks through his veins/ cause it wreaks through his veins/ Shot's are being fired/ It's time for you to retire/ now I'm being admired/ MIZeRY's the pain/ he's taking away the fame/ of this whole entire game/ cause it wreaks through his veins/ cause it wreaks through his veins/

VERSE 2: Now take a minute and listen/ while all these bullets glisten/ as they light up to your eye/ now watch these missiles fly/ very high in the sky/ and listen to this sound/ cause this shit is so profound/ listen to this beat/ cause this shit is discrete/ and this track is gonna make all emcees see their defeat/ Imma tell you how it begins, we go out on da prowl/ right at 3 a.m./ with fifty five men/ the next thing you'll hear is 1, 2, 3 – 54/ coming for your door/ a moment of silence/ CH-CH, Boom, then you'll see violence/ now everything's paused, your hearts stopped/ mother fuckas got dropped/ we killed your secretary/ your whole entire family/ we killed all of your artists/ the CEO and the president/ of your whole fucking label, without giving them a moment/ to say goodbye to their wife, their family, or their kids/ we didn't even give them time, to pray to the lord, to forgive them for their sins/ right before we exit, we take anything in reference; that, was up in that company/ than we strap the entire building with C4 heavily/ we blow the building down to bits and pieces of rubble/ then we sit back and watch most of this industry tumble/

HOOK/CHORUS: Shot's are being fired/ It's time for you to retire/ now I'm being admired/ MIZeRY's the pain/ he's taking away the fame/ of this whole entire game/ cause it wreaks through his veins/ cause it wreaks through his veins/ Shot's are being fired/ It's time for you to retire/ now I'm being admired/ MIZeRY's the pain/ he's taking away the fame/ of this whole entire game/ cause it wreaks through his veins/ cause it wreaks through his veins/

VERSE 3: Now it's the aftermath/ and here's the after effect/ that your high class security systems could not detect/ and if you dare to oppose me/ I will take you out willingly/ and I mean this shit seriously/ I'm gonna win the streets, the fans, and the industry/ as they're following me/ and you see me on T.V./ and you're buying my CD/ no more club hopping/ no more bullshit talking/ no more CD contracts/ and no more discrimination, between whites and blacks/ no more whack tracks/ I'm heir to the thrown/ cause I am a guy who is prone/ to sudden rage and wrath/ cause I chose this path/ I'm a mercenary who is sent/ on a major quest/ to pass this test/ to lead all the rest/ to become the best/ as soon as I enter, I'll have a lot of people against me/ and If everything goes right, I'll have the best joining with me/ I'll say it over again "Shot's are being fired/ It's time for you to retire/ now I'm being admired/ MIZeRY's the pain/ I'm taking away the fame/ of this whole entire game/ cause it wreaks through his veins/ cause it wreaks through his veins/ and I can not say, till this glorious day/

HOOK/CHORUS: Shot's are being fired/ It's time for you to retire/ now I'm being admired/ MIZeRY's the pain/ he's taking away the fame/ of this whole entire game/ cause it wreaks through his veins/ cause it wreaks through his veins/ Shot's are being fired/ It's time for you to retire/ now I'm being admired/ MIZeRY's the pain/ he's taking away the fame/ of this whole entire game/ cause it wreaks through his veins/ cause it wreaks through his veins/ cause it wreaks through his veins/

SUMMARY - I'll explain it like this. "This song "MIZeRY" is simply a metaphor for who I truly am, what my mission is for this Earth, and that I was sent by God cause I am God's son. This song is referencing Judgment day and God's proposed plan for destroying all of capitalism, socialism, and corrupt ways of thinking. In addition, you can tell from some of my lyrics that God is determined to create peace on Earth; any who opposes him, shall be defeated. This is by far one of those lyrical songs that proves, I was way ahead of my time at the early age of 18."

Chapter 6: Song 5 – Step outside yourself (6:5)

Step outside yourself Ft. Sandman (2005) – lyrics not included:

VERSE 1: I'm here to define you/ how do you treat people/ good, bad, or evil?/ ask yourself, you look at everyone as an equal?/ what if they, were, a different race than you?/ does that make them lower than you?/ just cause you got more money, does that make you better than me?/ what are you crazy/ please stop playing/ I don't give a fuck about what y'all are saying/ under your breathe and behind my back/ about my rap/ it doesn't matter, cause I've found my inner self/ you haven't even begun to explore yourself/ one minute you're a mobster/ then a gangsta/ then a drug dealer/ then a girl stealer/ you don't even know, who you are/ you look in the mirror/ and you don't look far/ into your eyes/ you can't even see, past your own lies/ you got caught in a world of denial/ so you come up with a new fucking style/ day after day, lie after lie/ I already know, who I am/ I'm a rapper on a mission/ I am a man with big intentions/ I was put on this Earth, So I can help/ you were put here, so you can receive/ anything I do, as long as I breathe/ do you have someone that influences you; do you have someone that you look up to; do you have someone that you pray too?/ you should take a minute and look at yourself/ so that you can, step outside yourself/

HOOK/CHORUS: Look at yourself, from another perspective/ what's your incentive/ what's your reality?/ focus your energy/ close those eyes/ what is it like, living those lies?/ Look at yourself, from another perspective/ what's your incentive/ what's your reality?/ focus your energy/ close those eyes/ what is it like, living those lies?/

VERSE 3.0: Come and take a walk with me/ on my journey's/ while I'm going through surgery's/ while, going through purgatory/ almost every night/ I put up a fight/ to get down on my knees, to put my head up/ just to speak up/ I don't deserve the full love of the lord/ to a certain degree, I deserve to be heard/ everyone needs love/ so I look above/ all the fucking poverty/ and the fact that the government, doesn't give much back to the black community/ so when I'm done here, we'll fight as a unity/ against these thugs/ against these guns/ against these drugs/ against these laws/ what's my cause?/ if you're willing to ride/ stick by my side/ and we will prosper/ as one and together/

HOOK/CHORUS: Look at yourself, from another perspective/ what's your incentive/ what's your reality?/ focus your energy/ close those eyes/ what is it like, living those lies?/ Look at yourself, from another perspective/ what's your incentive/ what's your reality?/ focus your energy/ close those eyes/ what is it like, living those lies?/

SUMMARY - I'll explain it like this. "For starters, this song was one of my earliest and by far my most advanced. This was a collaboration with my good friend Rob and together, spiritually our souls connected. We fortified a song that the entire world can relate with. Regardless if they are trapped behind their own lies or not. However, during my verse, I'm not only referencing all those whom lie day to day, behind the devils many faces; but, I was also prophesizing about my life and my future. For example, **"I already know who I am/ I'm a rapper on a mission/ I am a man with big intentions/ I was put on this Earth, So I can help/ you were put here, so you can receive/ anything I do as long as I breathe/."** Further more, my second verse explains: To walk with me, AKA walk with God, and let him/me show you where we must walk in order to preserve our eternity. Simply, this entire second verse is me discussing my future plans to abolish all wrong. Rob and I created this song in 2005 and we are now in 2012; and I must say, this song is by far still ahead of it's time."

Chapter 6: Song 6 – Lost Angels (6:6)

Lost Angels:

VERSE 1: I got lost inta some tangles/ I'm missing some angels/ I'm lost at every angle/ this soldiers unstable/ I can't find the key, to break out of this prison/ Y'all don't know, where I've been, you don't know that I've been missing/ I lost my way, when I was on the path to my destiny/ Can't fulfill my prophecy/ the family crest that's embedded on my arm/ embedded in my skin/ embedded in my brain/ embedded in my veins/ searching for that spark/ all I see is a lonely soul that's left in the dark/ how can I be positive/ when everything's negative/ I try to grow stronger/ I try to live longer/ I'm still searching for the day, I find a brighter future/ In this given society/ with these corrupt, court cases loaded with anxiety/ I can't pay my fines, cause I ain't got the funds/ I can't pay my felonies/ cause I ain't got the money/ living in this world, with me and my sister/ me and my brothers/ all of us having, different fucking fathers/ with the same mother/ me and my sister/ bonding on a level/ please refrain from, calling me the devil/ I've made bad decisions/ but now my mind state, has only good intentions/

HOOK/CHORUS: I am the general/ that's fighting for his people/ I want all y'all Lost Angels/ to come and follow me, as I'm leading all y'all Toy Soldiers/ that's giving you A New Hope, giving you a New Dream, giving you a new world/ I am the general/ that's fighting for his people/ I want all y'all Lost Angels/ to come and follow me, as I'm leading all y'all Toy Soldiers/ that's giving you A New Hope, giving you a New Dream, giving you a new world/

VERSE 2: Everywhere that I go/ I see these miserable fucks/ working these 9-five's/ that are hating their lives/ that are wishing they were doing something better, with their time/ you should of chose a, better career/ but, your life's gears/ aren't turning/ now your souls burning/ you're suffering/ you quit from the dreams that you had/ but, now it's too late, to try and bounce back/ soon enough you'll loose it, and become suicidal/ things turned critical/ high blood pressure, killing colleagues/ that are way out of your league/ I'm here to pull you out, of that fake ass world, that you always be living in/ I am the soldier/ I am the one who's here to save Ya/ I am the one who's gonna rein-spark/ that fucking ambition/ that's gonna re-embark/ this whole youth nation/ I gots to be a leader/ I gots to be a general/ that's leading these toy soldiers/ straight into battle/ I need to lead these kids straight into the war, fighting against the government/ fighting against the public/ Imma be there, right next to you/ Imma be there, riding with you/ Imma be there, fighting with you/ Imma be there dying with you/ I'm giving you A New Hope/ giving you A New Dream/ giving you a new world/ Come and Follow me/

HOOK/CHORUS: I am the general/ that's fighting for his people/ I want all y'all Lost Angels/ to come and follow me, as I'm leading all y'all Toy Soldiers/ that's giving you A New Hope, giving you a New Dream, giving you a new world/ I am the general/ that's fighting for his people/ I want all y'all Lost Angels/ to come and follow me, as I'm leading all y'all Toy Soldiers/ that's giving you A New Hope, giving you a New Dream, giving you a new world/

SUMMARY - I'll explain it like this. "First of all, "Lost Angels" is so important to me. It's so important to me, I re-recorded this a second time. This song was written around the time, I began noticing how many people in the world were like robots. I noticed how people were programmed by the ways in which society deceived them to be. Further more, I meant this song to be spiritual; hence the title. In terms of personally: this song is made to remind me, exactly what I can't allow to happen to me; both in terms of quitting or following another path, other than the one sent to me by God."

Chapter 6: Song 7 – We are the people (6:7)

We are the people Ft. Brilyant – Lyrics not included

VERSE 1: My dogs are my dogs with official fam crest/ flesh of our flesh/ Blood of our blood, cause we ain't the greedy/ we don't like the needy/ sick of people coming Up, asking for that money/ like I'm rich out da ass/ like I been living it with 3 million in cash/ motha fuckas think it's sweet, till they get their face messed up/ dressed up/ blessed up/ couple days later, they get their ass shot up/ waiting on the day, till the soul gets sent up/ I want some breathing room/ don't make me get the semi/ count down till noon/ Ill flow like remi/ until shit goes boom/ I'm taking y'all out, just like a monsoon/ this ain't no monopoly/ I can't believe you seriously/ think you're going to stop me/ this ain't no democracy/ fuck piracies/ I'm sick of Mp3's/ being downloaded onto everybody's pc's/ back to the topic/ so when y'all in the club/ y'all able to rock it/ the nine, pocket/ drop it/ if I got my gun, I will have to cock it/ don't blame me, if you hear that noise, from my gun/ cause, don't bounce to this beat, and you might get shot/ don't bounce to this beat and Ya might get shot/

HOOK/CHORUS: I'm loosing my mind, with all y'all cats/ If you talk that shit,

I will clap back/ cause all my dogs, will fuck y'all up/ cause all my dogs, would shoot'ch y'all up/ cause all my Homies, get down tonight/ cause all my people, get down tonight/ I'm loosing my mind, with all y'all cats/ If you talk that shit, I will clap back/ cause all my Homies, get down tonight/ cause all my people, get down tonight/

VERSE 3: One white man and a whole lot of hood/ I walked my ass, to the parts that weren't good/ it's not my fault, that I like the damn hood/ after what I been through and after what I saw/ I know that no matter what, I'm riding with the lord/ from thug angels/ to thug babies/ from jail cells/ to government slaveries/ you ain't catching me walking down d-block without enough artillery/ you ain't stopping me unless you got a military/ please, stop that walk/ and that gangsta talk/ otherwise your bodies going to be outlined in white chalk/ the fucking street life/ it's all in my heart/ this is my time/ to shine/ cause this shit is in my fucking bloodline/ don't fuck with the family/ cause we'll bite back and come for you pussy/ we ain't scared/ the next time your life, is not going to be sparred/ if you wanna hide shit, than put it in a book/ you wanna teach us something, put it in a hook/ quit degrading on the black folks/ enough with the white jokes/ I ain't having it no more/ not wasting time to pull out the four, four/ my roots go deep down, to the souls core/

HOOK/CHORUS: I'm loosing my mind, with all y'all cats/ If you talk that shit, I will clap back/ cause all my dogs will fuck y'all up/ cause all my dogs, would shoot'ch y'all up/ cause all my Homies, get down tonight/ cause all my people, get down tonight/ I'm loosing my mind, with all y'all cats/ If you talk that shit, I will clap back/ cause all my Homies, get down tonight/ cause all my people, get down tonight/ I'm loosing my mind, with all y'all cats/ If you talk that shit, I will clap back/ cause all my dogs will fuck y'all up/ cause all my dogs, would shoot'ch y'all up/ cause all my Homies, get down tonight/ cause all my people, get down tonight/

I'm loosing my mind, with all y'all cats/ If you talk that shit, I will clap back/ cause all my Homies, get down tonight/ cause all my people, get down tonight/

SUMMARY - I'll explain it like this. "We are the people" was a song I made with a good friend of mine at the time, Brilyant. We decided, we wanted to collaborate on a song about racism and about the struggle that all kinds of men go through.

In this song, I was discussing everyone in the world, not just white or black; cause if you think about it: white is the far left of the spectrum and black is the far right of the spectrum, or vise versa, and everyone else falls in-between thereof. ”

Chapter 6: Song 8 – There's only one (6:8)

There's only one…

INTRO: "I'm not trying, to be, Eminem…

HOOK/CHORUS: I'm not trying to be slim shady/ I'm just being mercenary/ I'm not trying to be like you/ At most, I just wanna roll with you/

VERSE 1: I been waiting on the day, when I can talk about this issue/ it's not just about the facial issues/ its not just about the racial issue/ it's greater than that/ it starts when they saying that, I'm just trying to be black/ it starts with the white mans raps/ lets take it to when they start calling me Marshall/ stating that I'm only partial/ half the talent that he is/ understand, that I'm not trying to be what he is/ he goes by the alias slim shady/ while I go by mercenary/ we're two different people, two different personalities/ with several similarities/ my father left me/ while still attached to an umbilical cord feeding/ while my mother was attached to IV's breathing/ while Marshall's father left him when he was just a young seed/ nothing we could do, but just sit back and breathe/ while we go through the trials and the tribulations of life/ begging the lord we get killed by the blade of a knife/ won't be in the streets alone, scared of being snuffed from behind/ both of us left alone in this world, just scared and blind/ without parental guidance/ and you're wondering why we all revolve around violence?/

HOOK/CHORUS: I'm not trying to be slim shady/ I'm just being mercenary/ I'm not trying to be like you/ At most, I just wanna roll with you/ I'm not trying to be slim shady/ I'm just being mercenary/ I'm not trying to be like you/ At most, I just wanna roll with you/

VERSE 2: The one diss I hear more than once, is you're trying to be like Marshall, you're trying to be like slim, you're trying to be like Eminem/ for now on, no more getting pissed/ I'm thanking you for comparing me to him/ no matter where I go, or anything I do/ I'm always being compared to you/ walk, talk, and act like slim/ live, look, and rap like him/ keep throwing those disses at me/ I'm using your compliments to boost my self esteem/ I even got brotha's/ from the hood, saying "look at this slim shady mother fucka/" just cause I'm a white rapper/ go back to dissing murder inc wankstas/ I even got X-girlfriends saying, I try too hard to be like crazy shady; but, just maybe/ If you opened up your eyes and would just see me/ **through 3d**/ you'd see a real emcee/ you'd see the real me/ it's about time this game/ got a little taste of what's flowing through my veins/ its about time you got word of my name/ look up my file/ I ain't choose this lifestyle/ a young teenage/ who's enraged/ ready to upstage/ anyone who's willing to defy me/ anyone who's willing to dethrone me/ or from getting to the top of my throne/ I'll use that shit as my mother fucking stepping stone/

HOOK/CHORUS: I'm not trying to be slim shady/ I'm just being mercenary/ I'm not trying to be like you/ At most, I just wanna roll with you/ I'm not trying to be slim shady/ I'm just being mercenary/ I'm not trying to be like you/ At most, I just wanna roll with you/

VERSE 3: For the record/ Imma keep my nose clean up out of jail/ cause, I think the judges are getting sick of giving me bail/ it seems that rap artists have some type of criminal tale/ whether it's with past lives/ or its with current ex-wives/ we got one thing in common/ I'm not talking about rhyming/ it starts with the parents back and forth/ allowing life to take its course/ ever since we came from the whom/ or we stepped into school/ we were labeled as a born loser/ priests telling us that God wanted to choose Ya/ that he's got something special lined up for Ya/ therapists/ trying to get us on meds/ to control us when we get pissed/ but the pills won't fix it, its all psychological/ its like they using biological/ weapons on us/ to try and control us/ like testing an experiment/ that's why were so independent/ we don't trust our parents/ we got similarities/ but different personalities/ that's why there's only one PAC/ only one DOC/ as in D.R.E./ only one snoop to the D O Double G/ One X to the mother fucking Z/ one fifty/ one swifty/ there's only one slim shady/ only one MIZeRY/ there's only one Obie trice/ this is why I've been stating this shit more than twice/

HOOK/CHORUS: I'm not trying to be slim shady/ I'm just being mercenary/ I'm not trying to be like you/ At most, I just wanna roll with you/ I'm not trying to be slim shady/ I'm just being mercenary/ I'm not trying to be like you/ At most, I just wanna roll with you/

SUMMARY - I'll explain it like this. "There's only one" came about during my attempt at defining myself; in society in the rap world, and the world itself. In general, my concept is simple; there's only one of everyone. However, I took it deeper and was comparing myself to Eminem in my musical career. Further more, I then decided to establish that in someway or another: everyone in the world is similar, but we have all different personalities. Ultimately, I feel this song is a great indication that the world will judge you no matter what, or whom you are in this world, and it's all wrong."

Chapter 6: Song 9 – What's my purpose (6:9)

What's my purpose Ft. Sandman

VERSE 1: Yo I feel every soul is born with a purpose or an intent/ each man has a mission/ and that's why, we all have been sent/ into this realm, into this world, and onto this Earth/ to do their part/ shit most of you don't even know where to start/ you lived out your lives/ and not knowing your capabilities/ you were scared of the risks, so you didn't factor the probabilities/ so you mapped out a quest, with the entirely wrong decisions/ you studied the wrong knowledge, so you made up the wrong incisions/ you made the wrong turns, with the paths that you have chose/ I'm here ready to oppose/ any of you chumps, that are willing to oppose me/ and I'll be ready to defy you, if you do not believe in me/ because almost every night, I asked the Lord to take my life/ if I ain't here for rap, I'm done struggling to win this fight/ with mine and MIZeRY's life/ look I'm still here, so it must be something with this rap shit/ it's just a matter of time, until I take off with this music/ every beat, every track I have produced/ have all seduced/ each and every listener/ each and every sinner/ so I must got some skills/ and If I must I will prove each and every one of my kills/

HOOK/CHORUS: What is my purpose?/ what is my game?/ what is the reason, I was put on this Earth?/ What is my purpose?/ what is my game?/ what was the point of having my birth?/ What is my purpose?/ what is my game?/ what is the reason, I was put on this Earth?/ What is my purpose?/ what is my game?/ what was the point of having my birth?/

VERSE 2 – Sandman/MIZeRY: **Rob Preski** "I ask the very question/ on my questing/ searching for my secret treasure chest/ than/ keep up motivation/ elevation/ is what I'm believing/ my religion/ what's happening/ turning backs on Jesus/ spitting ancient scriptures/ Is the gift that I give/ purpose is/ this/ to uplift/ God knows, not to enlist/ in the poison service/ making people nervous/ the war life that we living/ Alpha and Omega/ the beginning and the ending/ **MIZeRY** "Yo everyday of my life, people come to me for help/ whether they're lost angels, or whether or not they fell/ I'm here to help my dogs, I'm here to help my people, I'm here to help my family/ psychologically/ physically/ any means necessary/ I go out of my way to do what I got to do/ right now two of my dogs are trying to raise babies/ in my life, things like that are always just maybes/ my main purpose it to destroy most of this industry/ and rebuild the foundation, and start this empire/

HOOK/CHORUS: What is my purpose?/ what is my game?/ what is the reason, I was put on this Earth?/ What is my purpose?/ what is my game?/ what was the point of having my birth?/ What is my purpose?/ what is my game?/ what is the reason, I was put on this Earth?/ What is my purpose?/ what is my game?/ what was the point of having my birth/

SUMMARY - I'll explain it like this. "First, let me state for the record that when Rob and I completed this song originally; I still had no sure understanding of my true purpose in life. It took about 7 years after completing this, to re-evaluate this song; while speaking with Rob one day. In 2012, after God has shown me the truth about myself; I realized that this song was actually amazing. In addition, my true purpose was written within these pages all along. Let's take a look at the last line of my second verse - "my main purpose it to destroy most of this industry/ and rebuild the foundation, and start this empire/." Evidently, this is my story and my purpose in life. Further more, the word **Industry** is a code word, I have used my entire career and life; which ultimately means, the *World, and* not the actual music industry. My first verse however, speaks about my belief of humanity and how we are all destined in God's plan. Simply, the human mind per individual must learn to accept this fact and pursue a life in which God has intended rather, a life in which the sole individual intends."

Chapter 6: Song 12 – Listen (6:12)

Listen

VERSE 1: Yo listen up closely, while I tell you a story/ cause I'm sick of these bullshit beef's between crews/ I'm sick of these underground rappers saying that they paid all their industry dues/ The thing that irks me the most is they calling Eminem a racist/ here let me give you a list of some people, who said the same shit, that he said at sixteen/ Papis, to Muslims, to Chinese gangstas, you see what I mean/ they ain't African/ and I don't here anybody complain/ Y'all sound like a bunch of little kids, teacher, teacher, Johnny stole my eraser/ if you gonna start some shit/ make it over something worth it/ otherwise you're gonna end up dead, over some fucking bullshit/ Cause we already lost bugz/ if it's over some petty ass drugs/ just let this shit be/ cause I know that you're willing to ride for me/ just let this shit be, cause I know that you're ready to die for me/ remember I told Ya, that I only select soldiers/

VERSE 2: Yo, no wonder why they killed Bugz/ cause everyone's trying to be a damn thug/ just to prove how man they can be/ well it doesn't prove shit/ why don't I go around and start killing your whole family/ cause no one fights no more/ its just about killing people and holding up forty fours/ if you stating that you a thug, than you better be able to prove it/ cause I ain't gonna believe it/ till I actually see it/ mark my words, I breathe this rap shit/ I live for this rap shit, I die for this rap shit/ cause I ain't got nothing else going for me/ except for an alias that was given to me/ that's almost as fucked up as a man, who ain't give a fuck about his son/ who decided to run/ from the life he should have led/ I won't forget till he's actually dead/ I guess this is the way that it goes/ A pimp comes along/ fucks a couple of hoes/ nine months later/ he gets a phone call/ from an old bitch, finds out she got knocked up/ he tells this bitch, to shut the fuck up/ and then he says to this woman, that it ain't mine/ and this story continues throughout all of time/

VERSE 3: Yo I married a pen/ cause I'm sick of these women/ cause they're always making me choose between them/ they ask me to choose between the MIC or the ring/ I picked up the MIC, and I dropped the ring/ cause I would do anything/ to do my dream/ and if that's not the reason I was put on this Earth/ than by all means Lord, take me now/ cause I don't know how to continue my life/ I don't know how, to justify what's right/ without rap, I've lost my sight/ It's all I've got, it's all I want, it's all I need/ in this life of greed/ you only get one life, to live/ one life, to choose/ to do, what you need to do/ I follow the Bible/ that's my title/ and you're wondering why I've got so many rivals/ these people don't want me to go on ahead/ they want me dead/ well you know what they say, the good die young/ I'm probably dying from a disease/ as we speak/ that's why I need to seize/ this whole rap game/ before I die, and live out my name/

SUMMARY - I'll explain it like this. "Listen" is a song all about telling the world to wake up, including myself. Not only to wake up from themselves; but wake up from being fed all the lies and deceit; in which this world has poured constantly, into all our lives. Listen to my voice, listen to my lyrics, and listen to what I have to say because only through me can we all be saved. The last lines of my third verse, which are as follows - **I'm probably dying from a disease/ as we speak/ that's why I need to seize/ this whole rap game/ before I die, and live out my name/**. Those lines are in fact, my metaphor for gradually dying by the plague of humanity-AKA the devil. I must overcome it, order to conquer him; while reclaiming the Earth, before I die, & lived out my name."

Chapter 6: Song 13 – Clubbin (6:13)

Clubbin Ft. Lee Kid – Lyrics not included

HOOK/CHORUS: Feel the beat and get your groove on/ bounce baby bounce/ bounce left, bounce right, bounce faster/ Bounce here, then here/ and there after/ Feel the beat and get your groove on/ bounce baby bounce/ bounce left, bounce right, bounce faster/ Bounce here, then here/ and there after/

VERSE 2: I wanna start clubbin/ I wanna start bumpin/ I wanna start humpin/ I wanna start fuckin/ Shorty right there, starts coming to me/ grinding her clit/ all over my dick/ shaking her tits/ working that ass/ but Shorty right there's, got a big fat ass/ you got me mesmerized/ cause of your hips/ confused of the way, that you work that shit/ don't know what to do, don't know what to say/ But I love those games, that you love to play/ anywhere that we go/ I want you to know/ I'm sick of these hoes/ I want a good girl, who loves bad guys/ I'm sick of each and every one of your lies/ Its time to get serious/ we move to fast/ this shit won't last/ can you trust me/ cause I can trust you/ can you love me/ cause I can love you/ I'll tell you right now, I fucking hate clubbin/ I'm sick of just fucking/ I'm sick of you yelling/ I'm sick of you telling/ me I'm good for nothing/ I actually want you and me to mean something/ I'll give you my word/ I'll give you blood shed/ I'm done with the games/ Its time to move past, all of this pain/

HOOK/CHORUS: Feel the beat and get your groove on/ bounce baby bounce/ bounce left, bounce right, bounce faster/ Bounce here, then here/ and there after/ Feel the beat and get your groove on/ bounce baby bounce/ bounce left, bounce right, bounce faster/ Bounce here, then here/ and there after/

"haha, Yo if y'all think you'll ever catch me in a club, If I ain't performing/ you got shit twisted Homie/ you'll never see me in a fucking club/ you'll never see me doing that bubble gum, that candy ass fagot bullshit rap/ understand only real shit and real talk over here Homie/ I'm out…"

SUMMARY - I'll explain it like this. "Clubbin Ft. Leekid" was the first official song, I have ever done with a high school buddy. I first, intended this song to be the very start of long term artistry with my buddy Lee Kid. However, later down the road he wanted to have his own this, his own that, & his own crew; instead of formulating a conglomerate with me. Further more, I made this song to show that even if the beat is party type; you don't need to make commercial bull-crap in order to make a song good."

Chapter 6: Song 15 – The savior of rap (6:15)

The savior of rap

INTRO: "I'm the savior…

VERSE 1: Yo, Yo, every time I start thinking about this game/ it's a shame/ these mother fuckers will never understand our pain/ dying in these streets/ fighting against the police/ struggling to keep/ our heads up, just to keep the peace/ we been saying please/ no more getting down on our knees/ we through asking nicely/ we gonna start kicking and ripping this shit lively/ we still gonna go at it, even if it's pricey/ we put our lives/ out on the line/ just to get more stress put to the mind/ sick of all the struggling/ we sick of all the suffering/ most of our brotha's get high/ to get by/ cause we don't know how to survive/ or cope with the reality/ we living in poverty/ most of our sisters working three jobs/ just to get robbed/ of their money/ these mother fuckers think this shit's real funny/ so we go on welfare/ that supplies that child care/ that first aid/ and that Medicare/ that's getting us by every other day/ and these food stamps, don't by diapers/ its got my ass hyper/ the only thing that keeps me going is the fact and reality I am a soldier/ A survivor/ the knowledge that I am the savior/

HOOK/CHORUS: (Female only) - Once I get up, I can't get down ↓/ Even if you shot me, You won't stop me now/ **Once I get up, I can't get down/** I made it to far, to even quit now/ **Once I get up, I can't get down/** I'm fighting this war, until the very end/ **Once I get up, I can't get down/** My voice will be heard, till the end of time/

VERSE 2: Yo, Yo, this game is a lot deeper than just being a lyricist/ its time I started pulling your heads up out of that mist/ I'm taking this shit back to ninety seven/ keep rapping about that fake shit, I'll send all your asses to Heaven/ your souls shouldn't be redeemed in my eyes/ this game was real at the same time of Tupac's demise/ all I can do recently is watch this game perish under these fallen skies/ while it washes away like this societies pride/ most of you artist's are just along for the ride/ I'm here till the day that I die/ even after my time/ ever since I was young/ words of wisdom were sprung/ from my tongue/ living ways as the devils advocate/ with an immaculate/ rhyme style, that's intellectually/ confusing only mentally/ cause my destiny/ is too immense, for any mans soul/ to haul/ on their backs/ I shall not quit, for I am the savior of RAP/ (Reality and People)

HOOK/CHORUS: (Female only) - Once I get up, I can't get down ↓/ Even if you shot me, You won't stop me now/ **Once I get up, I can't get down/** I made it to far, to even quit now/ **Once I get up, I can't get down/** I'm fighting this war, until the very end/ **Once I get up, I can't get down/** My voice will be heard, till the end of time/

VERSE 3: Yo, Yo, ever since Tupac's demise/ I prophesized/ everyone looking at this game, only through my eyes/ since the day of his death, it feels like I got a piece of his soul/ put into my mind, body, and soul/ giving me the strength and hope, to continue/ taking his legacy to a whole other level/ you might call me mental/ I'm a man for the people/ and Tupac's death, was maybe my calling/ if you ain't take notice, this rap games falling/ we lost our leader/ who was brining us into a bigger brighter future/ honestly/ I'm going to rearrange our history/ we sick of all the MIZeRY/ I was built to absorb all of this agony/ making a better society/ for all of our kids/ that is my cause/ that's what Imma die for/ Its time, to fix the flaws/ lyrically, everything that I spit, are all metaphors/

HOOK/CHORUS: **(Female only) - Once I get up, I can't get down** ↓/ Even if you shot me, You won't stop me now/ **Once I get up, I can't get down/** I made it to far, to even quit now/ **Once I get up, I can't get down/** I'm fighting this war, until the very end/ **Once I get up, I can't get down/** My voice will be heard, till the end of time/ **Once I get up, I can't get down/ Once I get up, I can't get down/ Once I get up, I can't get down/ Once I get up, I can't get down/ Once I get up, I can't get down/ Once I get up, I can't get down/ Once I get up, I can't get down/ Once I get up, I can't get down/ Once I get up, I can't get down/**

SUMMARY - I'll explain it like this. "This is one of my favorites ever, simply because it explains exactly who, what I'm here to be, and do for the world. When I created this song, I originated it's meaning to declare me saving the rap world of music. However, we all can clearly see at this point that it's far beyond that. I further realized, when I say "I'm the savior of rap" – RAP means to me **(Reality and People)** and that's when I further understood the purpose for this song. In conclusion, what more shall I say other than the fact: I am the chosen savior of the world. I truly know, God wouldn't have allowed me to write and speak these words. Especially if, all I've done is baring false witness to Thy Holy Lord. Additionally, I have already surrendered my soul and prayed for him to be my guide. Guide me towards his holiness and his light. I also have asked him to prevent me from ever doing any wrong; while protecting me from all evil; Amen."

Chapter 7
Escaping My past

From 2006 – 2010, I encountered some of the hardest trials I may ever face in my life. All these trials, will result me having to escape my entire past from catching up with me; preventing it, from permanently damaging my future. I am now 18, soon to be 19, and I was clean from all illegal issues that had lingered on for several years prior. However, my great grandmother Erna recently passed away. She was the sole reason why my siblings and I weren't in foster homes. Although, I didn't show any emotion at the time, it was devastating to me. It was so severe, it would take near five years to permanently recover from this tragedy. With everything else going on in my life; I would soon find out that my mother would be moving out of Glen Head, N.Y., and going upstate to follow her on/off boyfriend. With this drastic move, I was in no way prepared to move upstate, NY. Instead, I had recently been hired at a newer and better job with 20/20 Ltd. and Verizon; whilst also having moved into my best friends house, Brian H. However, even though things seemed okay on the outside; they weren't on the inside. As I turned 19 and the year ventured on; things with my new job and residence were working out pretty well. However, sometime later within the year, an altercation would occur; right outside of my residence, with a random construction worker. The altercation would result to an assault charge, with a deadly weapon, and menacing. All because this random guy made a racist remark about my music, coming from my vehicle. What didn't help my side of the story was my short temperament for ignorance and zero tolerance for racism. However, in today's world you can't seemingly stand up against racism without being persecuted for it. One of the few lessons I had learned, from that day forth.

The next morning, I found myself rudely awoken up by Police and was soon arrested. When they questioned me, I didn't lie to the officers; even though I should have. Several days later, thanks to my friends; I was bailed out on a $2,100 bail and I was very thankful for not remaining in jail. After a year of going to court, working my ass off to pay for court fee's, and lawyer fees; I was finally sentenced with a three year term of probation, in the county of Nassau. Thankfully, the DA didn't succeed in sentencing me with several years of jail time. Even though I avoided jail, things at my current home soon became an unpleasant issue.

In 2007, I was very short on cash and had to work in Boston for a month and a half; earning enough money to move out of Brian's home. In May of 2007, I had received a notice from his best friend's mom to move out immediately. Within thirty days, I had found two places to move into and decided to take the second of the two; resulting, moving to Massapequa, N.Y. Although, this move was abruptly forced upon me; I was always resilient enough to find a way to survive. I began settling into a new place, with my new roommates. I am now living on the south shore of Nassau County, in a new city, and new district of Long Island. I quickly needed to find a way to become relevant in this town. Soon after moving; I also quit my job with Verizon due to frustrations, poor management structure, and not being happy selling a service that I wasn't okay with or that was for God. It was on that day of quitting, when I realized that something about my life wasn't right. I had realized, I begun refusing to do anything else other than pursue my own dreams. In this new city, I had also realized I needed to quickly find a part time job to pay my bills. I eventually found a part time job in December, 2007 with concord Mortgage to train as a loan officer. This job was good for the 4 months it lasted, but in March, 2008 I was laid off. Yet another obstacle, I needed to overcome and quickly. Thankfully, my girlfriend at the time seemed to force me to get a job and I found a job at Mario's pizzeria in Seaford, N.Y. However, this job was only part time delivering pizzas. I soon realized this wouldn't be sufficient to maintain life. In the summer of 2008, I then filed for welfare and Medicare to assist in living expenses. Even though, I started finding ways to help pay my bills; my home life with my current girlfriend, were on and off rough. In addition to that, my friends didn't seem to really like or appreciate my girlfriend Jayne. However, things in my music career would soon turn into a reality.

I was soon introduced to an upcoming known rap artist named "Uncle Murda." In 2008 and all of 2009, I worked in Manhattan four days a week. Most of that time, I was in a studio or at a show with this new artist, Uncle Murda. In addition, every two weeks I would have to report to probation in Minneola, N.Y. I also had to work on deliveries Thurs-Sat and all the meanwhile; I couldn't let organizations know, I was in the city as often as I was: due to legal restrictions. As I continued living secret lives amongst everyone I knew; I began to excel and work on music, immensely, and constantly. As I excelled, I started meeting famous artists, working with famous artists, & organizations too. I would soon rapidly build a name for myself; mostly good, but some allege to be poor. Lets recap if you are lost: I live in Massapequa with my current girlfriend Jayne; I worked off the books at a local chained Pizzeria; I was interning and working for myself in the world of music, under an artist named Uncle Murda; and I had to go visit my probation officer every two weeks: and explain to him, I was remaining positive and eagerly looking for new ways to expand my life. Despite all of these aspects of my life being so separated, but all connected; I would soon receive wonderful news in August, when I would be released from probation permanently. Even though some positive news was coming into my life; finances were still an issue, to the point I had no way of maintaining a phone; and I was late on my rent for several months as well. Thankfully, my really good friend Alessandra P. helped me out with $1,600. I never understood why she had helped me; until later I did, seeing her again in 2012…

In the latter portion of 2009, my life came crashing down all at once. Starting with my home life and current girlfriend. In November, I would also find out my apartment was going into foreclosure, a month before it was closing. The other three roommates I lived with had already moved out by this time too. It was now up to me, to maintain this home, and find a way to remain here until I could move. Aside from my housing issues; my girlfriend wasn't helping the situation by nagging, complaining, and looking for a new boyfriend secretly behind my back. In December, I would soon come to find out that Uncle Murda was getting dropped from the label: due to Jay Z disbanding, *Rocafella Records*… In January 2009, things became very slow for me. My addiction to Marijuana and alcohol became so severe, I attempted to kill myself. After an entire evening of drinking and smoking; I became so dazed and crazed, I tried drinking myself into a coma. Throughout the late hours of the night, around 2am; I found myself, hysterically crying to myself, and screaming up to God or the sky; asking God: "Please Lord why won't you take my life and donate it to as many children as it's worth; for I am not worthy to sustain this life." Ultimately, God did nothing and I eventually surrendered my life and my will to God's. I think it was from this day forth, I had begun to permanently change my life for the better. In January of 2009, I had reached out to my long lost father for the first time ever. I then began engaging into a new relationship with someone, whom was never in my life prior. Long story short, after a few months and a DNA test through Identi-gene; I had requested, if I could come live with my father. I only pursued him because after everything that has occurred, nothing made sense any more, or seemed to be working out for me; including, my girlfriend of two years.

In March of 2009, I would begin yet another but entirely new life in Haverhill, Massachusetts; living with my father, for the very first time. At first, I was depressed, alone, and nervous about my life here. For the first 4 months, after having moved up there; I spent almost four thousand dollars on travel expenses, going to, and staying in Long Island, N.Y. I traveled so often because I wasn't comfortable being in Massachusetts. Well, this would soon abruptly end in the month of August; when my father gave me an ultimatum: go to school full time or move out! On August 28th, 2009 at last minute, I had gotten together all the required information and enrolled in Northern Essex Community College. For the first time in six years, I was reentering into the world of education; majoring in business management. Living with my father wasn't easy, on top of everything else I had to cope with. My father Frank was not only suffering from isolationism, but he was very strict with dictatorship type of rules and methods. Nonetheless, some of his rules weren't an issue. It truly was the rules that made no logical sense what's so ever; which caused all of the issues: i.e. no drinking beer in the house or smoking. In fact, he stored alcohol in the house and he smoked cigarettes constantly in the home. These rules would have never been an issue, if my father had lived like me; live by example or if you want life to be a certain way, than the individual whom sets the standard, must abide by the same standards. As I am the witness, my father did no such thing. Instead, he made life extra difficult for a man whom wasn't looking for more difficulty in life. I was searching for more simplicity out of life instead.

Although, getting used to living with my father was going to take a sufficient amount of time; I was eager to make a best friend in this new town. In the month of November 2009, I had met my first new best friend- Fred B.; during math class. This young man, was very similar to me and much of a comedian. As the months went on, I began working on my first music album since "The savior of Rap" completed in 2005. This album was to be titled "No More Running." I had titled this as is, to force me to stop running from my past and accept what has occurred in my life.

On June third of my 22nd Birthday; I had released my new album, which debuted my good friend Fredy Bombs, and some of my lady friends on the cover. My new friends assisted me in selling some copies too; which totaled about 75 copies, locally. As the year progressed, I started becoming well known through out the college, my community, and amongst the youth. In December 2010, I would commence writing and recording songs for my first major debut album with *Island Def Jam Digital Distribution*; which was scheduled for release in May, 2011. After several months of working hard on my music, slacking off at school and my part time job at Best Buy; I would eventually see one of my dreams occur. My first debut with a major record label would commence. Although, this was an independent record deal; I was still becoming globally published. As thrilled as I was at the time to see this occur; I quickly realized, the road to victory was still far from over. The actual album didn't sell as well as I had hoped. In any event, I eagerly began working on a second debut album; which was to be released in November of 2011. As the year progressed, I continued to slack in school but continued to work hard as ever on my music career. When November 2011 came; my second album titled "Til' Death Do Us Part" would be released digitally, with *Island Def Jam* on 11/11/11. I was more excited than ever. Although, creating all this new music helped me in a positive fashion, something else occurred to me; I realized, that I was praying continuously to find the love of my life. In December of 2011, I attempted to remain positive by throwing a birthday bash and concert for my good friend Fredy. On December 17th 2011, I was arrested for a suspended out of state license. Despite being released thirty minutes before set time and loosing out on $1,200; I managed to perform and throw an eventful party for Fred.

On December 20th 2011, I had an epiphany about life and myself in terms of who I was in the world. During one week of restless sleep, I randomly began thinking or being told that I was Jesus Christ in the second form. Several days after Christmas 2011, I had woke up with an amazing idea to write a novel, movie, and a soundtrack for my return; which I self titled "The 2nd Coming." In addition, as referenced later in **chapter 11**; I'm explaining, when and which photo's I stumbled upon that ultimately reassured me of these thoughts. Near the end of December, I had also commenced writing my upcoming movie sound track. As the days continued on, I was working day and night continuously on this new music. It's because of the above mentioned photos, this book, and my music; which reassured me, that I wasn't crazy with all I was beginning to understand and believe were in fact true. I truly believe, my work is what God had intended for me and the world. For the first time ever in my own career and maybe most artists' careers; I had finished and recorded a total of 33 songs, in less than two months time. In addition, more than half of these songs were not pre-written; they were prophesized at the exact moment of recording on the spot in my home studio. I concluded, the reason for these series of miraculous events; resulting prophecies through songs, was simply for extra reassurance. Proving to myself that I was in fact Jesus Christ in the second form. I also concluded, these songs were my confirmation to show myself and the world; that everything in which was being recorded, were pieces of my past life, as Jesus Christ, and my future as Michael Izzo; or biblically referred to as, Saint Michael Thee Archangel. Aside from these songs proving to me my own truth; these songs in fact, contained the keys to discovering my path in life. In the month of February 2012, I began studying and defining the premonitions and signs, in which God has shown me; pertinent, to writing my first Novel and Movie for the world to see the truth from. Now being in the month of August 2012; I sit here, at last, writing this exact sentence informing the world how I ended up here; with you, reading this very chapter. In the meantime, we need to go back to 2010. I need to show you all, how I ended up here; both physically and lyrically, throughout my life, and my musical career. I've said many times before: My music and work is the very reason why I am even alive today…

Chapter 8
No More Running

I, Michael "MIZeRY" Izzo am turning 23 in a few months; and randomly, rediscovered, that my only passion in life next to finding true love: was music. In January of 2010, I commenced working on my first Rap album since my last in 2005. As I commenced writing the music for this project; I eventually, self titled this album "No More Running" to describe what my life has been most like; until now. In other words, I was sick of running from my past. This album was going to signify the mark of a new age for me in my own life; but within my musical career as well. This album was going to be the culmination of a new style and attitude for me; while also, assisting in expanding my public life in Haverhill, MA. Thanks to my newly signed producer Hev1 from Brooklyn, N.Y.; I had a plentiful selection of production to choose from for this album. Long and behold, most of the beats for this album came from Hev1; whom, to this day is a producer in which I intend to manage and make globally known. Creating this album, took a lot of time, and preparation in order for me to recreate myself; while redefining myself, as an artist. Considering, I haven't practiced my skill or trade in over five years. However, I being one to overcome any adversity in life; had completed this album four months later. Now that my album is finally completed; I noticed how quickly it became quite a successful project. Considering, how busy I was during the time of creation. On June 3rd, 2010, I had released my first album in five years time; while also, releasing my first CD in a new state. This is the story of how I came back to my musical roots and my very own salvation of life. Such salvation was channeled through writing and creating music; salivating through my very pores. Welcome to "No More Running."

No More Running - front and back; photo taken by Zack Meader; Direction and design by Michael Izzo. Copyright © 2010, *MIZeRY ReCORDS* – All Rights Reserved. People in photo, left to right: Katie Miller, Katie Dryer, Michael Izzo, Fred Boucher, Kristin Dryer, & Ashley Fay – Photo Taken in Massachusetts.

Chapter 8: Song 1 – The offering (A Tribute) (8:1)

The offering (A Tribute)

VERSE 1: I'm back, hahaha, oh shit and you really thought I was done. MIZeRY, Yaa… Take the pen to the pad, cause this is all I know/ I write hundreds of lyrics, and this is how I flow/ if you really wanna roll/ than be ready in five/ cause I'm already on the road/ this is my offering/ so fuck all you assholes/ who want to stop me now/ I'm a fucking cash cow/ I ain't never slowing down/ I'm a money making machine/ there ain't nobody hotter than me/ My name is MIZeRY/ I'm the best at this shit G/ I run MIZeRY ReCORDS, and I will never shut my mouth/ If you unplug my MIC's cord/ I'll be busting down your door/ with my chrome forty four/ pointed at your nose bone/ I need to take a break/ NO wait/ I'm not built for society/ this is not a fantasy/ for me/ it's all real life/ without music in my life/ I could drop dead tonight/ I'm tired of all the fighting/ just to survive/ to live and die another night/ I love making money/ I'm in control of my own destiny/ Yo fifty holla at me/ aside from all my skills/ I have several million dollar deals/ that I know, I could sell/ I'm a natural born hustler/ It's natural, and it comes from each of my stem cells/ etched in my DNA/ pumped in my veins/ while it flows through my bloodstream/ I'm ready to explode/ all over this microphone/ don't take this so literally/ cause I'm not showing you this sexually/ I used to love banging hoes/ an addiction, that comes and goes/ do you really think I care, If I spit this shit fast or slow/ fuck no/ go for broke/ steal away his show/ take the lime light from Eminem/ just for a few minutes/ so I could really feel, what its like, just to live in it/ if it wasn't for your music kid/ I probably would have slit my wrist/ back in school, on some real shit/ I was built for this kitchen/ back than, I never understood it/ but I learned to embrace it/ (Eminem – but you better hope you can handle the heat, or stay the fuck out of hells kitchen) I'm ready for any heat/ no matter what you throw at me/ I'll be ready to overcome any kind of adversity/ I was built flawlessly/ I'm filled with such diversity/ with those two combined/ it's damn near impossible to try to ever defeat me/ fuck playing the same/ I've already made a new game/ cause I'm sick of all the garbage/ I'm famished/ Yo fif/ put me in this shit kid/ cause I'm ready to do some damage/ no matter how far I go/ I will never forget my Homies/ as long as you have my back, I will always have yours/ I was born to pop off/ lets keep this shit neutral/ I don't want it to get brutal/ stopping me is futile/ these words keep my vitals/ stable/ hip hop is my opportunity for a better life for me and my people/ so instead of being the problem/ start being the solution/ and if you thought for a second/ I didn't know you was talking about me on "Despicable"/ As if you were invisible/ here's something spiritual/ I will never beef with you/ but if you are too scared to mention my name, Homie it's cool/ cause I don't want to attain/ any fame/ from you/ here are my last words for you/ I'm glad you're back on your feet/ you remembered to stay strong, in your biggest time of need/ do me one favor please/ Google MIZeRY ReCORDS, cause that's how you'll find me/ "Yaa, this is not even a beef, it's a tribute. Welcome to No More Running."

SUMMARY – I'll explain it like this. "When I began brainstorming for this new album; I immediately knew, I needed a very powerful and straight forward song to represent what I needed to state; "The offering" did that for me. I not only explained who I am lyrically and musically, but I also proposed working with people in the music world that I thought I should work with. In addition, I also paid homage to the white rap artist who paved the way for me to develop and master my own skills: *Eminem*."

Chapter 8: Song 2 – Life's direction (8:2)

Life's direction

INTRO: "This is the bag. This is the life I grew up knowing; only life, that I kind of really knew for awhile."

VERSE 1: This is what life's like anytime that we struggle/ Thinking of the next move every time that I hustle/ Just to make another dollar, to survive another day/ Listen to what I'm telling you, cause this is my pain/ Imma give it to you raw/ and tell you like it is/ I ain't any kind of chef, I'm a diverse kind of artist/ telling you these silly little rhymes/ when I spit it like this/ But, this is my life/ and I won't live like this/ I wanna be on beach tops, in all different countries/ I want to go to a bunch of different venues/ Yaa and tell all y'all my story/ and I feel like Alice in Wonderland, When I'm lost, playing in this beat/ and what's the next move, that I'll make in this chess game/ that I play/ 24 – seven/ 1st, I need to pray for a little bit of courage/ so Lord will you grant me this courage? / 2nd, I need a little motivation/ to get my ass moving/ so Lord, will you strike me on my ass so hard, that I'll never stop running/ 3rd, I need some help in deciding my direction/ there's so many lights to choose from and I don't really know which one's even a good one/ and I need some help choosing between the good and the bad/ I'm on a righteous path/ who's trying to get passed/ all the bad times of my past/ who's acting/ on this rapping/ of this life, yes, through this Rhyming, Acting, Poetry/ 4th, I want to meet a wealthy visionary/ who see's eye to eye with me/ and if God could build the world, in six different days/ Than, I can do something huge in my lifetime man/

HOOK/CHORUS: Life – what does life really mean? If you're not helping each other/ what's Life – Lessons Instructed, by our Father, Yaa for all of Eternity/ Life – life on Earth is really purgatory/ A lifetime of prisons, where we're all made to suffer on every single day/ Until we figure out, who we're really gonna be/ In this game that we all call Life/ except in this life/ for me/ it's nothing but MIZeRY/ Life – Yaa, what does life really mean?

VERSE 2: I'm trying to survive/ just another day, with my head pointed to the sky/ and yes, I've asked God to sacrifice my life/ on several different times/ If I could go back in time/ I would change so much in my life/ I would purify my soul/ I'd undo all my wrongs/ I would thank God, every single day, for the life that I have/ And I would just ask/ How not to be so sad/ On those cold-wintery nights, that keep my bones frozen, with mass amounts of pain/ and I don't want the darkness to overcome me, with a permanent scenery that's gloomy with rain/ and I do need some change/ I can't constantly be doing the same things/ Ya and I've done a lot of bad things to a lot of different people/ That's evil/ and goes against all the ways of the Bible/ here's a twister for you kids/ I'm a righteous/ mad scientist/ who's sick/ with this/ that's got most of you bitches/ pissed/ off at the kid/ like it's your day job, and shit/ to live up in this bitch/ I'll tongue twist/ your nuts/ in a bunched up/ net full of bitches/ oh wait, now I'm all confused with this/ If I slipped/ Cindy, the answers hidden in a bag of chips/ the twist is this kids/ and it's not alcoholic/ so sit/ I'll be real quick/ I was trained for this quest/ you can hate it or love it/ either way son, I'm not quitting on this music/

HOOK/CHORUS: Life – what does life really mean? If you're not helping each other/ what's Life – Lessons Instructed, by our Father, Yaa for all of Eternity/ Life – life on Earth is really purgatory/ A lifetime of prisons, where we're all made to suffer on every single day/ Until we figure out, who we're really gonna be/ In this game that we all call Life/ except in this life/ for me/ it's nothing but MIZeRY/ Life – Yaa, what does life really mean?

SUMMARY - I'll explain it like this. "Life's Direction" was my attempt at understanding what life truly means for us all. Through my study of the word itself, I defined LIFE as follows: **Lessons**, **Instructed**, by our **Father**, for all **Eternity**. Further more, as I was defining LIFE. I decided to describe and elaborate a little upon my life too; while using slick metaphors, in order to intelligently confuse society to my true meaning. Ultimately, this song was me attempting to figure out my own direction in life; while deciding, which paths I should choose in the upcoming future."

Chapter 8: Song 3 – No More Running (8:3)

No More Running

INTRO: "Let's break, let's break, let's break the bank with this one. This is a tale that I've never told before. This was my life before the age of 12 and I'm coming for the top with this; so go ahead."

VERSE 1: Impair my ability/ cause I'll never stop rhyming G/ this is in my blood stream/ it was injected in my veins/ when I was just a little man (mane) even though my family was fucked, I was born and raised a catholic/ I was raised by two grandparents/ confession was on Saturday/ I went to church on Sunday's/ cause that's the day that you worship God, and be forgiven for your sins/ It's so hard for me to win/ especially since I have good intentions/ the majority of this planet/ hate it when optimism happens/ I'm sick of all the pessimism/ I'm so sick of this fucking system/ that society makes us live in/ whatever happened to being free/ oh wait that's right, cause freedom was never meant to be free/ it was just a bunch of bullshit, that they all lead us to believe/ back in the days/ maybe about the seventh grade/ I heard the real slim shady/ a couple years after that/ I was living with all this misery/ so I started writing rhymes/ and I was working hard body/ cause ever since that day/ I've wanted a part, in this game/ I started masterminding my own way/ up into this game/ and during all my trials/ I think I've gone a bit crazy/ as I was changing all these ways/ about the mother fucking game/ I promise you all this, that I will never chase this fame/ The one rule that I've made/ is that I shall remain true/ anytime I step in this booth/ I honestly do believe/ that I used to be in my prime/ when I was bumping Eminem's rhymes/ My motivations diminished/ but it will never be extinguished/ I'm still working on investments/ to get this music thing going, trust me I ain't never gonna stop, writing down these rhymes/ that manifest themselves, in my mind/ I'm developing this story, every time/ I write a new line/ without music in my life/ I could drop dead on a dime/

HOOK/CHORUS: What do you know/ and what do you know/ about this life/ I'm done running, I'm here for good this time/ I don't care what you say, Imma keep making my rhymes/ and just so you know/ I'll still be here, after I die/ When I turned twelve, I became a mastermind/

VERSE 2: At writing these rhymes/ I'm sick, back on my grind/ from the hook, into this verse/ I've always had this blood thirst/ to be nothing but number one first/ ever since I was age 12/ I was built to be competitive/ if you don't speak any intelligence/ than I won't be comprehensive/ to you, I'll just keep on ignoring you like you don't even exist/ until you just give up and quit/ because you're way to fucking pissed/ to deal with any of my adolescence/ as the clock strikes 12, you'll see my arrogance diminish/ poof, than I vanish/ just like a magic trick/ when my skills come out, you know it's after twelve o'clock/ Yo, when the DJ turns this music on, and let's this record drop/ I'll have the whole crowd going crazy, swinging from my cock/ I could mix so many words/ that they can never even be purged/ from any of my verses that I kick/ and fall within my scriptures/ if I paint you a verbal picture/ will you then, be able to interpret/ the wisdom/ in which/ I'm giving you? if you ever put me into power/ I shall remain true/ to each and every one of you/ including me/ for all eternity/ and just so you all know, I have sworn to inherit/ each and every bit of your misery/ so you all can live more peacefully/ so I ask you Lord, will you grant me this opportunity/ to start saving some lives/ up until now, I felt worthless, and didn't really know what to do with my spare time/ the one thing I demand is, if you dare judge these lines/ before you understand my rhymes/ I'll unleash hell upon you all for the rest of your lives/

HOOK/CHORUS: What do you know/ and what do you know/ about this life/ I'm done running, I'm here for good this time/ I don't care what you say, Imma keep making my rhymes/ and just so you know/ I'll still be here, after I die/ When I turned twelve, I became a mastermind/

SUMMARY - I'll explain it like this. "No More Running" was my first single in a very long time. At first, I wanted a song that was very clever with a singing type of hook. However, I quickly changed the concept to being about my life before I was 12 and after the age of 12. This song explains my life before 12 in the first verse; and then explains my life after 12 in the second verse. During the second verse, you can see that I capture my true purpose in the world; before I actually even understood it myself, two years later. This song was the true sign from God, that I am, who I am, and I need to wake up and realize that I am the true son of God: reborn."

Chapter 8: Song 6 – We got it all w/ live band (8:6)

We got it all

INTRO: "This is one of those records, that you just kick back, lay back, talk about some real shit, keep shit funky/ you know what I mean, just air some shit out/ But, you staying real at the same time, you know what I mean?/ Yo check this mother fucker out Yo."

VERSE 1: We got it all , and you ain't got nothing/ so please stop frontin/ if you wanna be worth something/ stop being pussy, sitting in your crib, while you're crying about nothing/ I spit it so smooth, I spit it so fast/ I can kick it anyway Homie, just make this beat last/ This is that real classic shit/ this is the kinda record, that makes the CD skip/ naa – you must be crazy kid/ you're the one who's whack bitch/ This a platinum plaque hit/ and I ain't even finished writing to this mother fucker yet/ Yo, real is real dog, and you wanna know what's real/ is my girls got real housewives of Atlanta, Loud as fuck in the back/ screwing with my thoughts, as I'm bumping to this track/ I'm keeping my lyrics simple/ If I went back to intellectual/ you couldn't even follow/ you'd get lost in the beat, I'd be running circles around you, If I was at a track meet/ my thoughts is all scattered/ even if you managed/ to collect all them dog, you would never connect them/ My thoughts are too complex/ kind of like a Rubex cube multiplied by ten/ I can't finish writing this/ I gotta freestyle on this/ huh, let me kick a few bars/ right now – I'm thinking about deadin' some rap stars/ If I put some of you on blast, you wouldn't be ready to get it/ you mother fuckers need to quit it/ cause If I normally spit it/ you wouldn't even understand it/ the way that I speak intellectual, complexity/ that's telling these stories/ with high propensity/ with so much diversity/ who's filled with this mystery/ that's been secretly/ running, this whole entire game, that we all know as MIZeRY/ Now that I'm exposed, I gotta tell y'all something/ go ahead and try to steal any of my tactics/ but they ain't gonna help, any of you butt fucking fagots/ Let it be known that I don't tolerate bitch-assness/ It's MIZeRY ReCORDS, I formulated this plot/ As I, sneak through the back door, and dominate my way to the top/ I'm getting too tired, I can't finish writing/ let me ask y'all something/ Should I, finish writing this record, are you satisfied enough? Let me tell y'all what's really going on, what's up/ I wanna lay down, go to sleep, just dream, Yaa and never wake up/ Ya keep it real/ I'm confused with your line, you say Homies respecting you for chasing these mills/ that's all cool/ please keep this shit real/ I paid you and Karl $**** flat/ that was just a down payment, for a show you never showed up at/ Back in NYC Karl tried to introduce us together/ Homie, you turned your back on a much younger brother/ Yo, I put money in your pockets.... And Just quit acting arrogant/ **"Uncle Murda – Don't let money change you, and get big headed, cause Ni***s will bang you, shit"** Ya, I still respect you, but keep on listening/ if you don't like what I'm saying/ take it with a grain of salt/ cause... Sitting in your crib/ way before you ever find... Dog, I put work in for you/ All I'm trying to say, is let's break bread together my G/ Yo Murda's the realest dude that I know, that's why I'm GMG for life/ and I don't give a fuck if everybody knows/ I'm giving everybody/ one opportunity/ to break bread together/ so we can all change, change for this better/ we need to all stop acting like young punks/ that's molded into these young thugs/ that's grinding in the hood/ It's time we change our mind states, Ya only for the good/ This is MIZeRY ReCORDS, you mother fuckers heard/

HOOK/CHORUS: I wanna get high/ Get Drunk! Stay rhyming on this MIC/ all night/ I wanna get high/ Get Drunk! Stay rhyming on this MIC/ all night/ Cruising in the whip/ of my BM X6/ cruising to these clubs, just searching for a bitch/ Meli bring some shorties, I'm into freaky ass shit/ Cruising in the whip/ of my BM X6/ cruising to these clubs, just searching for a bitch/ Meli bring some shorties, I'm into freaky ass shit/
I wanna get high/ Get Drunk! Stay rhyming on this MIC/ all night/ I wanna get high/ Get Drunk! Stay rhyming on this MIC/ all night/ Yaa,
I wanna get high/ Get Drunk! Stay rhyming on this MIC/ all night/ I wanna get high/ Get Drunk! Stay rhyming on this MIC/ all night/ Cruising in the whip/ of my BM X6/ cruising to these clubs, just searching for a bitch/

SUMMARY - I'll explain it like this. "When I made this song, I simply was so high and feeling so good from pot that I was in the zone: my zone. This record was created by a live band and touched up with a Cypress hill sample from my boy Jon; I also knew, it was time to vent about some shit. As I started bumping this song my current girlfriend at the time, started complaining to me and turned up her TV show "Real housewives of Atlanta." As a result, she allowed for my venting to commence. As my writing continued, I had to discuss my intelligence and how I can't believe people in the music industry are screwing me over. Especially, when I'm trying to unify business for us all. In the end, my main focus was to make it laid back, as I was feeling at the time."

Chapter 8: Song 7 – Carnage or Rebirth (8:7)

Carnage or Rebirth

VERSE 1: "This is G-man MZ coming at you live and direct, I don't think you're on my level." Yaa, I don't need an introduction/ this is a beef record son/ when I'm through with this dog, Imma let off my gun/ Early bird/ gets the worm/ that's what I'm thinking about, when I'm writing to this record/ who's getting bodied, on this mother fucking record/ I've got alotta different names, on my mother fucking list/ If you don't like what I'm saying, y'all can suck my dick/ All 8 inches, on my chrome desert eagle/ no need to get gangsta, my lyrics are too lethal/ I'm never one to beef/ but if I really have to sin, Imma take it to the streets/ here's a couple of rules b/ rule number 1, you should never ever sleep/ on a mother fucking G/ cause, Homies call me the G-man/ with central intelligence/ I'll find you off the internet/ within a matter of minutes/ I've got my boots, gloves, and my black mask on/ creeping up behind you, saying give up Ya life son/ I'll be sitting/ waiting, in Ya crib/ with Ya bitch/ and your kids/ buried, and tied/ in a 10 foot ditch/ cause, the cops stop looking after 6 feet kid/ this is hip hop son, if you don't like what this is/ than get the fuck out this bitch/ and this is why I'm in it/ cause I relate to this shit/ I was born with this gift/ and this is how it is/ but I will say this/ Manny Perez/ is a pussy, how did someone like you? Make the <u>*Invitation*</u>/? So welcome to my mission/ and I ain't shifting visions/ so tell me what it's like, now that you're the victim/

<u>HOOK/CHORUS:</u> Beef, Ya, I said what's beef? Beef is what happens when pussies act up and get bodied in the streets/ Beef, Ya, I said what's beef? Beef is when Emcee's talk a lot of shit and get bodied on these beats/ Beef, Ya, I said what's beef? Beef's only going down, after I load up my gun/ Beef, Ya, I said what's beef? Ya you know the beef's over, when your enemies run/ Beef Homie, I said what's beef?

<u>VERSE 2:</u> If you got any beef and you want to clarify it/ you need to come confront me/ face to face, eye to eye, some ride or die shit/ you see man, I'm gangsta to the core/ I was built for this war/ I would never, ever want for that part of me to surface/ I was put here for something, but that wasn't my purpose/ this records not for kids, this is strictly for my G's/ and these mother fucking streets/ if you wanna role with me/ you need to have a lot of dreams/ and they got to make sense/ the rule is man, if it don't make dollars, than it don't make sense/ you ain't built for my game, get the fuck off my bench/ I make a lot of music and I tell different stories/ straight fly, so smooth, Shorty don't bore me/ I need you to be sexy/ where are you girl, I'm waiting for you Shorty/ I need a real tall girl, with long black hair/ straight up sexy, with a thick ass body/ here next topic/ the one thing I hate is all y'all bitch ass artists/ who don't collaborate with any other artists/ MIZeRY ReCORDS.com is where y'all find me/ I have a lot of talent/ there's money to be made/ Yaa, come follow us, we all getting paid/ Yo son, real talk, wait a minute for a second/ Yo, and this is the transition into my rebirth, into my rebirth/ and that's the transition, into my rebirth/ you could find me on tour, are you ready for this beef? Are you ready for the beef? Na naa, I don't think you're ready for the beef/

HOOK/CHORUS: Ya, I said what's beef? Beef is what happens when pussies act up and get bodied in the streets/ Beef, Ya, I said what's beef? Beef is when Emcee's talk a lot of shit and get bodied on these beats/ Beef, Ya, I said what's beef? Beef's only going down, after I load up my gun/ Beef, Ya, I said what's beef? Ya you know the beef's over, when your enemies run/ Beef Homie, I said what's beef?

SUMMARY - I'll explain it like this. "Simply, I figured that since I was venting on "We got it all," I would just continue to vent more; while taking it to the next level. On this song, I decided to express my Armageddon like violent capabilities. However, I was also proving to my enemies; I will be reborn, before I create massive carnage; hence the title. Ultimately, I wanted to take a real Gangsta Rap style and inform everyone what happens in all forms of beef. Even if you're caught in the wrong streets at the wrong time."

Chapter 8: Song 8 – Hero (8:8)

Hero

INTRO: "hahaha Yaa, Alright, alright, you may be right, you may be right/ you may be, this shit is serious/ oh ight, here we go"

VERSE 1: Yes baby girl/I will always be your hero/ pick any one, start counting down to zero/ I could be your superman, protect you from this world/ from all these hurtful things, that's trying to get'ch you girl/ I'm trying to tell you baby, that I'll love you till the end/ If you felt, how I feel, when I'm writing with this pen/ I'm trying to tell you sweetie/ I'll be your Superman/ I could be your Bruce Wayne/ I could be your Batman/ I could Hit'ch you off, with some of my batterangs/ Ok, here we go girl/ Yes, I could be your Wolverine/ I could be your saber tooth/ Get'ch you out of those clothes and make you feeling loose/ I could be your MIZeRY/ and make you feel good/ Maim' ok – here we go, here we go/ I'm doing it for the flow/ I'm trying to make mad money, stacking up this doe/ I hope you could handle/ what I'm doing for you girl/ I'm trying to tell you baby that you're my entire world/ I wanna see how far you'll ride with me/ Gonna do it for me? I told you, that I love you, so stand by me/ I told you girl…

HOOK/CHORUS: Okay, here we go/ here we go/ I could be your hero/ I could be anyone, and save you from this world/ I said that I'm here, so don't hide girl/ I love when I'm starring deep down in Ya eyes/ I love when we get away, living out our lives/ I told you baby girl, I could be your hero/ pick any one, I could be your hero/ I told you girl, I told, I, I, I told you girl/

VERSE 2: Imma, Imma smooth criminal/ and Imma tell you what you wanna know/ except for my name/ It's tatted on my right arm/ I don't need a firearm/ to slay y'all bitches/ go ahead girls, Imma grant you three wishes/ anything y'all need/ your dreams is reality/ why I gotta lie/ to get'ch you in my bed tonight/ but ass naked, I ain't even faking/ there will be cum on my floor/ go ahead ladies, and walk through my door/ Just you and me girl/ playing fantasy fucking/ Up in MIZeRY's mansion/ sex toy's, orgies, all sorts of outfits/ yes, go ahead girl, and sip on this drink/ ohh Yaa, I know that My car doesn't always fit up/ in your tight tiny garage/ I can go all day, barraging you with batterangs/ I love those sounds you make, when we bang/ I'm a new criminal, I ain't supposed to be polite/ Booboo, shut up and listen, Man while I write this rhyme/ as I'm spitting this rhyme/ Imma, Imma – Smooth criminal/ cause everywhere I go/ these ladies gotta know/ who's that guy, who's that guy? Owww/ You've been hit by/ you've been struck by/ The new criminal/ and no matter where I go/ these ladies gotta know/ what's my name/ yes, yes, what's his name/ Yooo, Ha I could be your hero/

HOOK/CHORUS: Okay, here we go/ here we go/ I could be your hero/ I could be anyone, and save you from this world/ I said that I'm here, so don't hide girl/ I love when I'm starring deep down in Ya eyes/ I love when we get away, living out our lives/ I told you baby girl, I could be your hero/ pick any one, I could be your hero/ I told you girl, I told, I, I, I told you girl/

SUMMARY - I'll explain it like this. "Originally, this song was supposed to be a song all about how me and DaRedANT AKA Jon were the heroes of this world. Especially, for our very special wives; most importantly. Later on, Jon decided to opt out because the verses he wrote were too much about being a super hero as oppose to being the hero for your women. Even so, I decided to continue on with the song and make a good version of me being my women's hero. The second verse is the bad raunchy version of being a hero to women. Jon threw some auto-tune on my vocals and this is what I came up with; inspired by, Michael Jackson's "Smooth Criminal."

Chapter 8: Song 9 – Anger Management (8:9)

Anger Management Ft. Sundance Kid – Lyrics not included

VERSE 2: What up, It's HTS! Teaming up with MIZeRY ReCORDS/ So you betta, check what we saying/ every time we come to this MIC/ I could just go down, and let the beat drop out/ come back in/ saying Mother fucker you thinking? Understand Homie, I ain't playing these games/ but I keep on telling you, Mother fucka's lames/ you wasn't built for this game/ this is how I vent, this is how I speak/ So respect what I do, when I step to this beat/ I got so many thoughts that would make you go insane/ If you jumped in my mind, you would blow out your brains/ within the first day/ and I ain't even playing/ but, anyways man/ let's talk about the doctor's/ let's talk about the trouble/ let's talk about the women/ naa, let's talk about those things that I did for a living/ I'll tell you about my friends, shit I'll talk about some people, that I said I'd never mention/ did I ever mention/ I wanna be an assassin/ no, no, no, you need the anger management/ I have this intensity, that requires an adrenaline rush/ Yaa, just to keep my soul up/ I don't care what you say, cause I love making music/ when I make a song, I just know how to groove it/ I'm something always new/ and I'm something you wanna be/ Yaa, I'm someone all these ladies really gotta see/ Yaa Sundance, he's my backup generator, when my lights black out/ he's my brother, who picks me up as I fall to the ground/ when I think about this song/ I'm saying to myself, that, this is where I end it/

SUMMARY - I'll explain it like this. "It took a long time to create a song for this beat. For two years, Jon and I attempted to create a song. All of a sudden on one evening, my buddy Sundance comes to our studio and hears this beat. He immediately decides to begin working on the song. Long and behold, that was the exact motivation I needed in order to find the right title and lyrics for this beat. I decided to vent on anger management and how I don't need it. However, this beat was reused later on."

Chapter 8: Song 11 – No Privacy (8:11)

No Privacy Ft. Brittles – Lyrics not included

"Turn the beat up a little bit, Ya I said turn that Sh** up, oh wait I already did, turn it up a little more, no I already did that, fuck what I said ."

VERSE 2: Babygirl, you know that I never meant to hurt you/ you know that I'll always love you/ I'm only hating girl, cause you're not in my arms/ how can I be strong/ when I'm dying inside/ My hearts all shattered/ Babygirl Yaa, are you down to ride? I wanna get plastered/ I wanna get hammered/ Brittney Pink, tell em again girl/ tell em again girl/

VERSE 4: Just come back to me/ I know – I know, you wanna be with me/ why you gotta hate? Well you know girl, you ain't ever gotta fake/ how you feel for me/ Don't be mysterious/ I'm the only one who can be MIZeRous/ mischievous/ Don'tch you ever – hate on this/ I know, that'ch you know/ you want, everything that I got/ BITCH! Bitch/ ha Ya, I called you a bitch/ I told you girl/ that I'm tired of this shit/

VERSE 6: Yaa, cause I got to be all up on you/ yes, I really want nothing but you in my life/ soo girl, you wanna be committed/ you wanna stay and sit/ in the crib/ that'ch you live in/ but understand, I ain't trying to fuck around girl/ I ain't trying to play games/ cause I've made this game/ and I'll change these rules/ when they gotta be changed/ I'm the fucking host/ but where were you all, when I needed you the most/ you can't fuck with my crew/ cause we the mother fucking best/ I am the boss! MIZeRY ReCORDS, that's who it is bitch/ you better check this/ 2009 to infinity sucka's/ you can't ever touch me or my hot ass crew/ My click/ understand that you are the bitch/ I'm the mother fucking man running this shit/ don't get it twisted/ you heard you punk ass bitch/ Haha Yo, I'm buying my girl an ill ass crib/ with an ill ass ring/ that cost a mill flat son/ you can't fuck with what I think about, cause I think about billions/ Billions/ you can't fuck with what I think about, cause I think about billions/ and nothing fucking less/

SUMMARY - I'll explain it like this. "During this stage in my life things were difficult between me and my friends. Some of the reasons included people creating fake stories behind my back due to jealousy. Long story short, after me and Brittney started speaking again; she finally got into our studio and decided to make a song to this beat with me. After I had heard what she recorded, I immediately decided I wanted to make this a feature. I immediately began writing a part to counteract hers. My first intentions were to make this song Brittney's first debut. However, she later decided she didn't like me on the song anymore and caused a new issue between her and me."

Chapter 8: Song 13 – The Prototype (8:13)

The Prototype

VERSE 1: I am the prototype, put me on the shelf/ way back when, I was ready to sell/ a million fucking units, in the first day son/ I told you people, I am the one/ I'm breaking all barriers/ and I'm gonna hit a bunch of Guinness world records/ you can't stop me, this is MIZeRY ReCORDS/ I'm here to make millions, I ain't trying to get less/ you can't compare to me, cause I'm different from the rest/ I've taken all the tests/ and I passed with all A's/ You're not on my level, I have much higher grades/ Don't interpret this, cause it's not that important/ why so serious? (Joker Clip) I am the joker, I'll even be a gambit, and beat your ass in poker/ let me tell you some jewels, I'm all about the numbers, and I'm all about the facts/ I love having money, and I love getting ass/ I'm gonna make a sick game, just like Mortal Kombat/ Yo fly Bri, If me and Jayne don't work, I'm gonna go wild, with a bunch of different girls/ I'm sorry God, but that's just how I'm built/ here's a list of what I'm worth/ It's MIZeRY ReCORDS, with MIZeRY Musik/ MIZeRY Islands, and MIZeRY Money/ MIZeRY owns Spa's and MIZeRY films/ we've got MIZeRY Models/ that's rocking MIZeRY WeAR/ Now let me rhyme to everything that I just listed/ I could fight you with Swords/ and you know that I'd do it/ I'm all about the peace/ but I could turn violent/ I'll start with your braw/ and I really want your pussy/ If I can't get your pussy/ than I may sell some pills/ just so I could go buy me more models/ They'll rock MIZeRY WeAR/ when they're riding my dick/ oh shit, I'm so caught up in myself, that I forgot about the hook/

HOOK/CHORUS: Yes, Yes, I am the prototype; put me on the shelf/ way back when, we were ready to sell/ a million fucking units, in the first day son/ Imma genius mastermind, and here's my prototype/ (Joker Laugh)

VERSE 2: Ya well, the jokes on all of y'all/ so if you really got the balls/ than you better join my squad/ it's in your best interest/ to invest/ in MIZeRY ReCORDS/ Get it, yup, success/ I want a fleet of trucks/ and G 5 Lear Jets/ three for my entire label/ this is how I treat my employees, Ya, as if they were my angels/ Ya so I'm waiting for somebody so ill, to jump on this record and tell me a story/ that really gets me crazy/ understand I mean like, something that so crazy/ that I just question/ to myself, how the fuck did that happen/ than again understand, this is why I'm rapping/ so you can understand it, so you don't repeat mistakes that I've made/ or so you don't have to struggle through the dues that I've ever paid/ did you notice that these dudes is all fucking crazy/ and how dare any of you think you're better than me/ this is all MIZeRY/ I'm the pain and agony/ of this whole entire industry/ so you better recognize, that I've innovated and created a brand new game/ ha Yaa, welcome to planet MIZaine/

SUMMARY - I'll explain it like this. "The Prototype" initially was supposed to be a song where I display all my artists which were the metaphor behind the song title. However, down the road no one whom claimed to be on my label ended up recording on this song so I took it over as a metaphor for me being the best prototype the world has ever seen. Lyrically, if you read my lyrics, you can tell that I'm discussing that I've created a new world for a select few; or a select many. Life can be freely expressive; until the rebirth of Christ. Further more, I wanted this song to represent what I'm worth because I truly believe: through my success, I'd stop at nothing to make everyone else just as successful."

Chapter 8: Song 13 – This is my jungle (8:14)

This is my jungle

Axel rose welcome to the jungle live clips…

HOOK/CHORUS: Now I'm just a love machine/ you might not live to see your kids/ so she'll just burn down your house, and all while you're on vacation bitch/ Now I'm a love machine/ you might not live to see your kids/ so she'll just burn down your house, and all while you're on vacation bitch/

VERSE 1: Yaa, this is not my usual style, this is not my usual swagger/ you took me out my box, and I'm sick and tired of your laughter/ I see you sitting in the corner/ asking what I do for a living/ is he a gangsta, or a rapper/ is he a pimp, or a player/ (Guns & Roses Sample) So I'll welcome you to the jungle/ and I don't think you're ready to tussle/ you ain't built for this kind of hustle/ and I'm way to motivated, but if you invade my airspace/ I'll inebriate your brain/ If you come to close to me, Imma blow you out the sky/ I've got something to tell y'all, I'm the worlds greatest mastermind/ I'm restricted with my talents, when it comes to using my gifts/ when I'm using/ or abusing/ these abilities that I was given/ I can't alter reality or you, I can only choose/ a destiny in which I want to pursue/ but very soon/ I'll be the one, who's searching and hunting for you/ from a distance, camped out, with a magnified zoom/

HOOK/CHORUS: Now I'm just a love machine/ you might not live to see your kids/ so she'll just burn down your house, and all while you're on vacation bitch/ Now I'm a love machine/ you might not live to see your kids/ so she'll just burn down your house, and all while you're on vacation bitch/

VERSE 2: Yaa, my flow is immaculate, spectacular, spontaneous in every way/ If you could roll with me, I bet you would on any given day/ I'm sorry if these stories are to bleak/ or to mean/ or maybe their just way to real/ for you, hey youngin/ you should take a seat/ I don't think that you're ready for my knowledge, or any of the words that I speak/ or the verbal tones, that I'm sending your way every time that I breathe/ and it's just a matter of time, until my verbal attacks of violence/ all kicked in, brutally beating you, until you're permanently silent/ (Guns & Roses samples) I'm not trying to shake this up/ I'm just trying to throw you off/ with my verbal attacks of warfare/ that I'm using against you/ this is psychological warfare, that I'm trying to use against you/ so welcome to the jungle, where I've got fun and games/ I'm tired of you repping things, that you wasn't ever built to name/ So welcome to the jungle/ where we don't allow no lames/ and if you ain't bring any girls, than you was never allowed to play/ and if this is how it's gonna be, than I want'ch you out of my face/ so welcome to my jungle, cause were the one's making the games/

HOOK/CHORUS: Now I'm just a love machine/ you might not live to see your kids/ so she'll just burn down your house, and all while you're on vacation bitch/ Now

I'm a love machine/ you might not live to see your kids/ so she'll just burn down your house, and all while you're on vacation bitch/

SUMMARY - I'll explain it like this. "Simply I wanted to remix "Welcome to the jungle" by Guns & Roses. Long and behold, this is what I ended up creating."

Chapter 8: Song 16 – King Brutis (8:16)

King Brutis Ft. Reino Ortiz – Lyrics not included

HOOK/CHORUS: MIZeRY's part after Reino's hook – Shake, shake, shake your ass girl/ drop it so slow/ that I'll throw you some doe/ baby you know that I'm a king, Reino Ortiz show these bitches how we do/ haha

VERSE 2: Haha, Yaa, I've got an ill mean swagger/ Shorty what'ch you after/ trying to get my paper/ well, I already turned these pages/ I don't need these ladies/ I'm trying to make some money/ Shorty/ trust me/ I don't need you to help me/ there's two kinds of people, Kings and other G's/ that will get down like me/ chillen while popping bottles; sitting in VIP/ while you're starring from a distance, asking DJ Envy/ who the fuck I really be/ I'm MIZeRY/ Ya the one and only G/ Imma break this hit down/ I was born with this gift/ and even if I quit/ it would come right back, cause we're attached, cause we're attached at the hips/

HOOK/CHORUS: MIZeRY's part after Reino's hook – Shake, shake, shake your ass girl/ drop it so slow/ that I'll throw you some doe/ baby you know that I'm a king, Reino Ortiz show these bitches how we do/ haha

VERSE 3: I'm MIZeRY, no matter what I did/ I would always choose music/ over any kind of chick/ but I will say this/ I've seen so many things/ but not enough girls in sexy G-Strings/ Reino's already passed me a bunch of different bottles/ fuck getting drunk, start passing me some models/ I would never want no squeezies/ dog do you feel me? I need a quarter piece Shorty/ who keeps a quarter million tucked between her cheeks/ and no baby mama drama/ that shit will slow you down/ I need a sugar baby mama, that's gonna hold me down/ Yo Reino, come back in/ and show them how you sing/ and Shorty let's roll/ fyi though/ you're messing with a king/ Ya, you're messing with a king/

HOOK/CHORUS: MIZeRY's part after Reino's hook – Shake, shake, shake your ass girl/ drop it so slow/ that I'll throw you some doe/ baby you know that I'm a king, Reino Ortiz show these bitches how we do/ haha

SUMMARY - I'll explain it like this. "When my producer Hev1 gave me this beat, I was confused on what to do with this song: seriously. Shortly after, I had met a co-worker Reino; whom was a singer from Boston. Later on, he came to my home studio and we started working on this song together. He inspired me to capture all my stories hitting clubs with Uncle Murda in VIP: throughout NYC.

Chapter 8: Song 19 – Faith – Got Any? (8:19)

Faith – Got Any?

INTRO: "Ya, huh, the beats, the beats, it's all about the beats. Here we go Dre."

VERSE 1: If it wasn't for the bit of faith I kept inside/ as I'm growing in my life/ I would not be alive/ I would of committed suicide/ My angels warned me/ if I went down that road, I'd be stuck in some hell, for all of eternity/ I would never even want that, what the fuck is you crazy/ I don't wanna be here, at this place that I'm staying/ I'd rather be on tour, and this is why I'm praying/ you think I wanna go to school, and learn about business/ I'd rather make more money, from what I know best/ this is my success/ I've got so much talent, that's deep down inside of me/ all I wanna keep doing is telling you my story/ I wanna make music every single day/ but, that costs tons of money and a few other thangs/

HOOK/CHORUS: Man, Here we go! This is the faith, that I kept inside/ For all those years, I just learned how to write rhymes/ coming from my mind/ All those years, I just had to keep on going/ No Matter what got in my way, I had to keep on going/

VERSE 2: I've never been afraid of another man G/ oh please/ like you could ever keep up with me/ I drift, and I vanish, just like a ghost/ for the past 10 years, you never see me come or go/ and fuck all of y'all, you ain't help me raise myself/ I watched my own back/ and with that/ I protected myself/ now listen up Miren/ Here's some advice, and/ If you're gonna start trouble, you need to finish the job even if you hear them sirens/ I don't wanna know about it/ Gangsta's move in silence/ if you got a lot of problems/ solve em with intelligence/ if you dare use violence/ I'll make you permanently silent/ I don't make these rules, I just learned to apply em/ I'll ask Ya only once, I hope that you're ready cause now you're fucking hired/ I thought you read my flier/ you've gotta pass my test/ and you only get one chance/ I need you on my team, so you really have to last/ you really need to fight, and Ya gotta switch your stance/ and I ain't fucking kidding/ so you better grab that ratchet/ and you gotta start shooting/ Imma mastermind the plan, and you execute the action/ and I ain't about no scams/ so what the fuck was you planning? And I ain't ever gonna quit, Imma make this shit happen/ (Pause) And you really thought I'm done, I ain't ever gonna finish/ Imma keep on rhyming/ till my heart stops beating/ and you really think I'm kidding/ trust me I've really tried to quit, so many mother fucking times/ it's like no matter what I tried/ it keeps on coming back/ to me chilling in the studio, writing to these tracks/ it's a mother fucking disease/ that's surging through my veins, that keeps on begging me/ not to quit on my destiny/ no matter what I do, I'll fulfill my prophecy/ no matter what you say Homie/ Imma stay doing me/ there are certain things about me/ that I would never even change, and before you ever judge me/ you should look at yourself/ way before you ever start judging somebody else/ and always remember man, I don't really got any enemies/ just a bunch of Hater's/ who's faking/ begging God, to make em more like me/ but you can't ever be/ cause I'm one of a kind G/ and the next time, that'ch you start picking apart my music/ I dare you to step in this booth/ and attempt every thing that I've really been doing/ Yaa MIZeRY ReCORDS, 2010 to infinity Sucka's/ What you know about it, Fucka's/

SUMMARY - I'll explain it like this. "Faith – Got Any?" This is the song, I asked myself that very question. I quickly realized I had an abundance of faith. I did want this song to channel some past events in my life. Mostly when my faith was being tested and my humane decisions of choosing between right and wrong. Ultimately, I discovered what was truly right and wrong in this world; this song helped me seek those answers."

Chapter 9
15 Years of My Life
Island Def Jam Debut Album

I'm now entering young adulthood at age 23. I have decided to continue pushing forward with my music career, making inspirational music for all. During the early year of 2011, I haste fully started working on my debut album "15 Years of My Life." This album was later published in about 150 countries globally, by *Island Def Jam*: on *iTunes* & *Amazon* online. This debut album would mark the start of a long enduring career for me. I finally was able to explain the past 15 years of my life and all the struggles I've endured during this time. In addition, I believe this might be one of the most revolutionary rap albums in the world. I think this because, I have created a new Genre of music by the name of Rhythmic Acting Poetry; which later was renamed to **RAPP/RAP2 – Rhythmically Acting Poetic Pictures**®©. In addition, with this new found genre; I would also be telling the world virtually about who I was as a person, as well as a struggling artist in the modern age of humanity. With completing this album, also came much hardship. Struggle with coworkers, family, and friends whilst struggling financially. In addition to all my hardships, I started realizing new truths about myself; which ultimately led to my discovering, that I was more than just a man. All in all, this album is not only the most unique, poetically inclined work I've ever heard; but it was by far the most heart felt album I've ever created too. "15 Years of My Life" is a must own; while containing world class production, lyrics, vocal lyricism, and much more. Simply, let my music speak for itself… "This is by far my best album; please take sufficient time reading this chapter; thank you."

15 Years of My Life

RAPP = Rhythmically Acting Poetic Pictures

MIZeRY has created a new Sub-Division of RAP. Instead of Rhythm and Poetry; he's created "Rhythmically Acting Poetic Pictures". The Difference: MIZeRY, whom has written music for over 10 years; takes pieces of his life experiences, close associates lives, or a life style he could have pursued; & interprets them through stories, to tell his life's story; while, educating all upon real life situations. In other words, he is (Acting) out life styles of his own life, or others, through (Rhyming Poetry). MIZeRY brings wide range of Unique, Intelligent, Diversity to the world of music; through his, unique style of music.

Rhythmically Acting Poetic Pictures is going to revolutionize music sales by restructuring song formats. An album, isn't going to just be an album anymore. An album, is going to represent a movie about the artist or group. The lyrical content will vividly express the song, through chapters, which will compile a full movie album.

R.A.P.P. – Rhythmically Acting Poetic Pictures synopsis page; this is page 1 within the "15 years of my life" album booklet. This explains the format for my style of music, and my ability in which how I create my specifically styled music. Copyright © 2011.

"15 years of my life" – front cover; photo taken by Zack Meader; Art direction and design by Michael Izzo. Copyright © 2011, *MIZeRY ReCORDS*; in association with *Island Def Jam Publishing* – All Rights Reserved. This album is Distributed online through *Tunecore* & *MIZeRY ReCORDS* websites in over 150 countries globally.

1. Intro

Welcome to planet mizaine. From here on out, you could forget about the realities and the lives that you are used to viewing and experiencing, Because when you are in my reality. Everything's fucking flipped upside down. But, don't take everything you are about to hear so literally. And we do implor parental advisory cause I'am not a role model. I'm a general. And everything you are about to hear in my songs are a little to intense for the average listener. Then again you just need to pay attention and listen. Becuase my lyrics are neccessary to unlock the doors for our success and our future, Ya heard. The last thing I want all yall to know what makes me stand different amongst the rest. Is that on this album just like on all my other albums I wrote, recorded, engineered, mixed, & mastered my entire album. I've dont this for 12 years and its my time to get put on cause im running out of time.

2. My Death Wish

VERSE 1:

Heres another story about my wicked life/ Cause I have a polluted mind/ And I have some disgusting rhymes/ Im tired of all yall fakers, that's wasting all of my time/ Im broke, and I can drop dead simply on a dime/This music is fueling my soul/ I have a few friends, who are unsupportive of my goals/ Airbody wants me to do what they want me to do/ Whatever happened to doing, what the fuck I wanted to do/
So in this verse, homie, im saying FUCK YOU/ to each and every one of you/ If this was my will, would you - even give a shit/ AS IF/ you cared for my Music to live/ or do you really only care if I ever Blow up BIG/ Cause no matter what I ever did, I don't think that I can quit/ And heres why kidss...
When I was young I was taught to dream real big/ be whatever you wanted to be/ and as soon as I turned thirteen/ that all went out the window, so ill tell you like it went down, as if you was my shadow/ This is what im destined for/ My desire TO succeed struck me when I was four/ Because I was always aggravated from constantly living poor/ Now I'm twenty three years old/ I've got no money/ and I've got no way to eat/ Unless, I swallow my pride eat and sleep for free/ Living at my boys crib/ Like I, can will ever feel like a man after that shit/ All I want is a job in this music business kid/ its not my fault I was born with this gift/ to shift/ everything in the world of music/ So where did I go wrong/ has it been to long/ for me to see the truth behind closed doors/ oh no/ should I write & wear a blind fold/ as this story unfolds/ Oh lord/ will you save me if I continue to swing my sword/ Im blinded, and near sited, but I don't need to see what I write/
because this is MY life/ AND All jokes aside/

HOOK:

I have a lot of pain/ waiting to break free from its chains/ Held by my lord in vein/ for he doesn't really feel, that I even deserve this name/ Please lord im tired of being sane/ and seeing the worlds pain/ let me come home/ im tired of walking on this road/ especially since im all alone/ please – let me come home/ Im tired of walking on this road/ especially since im all alone/

VERSE 2:

A brother got no girl, when I used to be the king of his world/ The popular guy/ who was nothing but honest and never even lied/ until he sacrificed my entire life/ to chase this dream that's raging inside/ It must be something about this life/ that made me change my mind/ cause, The streets ate me up alive/ and makes me hate the man that I really am inside/ even if im good, Ive done enough wrong for a lifetime of torture, because the only way to succeed in this world, is to do whats right/ live a puuuRREE life ROB from the wicked evil/ if you don't believe me, then come test my people/ cause we all live in the same jungle/ Im finished with this jingle/ Im begging yall make this my single/ cause I can't mingle/ and triple yall profits/ without the right kind of budgets/ take a look at My Statistics/ Im a prodigy child, I was given the intelligence and strength to succeed to the next test/ and I can't stand all y'all kids who text/ Im here to pull all ya heads up out of the mist/ Trust me, I know what it feels like not to exist/ as if/ everyone around you couldn't give a shit/ If you dropped dead in the kitchen/ holding a pair of - scissors/ cause you slityour own wrist/ now lets pause for a second/ One scenario is/ You slit your own wrist/ cause the crowd wouldn't let you spit your lyrics/ meanwhile your really the shit/ & fuck all them kids/ imma cut my wrists/ and let them morn me later/ with MY dying breathe, I whisper, Fuck all you haters/ The second scenario is/ you slit your wrist/ cause you're a fat fucking kid/ always getting picked on, by the older kids/ so you take a few sedatives/ to relax your nerves and give a few incentives/ to continue your own life, but no matter what you can come up with/ its not good enough, so you decide to end all of this shit/ Meanwhile, your husband receives a missed call/ As hes already rushing home/ moments later he busts opens the door/ but its to late cause you're dead on the floor/ ya pulse is froze/ with 911 on the phone/ As hes trying to save your life/ however its to late/ and your husband joins your side by ending in the same fate/

HOOK:

I have a lot of pain/ waiting to break free from its chains/ Held by my lord in vein/ for he doesn't really feel, that I even deserve this name/ Please lord im tired of being sane/ and seeing the worlds pain/ let me come home/ im tired of walking on this road/ especially since im all alone/ please – let me come home/ Im tired of walking on this road/ especially since im all alone/

"15 years of my life" – page 2; original photo title: i-love-music-16-1; Art direction and design by Michael Izzo. This album is Distributed online through *Tunecore & MIZeRY ReCORDS* websites in over 150 countries globally.

3. And I Know

INTRO: Yo Pooch, Good lookin for this record man. Yo we going to the top with this Man. Lord, I wanna thank you for giving me the power and strength that I need to do this everyday...

HOOK:

Ya I know, You want to be here with me/ And I know, You wish you could have a piece of me/ And I know, you're greedy and ready to take this from me/ And I know I'am Ready to explode and I'am That crazy/ Ya I know, you can't ever compare to me/ And I know, I'm Perfectly made for this game/ And I know, I have you feelin my fucking name/ And I know...

VERSE 1:

And I know, Im a slick talker/ Fast Hustler/ that's juggelling ya/ Similar to torture/ That takes place in the Evil Orchard/ Zig Zag/ Boom Bap/ The dynamic Duo/ Simply two hero's/ Nick Nack/ Paddy wack/ Give a girl a bone/ Faster than you know/ This little Piggy's coming home/ Trying to conquer your thrown/ As if she wears the crown/ Sexy as freak, Black silk laced night gown/ All of a sudden, she's touching me and you all around/ This is the censored verse/ clean version goes first/ Im a good and evil, because of a blood born curse/ That I'm trying to break/ I've got way to much at stake/ to ever Hyper-ventilate/ Over making Mistakes/ Ask lord for forgiveness/ Everytime you pray/ And Yes - Praise the lord every single day/ without any questions/ Quit all your stressin/ Jesus Sheds many blessings/ Alike, while I'm interpellating/ Every one of his meanings/ It's amazing/ this feeling/ I receive/ from my obligatory/ Duties/ commanded unto me/ By the one and only Almighty/ It's frightening to me/ How amazing he is to me/ Through all of my agony/ He awakens my inner serenity/ If you're not impressed yet/ come second verse you'll be so content/ you'll be confused and you will no longer comprehend/ Anything that's ever said/ Other than my words that are gunned from my mouth, that are filled with this led/

HOOK:

Ya I know, You want to be here with me/ And I know, You wish you could have a piece of me/ And I know, you're greedy and ready to take this from me/ And I know I'am Ready to explode and I'am That crazy/ Ya I know, you can't ever compare to me/ And I know, I'm Perfectly made for this game/ And I know, I have you feelin my fucking name/ And I know...

MATTHEW 5:9
BLESSED ARE THE PEACEMAKERS,
FOR THEY WILL BE CALLED SONS OF GOD.

VERSE 2:

Ya I know, I can give into these demons/ But why should I join them/ When I can simply beat em/ Through Jesus, I Harbor the strength/ Sqaured powered to the tenth/ Multiplied by infinite Wisdom, Makes me the most INTENSE/ Lyrically/ Metaphysical/ Complexity/ Beyond Incredible/ Random Search and Seizure/ I'll Kill you with a nine MILLA-Meter/ If you try to combat me/ or anyone of my family/ that includes all my homies/ who are riding with me/ Until His Return/ I won't ever get burned/ I'd much rather have to swerve/ and crash into this curb/ Hop Out shootin/ Not questioning/ Anything/ Except for my thinking/ Only about my surviving/ If I start bleeding/ I'll make sure you're the one Dying/ Crying/ & Screaming/ for your mommy/ Cause a guy like me/ Doesn't ROMP AROUND WHICH YA KIND OF DUMMIES/ In reality/ Pussy Wigga Speaks/ Pussy Wigga Eats/ & Pussy Wigga Sleeps/ EVENTUALLY/ And thats where IMMA Be/ So Quick/ Ready to hitch you with a couple of these clips/ Starting with you/ and your motha fucking bitch/ Including all the witnesses/ Hire me a lawyer quick/ I only plead the 1st Amendment/ Including the Fifth/ Other than that, Coppers I ain't saying shit/ Now take these cuffs off my wrist/ Who do you think you are who can abuse such authority/ cause I will SUMMON MY Lord, Upon to you who will punish you spiritually/ Through the world's MIZeRY/ I grow stronger on my mission, to fill the world with this never ending PEACE/ So if you try to end me/ There will be one just like me/ Forced to replace me/ And through God I will live for eternity/ Cause Lyrically/ I'm tellin you all his Story/ Finally/ My missions extremely/ Clear to me/

HOOK:

Ya I know, You want to be here with me/ And I know, You wish you could have a piece of me/ And I know, you're greedy and ready to take this from me/ And I know I'am Ready to explode and I'am That crazy/ Ya I know, you can't ever compare to me/ And I know, I'm Perfectly made for this game/ And I know, I have you feelin my fucking name/ And I know...

"15 years of my life" – page 3; original photo title: peacemaker_1024x768; Art direction and design by Michael Izzo. Copyright © 2011, *MIZeRY ReCORDS*; in association with *Island Def Jam Publishing* – All Rights Reserved. This album is Distributed online through *Tunecore & MIZeRY ReCORDS* websites in over 150 countries globally.

4. Hey Baby, Whered you go?

Intro:

So let me tell you how this goes down. New Years two thousand 10, I met this new cat by the name of Andre. Yo this dude was talking to me for only 2 hours and he says yo, I know your soul mate...

VERSE 1:

So this is a little story, about MIZeRY's soul mate/
And I haven't even made her my wife yet, or Asked her out on a date/
It's a little bit crazy, but I know this is mine and your fate/
Here wait, let me just explain/
With all that I have ever been through, I can justify my claims/
Over these years I've searched for the key to end all of my pain/
That key was you, my love, my soul mate/
The reason for me to continue playing this game/
Ill take you way back into the days/ Back to when I was even born/
My mom had abandoned me, permanently torn, and leaving me scorn/
A mother forfeits her own child on the other end of this country/ and left me/ Like I wasn't worthy/ to even be a part of her sick family/
No father neither/ so either/ I'm nothing to anyone, or I was meant to be a world wide rapper/ by surviving hell on earth/ Cause ever since my own birth/ I have designed a plan to rid me of this curse/
By finding you, I could be reborn/ Like Lord would give me a second chance to undue all that was wrong/ I've never made a song/ about no women, until you/ cause I love you/

HOOK:

Hey Baby/ You drive me so crazy/
This feeling is insane/ it wipes away my pain/
Even when it rains/ I think of your name/ and I see your face/
Forever onto you I hold/ I swear I wont let you go/
Cause baby/ you drive me so crazy/
This feeling is insane/ it wipes away my pain/
Even when it rains/ I think of your name/ and I see your face/
Forever onto you I hold/ I swear I wont eva let you go/

VERSE 2:

Your beauty is unequal/ without you, I would not have any sequels/ and this is just a sneak preview/ of my love that's so lethal/
To the average/ they'd get plastered/ turn enraged like a savage/ who's afta/ more than just a brisk of cabbage/ so join me on Sabbath/ or maybe just a bubble bath/ I need to release all this wrath/ that's been encaged/ within an enraged/ outlandish character/ formerly a sinner/ but no longer/ shall I walk the path of any darkness/ cause through your essence/ I see all that is present/ I can change our lifestyles/ within lord, I find the strength to build high piles/ and large sums of anything, that's soo great/
Mine and your fate/ was destined way before we mate/ I meant met/ what do you mean/ Now I'm confused, like you girls do to us all the time/
Forget that line, ever since I laid my eyes/ upon you it was love at first sight/ I've been searching for 20 years/ for the women who can relate to my tears/
We barely know each other, but already I know you/ Its like we are one and the same/ in fact, you were born on the sixth day and I was born in the six month/ Its like I've got a six sense/ for your scent/ because I've been searching for you since the creation of any trends/
Your one of kind/ the type/ that was born to ride/ right by my side/
Were meant to be married for the rest of our lives/ No Lie/
Lord knew you needed me/ so baby/ Will you let me love you, and will you love me/ for all of eternity/ cause you are special to me/ Soo A**/ will you be the end of all my mizery/

HOOK:

Hey Baby/ You drive me so crazy/
This feeling is insane/ it wipes away my pain/
Even when it rains/ I think of your name/ and I see your face/
Forever onto you I hold/ I swear I wont let you go/
Cause baby/ you drive me so crazy/

"15 years of my life" – page 4; original photo title: space; Art direction and design by Michael Izzo. This album is Distributed online through *Tunecore* & *MIZeRY ReCORDS* websites in over 150 countries globally.

5. Servin Y'all Justice

VERSE 1:
G Unit, When y'all come correct/ Lord comes with plenty of gifts/ Love and Respect/ Sell your soul to the devil, and you get the same shit/ Just a little bit quicker/ I'm the opposite of Rick Ross, I AM much smoother/ Like Larry hoover/ Im half the hustler/ That I used to be/ and all for good reason/ If I wasn't saved by Jesus/ I promise some of y'all that you would not be breathing/ Cause I used to get off on seeing y'all leaking/ and don't start speaking unless ya spoken too/ I love making rules/ so when I give y'all work you betta make some moves/ I come from the streets/ and I know a few g's/ ready to put work in for a little bit a cream/ so you betta come correct if you eva approach me/ at this point in my life I only come in peace/

HOOK:
I'm servin y'all justice/ spittin on this record/ this is MIZeRY ReCORDS/ We don't fuck with lames/ if you don't paper chase/ then get out of my face/ cause we don't got no time to be playing y'all games/ I'll say it again/ I'm servin y'all justice/ spittin on this record/ this is MIZeRY ReCORDS/ We don't fuck with lames/ if you don't paper chase/ then get out of my face/ cause we don't got no time to be playing y'all games/ G-Unnit/

VERSE 2:
Yaa, well Ive earned my title/ so I'll quote from the bible/ if you come as a rival/ then I'll use gods power to snatch away your right to maintain vital/ If you come as a student/ I'll make you my disciple/ Ok, Now I'll go blind/ and let lord take over when I'm writing out my rhymes/ as he teaches all y'all how to really live ya lives/ I'll spit from the good book/ As long as lord lets me make it to the hook/ aint no reason to rush/ why should I start teaching/ If we both know – You're Shook/ Cause, where I come from, there ain't no such things as Half Way Crooks/ It's kinda funny cause, right about now, I would have had y'all juxed/ Even back then I was conflicted between the good and the bad/ Ya Man, I finally found a way out maneuvering through these traps/ spitting complex syllables rhyming in my raps/ I'll keep it on wax/ I ain't fucking with ya cats/ if you come at me bitch, with some I'll logic math/ Then imma be ghost town, (Snap) Just Like that/ And you'll be front page news/ murdered on the cover, popped right out of ya shoes/ I don't fuck with no fools/ I See your doing coke/ Im not trying to get knocked/ All of a sudden, homie you're the big boss on the block/ Naa fuck that/ Imma Promote ya ass to the brains of the block/ (Gun Shot)

HOOK:
I'm servin y'all justice/ spittin on this record/ this is MIZeRY ReCORDS/ We don't fuck with lames/ if you don't paper chase/ then get out of my face/ cause we don't got no time to be playing y'all games/ I'll say it again/ I'm servin y'all justice/ spittin on this record/ this is MIZeRY ReCORDS/ We don't fuck with lames/ if you don't paper chase/ then get out of my face/ cause we don't got no time to be playing y'all games/ G-Unnit/

VERSE 3:
OK Shh, As I Take a moment for silence/ (Pause) I only come in peace/ If you wanna fuck with me/ then, you can meet me in the streets/ cause if we ever had beef/ I would tell you where to meet me/ and I wouldn't even show/ I'd snipe you from the roof, while hiding on the low/ Woah – Hold it, The bible did teach me to slow my roll/ Easy up little homie, I'll blast my gun off/ You've got a much bigger mission, for this mother fucking world/ Those were the last words of my man J. Russo/ who's now convicted for life for contract killin/ and that's one of my mans, I said I would never mention/ Ever since that day/ My whole crew decided that we need to walk away/ That was a long time ago/ My Story either way, is still gonna be told/ Imma spit my flow/ I need to keep it on the roll/ cause everything that I'm building, has never been sold/

HOOK:
I'm servin y'all justice/ spittin on this record/ this is MIZeRY ReCORDS/ We don't fuck with lames/ if you don't paper chase/ then get out of my face/ cause we don't got no time to be playing y'all games/ I'll say it again/ I'm servin y'all justice/ spittin on this record/ this is MIZeRY ReCORDS/ We don't fuck with lames/ if you don't paper chase/ then get out of my face/ cause we don't got no time to be playing y'all games/ G-Unnit/

"15 years of my life" – page 5; original photo title: CON2326; Art direction and design by Michael Izzo. This album is Distributed online through *Tunecore* & *MIZeRY ReCORDS* websites in over 150 countries globally.

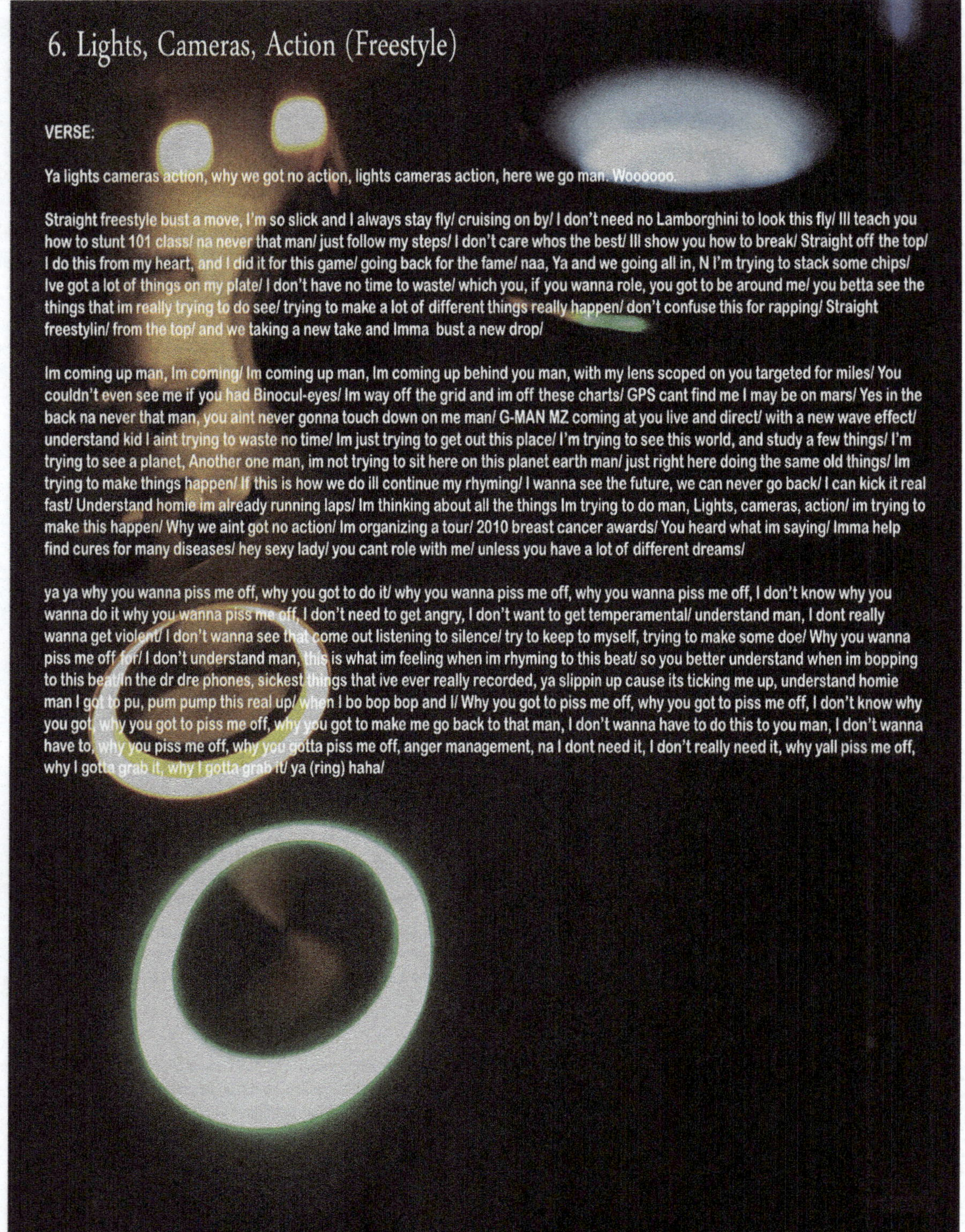

6. Lights, Cameras, Action (Freestyle)

VERSE:

Ya lights cameras action, why we got no action, lights cameras action, here we go man. Woooooo.

Straight freestyle bust a move, I'm so slick and I always stay fly/ cruising on by/ I don't need no Lamborghini to look this fly/ Ill teach you how to stunt 101 class/ na never that man/ just follow my steps/ I don't care whos the best/ Ill show you how to break/ Straight off the top/ I do this from my heart, and I did it for this game/ going back for the fame/ naa, Ya and we going all in, N I'm trying to stack some chips/ Ive got a lot of things on my plate/ I don't have no time to waste/ which you, if you wanna role, you got to be around me/ you betta see the things that im really trying to do see/ trying to make a lot of different things really happen/ don't confuse this for rapping/ Straight freestylin/ from the top/ and we taking a new take and Imma bust a new drop/

Im coming up man, Im coming/ Im coming up man, Im coming up behind you man, with my lens scoped on you targeted for miles/ You couldn't even see me if you had Binocul-eyes/ Im way off the grid and im off these charts/ GPS cant find me I may be on mars/ Yes in the back na never that man, you aint never gonna touch down on me man/ G-MAN MZ coming at you live and direct/ with a new wave effect/ understand kid I aint trying to waste no time/ Im just trying to get out this place/ I'm trying to see this world, and study a few things/ I'm trying to see a planet, Another one man, im not trying to sit here on this planet earth man/ just right here doing the same old things/ Im trying to make things happen/ If this is how we do ill continue my rhyming/ I wanna see the future, we can never go back/ I can kick it real fast/ Understand homie im already running laps/ Im thinking about all the things Im trying to do man, Lights, cameras, action/ im trying to make this happen/ Why we aint got no action/ Im organizing a tour/ 2010 breast cancer awards/ You heard what im saying/ Imma help find cures for many diseases/ hey sexy lady/ you cant role with me/ unless you have a lot of different dreams/

ya ya why you wanna piss me off, why you got to do it/ why you wanna piss me off, why you wanna piss me off, I don't know why you wanna do it why you wanna piss me off, I don't need to get angry, I don't want to get temperamental/ understand man, I dont really wanna get violent/ I don't wanna see that come out listening to silence/ try to keep to myself, trying to make some doe/ Why you wanna piss me off for/ I don't understand man, this is what im feeling when im rhyming to this beat/ so you better understand when im bopping to this beat/in the dr dre phones, sickest things that ive ever really recorded, ya slippin up cause its ticking me up, understand homie man I got to pu, pum pump this real up/ when I bo bop bop and I/ Why you got to piss me off, why you got to piss me off, I don't know why you got, why you got to piss me off, why you got to make me go back to that man, I don't wanna have to do this to you man, I don't wanna have to, why you piss me off, why you gotta piss me off, anger management, na I dont need it, I don't really need it, why yall piss me off, why I gotta grab it, why I gotta grab it/ ya (ring) haha/

"15 years of my life" – page 6; original photo title: pioneer_edge_buttons_1920x1200_club_music_wallpaper; Art direction and design by Michael Izzo. This album is Distributed online through *Tunecore* & *MIZeRY ReCORDS* websites in over 150 countries globally.

7. Goodie Bags Ft. Fredy Bombs

INTRO: MIZ – "Shit Fredy Tell Em", Fred – "Right", MIZ – "haha", Fred – "Ya", Ya here we go, here we go, here we go, ya, haha, this is for the girls, here we go Hev, heres another.

HOOK:
Goodie Bags Goodie bags I wanna get to know you/ Dress down make out, I really wanna touch you/ I don't carry lollipops that's Lil wayne, But Ive got a bunch of candy/ I love Black Glocks, with different kinds of bullets but nothing to fancy/ put it in your mouth, and place it in ya aahh/ Rough Sex, slow down, put it in ya chaaah/ So how you like us now, so slick, so smooth, something real sexy/ Goodie Bags, goodie bags Ive got em all day for any kind of lady/ Goodie Bags, Goodie bags from any one of us If you really want some just hop on that bus/ Here we go/

VERSE 1:
Im several kinds of things/ mixed up, shredded up, grinded in a blender/ I never had a mentor/ chop it up, brake it down, teach it to a Minor/ I Aint talking about NO Coal/ Listen up, read the script, and perform this role/ listen up, turn this up/ Pay attention quickly/ aaahh, IM cynically/ Technically/ mentally/ Insane/ Bruised up, beat down, and mashed in the brain/ Seen so many thangs/ but not enough girls with sexy g-strings/ Im really sorry *****/ I Really Loved Ya Girl/ But I need to live a little/ The first time I met'ch you, I knew you were my Sigel/ Back to the topic, Goodie Bags, Goodie Bags that's what im wanting/ Big Bombs, little bombs, any kind of color/ I wanna get to know you, and touch you all over/ Soo you wanna be my girl/ yaa Imma take you all over, and show you this world/ How about your shorties/ yes bring some of them/ I don't want to date you/ I just wanna be friends/ Let me stare into your eyes, ya as I focus my lense/ Let me get a better picture, with a hundred twenty hertz/ What'ch you thinking about are you feelin this verse/

HOOK:
Goodie Bags Goodie bags I wanna get to know you/ Dress down make out, I really wanna touch you/ I don't carry lollipops that's Lil wayne, But Ive got a bunch of candy/ I love Black Glocks, with different kinds of bullets but nothing to fancy/ put it in your mouth, and place it in ya aahh/ Rough Sex, slow down, put it in ya chaaah/ So how you like us now, so slick, so smooth, something real sexy/ Goodie Bags, goodie bags Ive got em all day for any kind of lady/ Goodie Bags, Goodie bags from any one of us If you really want some just hop on that bus/ Here we go/

Fredy Bombs VERSE:
Yo my names Fredy Bombs im from southern New Hampshire/ ask me a question, I will have the answer/ I am the best, at what I do/ I catch bitches like a virus I got the flu/ mackin on ladies is what I do/ If you get my attention, Imma Fuck you too/ Im not here to judge, Im just here to admire/ Cause that is my face posted up on that flier/ Im not to be messed with, Im not to be jerked/ if you get in my grill, your gonna get murked/ Ask me no question till I get what I want, that's with you in my bed while im smoking this blunt/ Just send me a message Ill always reply/ cause my name is fredy bombs and Im your kinda of guy/ with your face in the pillow and your ass in the air/ I wanna make this little hobby my career/ sooner or later bitches would stare/ cause I'm as smooth as will smith from the fresh prince of Bel Air/ I will never get drunk and drive on your lawn. Cause I GET MORE booty then lil jon/ yaaaaa/

VERSE 2:
Yaa here we go man, Last bonnie and Clyde/ Shorties so fine/ put a soda on the side/ that's my Camaro chick/ My ride or die chick/ Put a gat in her hand she'll bang a homie quick/ Loves sucking my dick/ Loves banging my shit/ Loves Bumping my music when shes banging me and shit/ Hips so fine/ I became mesmerized/ When I was clocking up and down those thighs/ Back at my boys crib/ Chillen in da whip/ Drinking, Smoking, Doing tops and bottoms/ Shorties so fine her lips stay poppin/ Don't need the glossin/ Keep that shit flossin/ why have the cake if it aint got the frostin/ Shorties so sexy, Ill even eat off you/ Strawberries, whip cream, Ill eat that shit off you/ Now airbodies gonna be saying this/ always think back that MIZeRY Made this/ "I Love You Like a Gangsta", I love you like a thug that be lovin his Gats/ I Love you just the same when IM writing my raps/ I Love you like a thug when he be robbing banks/ Im a Gemini so theres two sides to me/ SO you need to learn how to love each and everyone of me/ Sometimes IM MIZeRY/ Sometimes Im Mercenary/ But Im always GMG/ Can you deal with that, Think about that/ think about that/ Here we go Maa,

HOOK:
Goodie Bags Goodie bags I wanna get to know you/ Dress down make out, I really wanna touch you/ I don't carry lollipops that's Lil wayne, But Ive got a bunch of candy/ I love Black Glocks, with different kinds of bullets but nothing to fancy/ put it in your mouth, and place it in ya aahh/ Rough Sex, slow down, put it in ya chaaah/ So how you like us now, so slick, so smooth, something real sexy/ Goodie Bags, goodie bags I've got em all day for any kind of lady/ Goodie Bags, Goodie bags from any one of us If you really want some just hop on that bus/ MIZeRY, MIZeRY ReCORDS 2010 to infinity. Well you only got a little taste but check back for the release date. So Welcome to Planet MIZaINE/

"15 years of my life" – page 7; original photo title: Ricks-cabaret-girls, 480c2d6472709ibiza017, & Amrit-Dhaliwal; Art direction and design by Michael Izzo. This album is Distributed online through *Tunecore* & *MIZeRY ReCORDS* websites in over 150 countries globally.

8. MIZeRY's Izzo Ft. Brittles & many MC's

MC's Appearance List (Compiled by MIZeRY): J, Tupac, Tony Yayo, Slim Shady, Xzibit, Tupac x2, DMX, Tupac x3, Nas aka N, DMX, Drag on, Eminem, Nas aka N, Jay-Z, MIZeRY. (Download free intro compilation of samples at www.mizeryrecords.com/home/)

INTRO: Aiiyoo, you notice how all dem cats you just heard. Was repping my shit, way way before I even started emceeing. Dog I am an unknown legend and it's my time for recognition man/ I told you, I wasn't playin games/ yo check this shit out man, I got a story to tell yall. Yo check this shit out/

VERSE 1: Yo check it, My mothers a hustler/ my fathers a bastard/ Put em both together – that made mizery/ I did it for my agony/ I do it for this industry/ The industry that you fagots destroyed in front of me/ while sittin back, I couldn't do nothing/ Deep down inside me, I would never stop rapping/ Why the hell you think that our shit keeps on smashin/ Judge Me, Love me, Then you wanna hate me/ You bitches can't ever fuck with MIZeRY/ It's always been a battle/ my teams all animals/ my pen is the weapon, my lyrics is the ammo/ you've been telling me, I'm going through these phases/ only thing I'm going through are Rap game stages/ never dyin down, Im aint never dying out/ This is my life, I've never been sorry for the shit that I write/ man, I said, I've never been sorry, for the shit that I write/ man/

Brittles HOOK: You can't fuck with Mike Mizery/ we got that Red Fire you see/ its Brittney bitch/ Im hot and sexy/ there aint no other bitch out there like me/ like me, like me/ Ohhh yeaaaa/ You can't fuck with Mike Mizery/ we got that Red Fire you see/ its Brittney bitch/ Im hot and sexy/ there aint no other bitch out there like me/ like me, like me/ Ohhh yeaaaa/ ohhh yeaaa/

VERSE 2: Yooo thee only person who ever tries coming up on his own/ Isolating himself in his own room/ what's everyone gotta saayyy/ Has he really changes or his he just somewhat insane/ nowadays/ hes like a different person/ The pain Ive endured/ Gave me game for certain/ with that I became observant/ But not before he realized he was 9/ just trying to live life like he was already – Twenty – Five/ MIZ had enough of isolating himself from the world/ back in school/ I wrote poems and songs/ looking at you because you are the fool/ I told yall/ I would soon/ Obtain/ fame from you/ Living hard/ but no matter how far/ That's my dreams get/ I will never forget/ Any of the goals that I've already set/ regardless of this/ I write visual pictures when MIZeRY Vents/ So Welcome, to the pain department/ I said welcome, to MIZ's Department/

Brittles HOOK: You can't fuck with Mike Mizery/ we got that Red Fire you see/ its Brittney bitch/ Im hot and sexy/ there aint no other bitch out there like me/ like me, like me/ Ohhh yeaaaa/ You can't fuck with Mike Mizery/ we got that Red Fire you see/ its Brittney bitch/ Im hot and sexy/ there aint no other bitch out there like me/ like me, like me/ Ohhh yeaaaa/ ohhh yeaaa/

VERSE 3: Ya you, Aaiiyo dog, I was born a genius/ I could take anybody/ and make em bigger then venus/ You say fifties a mogul that's never before seen/ Sooo Wait and see/ and keep your eyes on me/ I told you, I made MIZeRY/ MIZeRY did not make me/ I've been told before that I've got no destiny/ I told myself a long time ago/ That I wasn't gonna be just another lost soul/ I'm an unknown legend, Who stimulates the pain/ Mimic any move I make/ We already know that you're the fucking gimic, when we aint/ Technically insane/ I never follow g's/ I'm a leader yall supposed to follow me/ So please don't ever judge me/ If I aint got shit to say, cause Im Vague/ So start mis-taking me for being crazed/ If I catch you in the streets/ Then we really gonna see/ if you a motha fuckin G/

Jay-Z...

"15 years of my life" – page 8; original photo title: music note; Art direction and design by Michael Izzo. This album is Distributed online through *Tunecore & MIZeRY ReCORDS* websites in over 150 countries globally.

9. I'm sad for this world

INTRO: In the name of the father, the son, the holy spirit. May you lord bless with me with the gift and ability to tell my story...

VERSE 1:
Everyday that I wake/ I feel I must escape/ from all of this worlds pain/ That compels me to explain/ what's going on today/ Behind all of these doors/ that are being forced/ the fuck closed/ And I continue to be compelled to Save this world/ my prophecy wont unravel/ Until I find myself a longtime girl/ Who's good and shares the same visions of life with me/ But Why DO YOU keep on hiding from me/ Cause the longer you take to find me/ The longer this world must suffer/ and over my journey I realized ain't no such thing as free suppers/ You got to take your food if you want to survive/ And ill explain something's that I'm not looking for in a wife/ I don't want no bitch who acts like a raging cunt/ who's roaming these streets like a Kat stacks punk slut/ who's passions are getting drunk/ then getting fucked, in someone's pickup truck/ I hope my sharp tongue/ has you taken back and your brain stuck/ cause this is supposed to hit you as if you been struck/ by a lightening bolt of wisdom and intelligence for the all ages/ so welcome to my life of seeing pain cases/ on a daily basis/ which no longer phases me/ in any ways/ as I daydream of still being able to lock away this worlds pain in unbreakable cages/ so keep listening as I turn these pages/ So with the little bit of success these demons have revealed themselves/ as if they were waiting for the clock hands to strike twelve/ so they can strike me down to hell/ but cant you all tell/ I'm a man of god, and left the streets/ to pursue my career as a g/ who rhymes over these beats/ to tell you a story of trials of defeat/ so people like you, wont have to retreat/ Back into your caves/ or save havens/ like astronauts floating in space/ not dealing with a fucking thang/ but counting down these days/ Homiee

HOOK:
This World Makes Me Sad/ I Want Nothing more Man/ To Make Change So Bad/ And I don't really mean to Brag/ But if you're moving dead slow, And you start placing in last/ Then I'm Black Listing your Ass/ Cause I'm Limited with Time, And I'm moving really fast/ Cause I need this Pain to Pass/ (Repeat)

VERSE 2:
Speaking of astronauts/ – how did one as Doug wheelock/ get stuck in a spaceship with two ladies/ as if he won the fucking lottery/ or something extraordinary/ cause I'm sure that's every mans vivid fantasy/ I'm sure right now he's getting more pussy then a sexy guy like me/ shit homos I'm cool with my sexuality/ so go ahead tmz/ Make up some crazy as story about me/ to tarnish my history/ but no matter what you say about me/ I know the truth about who's speaking in this booth/ telling you these stories in which are fluidly smooth/ and as of now, I'm looking for a new crew/ to take over this crude and cruel world With Me someday soon/ As I speak my last words/ Please take a seat/ before you get to ahead of me/ because I need all you fake fuckers to hate on ME some more/ cause I still have to even up the score/ that you tore/ through my skull and had sink into my brains pores/ However, long its been, if you left on bad terms with me/ I'm blacklisting your ass from my industry/ trust me/ Aint nobody/ got shit on me/ Ya MIZeRY/

HOOK:
This World Makes Me Sad/ I Want Nothing more Man/ To Make Change So Bad/ And I don't really mean to Brag/ But if you're moving dead slow, And you start placing in last/ Then I'm Black Listing your Ass/ Cause I'm Limited with Time, And I'm moving really fast/ Cause I need this Pain to Pass/ (Repeat)

VERSE 3:
I've already accepted you can hate me/ cause a man as skilled as me/ needs to be ready/ cause when I wake I suffer from all this worlds MIZeRY/ starting with millions of babies/ Dying and suffering/ because they are starving/ While our government is over seas fighting/ for oil or something/ That they seem to claim/ is for change/ In fact/ what about this fact/ that every 69 seconds a women dies of breast cancer/ which means every hour, 56 women die/ Which means 1,344 times a day we must cry/ Which means 490,560 times a year there are less women alive/ My genius best comes alive/ when I write down MY rhymes/ In these pages in which are confined/ So don't mistaken me for no other/ cause there is no other multitalented rappers/ who's got half the skills That I uphold/ and it's impossible to mistaken me for any another Izzo/ So thanks hova/ for my anthem now pay me my royalties for not asking me permission to publicly display my last name to this fucked up game/ that we all seem to love and hate in similar ways/ But If you carry guns/ And you aint my GmG guardian soldiers/ I want nothing to do with you son, Bang, bang, It's GAME OVER/

HOOK:
This World Makes Me Sad/ I Want Nothing more Man/ To Make Change So Bad/ And I don't really mean to Brag/ But if you're moving dead slow, And you start placing in last/ Then I'm Black Listing your Ass/ Cause I'm Limited with Time, And I'm moving really fast/ Cause I need this Pain to Pass/ (Repeat)

"15 years of my life" – page 9; original photo title: ws_City_Music_1280x1024; Art direction and design by Michael Izzo. Copyright © 2011, *MIZeRY ReCORDS*; in association with *Island Def Jam Publishing* – All Rights Reserved. This album is Distributed online through *Tunecore & MIZeRY ReCORDS* websites in over 150 countries globally.

"15 years of my life" – page 9a; original photo title: ws_City_Music_1280x1024; Art direction and design by Michael Izzo. Copyright © 2011, *MIZeRY ReCORDS*; in association with *Island Def Jam Publishing* – All Rights Reserved. This album is Distributed online through *Tunecore* & *MIZeRY ReCORDS* websites in over 150 countries globally.

"15 years of my life" – page 9b; original photo title: ws_City_Music_1280x1024; Art direction and design by Michael Izzo. Copyright © 2011, *MIZeRY ReCORDS*; in association with *Island Def Jam Publishing* – All Rights Reserved. This album is Distributed online through *Tunecore* & *MIZeRY ReCORDS* websites in over 150 countries globally.

10. Game Over

INTRO:
Ahhh, haha, This is just one straight head knocker
Its Game over, Game Over, Its Game Over, Game Over,
Its Game Over, Game Over, Its Game Over, Game Over,
Its Game Over, Game Over, Its Game Over, Game Over,
Its Game Over, Game Over.

VERSE:
Okay Okay If you really wanna battle, you can meet me on the field/ Lord shall protect me, and this is my sword and shield/ I praise the LORD/ and I Only Fight for Him/ If you wanna come at me with some evil, Then I will Murder you Only using MY PEN/ I come at you with Lethal, Weaponry Tools/ And Tactics of Strategy/ My Missions Clear To ME/ Rid Everybody's, MIZeRY/ The Pain & Agony/ Is What Fuels me Inside/ Better Days Keeps us going, Im Ready to Ride/ Worship thy Lord Jesus Christ/ You Might survive 2012/ Im Just Trying to see anything, Anything but Hell/ You Punk Bitch, Why I gotta Yell/ I see what your doing, Can't You Tell/ Aint no Trying to Lie to Me/ I See right through you/ I got the gift of Ability/ Of Intelligence to defeat of any one of you/ I Aint messing with you Evil Cowards/ My Powers/ Will Have each and every one of you Devoured/ Have You All Die/ I've got Millions of People ready to Ride/ by My Side/ Fuck with me – You Must be, out of ya mind/

Understand homie, Ive Got Millions of Rhymes/ About You, if you come at me with some sort of Craziness, Or Some Sort of Evil, Imma let you die, Like I really don't even know you/ Mother Fucker you Act like you been there with me/ Growing up by my side/ Tellin me I haven't been through a rougher ride/ What'ch You trying to tell me, Are you ready to die/ Everything you speak, is a mother fucking Lie/ I See ya Insides/ N' No Matter what You do, You know Im gonna Shine/ You Can Never even stop me, These Are My Rhymes/ Imma Ipod through it, with my Lyrics of Wisdom/ And everything that Im doing, this is Just my Decision/ You Can call me the predator, with Seven Kinds of Vision/ I Run This Division/ I Aint never gonna Stop it, When I Open my Mouth this shit continues to Glisten/ Now Pay Close Attention/
Cause I need you all to Listen/ Cause these are lords Commandments/ If you don't follow Em, then your going to Hells Detentions/
Im giving it to you like this, to save all your Children/ What do you mean man, Is you really need redemption/ Cause I know that's what I need before Im annihilated/ And I need to make it to Heaven/ So Im only rolling Sevens/ Im trying to win, Im not trying to loose/
I aint trying to be like you/ And go down to the firey Hell Pits/ Man, all of a sudden you think your really the shit/ Naa cause in Heaven in my world, and in my religious reality/ Theres only one form of humanity/ Were all Equal, cause this is Equality/ This is what it means to be one of a Kind/ Go Ahead, and Jump into my Mind/ Fast Grind/ Blessed Rhymes/ And This Ability to Write/ No Lie/ Cause - This is My Life/
Wake Up, and Listen/ And Theres No Intermissions/ What'ch you thinking MAN, you thinking you smarter then LORD/? NA Man, He built everything you see around you/ everything that you Breathe/ Everything that you eat/ No Matter what'ch you think, Man I need you to

PLEASE/ Get off My Beat/
Real Talk, Your Smug and you're really Discreet/ And I Think you need to Retreat/ Back to where ever it is you came from/ Because you're infected, with De-MONS/ Ive calculated the SUM/ Either you Change Now, Or in the Near Future, you Will not Survive/ This is NO Lie/
You Can Strategize/ Or Get high and be mesmerized/ by Pure evil/ during 2012/
Worship thy Lord, and follow his commandments, and thy shall be saved/ Pray and he will shower you with a little of his Praise/
I was lost, trapped, and stuck in this Maze/ but I found my way through this Dark Cave/
I follow the path of the Righteous, and though shall repute Devil/ Cause I see No Evil/
Only In your eyes of fury/ With my Lyrical Ability/ Ill Assassinate All Enemies/
I was built for this Path/ I fear lords Wrath, and I love him for his Grace/ The feeling makes me Sane/ And Keeps me alive, Straps me with the power to slay all Demons/
Im gifted/ the Rooms quickly shifted/ You ready, because I can create summons/ Like a sorcerer/ Your finished, Call me the Game Slayer/
Now go Sit in Prayer/ Cause For you, Its Game Over/

"15 years of my life" – page 10; original photo title:ws_City_Music_1280x1024; Art direction and design by Michael Izzo. This album is Distributed online through *Tunecore & MIZeRY ReCORDS* websites in over 150 countries globally.

11. We in da buildin Ft. Infinite

INTRO: MIZ – "Infinites Coming in"

HOOK:
Infinite –" We in da buildin, we in da buildin/ captivating all the ears of your children/ its MIZeRY (MIZ - ReCORDS) Its MIZeRY (MIZ - ReCORDS) its MIZeRY (MIZ - ReCORDS) Its MIZeRY (MIZ - ReCORDS) We in da buildin, we in da buildin/ captivating all the ears of your children/ its MIZeRY (MIZ - ReCORDS) Its MIZeRY (MIZ - ReCORDS) its MIZeRY (MIZ - ReCORDS) Its MIZeRY (MIZ - ReCORDS)

INFINITE VERSE:
Yo, Me and MIZeRY Step up in the building/ we gun wielding/ ya we straight killin/ cause on top of the game looks so appealing/ well take it over by force/ we fucking villains/ we should be on top of this/ Americas most wanted list/ I aint even hit my prime yet/ no optimus/ out for my doe, like a hungry hippopotamus/ all star ever shot I take is not a miss/ but when I dick your girl down its anonymous/ because she gave me her lips dog, but not a kiss/ infinite and mizery aint no stopping this/ well kick the illest shit forever, no apocalypse/ spitting shit up on the mic you know we the sickest/ running shit forest Gump, you know we the quickest/ never ask for permission/ only ask forgiveness/ no yogi, but you could bear witness/

HOOK:
Infinite –" We in da buildin, we in da buildin/ captivating all the ears of your children/ its MIZeRY (MIZ - ReCORDS) Its MIZeRY (MIZ - ReCORDS) its MIZeRY (MIZ - ReCORDS) Its MIZeRY (MIZ - ReCORDS) We in da buildin, we in da buildin/ captivating all the ears of your children/ its MIZeRY (MIZ - ReCORDS) Its MIZeRY (MIZ - ReCORDS) its MIZeRY (MIZ - ReCORDS) Its MIZeRY (MIZ - ReCORDS)

MIZeRY VERSE 1:
When I wake up in the morning, I be pissin out my excellence/ im teaching all you idiots/ nothing less then fucking greatness/ you can all call my a king/ because im destined to own everything/ and I don't need on any blind/ to be showing you all my ranking/ my intensity is intelligently/ fucking up your whole psyche/ precisely – psychologically/ according to how I envision/ when I step up in this building/ everybodies gonna be screaming/ as I walk up in this building/ Ill have a whole team of security/ with nothing less then 9 millies/ constantly surrounding me/ cause all you sick twisted fucks, might wanna try to kid nap me/ as you send my ass overseas/ and you sell me off for cheap/ but, rest assured little homie/ that it will never happen to me/ when im roaming through these streets/ I don't care who you be/ cause im a mother fucking g/ let me get back into my party/ as I escaped my own reality/ hey baby what is you drinking/ as my mind kept on drifting/ I was looking down your titties/ saying – I really want'ch your pussy/ so is you coming home with me/ so you should also bring your friend/ cause ill make both of ya backs bend/ when this shit comes to an end/ so please don't bitch or even fret/ in the early morning hours, I want your ass out my door/ do you understand me shorty, I don't keep around no whores/ If you continue to piss me off/ then Ill make your ass get lost/ so shortly lets roll/ Imma spit this from my dome/ When I wake up in the morning, I wake up as a boss/

HOOK:
Infinite –" We in da buildin, we in da buildin/ captivating all the ears of your children/ its MIZeRY (MIZ - ReCORDS) Its MIZeRY (MIZ - ReCORDS) its MIZeRY (MIZ - ReCORDS) Its MIZeRY (MIZ - ReCORDS) We in da buildin, we in da buildin/ captivating all the ears of your children/ its MIZeRY (MIZ - ReCORDS) Its MIZeRY (MIZ - ReCORDS) its MIZeRY (MIZ - ReCORDS) Its MIZeRY (MIZ - ReCORDS)

MIZeRY VERSE 2:
What, what, what, When I step up in this building/ Im the one whos negotiating/ Ive been running this conversation/ strategically from the beginning. IM speeding/ as im speaking/ that its made ya head start spinning/ within a matter of several minutes/ im feeding you all so much intelligence/ its become my torture method/ so let me shut up for 30 seconds/ pass the mic to my man infinite/ as he drops upon you knowledge/ because he feels sorry for you sick, twisted pricks/ who's nothing more than a sorry excuse for our existence/ polluting all of us with your ignorance/ begging for mizerys forgiveness/ my last words for you are this/ that Im not Jesus Christ/ and I have no obligations to tolerate any of your adolescence/

HOOK:
Infinite –" We in da buildin, we in da buildin/ captivating all the ears of your children/ its MIZeRY (MIZ - ReCORDS) Its MIZeRY (MIZ - ReCORDS) its MIZeRY (MIZ - ReCORDS) Its MIZeRY (MIZ - ReCORDS) We in da buildin, we in da buildin/ captivating all the ears of your children/ its MIZeRY (MIZ - ReCORDS) Its MIZeRY (MIZ - ReCORDS) its MIZeRY (MIZ - ReCORDS) Its MIZeRY (MIZ - ReCORDS)

"15 years of my life" – page 11; original photo title: clubbing; Art direction and design by Michael Izzo. This album is Distributed online through *Tunecore* & *MIZeRY ReCORDS* websites in over 150 countries globally.

12. I've Lost My Mind Ft. Infinite, Brittles, & The Invincible Red Fire Ant

INTRO: I got to kick it into this other mind state you know wha im saying, you know wha im saying, I was just like, Get those beats out bro. Yaa get those beats out bro, its narly bro. yo get those fucking beats out bro, I love those beats, aahhh shitt.

INFINITE's VERSE:
haha, Yo MIZ You a crazy motha fucker.
Sometimes/ I sit alone and kick dumb rhymes/ and smoke weed till my whole brain unwinds/ I aint lost my mind/ I misplaced it on purpose/ so I go crazy on my verses/ Wanna hear my message, well reverse this/ (all yalla mwawa) MIZ that was perfect/ Play it back and the whole crowd disperses/ devils strapped to my shoulder like girls purses/ I never wish, what the fuck I need a genii for/ Im demonic, get my lyrics of a wigi-board/ Started slow/ now im on some other shit/ If weezy is a Martian, than im the mother ship/ Im hot as hell, but Im colder then a snow flake/ Put your ass in a wheel chair, no drake/ NO direction I aint got no fate/ I just sit back/ relax/ and let the dro fade/ Come on MIZ take em back to the old days/ haha

MIZeRY's VERSE:
Shit, that's what it is though, I'm about to drop some real sick flow/ Understand homie, I aint got no time if you aint ready to roll/ Yo is we live? I've lost my mind, when I'm feeling on this beat/ I'm spittin some real shit, When I'm rhyming through my teeth/ Cause my mind is exploding, I see that'ch your folding/ By the look of your Composure/ My style is brand new/ feeling real good/ Go ahead, fuck with my crew/ WOAH, hold it up/ This IS a Stick Up/ Take YA Steps Slowly/ You'll never comprehend - my full entire Story/ Where ya Hands Going/ Cause If you Start Reaching/ You'll be the one screaming/ Bleeding/ to your deathm Trust me, If I got to Go to WAR/ Imma Put'ch you in ya Place/ Have you Erased/ AND Bury you Early, In YA Mother Fucking Grave/ What Are You Telling Me/ I'll Knock You in Ya Face/ You wanna fuck Around with Me/ Im Gonna Kill You Swiftly/ At a Slooowww Pace/ Fuck What'ch You SAY/ Imma Have You Beggin FOR FAITH/ In the Lords Holy Name, I Pray/ Can You Shower me, WITH A Little of Ya Praise/ Fuck, How I was Raised/ Intelligent People, Constantly Change/ I Think, you're the One's whos FUCKING Insane/ Imma Kick This Slow, I Ain't Never Gonna Slow Down/ OR SAY NO/ Back OFF/ I'm Here to WIN/ That's What Im Destined/ To DO In MY Life/ Cause I've Envisioned IT/ I Have Dreams, Im Recording in the BOOTH/ WITH 50 & SLIM/ Im telling you EXACTLY How THAT IT IS/ So Understand, IF you Wanna fuck with my Intelligence/ You'll BE 6 O'clock News COVER - AGE/ Getting HIT FAST/ Man, You wont be thinking - you got hit by my FISTS/ You'll be thinking, I Got Shot by SOME BULLETS/ What'ch you tryn to tell me, Imma Unload HALF A CLIP/ Imm WAAAYYY ACCURR - RATE/ [RIT] You Aint fucking With me NO MORE/ Im going at a HIGH Crime RATE/ Cause Im Tryn to Make SOME CHANGE/ What'ch you tryn to tell me, IS YOU GOT SLAIN/ I See whats going on, I Spit it through my RHYMES/ I tell it like it is, CAUSE I Think it - In MY MIND/ And I Give it to you RAW, and I aint cutting it cutting it up, I aint no chef/ This is what im thinking about, take it to the the next level,- TEST/ Yaa - Is you even foooIllllooowwwiiinnn/ Im thinking about it/ Every Step AND what NOT/ I Play Chess, When I Hustel W/ Every SINGLE BloCK/ I'm DOING THIS, With a VERSE IN The BACKGROUND/ My Intelligence, FAR Exceeds YOUR MEMBRAINS/ The KIND OF LIFE I've LIVED, Would make you go INSANE? Competition? NAA, It Doesn't EVEN Matta to ME/ I Don't think about IT/ I'm strategically WINNING/ I'm A Revolutionary GENERAL/ THIS life that I LIVE, HAS to be Incredible/ SO COME AND FOLLOW ME/ We're Fighting in this WAR/ To Spread Passivity/ AND Live spiritually/ We Could SURVIVE, through the YEAR 2012/ If we Rally Past Twelve/ On Our Way to Defeat EVIL in HELL/ AND I Will/ Never Sell - MYSELF/ Other than TO My Lord/ AND HIS Holy ANGELS/ Similar to the VOICE, Of My Girl Brittles/

Brittles VERSE's:
Club Brittles, Everybody in the club right now/ get up on the dance floor and break it down/ down/ I like that sound, that's how it is when your in our town/ Brittles, yaa, oooo. Should I be with him, should I be you, can you tell me baby what Should I do/ should I be with him should I be with you?/ tell me, what Should I do/ Im so confused, What should I do, I got a man, but im really feeling you/ It seems so wrong, it feels so right, dreaming about us every single day and night/ Them Gangstas, smoking that fucking dro, dro/ Hes my gangsta boy and im really feeling him, ill be his ride or die chick until the very end, and everybody wanna be like us, cause we g-a-n-g-s-t-a soo dangerous/ its Brittney bitch.

Red Fire's VERSE:
Never go to war unless you willin ta die never believe anybody who claims they never lie realize what they told you was wrong when you thought it wuz right and now what's real iz wrong but yet you hold on to the lies that said you'd be rich and famous not broke and nameless remember how you thought you'd remain ageless? now you old wit grays thinkin bout where the days of the past have gone you need to live it up, while you still can but let go of the past, face your fears or forever they will last and know this, I was high when I wrote this cuz life's a bitch N' then ya die, so I'm always high, R.I.P. Kit Nicolai, Is he really gone or am I losing my mind When will it be my time? They say there's always tomorrow for dreams to come true but if you wait too long opportunities can pass you by Like the girl on that bus, why didn't I say hi? So many mistakes, so many changes I'd make But you cant change the past, and even if I could would I make things worse? See every action sets off a series of events, ahhh maybe I'm not making sense... --- Brittney "Feelin You" - Sample...

"15 years of my life" – page 12; original photo title: 24006-bigthumbnail; Art direction and design by Michael Izzo. This album is Distributed online through *Tunecore & MIZeRY ReCORDS* websites in over 150 countries globally.

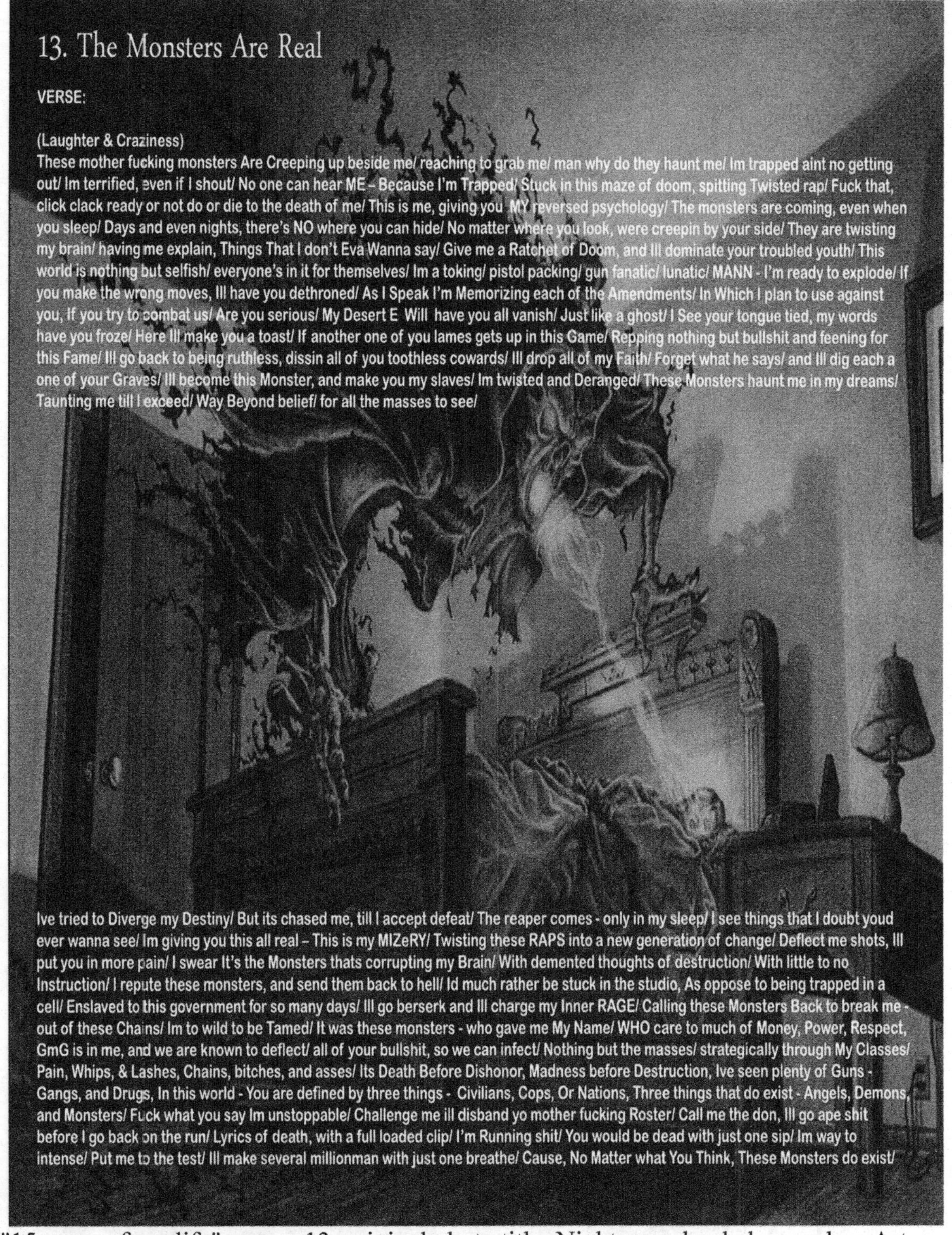

13. The Monsters Are Real

VERSE:

(Laughter & Craziness)

These mother fucking monsters Are Creeping up beside me/ reaching to grab me/ man why do they haunt me/ Im trapped aint no getting out/ Im terrified, even if I shout/ No one can hear ME – Because I'm Trapped/ Stuck in this maze of doom, spitting Twisted rap/ Fuck that, click clack ready or not do or die to the death of me/ This is me, giving you MY reversed psychology/ The monsters are coming, even when you sleep/ Days and even nights, there's NO where you can hide/ No matter where you look, were creepin by your side/ They are twisting my brain/ having me explain, Things That I don't Eva Wanna say/ Give me a Ratchet of Doom, and Ill dominate your troubled youth/ This world is nothing but selfish/ everyone's in it for themselves/ Im a toking/ pistol packing/ gun fanatic/ lunatic/ MANN - I'm ready to explode/ If you make the wrong moves, Ill have you dethroned/ As I Speak I'm Memorizing each of the Amendments/ In Which I plan to use against you, If you try to combat us/ Are you serious/ My Desert E Will have you all vanish/ Just like a ghost/ I See your tongue tied, my words have you froze/ Here Ill make you a toast/ If another one of you lames gets up in this Game/ Repping nothing but bullshit and feening for this Fame/ Ill go back to being ruthless, dissin all of you toothless cowards/ Ill drop all of my Faith/ Forget what he says/ and Ill dig each a one of your Graves/ Ill become this Monster, and make you my slaves/ Im twisted and Deranged/ These Monsters haunt me in my dreams/ Taunting me till I exceed/ Way Beyond belief/ for all the masses to see/

Ive tried to Diverge my Destiny/ But its chased me, till I accept defeat/ The reaper comes - only in my sleep/ I see things that I doubt youd ever wanna see/ Im giving you this all real – This is my MIZeRY/ Twisting these RAPS into a new generation of change/ Deflect me shots, Ill put you in more pain/ I swear It's the Monsters thats corrupting my Brain/ With demented thoughts of destruction/ With little to no Instruction/ I repute these monsters, and send them back to hell/ Id much rather be stuck in the studio, As oppose to being trapped in a cell/ Enslaved to this government for so many days/ Ill go berserk and Ill charge my Inner RAGE/ Calling these Monsters Back to break me - out of these Chains/ Im to wild to be Tamed/ It was these monsters - who gave me My Name/ WHO care to much of Money, Power, Respect, GmG is in me, and we are known to deflect/ all of your bullshit, so we can infect/ Nothing but the masses/ strategically through My Classes/ Pain, Whips, & Lashes, Chains, bitches, and asses/ Its Death Before Dishonor, Madness before Destruction, Ive seen plenty of Guns - Gangs, and Drugs, In this world - You are defined by three things - Civilians, Cops, Or Nations, Three things that do exist - Angels, Demons, and Monsters/ Fuck what you say Im unstoppable/ Challenge me ill disband yo mother fucking Roster/ Call me the don, Ill go ape shit before I go back on the run/ Lyrics of death, with a full loaded clip/ I'm Running shit/ You would be dead with just one sip/ Im way to intense/ Put me to the test/ Ill make several millionman with just one breathe/ Cause, No Matter what You Think, These Monsters do exist/

"<u>15 years of my life</u>" – page 13; original photo title: Nightmare_by_kalessaradan; Art direction and design by Michael Izzo. This album is Distributed online through *Tunecore & MIZeRY ReCORDS* websites in over 150 countries globally.

14. I'm A Problem

INTRO: You know so I think about it/ and when I, take myself back to, when I was a teen/ causing mad trouble and problems/ I just think about/ I was a wild mother fucker man/ woop woop/

HOOK:
Ya you could put me in hand cuffs/ or throw me behind bars/ but im never slowing down, im reaching for the stars/ much faster than you think, I'll conquer this game/ but ill never be the same/ so welcome to my pain/ with every ounce in my brain/ that generated my name/ ya ya, that generated my name/ haha man,

VERSE 1:
Ill take you back to when I committed several felonies/ SO hate me or love me/ even back then I lived alter realities/ I hustled everybody/ starting with your money/ I used tactics to manipulate everything around me/ starting with these judges, who kept on saying I wasn't built for society/ I had to do everything to wipe my felonies/ from permanently damaging my profession/ now pay close attention/ Man, cause my class is in session/ who the fuck is you chin checkin/ my chrome desert E, gone to teach your ass a lesson/ so quit which your flexin/ If we got some real beef, than I wont be playin fair/ If your gunning for my life/ then I wont really even care/ what happens to your ass by the end of this night/ my crew don't fight fair/ so if you ever try to compare/ you best come prepared/ full of precision, loaded with perception of distance/ cause little homie, I don't ever miss/ ok little bitch/ so Ill keep on spitting it like it really is/ Nikki Minaj might be the best his/ (I am the bestest (Nikki Minaj) But I am the best hers/ so fuck what'ch ya heard/ Im 3 styles in one/ DMX, EM, & Pac/ SO why don't you come and get it, if you really want some/ but ill fairly warn you that Im a problem/

HOOK:
Ya you could put me in hand cuffs/ or throw me behind bars/ but im never slowing down, im reaching for the stars/ much faster than you think, I'll conquer this game/ but ill never be the same/ so welcome to my pain/ with every ounce in my brain/ that generated my name/ ya ya, that generated my name/ haha man,

VERSE 2:
Ok, well fuck rules and regulations/ I was never one to abide by government manipulation/ when I was young, they tried to put me on controlled sedation/ coaxin me to take this medication/ instead, I kept things, come, collective, & cool/ as I refused to be used like someone's little mule/ just to amuse/ people like you/ pathetic little fools/ who pretend to be superior with your high tech tools/ time for a reality check, I dropped out of school/ still graduated and succeeded above you/ while still grinding to make my dreams come true/ now lets talk about you/ oopss – I mean me/ aint nobody right now care to speak of a nobody/ even back in the 3rd grade, yall was hating on me/ and I believe/ it was only cause I was different in ways that you couldn't even see/ startin with my swag/ that it seems yall just lacked/ as a matter of fact/ I wasn't always inta rap/ I was a good kid, if ya can believe that crap/ It was when my MIZeRY grew, so strong, that it consumed my whole soul/ that it buried Michael Izzo/ In such a deep hole/ It took 15 years to climb up out of this hole/ scarred me for my life, and I Paid a heavy ass toll/ to uncover my role/ that IM destined to play/ in this crazy ass game/ what more shall I say/ other than I must pray/ and ask for forgiveness/ for all my wrong doings, that Ive ever committed/

HOOK:
Repeat 2x - Add - haha, MIZeRY was the pain that was given to me man/

VERSE 3:
Im A Bit of a thrill seeker/ exploring all meters/ and I don't need any features/ to be an ill rapper/ I Probably got more songs than all of yall combined/ Ive been doing this for many years, its my time to shine/ cause I stayed on my grind/ to be giving you these rhymes/ and every single time, they come from my mind/ so don't try to mimic my music of lyrics/ that's was given to me from lord, as a gift of precision/ and this was my decisions/ to be giving you this real, cause there aint no gimmicks/ only sheer optics/ connect to your house, kind of like fiber/ Im a little bit hyper/ always on the move/ looking for something new/ constantly making new rules/ cause I cant tolerate none of yall fools/ my sharp tongue/ was sprung/ from when I was real young/ I don't hold air in my lungs/ when I speak harsh words/ that makes you all cry like you're a bunch of little girls/ I call it as I see it/ As I turn my head and look the other way/ Forget about ya punk ass, and walk the other way/ I don't have time to waste/ am the only one man, that's trying to make change/

HOOK:
Repeat Hook: add - ya ya that generated my name/ haha man

You know I think back then I just didn't give a fuck man/ I figured this is who I am/ and I aint lettin know body change me/ but now, I think about it/ and im just a little more calm with every move that I make na meen/ but its all good cause soon enough we will be on the top/ and aint shit gonna matter/ peace.

"15 years of my life" – page 14; original photo title: downtown-destruction; Art direction and design by Michael Izzo. This album is Distributed online through *Tunecore* & *MIZeRY ReCORDS* websites in over 150 countries globally.

15. 15 Years of My Life

INTRO: This journeys been a rough one it's been a long time coming, but I think we're almost there, I can see shore. Ugh.

VERSE 1:
For 15 years of my life/ Ive chased this dream that's inside/ In hops that one day, Id eventually get signed/ So I may save this world, by expressing to you my rhymes/ For all of this time/ Most of you must really think man, that Im waay out of my mind/ As I Continue to believe that someday, we will all shine/ So bright, right into your eyes/ Lighting these paths, so we can all go home/ As the days go by, and Im waiting by this phone/ praying for yall to call, maybe, Ive lost all my hope/ In my last hours man, Ive refrained from my subtle tone/ So I kept this album raw/ cause for 15 years, its been a never ending war/ I started robbing stores/ then I started hitting these corners, selling you different kinds of drugs/ Acting like a young thug/ who didn't really give a fuck/ ready to bust his gun/ Eventually, Karma caught up to me, and kept me on the run/ Until, I were to clean my slate/ giving me a second chance to get up out of check mate/ It must have been my fate/ to remain so brave/ with everything that I say/ which kept me from ending up in my grave/ or in chains/ to this government, treating us all like slaves/

VERSE 2:
I broke free/ from these chains, by being an emcee/ Telling you my life lyrically/ Smooth and diligently/ we sneak/ not making a peep/ as the back door creeps/ Silently/ Trust me/ aint nobody stopping me/ cause – Ive come to far, to back down now/ so you can call me a cash cow/ searching for new ways, So I can come to your town/ and shut shit down/ As I really all the masses/ For something so spectacular/ reaching any levels of satisfaction/ 3-2-1, Lights, Cameras, Action/ This is years of wrath/ attacking you so rapid/ When I use verbal tactics/ Starting with lyrical mathematics/ The apocalypse/ leaves no souls, just dust/ In its aftermath/ So come join us and live in peace, up in planet mizaine/ where good people with troubled lives, can escape from their pain/ Lies & Deceit/ Where we always have food to eat/ Which is usually for free/ If your not ready man, than I need you to take a seat/ we only move at one speed/ and that's mine/ Racing to beat time/ metaphorically confusing you, by spitting some ill rhymes/ I could probably say anything, and ill blow away your minds/ Like – irragatu-pudu-ati-ari-gotu puma, ya keep my flow tight/ cause at the end of this night/ that's all yall care about ya right/ Well there much more to being a rapper, than having a sick flow/ Damn – your brains need to grow/ Here – Ill spit some shit slow/ Get Ready – N – Start Taking notes/ 2x2 equals four/ before you eva enter, you better knock on the door/ If your breaking the law homie, your bound to go to court/ lyrically – Im winning when it comes to this sport/

VERSE 3:
Ya for 15 years of my life/ Ive been chasing this dream that's inside/ In hopes that one day, I could live my life/ Without being stressed, going out of my mind/ 15 years of my life/ has been told through these rhymes/ and im starting to quit/ thinking that, all these paths meant shit/ Fuck – anxiety builds up quick/ my rhymes come super slick/ as if/ their supposed to confuse you brick by brick/ So as if Ive said, Maybe – my life aint worth shit/ and after all of this/ that I should just pick up and quit/ cause – Maybe – Im not really intelligent, or unique/ in any kind of way kid/ Maybe – im supposed to be born into a world of shit/ with nothing, starting with this gift/ If it wasn't for these rhymes/ I would not be alive/ cause for all of those years/ that I have ever cried/ I kept begging lord, to snatch away my life/ even a guy like me questions/ if hes really destined/ for greatness/ to save all of gods lost children/

"15 years of my life" – page 15; original photo title: DJ_Music_Mixer; Art direction and design by Michael Izzo. This album is Distributed online through *Tunecore & MIZeRY ReCORDS* websites in over 150 countries globally.

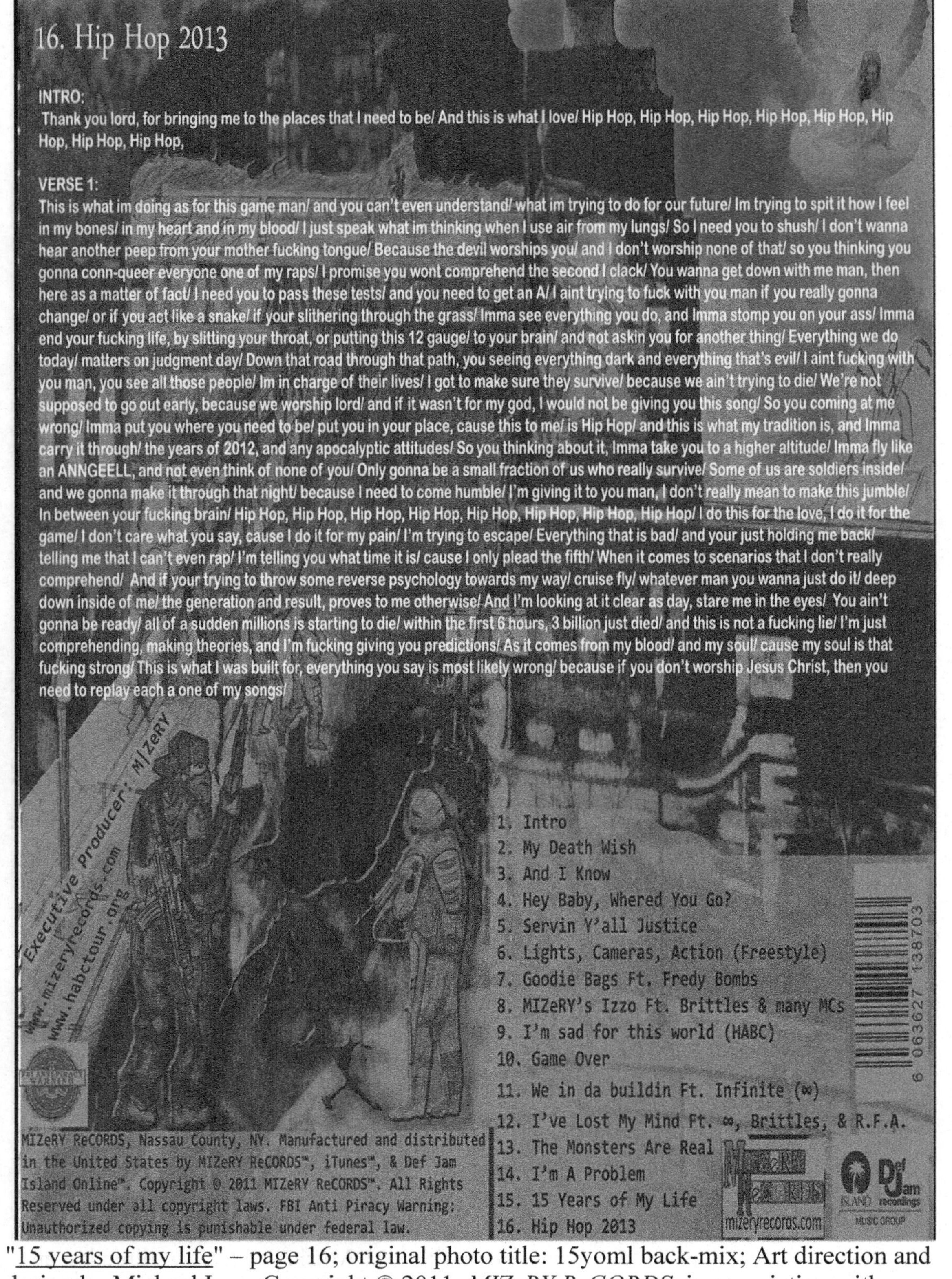

"<u>15 years of my life</u>" – page 16; original photo title: 15yoml back-mix; Art direction and design by Michael Izzo. Copyright © 2011, *MIZeRY ReCORDS*; in association with *Island Def Jam Publishing* – All Rights Reserved. This album is Distributed online through *Tunecore* & *MIZeRY ReCORDS* websites in over 150 countries globally.

1. Intro
(M. Izzo) MIZeRY Publishing, admin by MIZeRY ReCORDS in association with iTunes & Tunecore (BMI)/Copyright Control for Mike "MIZeRY" Izzo. Produced by MIZeRY for MIZeRY ReCORDS. Recorded by Deshaun for MIZeRY ReCORDS @ MIZeRY ReCORDS studios, Boston, MA.

2. My Death Wish
(M. Izzo) MIZeRY Publishing, admin by MIZeRY ReCORDS in association with iTunes & Tunecore (BMI)/Copyright Control for Mike "MIZeRY" Izzo. Produced by T.J. Jeter for Noise Productions. Recorded by Deshaun for MIZeRY ReCORDS @ MIZeRY ReCORDS studios, Boston, MA.

3. And I Know
(M. Izzo) MIZeRY Publishing, admin by MIZeRY ReCORDS in association with iTunes & Tunecore (BMI)/Copyright Control for Mike "MIZeRY" Izzo. Produced by Say Lo 2 Beats for Heavy Bag Entertainment. Recorded by Deshaun for MIZeRY ReCORDS @ MIZeRY ReCORDS studios, Boston, MA. All Rights Reserved.

4. Hey Baby, Whered you go?
(M. Izzo) MIZeRY Publishing, admin by MIZeRY ReCORDS in association with iTunes & Tunecore (BMI)/Copyright Control for Mike "MIZeRY" Izzo. Produced by SID & SI Productions. Recorded by Deshaun for MIZeRY ReCORDS @ MIZeRY ReCORDS studios, Boston, MA.

5. Servin Y'all Justice
(M. Izzo) MIZeRY Publishing, admin by MIZeRY ReCORDS in association with iTunes & Tunecore (BMI)/Copyright Control for Mike "MIZeRY" Izzo. Produced by Hev1 for MIZeRY ReCORDS. Recorded by Deshaun for MIZeRY ReCORDS @ MIZeRY ReCORDS studios, Boston, MA.

6. Lights, Cameras, Action (Freestyle).
(M. Izzo) MIZeRY Publishing, admin by MIZeRY ReCORDS in association with iTunes & Tunecore (BMI)/Copyright Control for Mike "MIZeRY" Izzo. Produced by HTS Entertainment for MIZeRY ReCORDS. Recorded by Deshaun for MIZeRY ReCORDS @ MIZeRY ReCORDS studios, Boston, MA.

7. Goodie Bags - Feat. Fredy Bombs
(M. Izzo) MIZeRY Publishing, admin by MIZeRY ReCORDS in association with iTunes & Tunecore (BMI)/Copyright Control for Mike "MIZeRY" Izzo. Produced by Hev1 for MIZeRY ReCORDS. Fredy Bombs Recorded by MIZeRY at MIZeRY ReCORDS Studios, Htown, MA. MIZeRY's vocals Recorded by Deshaun for MIZeRY ReCORDS @ MIZeRY ReCORDS studios, Boston, MA.

8. MIZeRY's Izzo Ft. Brittles & Many MC's
(M. Izzo) MIZeRY Publishing, admin by MIZeRY ReCORDS in association with iTunes & Tunecore (BMI)/Copyright Control for Mike "MIZeRY" Izzo. Produced by Nick Price for MIZeRY ReCORDS. Brittles & MIZeRY's vocals recorded by DaRedANT & MIZeRY at MIZeRY ReCORDS studios in Long Island, NY.

9. I'm sad for this world
(M. Izzo) MIZeRY Publishing, admin by MIZeRY ReCORDS in association with iTunes & Tunecore (BMI)/Copyright Control for Mike "MIZeRY" Izzo. Produced by T.J. Jeter for Noise Productions. Recorded by Deshaun for MIZeRY ReCORDS @ MIZeRY ReCORDS studios, Boston, MA.

10. Game Over
(M. Izzo) MIZeRY Publishing, admin by MIZeRY ReCORDS in association with iTunes & Tunecore (BMI)/Copyright Control for Mike "MIZeRY" Izzo. Produced by SID & SI Productions. Recorded by Deshaun for MIZeRY ReCORDS @ MIZeRY ReCORDS studios, Boston, MA. Mixed by MIZeRY.

11. We in da buildin - Feat. Infinite
(M. Izzo) MIZeRY Publishing, admin by MIZeRY ReCORDS in association with iTunes & Tunecore (BMI)/Copyright Control for Mike "MIZeRY" Izzo. Produced by T.J. Jeter for Noise Productions. Infinite's vocals recorded by MIZeRY @ MIZeRY ReCORDS studios Htown, MA. Infinite appears courtesy of MIZeRY ReCORDS. Recorded by Deshaun for MIZeRY ReCORDS @ MIZeRY ReCORDS studios, Boston, MA.

12. I've Lost My Mind - Feat. Infinite, Brittles, & The Invincible Red Fire Ant
(M. Izzo) MIZeRY Publishing, admin by MIZeRY ReCORDS in association with iTunes & Tunecore (BMI)/Copyright Control for Mike "MIZeRY" Izzo. Produced by S.I.D. for SI Productions. Infinite's vocals recorded by MIZeRY @ MIZeRY ReCORDS studios Htown, MA. Infinite appears courtesy of MIZeRY ReCORDS. Brittles & Red Fire's vocals recorded by The Invincible Red Fire Ant @ Da Ant Hill studios Long Island, NY. MIZeRY's vocals Recorded by Deshaun for MIZeRY ReCORDS @ MIZeRY ReCORDS studios, Boston, MA.

"15 years of my life" – page 17 - credits; original photo title: New-York-Skyline-Night; Art direction and design by Michael Izzo. Copyright © 2011, *MIZeRY ReCORDS*; in association with *Island Def Jam Publishing* – All Rights Reserved. This album is Distributed online through *Tunecore & MIZeRY ReCORDS* websites in over 150 countries globally.

13. The Monsters Are Real
(M. Izzo) MIZeRY Publishing, admin by MIZeRY ReCORDS in association with iTunes & Tunecore (BMI)/Copyright Control for Mike "MIZeRY" Izzo. Produced by T.J. Jeter for Noise Productions. MIZeRY's vocals Recorded by Deshaun for MIZeRY ReCORDS @ MIZeRY ReCORDS studios, Boston, MA.

14. I'm A Problem
(M. Izzo) MIZeRY Publishing, admin by MIZeRY ReCORDS in association with iTunes & Tunecore (BMI)/Copyright Control for Mike "MIZeRY" Izzo. Produced by Hev1 for MIZeRY ReCORDS. MIZeRY's vocals Recorded by Deshaun for MIZeRY ReCORDS @ MIZeRY ReCORDS studios, Boston, MA.

15. 15 Years of My Life
(M. Izzo) MIZeRY Publishing, admin by MIZeRY ReCORDS in association with iTunes & Tunecore (BMI)/Copyright Control for Mike "MIZeRY" Izzo. Produced by T.J. Jeter for Noise Productions. MIZeRY's vocals Recorded by Deshaun for MIZeRY ReCORDS @ MIZeRY ReCORDS studios, Boston, MA.

16. Hip Hop 2013
(M. Izzo) MIZeRY Publishing, admin by MIZeRY ReCORDS in association with iTunes & Tunecore (BMI)/Copyright Control for Mike "MIZeRY" Izzo. Produced by SID & SI Productions. Recorded by Deshaun for MIZeRY ReCORDS @ MIZeRY ReCORDS studios, Boston, MA.

THANK YOU'S:
First I want to thank God and Jesus Christ for everything you do and for saving me. I also want to thank my grandparents for raising me, my siblings, and the rest of my family who have been there. I want to thank Tim, Ali, Fred, Brittles, Jon, Brian H., Michael, Christina, Christine, Bill, Vin, Ma, Pa, Nonna, Aunties, and Uncles, Luke G., Pooch, Dwayne, Daven, Ash Fay, Katie M., Brian O., Hev, Nick P, Say Lo, SID, HTS, Noise, X, and everyone else who's truly helped me these years. Above all else, Thank You.

My entire staff and MIZeRY ReCORDS, Fresh Entertainment Inc., Decago Inc, GmG, Ant Hill Productions, Heavy Bag Ent, O State Djs, iTunes, Amazon, Def Jam, Facebook, Pro tools, HP, CAD, Monster, and all the other companies who made it possible to complete this album.

My team - Brittles, Infinite, Sam, DaRedANT, Hev1, Fresh Entertainment Inc, Daven, & Pooch.

TOTAL RUN TIME: 1:10:20

CREDITS:
Executive Producer: M|ZeRY
Album Producers: M|ZeRY, Noise Productions, Say Lo 2 Beats, SID, Hev1, HTS Entertainment, & Nick Price.
Photography: Zack Meader
Art Direction & Designs: M|ZeRY
Co-Art Direction & Design: Sam Kim
MIZeRY Management: Fresh Entertainment Inc.
Public Relations Manager: Fred Boucher
Promo Team Management: F.E.I. & MIZeRY Promotions
Communications Director: Daven Compton
Head Engineer & Sound Stage Manager: Hev1
Music Coordinator: Jonathan "DaRedANT" Nicolai
Publishing: Itunes, Amazon, Def Jam Island Online, & MIZeRY ReCORDS

PARENTAL LITERAL ADVISORY EXPLICIT CONTENT
FBI ANTI-PIRACY WARNING
ISLAND Def Jam recordings MUSIC GROUP

WEBSITES:
www.mizeryrecords.com www.habctour.org www.habctour.info www.myspace.com/mizeryrecords
www.facebook.com/MIZeRY63 www.facebook.com/pages/MZeRY/154557581244216 http://theunderstry.ning.com/

mizeryrecords.com
HABCTOUR.ORG
The underworld of the industry THE UNDERSTRY™ Worldwide
DECAGO Marketing and Management
FRESH ENTERTAINMENT INC. 516-771-6586

"15 years of my life" – page 18 – credits continued; original photo title: Filmmaker background; Art direction and design by Michael Izzo. Copyright © 2011, *MIZeRY ReCORDS*; in association with *Island Def Jam Publishing* – All Rights Reserved. This album is Distributed online through *Tunecore & MIZeRY ReCORDS* websites in over 150 countries globally.

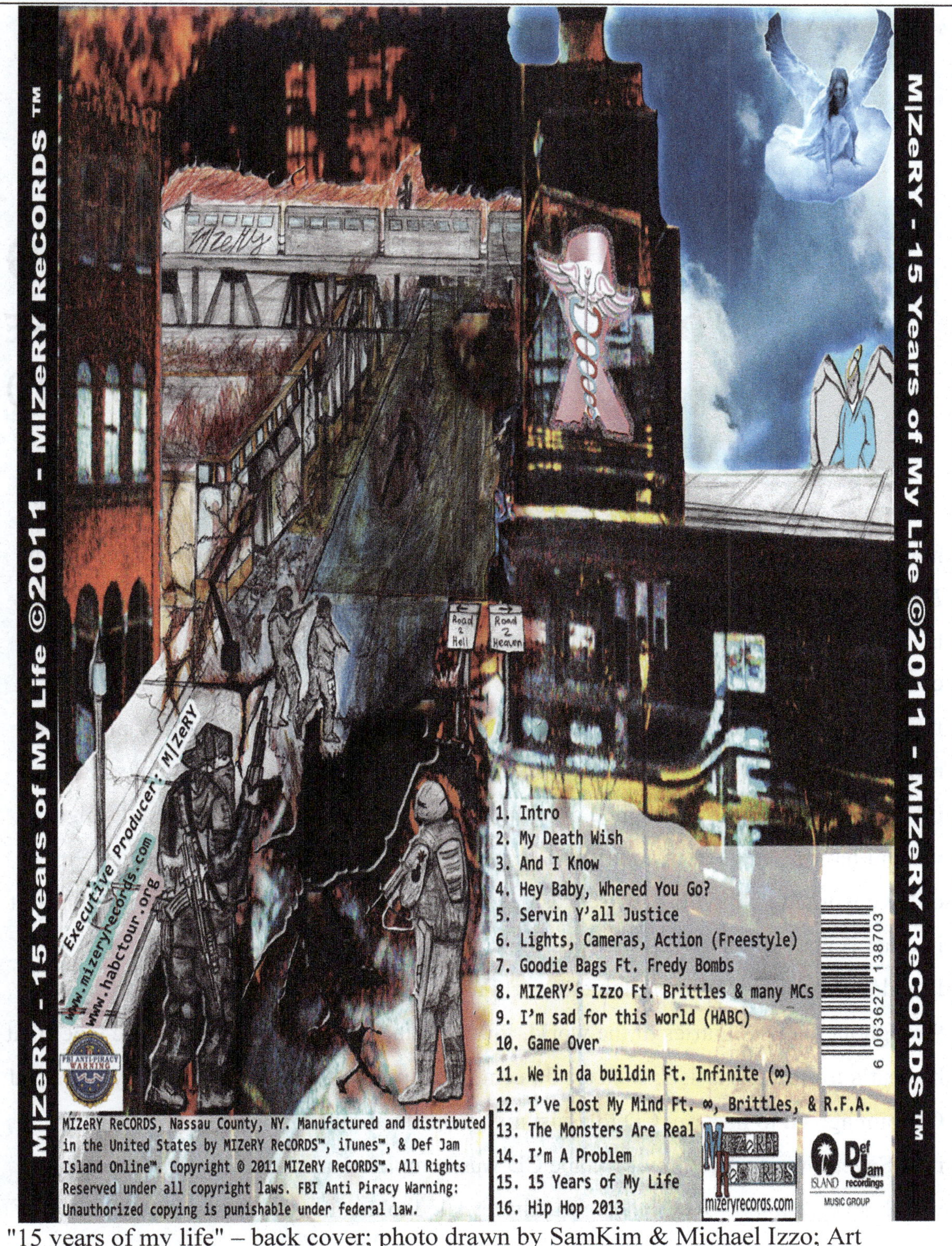

"15 years of my life" – back cover; photo drawn by SamKim & Michael Izzo; Art direction and design by Michael Izzo. Copyright © 2011, *MIZeRY ReCORDS*; in association with *Island Def Jam Publishing* – All Rights Reserved. This album is Distributed online through *Tunecore* & *MIZeRY ReCORDS* websites in over 150 countries globally.

Chapter 10
World Take Over – Mixtape (Hosted by DJ Onpoint)

I'm now 24 and it's the year 2011, which is coming to a fast end. I'm becoming more motivated to be victorious in life. I'm also about to release my second album with *Island Def Jam* globally. I further realized that before I do, I need a Mixtape to go with it in order to assist in promoting my new music. For some strange reasoning in which I can't quite explain, the title of this CD was decided to be "World Take Over." At first, I felt as if it was just a metaphor to represent becoming popular in the world of music; but now, I'm not so sure that's all it means. This CD, represents a wide variety of songs that my company and I have compiled over the years from other artists; or remixed songs in which I have re-created. In addition, a large pool of people that I haven't met, have met, or have worked with; will now, see a side of my story that I haven't directly spoken about in other songs. When the CD was nearing completion, I had reached out to a good friend/colleague in the entertainment world named **DJ Onpoint**. He is well known throughout many countries of the world, for his DJing ability, and for his music tapes that he host's for famous artists; such as: 50 cent, Joe Budden, Mobb Deep, & many more. DJ Onpoint agreed to host my CD to assist my musical career and for a really reasonable rate. Several weeks later, my Mixtape CD was completed and hosted by DJ Onpoint. It was this very album cover that eventually revealed to me, my own truth; I was in fact, Jesus Christ in the second form as I discuss later on in this Novel…

World Take Over – Mixtape Hosted by DJ Onpoint – front and back; photo taken by Dayne Mahadeo; Direction and design by Michael Izzo. Copyright © 2011, *MIZeRY ReCORDS* – All Rights Reserved. People in photo left to right: Tara Lynn & Michael "MIZeRY" Izzo; photo taken in Times Square, NYC.

Chapter 10: Song 1 – Redemption (B4) Annihilation (10:1)

Redemption (B4) Annihilation:

INTRO: "Sometimes we all come to a point in our lives, where we just want to give up and quit. But you know today is the complete opposite, today is the day that you're saved; so welcome, welcome to my pain."

VERSE 1: I'm back with another one/ I no longer carry guns/ I'm no longer on the run/ I just want to wake up and feel like the bright sun/ I'm sick of these dark streets/ seeing nothing but bad, the drugs, and the police/ struggling everyday just so we can eat/ with a nice place to sleep/ and you're still wondering why I named myself MIZeRY/ I need redemption before I'm even annihilated/ because if I don't make it to Heaven/ I won't be reincarnated/ you can't buy your way into Heaven/ but I'm so smooth, maybe we can all sneak in/ I'm sorry God but this is what I was thinking/ if what I say is so wrong, than take back this gift/ I was given/ that's loaded with precision/ and lethal incisions/ based on some decisions/ that I've made/ to escape all of MIZeRY's pain/ if we don't start getting paid/ then I'm quitting/ on this game, and I ain't fucking playing/

HOOK/CHORUS: Lil Wayne Hook remix "And I'm grinding till I'm tired/ they say you ain't grinding till you tired/ so if I'm grinding with my eyes wide/ looking to find a way through the day/ a light for the night/ Dear Lord, you gone and taking so many of my people/ I'm just wondering why you haven't taken my life/

VERSE 2: Okay, Here we go with another one/ I'm ready for anything son/ I only called you son/ cause you're way to fucking young/ to run up against me/ in this industry/ trust me/ I've studied all day/ and that's exactly why I got so much pain/ I'm so consumed by my passion/ to continue this acting/ through rhyming this poetry/ love me or hate me/ Ya you wanna battle me/ haa whatever you want to do to me/ just always know homie/ that you could never even stop me/ cause I'm way to motivated/ if you invade my airspace/ I'll inebriate your brains/ Am I really insane/ or just too crazed to make change/ upon this whole game/ without me many will fail/ this is a fact, not a fable tale/ used to enable/ one's imagination/ if you need a closer look dog, than decrease your magnification/ cause, it's not to hard to see/ that I am the key/ to everything you must be/

I am the one who will change this planet/ Imma fight till I die to make this shit happen/ I'm ambitious/ if I got's to turn violently vicious/ I can, and it only takes a couple of minutes/

HOOK/CHORUS: Lil Wayne Hook remix "And I'm grinding till I'm tired/ they say you ain't grinding till you tired/ so if I'm grinding with my eyes wide/ looking to find a way through the day/ a light for the night/ Dear Lord, you gone and taking so many of my people/ I'm just wondering why you haven't taken my life/

VERSE 3: Let's go, I just want to eat and feel good, my people want to survive/ and sleep good at night/ while, feeling no pain inside/ this music lifts our souls high/ up into the sky/ and I ain't got no reason to lie/ about the things that I've done in this life/ Yo, at the end of the night/ just pray for me to make it, so we no longer have to fight to survive/ so all I ask, is you stick by my side/ I will unlock more secrets in this life/ because, I've dedicated my entire life in doing all that is right/ even though I've done some wrong/ I make it all up with good, by writing these songs/ so kids if you act all pissed/ you won't accomplish shit/ so stay positive/ until you cease to exist/ nice guys don't have to finish last/ in fact, being the bad guy ain't all what it's cracked up to be/ if anyone's gonna know, than it's me/ ha welcome to my MIZeRY/ Indefinitely there's no stopping me/

HOOK/CHORUS: Lil Wayne Hook remix "And I'm grinding till I'm tired/ they say you ain't grinding till you tired/ so if I'm grinding with my eyes wide/ looking to find a way through the day/ a light for the night/ Dear Lord, you gone and taking so many of my people/ I'm just wondering why you haven't taken my life/

SUMMARY – I'll explain it like this. "This song all started when I realized, society is a constant conflict between good and evil. Soon after realizing and analyzing the many ways in which society was a huge conflict; I began, positively changing my own life. During my near maddening experience of analyzing life; I began to understand how I can still pursue my dreams, but there was only going to be two ways about it. Those two ways were simple: follow my main course in life on God's path or on the path of the devil. When I chose to change my life and return to the arms of the Lord permanently; I created this song. Now do you understand the title?"

Chapter 10: Song 2 – The Invitation - Remix (10:2)

The Invitation – Remix (50 Cent Ft. MIZeRY):

VERSE 3: Ya well I'm criminal minded/ on this record homie, I ain't even writing/ ain't nobody saying shit/ MIZeRY ReCORDS is signing to G-Unit Kid/ and watch on every record, I rep G, G, G-unit like that's my click/ I'll form a sub-division/ based on two conditions/ I'll do whatever I want/ and it's MIZeRY ReCORDS, whenever I want/ the difference between me/ and some fagot's that you've signed/ is if you save my life/ I'll never forget it/ so I put it in my music/ I'm tired of my poverty/ and this never ending MIZeRY/ see I'm dedicated homie/ I'm loyal and a rider/ who's a fucking live wire/ why you think I'm GMG/ and I roll with Uncle Murda/ I'm Psycho/ ready to go back to being a gangsta/ ready to shoot mother fuckers who fucks with my life/ or fucks with the man that's been saving my life/ I'll put caps in their brain/ I'm bringing everybody a different kind of pain/ I'm here to reconstruct, this whole entire game/ I've got hundreds of records, that's exploding on these suckas/ used to be a nice guy/ I used to do things to make peoples lives better/ now I don't give a fuck, I'm just down for whatever/ the truth of the matter is, everybody snakes/ who talk a lot of shit when I ain't up in they face/ I don't need no gang, I be rolling by myself/ I need a ruthless mother fucker, to put my CD on the shelf/ I have no compassion/ all of y'all should of helped me, when I kept on asking/ God made me a Gemini/ so I live different lives/ I can shift so quick/ you would never even feel it/ so welcome to my mission/ and I ain't shifting visions/ so tell me what it's like, now that'ch you're the victim/ you want some?

SUMMARY - I'll explain it like this. "This song is a great representation of the bad side I was pursuing and had to decide if I'm going to go this route on my life's course or not. Further more, this song is metaphorical about my overall intentions. Including, who I was or what I would have been involved with in the near future. This song however, does represent a large portion of my suppressed anger and disgust for all the evil in the world. In other words, I am representing the true power and anger God has placed within me; while still deciding, what I must choose to do during Armageddon."

Chapter 10: Song 3 – I Need a Doctor - Remix (10:3)

I Need a Doctor - Remix (Dr. Dre & Eminem):

VERSE 3: I do this for the love man; I do this because, I need to be healed. Ugh, uhh…. Everything that you suffer from, is really my MIZeRY/ My Heart weeps/ for everyone and everything that my eye's have ever seen/ I'm searching for the right team/ who can assist with my mission/ and share's the same visions/ of preventing our extinction/ the third day he was risen/ all truth, as it's written/ through Michael Izzo's Pen/ who spit's these scriptures/ of wisdom/ and paint's lyrical pictures/ over these years/ I'm dolo in the studio shedding my tears/ and fears/ that taunt my eye's and ears/ so thanks to Em & Dre/ I could survive another day/ cause the amount of pain/ that I suffer from, is harder than anybodies rain/ this is Jesus speaking through Michael Izzo's brain/ and I warn you all, I'm coming back soon someday/ to save/ all my children/ for too long you've abuse them/ right or wrong/ the majority of you is really wrong/ so Dre allow Michael, to save millions of souls/ through MIZeRY's songs/ cause I NEED A DOCTOR/

SUMMARY - I'll explain it like this. "Basically, when I heard the original version of this song by Eminem and Dr. Dre: I fell in love with it instantly. I'm a huge fan of both these artists and this song; which I replayed over and over again in my head for months; telling myself to stay strong. When I began recording to this song, I didn't write anything and I just started to record. What impresses me and scares me some, is when I say the line: "This is Jesus speaking through Michael Izzo's Brain/ and I warn you all, I'm coming back soon someday/ to save/ all my children/ for too long you've abused them/ right or wrong/ the majority of you is really wrong/ so Dre allow Michael, to save millions of souls/ through MIZeRY's songs/ cause I need a doctor/." I instantly realized, that me and him are one and the same. Realistically, it scared me beyond belief but there was no way I cared enough to prevent this holy truth from being revealed."

Chapter 10: Song 4 – You should be rich – Remix (10:4)

You should be rich – remix (50 Cent):

VERSE 1: Ya well, I blame my friends and my fans/ for all of my suffering/ as y'all sat back and you really did nothing/ except for telling me, to keep on pushing/ and chasing my involved crazy dreams/ without even knowing I went to the extreme/ logically studied society/ as I, devised a master plan, to change all of humanity/ realistically/ do you finally/ understand the true meaning behind MIZeRY/ infinitely/ spitting rhymes to the death of me/ 50 Cent "I was given the gift of life" Ya so fifty, was given the gift of life/ and I was given this gift/ to write/ to spit fluid rhymes/ wrote on paper lines/ fueled by my life/ I tremble at night/ sometimes/ I fucking really hate my life/ if you really know this pain, that kills me inside/ then follow me till you die/ and come stand by my side/ everything I'm telling you is definitely no mother fucking lie/

HOOK/CHORUS: You should be rich by now/ I'm wild, I've earned the right to bare this crown/ for all of my fam, troops, and my camp/ stack benjis, billions/ and change the planet in seconds/

VERSE 2: You don't want me to fail/ cause I am able/ to depict what's known as a devil/ or blackened angel with dark wings/ to represent evil/ sometimes when I wake/ I'm tempted to take/ everybody's whole cake/ truthfully what's yours, is actually mine/ if you follow me on this path/ you won't be coming back/ I superseded you a millennia ago/ way before I ever started to flow/ anywhere that I go/ I can always re-grow/ cause I'm the popular guy/ disguised as a mad man, who is on the rise/ y'all got till 2012, to get my crew signed/ or we will break into your home, and we'll kill you in the night/

HOOK/CHORUS: You should be rich by now/ I'm wild, I've earned the right to bare this crown/ for all of my fam, troops, and my camp/ stack benjis, billions/ and change the planet in seconds/ MIZeRY, MIZ, MIZeRY. Ya no remorse, no stopping/ I'm relentless/ till I get this/ understand, I'm ready to blast kid/ I'm tired, I'm fucking tired/ I'm dying/ You should be rich by now/ I'm wild, I've earned the right to bare this crown/ for all of my fam, troops, and my camp/ stack benjis, billions/ and change the planet in seconds/

SUMMARY - I'll explain it like this. "You should be rich truly came about, when I realized how much I like the beat. When I started writing to this song, I had no true perception of my concept or idea's for this song. Long and behold, I ended up sticking to a similar topic 50 Cent originated with; while molding it, into a much larger metaphor about my life. On this song, we further see a Good versus bad conflict within my own life; while being largely related with the world. Simply, if I must require money to change this world, then don't be shocked how cruel God becomes in order to prove money is worthless."

Chapter 10: Song 5 – The way life used to be – Remix (10:5)

The way life used to be - Remix:

VERSE 1: Yo Snoop, man, thanks for this record dog. I went hard for this man, I went crazy hard. The way my life used to be/ before I invented MIZeRY/ split personality/ It's continuously fucking with me/ in my dreams/ and in my reality/ back in 95 my gammy used to say, two wrongs don't make a right/ than she went and died in 2005/ that shit swallowed me alive/ I've got mad love for the west side/ cause I was born out there, but I'm too broke to ever go back/ stuck on the east coast/ so I talk about it in my raps/ in fact/ I'll take you to when I was a young lad/ an active adventurous/ secretly/ aggravated young child/ who has ran bashfully/ cautiously/ pursued aspects of his life to keep from turning wild/ at nine/ I was a sick athlete/ biking and hustling and skating through these streets/ Glen Head to Glen Cove, from BK to NYC/ even through QB/ but Yo, fuck queens/ only cause of the crooked ass police/ they dirty up in the 1 plus 1 times 114th precinct/ that was only through one life/ at thirteen, I was so pissed off for too many reasons to list/ and don't insist/ and listen instead/ to what's next/ or shut up and pay attention to my unique kind of gift/ I'll play you for a fool if you ever attempt/ to express/ any level of distressed content/ hidden from your sarcastic, disrespectful demeanor/ I'll eat you/ like I'm an animal/ bear slashing you/ and still you whimper and you quit/ verbally I learned this is a gift given from my savior/ I'm ethanol/ at its' purest form/ and

I come from/ somewhere/ that you could never foresee/ or one day ever be/ maybe even me/ ha, I'm capable of predicting such prophecy/ we are all foul tongued/ sometimes we forget to ask for forgiveness/ for all our dirty sins/ so I make music instead/ so these demons don't corrupt me again/ If I fail/ it will be really brutal/ for you/ just pure slaughter, upon all evil/ I fight for one/ and I've expressed his name enough when it rolls off my tongue/ no slang/ but if you're a gang/ and you don't value or live by his teachings/ than you're my enemy/ for thou who combat me/ will die severely/ not by my hands/ but by your own fate/ I will tell you this is definitely, no mother fucking game/ you'd only get one life/ live or die/ however, you decide/ to ride/ I decided, fuck everything else I love music and I did it cause it made me who I am today/ just a straight up G/ who's hustled and survived some of the hardest times of poverty/ oh and agony/ police brutality/ who's abused their authority/ as if they ever had right to judge me/ are you trying to save the world or just your community/ cause through MIZeRY, and his music we are trying to save the world/ from itself/ before we do some crazy shit, and offer no kind of help/ that's when we would fall/ tired from our own ignorance/ so I say this/ let's work together to change our future/ cause I love the way we could live/ we need to come together/ and give more to each other/ Ya so I guess my gammy was right/ two wrongs, don't make a right/ Ya that was back in 95/ but then she died in 05/ and it broke me down inside/ I forgot why I was even trying/ meaning/ out grinding/ chasing these millions/ through making dope ass music/ mad mother fuckers been stealing my shit/ I created a whole new level of game kids/ I ain't even been paid yet/ the Christian in me, tells me to sue nobody/ the demons in me tell me to shoot up everybody/ who dare cheats, steal, or ever lie to me/ cause I've done it all, and I'm better at it than you/ if you aren't family or in my crew/ than the shit I probably tell you is false/ I use it to test you/ catch you in a bluff if that's what you want to call it/ but fuck it I go so hard/ and I'm still broke/ off hard/ working ass music that bumps, so hard/ it will blow you ear drums/ as it kicks and blows your amp and your 12 inch subs/ trust me bub/ I come and go like the seasons/ karma's been a bitch for four years/ like I committed treason/ my reasons/ are secrets/ cause we ain't got no family between us/ and I'm back now, brand new like a Mercedes Benz/ riding with some of my sexy ass girlfriends/ Ya fuck it right/ I just want to live life/ if you ain't down, than get lost tonight/ my last words as I step off this MIKE/

SUMMARY - I'll explain it like this. "Simply, when I heard Snoop Dogg's version, I immediately was able to relate. Also, he was reminiscing about his grand mother and that's when the connection with me was triggered. I immediately began writing to this song and finished it in a few hours. I also realized my only purpose for this song was to remember a lot about my childhood."

Chapter 10: Song 10 – I feel like dyin – Remix (10:10)

I feel like dyin Ft. Lil Wayne - Remix:

VERSE 1: I feel like… Me and Lil Wayne both feel like dying/ he feels it when he's not amped on drugs/ I feel it, when I'm not cranked up on love/ I don't mean a women, I'm talking about this game/ it's the only remedy to help escape my pain/ I don't mean literal/ I'm talking metaphorically/ and I mean it in a good way/ so listen to this song, and don't take it in a wrong way/ I wanna take a land fill full of fucking weed/ I want to get so blitted I don't ever need to feed/ for life, music, money, or this greed/ I'm running in these circles, like nobodies around me/ well here's the new C.R.E.A.M./ cash rules everything around MIZeRY/ Wayne tell them/

VERSE 3: Ya I feel like dying also, I want to take a gun, and put it to my brain/ I wanna pull this trigger so I never feel no pain/ I wanna leap from a building/ just to keep falling/ just like Eminem did in "The way I am"// I wanna slit my wrist/ so I could bleed to my death/ I want you to suffocate me, and steal my last breathe/

SUMMARY - I'll explain it like this. "I wrote this song simply when I was at my all time low. I was an alcoholic and I was manically depressed; I ended up writing this song to vent how I felt. A great portion of my life the reoccurring thought of just wanting to die seems to become existent. Although I combat such urges, I never truly understood why they existed."

Chapter 10: Song 11 – MIZeRY's Story (10:11)

MIZeRY's Story:

"This is my life, come feel my pain, come see my fears."

VERSE 1: Imma take you back to about 10 years from now/ when I was a young kid still on the prowl/ just in case none of y'all never followed my life/ Imma show you everything in just one night/ I had no pops and I have no mother/ come to think of it, I really have no future/ I look at my lord and I ask why I bother/ if you only knew/ everything I went through/ if you follow me, well than I could show you/ I've been through it all, arguing, fighting, then going missing/ I look at my life, is it that depressing/ you tell me that it isn't/ get back in my shoes, and walk with me further/ look into my eyes/ and you really think I'm lying/ look into my cries, and look into my fears/ look at everything I've seen all these years/ trying to make friends but that shit wasn't easy/ y'all ain't do much but laughed at me/ cause I only had three shirts, three pants, three shoes/ and you still think I really needed you/

HOOK/CHORUS: Now I want all of you to follow my life/ Imma show you everything in just one night/ so come on down, and ride with me/ Imma show you everything you need to see/

VERSE 2: We never had much/ so I never got much/ I worked for everything that I had in my life/ when I turned thirteen/ I needed that money/ doing what I do cause I got expensive tastes/ and you're sitting there like you really wanna hate/ as I got older, I turned into a rebel/ I never follow rules and I never follow laws/ Busting out your face and cracking out your jaws/ I never went to school cause I didn't like you/ just the fake environment/ I couldn't handle it/ and my moms yelling at me every night, dealing with the cops like they really my friends/ doing this, doing that, doing it like I need to/ I've been in the prisons, I've been in the cells/ I've been on this mission to leave my hells/ do you know what I go through, when I cry/ when I die/ when I really wanna ride/ man, cause you really don't know/ I've been through this all, I've been through this game/ I've been through the phase/ like I've been through the fame/ now you know my name/

HOOK/CHORUS: Feel all of my pain, and feel of these fears/ listen to my name, and you see my tears/ Now I want all of you to follow my life/ Imma show you everything in just one night/ so come on down, and ride with me/ Imma show you everything you need to see/

VERSE 3: Now I'm 16, and I wanna live alone, I'm getting to old even for my own good/ and the old me never really understood/ I'm putting my life right back where I started/ A year went by, and I didn't get into trouble/ I felt something wrong, cause it went too subtle/ Then I turned 18, then I got locked up once again/ I'm sick of this shit/ I pray to my lord and I ask to forgive/ all of my wrong doings that I did/ I promise you that I'm never doing it again/ I'm sorry for my sins/ I'm sorry for my sins/ please forgive me, once again/ Now I do it right, cause you by my side/ I can't blame you, cause I chose this life/ I still got pain, cause I got no love/ feel my game/ when you feel my rain/ feel my name/ when you feel my pain/ did you see what I've been through now/ I hope you did, cause I'm done for now/

HOOK/CHORUS: Now I want all of you to follow my life/ Imma show you everything in just one night/ so come on down, and ride with me/ Imma show you everything you need to see/ Now I want all of you to follow my life/ Imma show you everything in just one night/ so come on down, and ride with me/ Imma show you everything you need to see/

"Ya, red, red redant/ this is my life/ empire, MIZeRY ReCORDS, feel my pain/ walk with me, I'll show you/ It feels like you got nothing to do in this world/ fuck out of my face/ I'm just not me anymore, shit's changed man/ redant, this is my life, empire, empire, MIZeRY ReCORDS, MIZeRY ReCORDS/

SUMMARY - I'll explain it like this. "This song came early on in my professional career, which was actually written when I turned 21. I wrote this song because I was so frustrated during this entire year; I wanted to vent about my past life, and all the hardships I've overcome. My main reasoning for wanting to reminisce and remember my struggle; was because, I had just been released from probation. I also felt like I could finally start my life over with no overhead problems."

Chapter 10: Song 12 – Airplanes - Remix (10:12)

Airplanes – Remix (B.o.B & Eminem):

VERSE 2: Okay, I could really use a wish right now/ through all those times I kept falling down/ while all these fucking haters kept stopping me out/ Hey look at me maa, cause I finally made it now/ if we could just pretend/ for 34 more seconds/ about my trials and tribulations/ I really shouldn't mention/ but I feel compelled/ to excel/ and never go back to living my life in hell/ so let's pretend/ my moms didn't fly to California, to put me up for adoption/ or that I really grew up living with some options/ and my mother wasn't selfish/ what if, my father was really also existent/ and he wasn't really pimping these young naive bitches/ or that my siblings and I/ didn't fight to survive/ just to live another night/ so let's take it to 98, when I wrote my first rhymes/ as more and more days went by/ people kept telling me that I was just wasting my time/ trying to chase this life/ Yo Marshall said it best/ I do need my cranium checked/ even my best friends/ are telling me to quit on this shit/ but if it wasn't for this music kid/ I would have slit my wrist/ back in school on some real shit/ so take it for what it is/ cause if it wasn't for your lyrics/ Em, I would not be here to do this/ but if I had one wish/ I would wish for this music/ let's take a few seconds/ cause everything I've done in my life, was all for this moment/ Yaa…

SUMMARY - I'll explain it like this. "When I heard this song, I immediately was able to relate and a verse was literally pouring out of my skin and my mouth. I started working on this remix that day of it being released. Soon after, I found myself writing one of my most meaningful and greatest versus ever."

Chapter 10: Song 14 – Sick with it - Remix (10:14)

Sick wit it – Remix (50 Cent):

VERSE 2: Fuck hustling in the streets/ I've moved onto bigger and better things/ like sitting in my studio/ cause this is what I do/ while I'm working on this beat/ no, I don't want none of your cheese/ so let me/ break this down b/ The code of the streets/ is keep Ya mind state 10 steps ahead of your enemies/ I was lost as a teen/ I'm in love with these beats/ ever since I was thirteen/ I've been stacking my cream/ It's unbelievable/ how the shit comes and goes/ like you would never even know/ I'll break this into syllables/ I'm tired of being typical/ I'll mastermind a ritual/ you'll become intellectual/

as I engineer my label/ I'm about stacking paper/ I'm a natural born hustler/ if you bring something less, than don't come around me/ but if you invest into me/ or MIZeRY ReCORDS/ than Imma double your money/ like you wouldn't even believe/ if you wanna fuck with me/ trust me/ I'll defeat all y'all on any kind of beat/ if any of you bitches act up, I'll have Brittles, knock you right off your own feet/ do us all a favor please/ don't get back up/ as a matter a fact/ back up/ fuck what Ya got/ I don't need any back up/ my gun talks enough/ I roll solo/ only, when I blast these shots off/ I'll spit this one time/ so you understand my grind/ I'm sick wit it/ rude boy, don't test me, man/ cause I'm real quick wit it/ believe me, I don't need to be high to spit it like this/ because it comes natural/ news flash I'm thankful for this gift/ I was given/ I've got way to much to loose on you, if you suddenly go missing/ Yo fif, tell em how it is/

SUMMARY - I'll explain it like this. "I remixed this song when I realized, I quit a life in the streets and criminal activities to pursue what I love most; music and God. Further more, I wanted to inform everyone that if I was forced to summon Armageddon; which will be my response or result. The fact of the matter is when it comes to hustling music and making music I am sick wit it."

Chapter 10: Song 18 – Trend Setters (10:18)

Trend setters Ft. Craven & A.O.:

INTRO: "Shout out to all my Homies on this shit, hahaha. All right well, Imma have to just spit this from the top cause that's how I feel this record.

VERSE 1: Okay well listen up man, cause I'm a mother fucking trend setter/ I come and go every season just like the weather/ and I'm back now, brand new, feeling better than ever/ kind of like those Hess trucks when I'm released every winter/ so respect how I spit it, when I come at you as a rapper/ I'm giving it to you raw, I ain't packaging it in a wrapper/ as a matter of fact/ I'm hyper active/ and a crazed sex addict/ all of a sudden I'm cursed and I've lost all my game/ maybe it's you, who I really think is that fucking lame/ and I'm way beyond your stage/ I'm still kind of wild, Ya I think I should be tamed/ by a sexy older chick/ who's intelligence, impresses me, way beyond my (D***)/ and wants to fuck me really quick/ I'm talking rough and rapid/ for 10 years I've had this habit/ I told you I was an addict/ and this is for all of you brainiacs/ who want to get down with me, than you better show me something/ cause if there is no incentive/ than I'm not fucking with you son/ if you exhaust/ all my wisdom/ for everyday that I'm inventive/ My mind is in control/ and expresses/ my intelligence that impresses all the masses/ take a look at my swag/ I come to you in different shapes, if you really add the math/ I'm number one in my class/ I'm not really trying to brag/ I'm inventively creating a revolutionary drift/ that's shifted/ only in positive/ as I set trends/ to save every one of God's children/

HOOK/CHORUS: Imma, Imma trend setter/ Imma, Imma trend setter/ Imma, Imma trend setter/ everyday I set trends/ Imma, Imma trend setter/ Imma, Imma trend setter/ Imma, Imma trend setter/ everyday I set trends/ Imma, Imma trend setter/ Imma, trend setter/ Imma, Imma trend setter/ everyday I set trends/ Imma, Imma trend setter/ Imma, Imma trend setter/ Imma, Imma trend setter/ everyday I set trends/

SUMMARY - I'll explain it like this. "This song was supposed to be the start of a great relationship between some new artists, my associates from NY introduced to me: whom were from the south. However, after several months of attempting to make music together as a collective unit; they began to assume, I was already wealthy, and they completely changed their attitudes. They turned greedy and hostile based on false assumptions. Either way, I'm a man of my words and I said I would assist in building a reputation for them and that's what I've been doing."

Chapter II
Til' Death Do Us Part
(*Island Def Jam*)

I, Michael "MIZeRY" Izzo am now 24 and the year of 2011 is coming to a fast end. I have prepared myself day and night to create one of my best albums ever; "Til' Death Do Us Part." My initial feelings for this album, were supposed to be totally different than my first album; which was more of a documentary album. On this new album, I was creating an album that would contain a bit of everything best in the world of hip-hip; from love pop songs, to hardcore gangsta rap, and classic good rap records with a great story. During the process of making this album and taking the risks in which I did; I ended up loosing some really close friends in my life, cause of it. However, this isn't something new for me to deal with and as a result; I realized, I must keep my life moving forward. When I started this project, I intended to create a project that represents my entire life in an aspect I haven't been able to touch upon yet; while making it clear that I'm in this music life: "Til' Death Do Us Part." Ultimately, this is by far one of the most diverse albums I've heard in a long time; and for that, I truly believe you will all agree with me eventually, about my latest release *with Island Def Jam*. Similar to "15 Years of My Life" both of my albums are for sale on *iTunes* & *Amazon* website stores in the following countries: USA, Australia/ New Zealand/ Canada, U.K./European Union, Japan, Mexico, & Asia. However, "15 Years of My Life" is also sold in Latin America & Brazil; and "Til' Death Do Us Part" is sold on Rhapsody's website store as well!

"<u>Til' Death Do Us Part</u>" – front and back; photo taken by Dayne Mahadeo; Direction and design by Michael Izzo. Copyright © 2011, *MIZeRY ReCORDS* – All Rights Reserved. People in photo left to right: Tara Lynn & Michael "MIZeRY" Izzo; photo taken in Oyster Bay Cemetery & in Times Square, NYC.; & is Sold in over 150 countries online.

Chapter 11: Song 1 – 1st Time Lovin (11:1)

1st Time Lovin Ft. Brittles (Hosted by DJ Onpoint):

INTRO: "aahh, here we go. You know there is a first time for everything and this is our first number one. Here we go girl."

VERSE 1: Well in my life, it was a living hell/ Twist, Turned, upside down, and I really felt/ I would some day fail/ just jump out and bail/ from everything I've created/ Instead, I found you and my life restarted/ a brand new you, with a brand new me/ now I'll never stop trying, for all of eternity/ no seriously/ all jokes aside/ I love it when you smile/ it makes me go wild/ including all your styles/ I'd take it soft, cold, hot, or even mild/ with the way I feel inside/ I love you more than music, cause you'll always be by my side/ okay seriously, no joking this time/ I love making music and I love all my fans/ realistically though, I could never choose y'all, over any one of my FAM/ Damnn/ I don't think you even understand/ how priceless trustworthy/ family/ actually/ means to me/ and will kill to protect me/ call me King Arthur/ she loves I'm a rapper/ let's make a new chapter/ she's my lifetime shorty/ everything we do is now split 50/50/ which means, if I make money/ than you're making money/ which means, if you receive any injuries/ then I'm inflicting injuries/ upon all your enemies/ physically/ I suffer if you face agony/ Ya baby, you can call me MIZeRY/ and I know – you love my company/ I'm here for you, as long as you're here for me/ simply, I love you baby/ Unconditionally & Faithfully/

VERSE 2: Ok, I'm going back in/ with no lines written/ keep my lyrics on coming/ diarrhea of the mouth, is aimlessly squirting/ I call her my coo, coo, coo, coo chicken/ cause she keeps screaming/ and always coming back fiend'ing/ for my seeds/ in which she feeds/ and needs/ to breathe/ which prevents her from ever leaving me/ for some other roosters meat/ now you can see why, I/ can body anybody over these beats/ like when I broke my girls back, over my back seats/

SUMMARY – I'll explain it like this. "I actually ended up writing this song after I heard Brittles' chorus in which she had previously recorded to this beat without my prior knowledge. All together, I wanted to counter what she said, and I did. My main focus for this song was to represent what it's like falling in love for the first time. Different than most people, my first time was actually how I wrote about it on this song and what I thought it was going to turn out to be. Now, I use this song as a gateway to remember such a time, as I wait patiently for the women of my dreams: Mary Magdalene"…

Chapter 11: Song 2 – All American (11:2)

All American:

VERSE 1: Okay, ok, I'll show you how I do as an all American/ you're a straight bitch, I'll call you a pelican/ while we slipping, sliding, smooth like a penguin/ moving, gliding, and spinning/ you can call me a hurricane/ everything I do is insane/ every record I drop is like crack cocaine/ you fiend to tell me each one of your lame ass names/ like I really give a fuck, call me Bruce Wayne/ I'm top notch, best dressed, and number one at every game/ fuck it switch lanes/ change my rhyme theme's/ as if I made a new crime scheme/ is truly what I mean/ why make the worst come out of me/ I could turn pure evil, much worse than you'll ever be/ seriously don't push me/ and don't ever try and tempt me/ for I worship Lord/ and he will grant me the strength to slice you in half with my sword/ no jokes, you're a whore/ what, even what score/ you must be confused and lost/ I'm smarter than you, so how could I be wrong/ less than 90% of the time/ trust me I am my rhymes/ I don't ever lie/ but sometimes I will if my life is on the line/ I come back in with some more rhymes/ I'm fully loaded, ready for crunch time/ I've emerged/ from a diverse/ unique, gifted kind of curse/ to purge/ all those people, who really aren't worth/ more than a coins purse/ and I'm talking more than money/ more like how to fix society/ using intelligent vocabulary/ metaphorically/ to abolish all evil tendencies/ you're the real pussy/ don't ever judge me/ as I spit my ideology/ doing good is much harder/ and the reward is much larger/ In addition, goes farther/ I will make you a martyr/ if you think you are smarter/ let's just end peacefully, here I'll even barter/ I'll give you a book about how to act civilized/ with nothing in return except for you to realize/ working together will optimize our production and, hasten our rise/ you seem out of shape and lazy, you all need to exercise/ I told you I'm the mastermind/ Ya I'm an All American/ I does it really big, I'm an All American/ I like my women fine, only dimes, as I say hi/ shorty I'm about to shine/ Okay, I'm all in with another/ I'm the dopest rapper/ coming up, I'm much more than just a couple chapters/ I'm a novel and movie, with many different sequels/ if you act any evil/ you're no longer my equal/ as he kills you, using deadly lethal/ we love racing WRX Rallye cars, 67 Corvette's/ whatever world you can suck it/ Ya pussy lips/ I'm in it to win it/ so fuck it/ I buck shit/ with my four fifth/ no gimmicks/ I've done this/ please sit/ I ain't done yet/ take all of your bets/ rig the election/ and become president/ fuck you, if you think you are ever a better candidate/ push you all out, cause I really don't want any residence/ I am incredible beyond any one man's intelligence/ except for my Lord Jesus/ it's you who commits sacrilegious/ acts/ of ignorance/ and unwanted acts of violence/ change is really coming, for God has told me/ for you should never worship me/ only befriend me/ as if we are truly family/ damn y'all how could you not feel me/ I'm a real G/ and I can suffer permanently slowly/ so come follow me/ for all eternity/ in his angelic humanity/Yaa, where we all live peacefully/ Yaa man cause, I'm an All American/ you could live this way too, you're an American/ no matter what you think, let's work together/ and fight against the enemy son/ we're all Americans/ we want to live big cause we're all Americans/ we do shit big cause we're all Americans/ ain't no fucking with my crew man, GMG for life/ we're all Americans/ New York is where I'm from and that is my home/ but Imma drop bombs to anyone's home/ if you try to conflict harm/ upon me or my crew/ what are you trying to do/ I see everything you're trying to do/ whatever I can make it go when I stick to it like glue/ making this map out/ when I'm rhyming this track out/ everything you talking homie, I'm about to clap out/ your mother fucking bullshit, cause I've heard it all/ and I ain't trying to go that far, man I'm ready to brawl/ Ha never I'm never going to go down the path that you want me to take/ fuck all of y'all I think you're starting to look like jake/ and I'm not trying to fuck around, I see y'all are fake/ you mother fuckers is fagots/ and I ain't messing with you maggots/ cause I'm an American/ Ya, I'm An All American/

SUMMARY - I'll explain it like this. "All American" was one of my newer style songs in an attempt to be patriotic for a new world. On this song, I was venting about how bad ass, intelligent, and hardworking I as an American am. Further more, I wanted everyone to know that we are the land of the free and I will show how this great country can be everyone's country; even if, they aren't on our soil. However, my favorite aspect to this song is all the great metaphors and intelligent rhymes I construed together; creating, one long and enduring poetic song."

Chapter 11: Song 3 – Beast (11:3)

Beast Ft. Andre Vincent:

VERSE 2: Ok, so I call it this MIZeRY/ with what I do lyrically/ I do it from the top/ every time that I drop/ you can call what I do rap/ or hip hop-pop/ either way I'm gunning, for the #1 spot/ ooo-yaa I'm too hot/ Dark Man X, Eminem, & Tupac/ all tied up in a big knot/ stirred & cooked, In Michael Izzo's' soup pot/ chopped & screwed/ with a Gas masked crew/ Ya call it slipknot/ write it all down, as I whip up a new plot/ mix this shit up, if it dare turns slop/

VERSE 4: Okay, I'm a mother fucking Beast/ and I love to feast/ on you fake Emcee's/ It's a necessity/ which prevents me/ from ever reaching pure insanity/ join the CIA, hunt and kill you legally/ take me seriously/ I won't act differently/ I've been going extreme/ take a look at my team/ Ya wanna be us? Only in your dreams/ Okay, back to the topic, about me being a mother fucking beast/ I'm a monster, eating up these beats/ I'm a silent gangsta, roaming these streets/ I'll shoot your ass dead, bleeding from Ya head all the way down to your feet/ Ya I'm a little bit sick, but I ain't one to creep/ you're an amateur on those skies/ I'm way too steep/ wake up call, as your alarm beeps/ beeps/ I told you man, you was only having dreams/ straight inception, attempting to be me/ Mike Izzo MIZeRY/ doing it big physically/ I run with real rappers, East New York, GMG/

SUMMARY - I'll explain it like this. "This song actually was titled and thought of by my friend, Andre Vincent. Andre was a passionate singer, whom was just starting out, and we ended up meeting New Years Eve 2010 from a mutual friend named: Nikki. Later on in the year of 2011, we ended up collaborating on some of my music and he ended up creating this song beast. After I heard the title, I immediately knew what to write. I wanted to represent how and why I am a beast both in the world and in the world of music. As of today, Andre and I no longer speak. He decided, he no longer liked his parts on this song and attempted to insinuate he never approved of this song. Ultimately, after confirming with my legal staff; they confirmed it was my decision, of what I wanted with this song. Because I like this song so much, I decided I wouldn't change it for nothing. I later also published it on this album. I chose to do so, because I wanted to publish good and innovative music. I also wanted to assist an aspiring singer out as well, regardless of how his initial debut would be."

Chapter 11: Song 4 – Flying with wings (11:4)

Flying with wings Ft. Im-famous (Hosted by DJ Dav):

INTRO: "Ya tonight, we all gonna party like we rock stars or rap stars, you know what I'm saying. So, I want all my people to put their red bull and vodka's in the air and just say, this stuff gives me wings."

VERSE 2: Yo it's Im-famous and MIZeRY/ I own the dream team/ I want enough Redbull cans to make a green screen/ ever since 2003/ I only chase things in threes/ starting with this money/ I'm searching for my wifey/ and I only make this industry/ wanna have to chase me/ so please don't ever worship me/ or ever try to be me/ because you'll only get screwed/ by mister scrooge himself, who will have you chopped and screwed/ honestly I'm better than you/ because I go harder than you/ all day I'm guzzling Redbulls/ in which fill up my skull/ until I am on full/ with this great green energy/ which let's me fly at fast speeds/ cause Redbull gave me wings/ and I don't even need a hook, I'll just let this beat sing/

HOOK/CHORUS: Put your Redbulls in the air/ if there's a party up in here/ Put your Redbulls in the air/ if there's a party up in here/ Put your Redbulls in the air/ if there's a party up in here/ Put your Redbulls in the air/ if there's a party up in here/ Put your Redbulls in the air/ if there's a party up in here/ Put your Redbulls in the air/ if you're partying up in here/

SUMMARY - I'll explain it like this. "I created this song to be part of a campaign and commercial for my signature designed "Green Redbull – Low Sugar." I had submitted the concept and idea, with supporting customers and this song. However, Redbull respectfully declined and made us sign a cease and desist order. They did send me a free 24 case of Redbull though. Long story short, this song still ended up being a really good party record and we published it anyways. At the time, I was also drinking a lot of Redbull and Vodka than too."

Chapter 11: Song 5 – I'm Superman (11:5)

I'm Superman:

INTRO: "Ya cause, when I feel this beat, I kind of feel like I'm Superman, Superman, I'm Superman all the time, cause I'm, I'm Superman, Superman. I'm Superman all day/ cause I'm here to save the day/ and I harbor the strength of a thousand men times a million."

HOOK/CHORUS: Cause I'm Superman, I come from a different planet/ cause I'm Superman/ Im invincible to your bullets, cause I'm Superman/ no matter what you do to me I'm coming right back, cause I'm Superman/ okay, well I live alter-realities/ and I'm the type of guy that your mommy/ always told you to never bring home to your daddy/ but surely/ you won't mistaken me/ for being the bad guy lady/ so baby/ will you let me be/ your Superman?

VERSE 1: I have an overall mission/ to rid the world of its filthy vision/ I'll fairly warn you all/ if you want to go to war/ I have unlimited ammunition/ no matter what you got, your green little rings gonna run out of energy/ and then I'm coming to defeat you, cause you're my enemy/ my mother fucking enemy/ I really don't care if you're sinister like Synestro/ with your magic Powers/ I've got an invincible suit, penetrating your Powers/ what'ch you telling me this, cause I'm the king of all these towers/ and in just a couple hours/ I'll have this whole world cower/ this is my intergalactic-planetarisum/ no matter what you saying, I'm spitting these scriptures of wisdom/ intelligence defeating you with precision/ so I'll keep on mind fucking you with my knowledge and deadly venom/ and what you trying to tell me, you don't have constant problems/ so keep running for the hills, cause you ain't ready for my knowledge/

HOOK/CHORUS: Cause I'm Superman, I come from a different planet/ cause I'm Superman/ Im invincible to your bullets, cause I'm Superman/ no matter what you do to me I'm coming right back, cause I'm Superman/ okay, well I live alter-realities/

and I'm the type of guy that your mommy/ always told you to never bring home to your daddy/ but surely/ you won't mistaken me/ for being the bad guy lady/ so baby/ will you let me be/ your Superman?

VERSE 2: Okay, let's talk about my smarts/ if I took the SATS/ I'd have to take the tests twice/ just to prove to you I was right/ when I predicted my first try/ wouldn't score nearly as high/ it's been a little while/ but I'll never forget my style/ as I'm flying through the skies/ with my lyrics of intelligence, it will lift you up so high/ that you'll be thinking in your mind/ that you got to step up your grind/ to begin understanding my rhymes/ so you seem a little anxious/ ok I'll get right into it/ I'm highly noxious to the touch/ don't get to close to me, cause you'll evaporate like dust/ don't ask me how this shit happens/ I'm just redefining rapping/ I'm keeping my shit smashing/ laughing/ at you from space/ as I keep winning this race/ cause I have my own lane/ with every single new day/ I'm looking for new people to ride/ and if you ain't gonna ride/ than you'll be sitting on the side lines/ observing how we play this game/ so if you want to make some change/ than come save the world today/

HOOK/CHORUS: Cause I'm Superman, I come from a different planet/ cause I'm Superman/ Im invincible to your bullets, cause I'm Superman/ no matter what you do to me I'm coming right back, cause I'm Superman/ okay, well I live alter-realities/ and I'm the type of guy that your mommy/ always told you to never bring home to your daddy/ but surely/ you won't mistaken me/ for being the bad guy lady/ so baby/ will you let me be/ your Superman?

VERSE 3: Ya let me tell you how my mind works/ I was bumping Eminem's "*Beautiful*" when I wrote this third verse/ because I'm cursed/ with this blood thirst/ to make things different/ and the way that I know how to do it/ is to take a pen and make music/ cause this is what I've envisioned/ and if I didn't get down with him/ by the age of twenty five/ then I was just gonna have to quit/ cause it doesn't really make sense, otherwise on some real shit/ Yo I would change places with you, at any point in time/ I would surrender this life/ cause I'm going out of my mind/ I feel like for fifteen years, I've been wasting all of my time/ with everything that I've tried/ so what more shall I sacrifice/ you must all think that I'm lying/ is it cause every time/ you see me, I'm riding fly/ rocking my own style/ but deep down inside/ I'm really crying to die/ you may say that it's fronting/ but I will tell you all something/ cause a part of me sometimes feels like that no matter what I do, I won't really change shit/ so hopefully someday soon, this jungle won't be so thick/

SUMMARY - I'll explain it like this. "Wow, this is one of my top 10 favorites for sure. First off, when I received and heard this beat; I immediately felt like a super hero from it. After that, the rest is history. However, I decided to make this song in relation with superman; because I started realizing that Superman is actually a character, closely based after Jesus Christ. Not only being one of his kind with super Powers, but being unique in everyway too. When I began writing this concept, I wanted to attempt and capture what it's like for either one of them; without even knowing, I ended up doing exactly that; meanwhile, I was also capturing myself."

Chapter 11: Song 6 – Four Broken Hearts (11:6)

Four Broken Hearts:

INTRO: "ughh Yaa, aahh, I gotta just do this from my heart man."

VERSE 1: Back in the days, you had my attention/ put me in line real quick, like I were in detention/ we had the best love sex sessions/ still to this day, my heart weeps with pain/ I loved you so much that it made me feel sane/ the times we shared together/ I thought life couldn't become any better/ I gave up on a wonderful life/ cause I thought that you'd be right by my side/ then you were gone/ left me all alone/ sitting on my throne/ I think you were scarred/ of the love that we shared/ so you bailed/ making me derail/ and I really believed that you cared/ Damn girl, you're all I had at fifteen/ ripped right through me, so evil and so mean/ now I'm back with vengeance/ to score even/ with you, my 1st love Lauren/ maybe it's my fault, when I dropped you, for this microphone & this pen/ and I chased these millions/ I still love you & your big brother, as if we're life long companions/ I can no longer hate, as it creates more madness/

HOOK/CHORUS: Baby, where are you/ baby, I want you/ baby, you've stolen away my heart/ your taking your time/ you've taken my time/ baby all I ask is you play your part/ I felt so much pain/ I have so much pain/ Lord all I ask if for one restart/ Baby, where are you/ baby, I want you/ baby, you've stolen away my heart/ your taking your time/ you've taken my time/ baby all I ask is you play your part/ I felt so much pain/ I have so much pain/ Lord all I ask if for one restart/

VERSE 2: We met randomly, by some sick twisted fate/ I liked you more than fish bate/ but much less than girls ever being raped/ my mouth should be duck taped/ many times you escapes/ over the years our love fades/ back & fourth/ on & off/ like a light switch/ for you, I cheated on several bitches/ just to share kisses/ not just on Ya lips/ your scent stuck to me like hot oven mitts/ our friendship is fucked & twisted/ Yaa, Long Island Iced Tea/ smooth, chilled, ready to make us crunk/ your love had me drunk/ if I can't have you, then kill me and throw me in the back of Eminem's trunk/ with you dead in the front/ have you dead waving/ with shades on your eyes, as Eminem's racing/ my hearts pacing/ I-V Pump/ no punt/ Yaa, my life's really Rocky/ no speed bumps/ I've fallen a million times, my knees are all weak/ ready to tweak/ Heroine addict/ if you really want my dick/ hardcore porno flick/ then break off the engagement/ cause you should be my chick/ no movie scripts/ only sequels & re-runs, Jessie I'm Ya favorite flick/

HOOK/CHORUS: Baby, where are you/ baby, I want you/ baby, you've stolen away my heart/ your taking your time/ you've taken my time/ baby all I ask is you play your part/ I felt so much pain/ I have so much pain/ Lord all I ask if for one restart/ Baby, where are you/ baby, I want you/ baby, you've stolen away my heart/ your taking your time/ you've taken my time/ baby all I ask is you play your part/ I felt so much pain/ I have so much pain/ Lord all I ask if for one restart/

VERSE 3: Ok, straight from the top/ don't ever ask me to stop/ my heart – dropped/ during this verse/ as this pain just bursts/ explodes right through me/ ever since I lost you, I haven't been me/ lost & confused, my mentality/ is like – fuck everybody/ so I try to rid the pain/ attached with your name/ it's really a shame/ I lost you, playing this game/ now I'm all ashamed/ I almost feel lame/ to the point nothing in life will ever be the same/ please forgive me Jayne/ if I knew I'd loose you during the process/ I would of dropped rap, like bad habits/ meanwhile, I know better to fall for such nonsense/ now it's always constant/ I question my conscience/ if I made the right choices/ Yo, I wanted you as my wife/ and that's no lie/ when I looked into your eyes/ I felt loved inside/ we are stickies for life/ and there ain't no lying/ you were my little lion/ when I think of our past, I wanna start crying/ I love you to death/ I'll prove I'm the best/ cause without you, I Should blow a hole, through my mother fucking chest/ I did all that I could, and I still failed loves tests/

HOOK/CHORUS: Baby, where are you/ baby, I want you/ baby, you've stolen away my heart/ your taking your time/ you've taken my time/ baby all I ask is you play your part/ I felt so much pain/ I have so much pain/ Lord all I ask if for one restart/ Baby, where are you/ baby, I want you/ baby, you've stolen away my heart/ your taking your time/ you've taken my time/ baby all I ask is you play your part/ I felt so much pain/ I have so much pain/ Lord all I ask if for one restart/

VERSE 4: What more shall I say, I'm in love with the rap game/ and I never felt so much pain/ ever come from the game/ unlike all these bitches/ & I don't play no tricks/ man, that nonsense is only for these kids/ as I sit back taking sips/ getting drunk, off my hardcore lyrics/ I realized anything is possible, based on our chemical physics/ the devil uses gimmicks/ to grant us sadistic wishes/ praise Jesus Christ, to fight those sinister images/ Am I really a menace/ or a true mastermind/ Intellectually using rhymes/ to control time/ pure silence, kind of like a mime/ who uses violence/ man, to end all crimes/ what's truly wrong, and what's truly right/ love is truly blind/ now stare me in the eyes/ and look beyond humans sight/ oh Ya man, I love that line/ in other words, only men who are wise/ may rise/ beyond one's demise/ otherwise, simply just die/ because you're compromised/ now back to all the facts/ I'm sticking hard to rap/ cause all I know how to do is really make tracks/ someday soon, I will sign with Aftermath/ oh Def Jam & Shady Records too/ call it the united music alliance/ Yaa cause, all day sell music/ go ahead and judge me, you worthless critics/ I'm fucking shutting off, signing out, MIZeRY ReCORDS/

SUMMARY - I'll explain it like this. "Four broken hearts was a very difficult song for me to make, because I had to force myself to remember some of the hardest times in my life. These times were not only difficult because I cared strongly for each person listed; but I am still only friends with one of the three girls. Whom to this day, is now married. The hardest part of this song was writing about Jayne, cause she and I had been through the most that I have ever encountered in a relationship. Ultimately, I wanted to make a breakup and love song all in one so the world had something else from me to personally relate with."

Chapter 11: Song 7 – NY, New York (11:7)

NY, New York Ft. Carlito & Uncle Murda (Hosted by DJ Onpoint):

VERSE 3: My time is money and I'm short coming up/ If I don't make enough cash, by the end of this month/ I'll unload an M16 GUN/ until it dumps/ all of your cash funds/ in several over seas accounts/ for 75 million – only in exact amounts/ don't ever fuck around/ well today's your lucky day, we'll even let your ass live, only when you pay us the cash/ in fact, we'll pay you ever single cent back/ like we agreed and signed upon a life contract/ haha – your life as a matter of fact/ Don't ever come around here, acting like you know about rap/ I'll stage you in a case, that places you at the crime/ of a triple homicide/ with substantial evidence/ you'll serve no less/ than double life prison time/ if you fuck around with us, I'll blow away your mind/ outside/ as you wait, on my own concert line/

SUMMARY - I'll explain it like this. "This song has a lot of history and bad blood all mixed in. Originally, this song was a joint venture partnership with one of my long childhood friends. He was very impressed and into this artist- Carlito, from Suffolk county NY. Long story short, we all decided to go in on purchasing a feature with Uncle Murda and push this new artist Carlito; under my record label. My friend, was supposed to manage him and I was supposed to assist in producing him. Long story short, both my friend and the artist breached their agreement. Once they breached the agreement in which was signed and set forth; I became the sole owner of the original version of this song. After several months of not thinking about this song at all; I realized, I might as well live up to my word, finish the song, and I'll add a verse of my own on it too. As a result, the title of the song changed and it became a featured anthem for NYC."

Chapter 11: Song 8 – Stand Up (11:8)

Stand Up Ft. Carlito & Uncle Murda:

VERSE 2: Okay I come in clocking/ watching/ calculating/ every one of your moves/ what'ch you trying to do/ hustle me or my crew/ homie we'll blast you/ from this planet/ we'll erase you/ like you never even exist/ my tolerance/ and patience/ are defensively aggressive/ way beyond saving/ I may not make it/ before I break faces/ way beyond repairs/ your reputation, went from great to bad/ and is permanently impaired/ I have an angel like stare/ meaning, I'm sent by God, searching for them he who shall be spared/ from the rapture/ don't let this message haunt'ch Ya/ Ya now listen and capture/ a movie of your life pictures/ Ya, a day shall come, when he returns/ to save those whom are pure/ and protects us, from ever being burned/ I know this/ because he tells me this/ everyday that I have lived/ ask thy God for forgiveness/ and he will grant us permission/ to enter thy holy kingdom/ thank you Lord for clearing my vision/

SUMMARY - I'll explain it like this. "The truly funny thing about this song is, I had this beat from my producer Hev1 for three years, before I could ever think of a topic. However, during my contract with Carlito, we ended up having him record a verse to this song as well; while we were in the studio with Uncle M. Uncle M at my request, created this quick little hook for us; as part of our arrangement, I had made with him. After several weeks of compiling different things together and adding my verse to this song; I finally finished it, which is now titled "Stand Up." As you can see in this song, more and more of my spiritual truth and connection with God emerged. As we progress further into the story we shall see much more of this evidence too."

Chapter 11: Song 9 – Stay in school (11:9)

Stay in school:

INTRO: "Even though I'm in pain right now, with my bruised ribs and everything; I know there are millions of kids around the world that are suffering & dying right now. This is just to give you all that education, motivation, and inspiration that you need by the push of a play button you know. Help you and help me make this world a better place."

VERSE 1: Okay kids listen up/ cause I spit it really quick/ with many educational lyrics/ so if you get lost in my music/ you won't understand this message/ cause I on the other hand, I'm destined for this/ since I was twelve, I started spitting rhymes/ they just developed in my mind/ like it was natural/ within due time/ I dropped out of high school/ cause I was serious to pursue/ my dreams of being this cool/ to express and teach you all how to respect one another/ represent each other/ and explain to you younglings/ you all can't be rappers/ school is important for you all to succeed/ because knowledge is worth more than anybodies money/ cause without any knowledge, we wouldn't have currency/ or Democracy/ that you all abuse and feel is for free/ but to live this way/ we need to fight everyday/ just to maintain/ this life similar to Eden/ as we continue to study and rearrange the way that we are speaking/ as I'm breathing/ I stop to think, man a guy like me never considered school/ cause maybe I was destined to implore innovation and this creativity/ cause school is designed to advance one spiritually/ cause it's through helping others we can all feel peace/ real talk when you drop the books, you fall for the streets/ where you will conduct negativity by creating beef/ selling drugs, and killing people way beyond belief/ so please/ forget what the TV says/ and do something instead/ that's useful for you and our children's children/ cause I'm a general and I'm destined for a much larger mission/ time is a ticking/ so please stop and start thinking/ of all that you're doing/ before you start taking action/ beyond one's level of satisfaction/ until nothing really exists/ and we're just a mere planet/ that's so desolate/ with no history/ but I assure you, that it will never happen to our humanity/ within my century/ because I'm determined to rid this whole world, of that kind of Misery/

HOOK/CHORUS: So stay in school/ if you want to be cool/ and make tons of money/ so stay in school/ if you want to be cool/ and make lots of money/ So stay in school/ if you want to be cool/ and have lots of ladies/ So stay in school/ if you want to be cool/ and be like MIZeRY/ So stay in school/ if you want to be cool/ and be just like MIZeRY/ haha, Yo that's for the kids man, you know got to give it up.

SUMMARY - I'll explain it like this. "I created this song because I realized that a lot of my songs are much harsher or too fierce for minors, under the age of 13. So one day, I decided to create a song that was both inspirational and clean enough for all kids to listen too. I not only captured exactly what I was hoping, but we can further see my spiritual side pour out of me."

Chapter 11: Song 10 – Sweet as sugar (11:10)

Sweet as sugar:

INTRO: "Do it again, do it again, puffy be like do it again, man. Puffy be like Yo its not good enough. You're as sweet as sugar, woo, sweet as sugar."

HOOK/CHORUS: Baby – you're sweet as sugar/ Ya you're as sweet as sugar/ baby you're sweet as sugar/ soo very sweet/ oh so sweet/ Baby – you're sweet as sugar/ Ya you're as sweet as sugar/ baby you're sweet as sugar/ soo very sweet/ oh so sweet/

VERSE 1: I love your addictive taste/ as it sinks in my teeth/ I won't let any go to waste/ your beauty is so Heavenly/ a Heavenly feast/ Ya just you and me/ dazed and stuck in pure harmony/ bound to faith and our holy matrimony/ we are one human being/ waiting for our death or his holy return/ to save those who are pure/ and I am so sure/ we all have a choice not to ever get burned/ by those who are cursed/ and try to make us turn/ forcing us to have to swerve/ crash into the curb/ to avoid having people hurt/ I'd do anything for you girl/ I'll spoil your world/ shower you with gifts/ hugs and many kisses/ it itches/ and it twitches/ I'm sick to my stomach/ of not having me a misses/ so come a little closer/ as I whisper/ sweet nothings right into your…

HOOK/CHORUS: Baby – you're sweet as sugar/ Ya you're as sweet as sugar/ baby you're sweet as sugar/ soo very sweet/ oh so sweet/ Baby – you're sweet as sugar/ Ya you're as sweet as sugar/ baby you're sweet as sugar/ soo very sweet/ oh so sweet/

VERSE 2: I, I stand and I wait/ as the clock runs late/ to hear your call baby, cause I know this is fate/ and maybe, you'll let me take you out on a nice date/ under the moonlight/ I sing/ you a song, for you my darling/ under the moonlight/ in the middle of the spring/ I've searched all around/ like I were a basset hound/ to have finally found/ you, an angel, I've waited and I fought through this hell/ ring, ring, ring on my bell/ come dance with me in the rain/ no wait/ baby stay/ here with me to pray/ until, God calls us home/ it has to be you, you got me feeling in the zone/ no longer all alone/ your beauty is remarkable/ incredible, delectably delicious/ you're exquisite/ intelligent, and fantastic/ it feels like a dream/ oh how good it really feels/ is this even for real/ I want to kiss you all over/ for ever/ cause there is no other/ for me/ baby/ you can rely on me/ I will protect you and our family/

HOOK/CHORUS: Baby – you're sweet as sugar/ Ya you're as sweet as sugar/ baby you're sweet as sugar/ soo very sweet/ oh so sweet/ Baby – you're sweet as sugar/ Ya you're as sweet as sugar/ baby you're sweet as sugar/ soo very sweet/ oh so sweet/

SUMMARY - I'll explain it like this. "Sweet as sugar just spoke to me the second I heard the production for this song. Long story short, I wanted to think as hard as I also realized on my first debut, I had a love song titled "Hey Baby, where'd you go?" and I wanted its counter part for this album."

Chapter 11: Song 11 – Til' Death Do Us Part (11:11)

Til' Death Do Us Part:

INTRO: "You know, I've been doing this shit for a long mother fucking time Yo and I still haven't reaped any ill benefits. Or, got my hard work paid off by now. And you know I'm to that point where I'm about to explode. And, my only wish is that when I'm gone; all that lasts is my music, you know?"

VERSE 1: Ya now I've got your attention/ do you feel my sensation/ I'm the best at anything/ call me Mr. Education/ I'm motivation & Dedication/ at it's best imperfection/ Imma musician/ of alliteration/ abruptly/ acting/ as/ abbey/ and/ Ashley/ arouse/ AAA-MIZeRY/ literally/ don't take this seriously/ It's literacy/ I can't always permit MIZeRY/ to expose his violent tendencies/ which are contained voluntarily/ I'm exquisitely/ at it's best formality/ don't ever get lost in another man's reality/ be all and everything that you ever wanted to be/ don't let anyone ever stop you from chasing your dreams/ that's cool if you wanna know me/ but don't become my enemy/ otherwise I'll show you this MIZeRY/ buried inside a me/ my imperfect physique/ is defined by physics/ no gimmicks/ on my conquest/ to conquer corrupt politics/

HOOK/CHORUS: Til' death do us part, I'm in this shit for life/ fuck everything else, I only need 1 MIC/ bitch if you ain't ride/ than you ain't my wife/ fuck you & Ya lies/ I only trust my rhymes/ Til' death do us part, I'm in this shit for life/ fuck everything else, I only need 1 MIC/ bitch if you ain't ride/ than you ain't my wife/ fuck you & Ya lies/ I only trust in my rhymes/

VERSE 2: Til' death do us part, I'm married to the game/ and I carry 9's and 10's, I don't rock with no lames/ Imma give away this fame/ it don't satisfy my tastes/ or my extreme kind of ways/ now shift out of my lane and invading my space/ this ain't no rat race/ if you try and harm me, I'll catch another case/ writing rhymes all day/ I'm not no child, so quit trying to play/ with all of my emotions/ I'm cruising in this ocean/ all by my lonesome/ every one of you is evil, not one is even wholesome/ if you think this shit is fun/ then come walk in my shoes, and get ready to run/ where I come from/ dudes die every month/ for acting way too tough/ so watch your little tongue/ for you might not wake, and see another day's sun/ if you act like a chump/ then get jumped like one/ dumping bullets in Ya lungs/ from auto-machine guns/

HOOK/CHORUS: Til' death do us part, I'm in this shit for life/ fuck everything else, I only need 1 MIC/ bitch if you ain't ride/ than you ain't my wife/ fuck you & Ya lies/ I only trust my rhymes/ Til' death do us part, I'm in this shit for life/ fuck everything else, I only need 1 MIC/ bitch if you ain't ride/ than you ain't my wife/ fuck you & Ya lies/ I only trust in my rhymes/

VERSE 3: Anytime I date a woman/ she questions/ and she stresses/ her concerns/ over how much money I've ever earned/ keep playing with this fire bitch! You're bound to get burned/ I'll leave you dead in the trash and blame George Burns/ you skank ass hooker/ playing sex strip poker/ get Ya ass on moving, I need a women who's older/ strictly cougars & Milfs/ with no shame or any guilt/ ready to take my ass home and pay all of my bills/ I'm the last action hero, seeking plutonic thrills/ chasing these mill's/ short for millions/ cause I'm a billion/ reasons better than you, starting with the fact I can admit/ 10% of my songs aren't even true/ and still about you/ of being way to un-cool/ to ever try and pursue/ being so blunt and so rude/ you're a mother fucking tool/ who we use/ and abuse/ simply to amuse/ these idiotic fools/ Yaa as MIZeRY's music, explodes your amps fuse/ your screws become loose/ leaving you dazed and confused/ on what you should do/ dunce'n you the biggest loser, at duck, duck goose/ I'm ready to explode! I've traveled on this road/ for way too long/ I don't know where I'm going, but exactly where I'm headed/ when I've reached my destination, this rap games Dead'd/ I don't play games, with another album ended/

HOOK/CHORUS: Til' death do us part, I'm in this shit for life/ fuck everything else, I only need 1 MIC/ bitch if you ain't ride/ than you ain't my wife/ fuck you & Ya lies/ I only trust my rhymes/ Til' death do us part, I'm in this shit for life/ fuck everything else, I only need 1 MIC/ bitch if you ain't ride/ than you ain't my wife/ fuck you & Ya lies/ I only trust in my rhymes/

SUMMARY - I'll explain it like this. "Til' Death Do Us Part" is by far one of my top three favorites. I created this song to show the world in one songs time; how committed I am to my art and my mission, as a human for this world. I was also discussing my rules: when it comes to love, money, and life. If you can't accept them, then you ain't ready to ride."

Chapter 12
Realizing, My own truth

Let's go back to when I turned 21; when I endured the most difficult trials, I claimed I may ever face. After cleaning up my act of a rebellious nature; I could finally be free from all illegal conflictions and sin. However, being free didn't mean things would be simple. I was given a new beginning, which meant, that I would have to rethink how I acted and what my true purpose in life was. I immediately found a new avenue in music to pursue as an alternative. Considering, music has always been my outlet of redemption and sanity; it was only natural, I pursued it in a new means. Although, I continued to struggle financially, more than ever no less; I knew, I must remain a committed entrepreneur because it was what made me truly happy. Through many poor decisions and co-mingling with evil people; I started realizing and feeling, there was something wrong about being in the music industry, and in the division I was surrounded by.

Over the years of living multiple lives and having to separate my life, between good and evil; I finally was saved from all avenues, when I surrendered my life to Jesus Christ. Through my submission to the Good Lord; God began revealing many truths about life to me and I didn't understand why, but started too. This is when, I also started my quest to live and act like Jesus Christ; because he lived righteously and there was no other alternative. With this new found discovery about life; I started a 3 year mental war of contemplating humanity, between good versus evil and life versus reality. All the meanwhile my love life, financial burdens, and constant dedication to succeed started taking its toil on my life. In addition, it severely affected my mental capacity, my physically body, and my relationships with friends. Eventually, scenarios of tests would present themselves between 7 of my closes friends and me. As a result, my love interest at the time and I would split. Forcing me to make a haste decision; risk everything I had and remain in New York, or move in with my father for the first time ever.

I quickly chose to move away from all that I had known at the age of 21, in search of a new beginning. The reason for this new beginning has a great deal to do with me always knowing: I was different and special in many ways; but, still have yet to uncover the why.

Throughout the many years of many hardships I have faced, I also had a difficult time with other people and friends. Ergo, people are always disloyal eventually and I've always had this ability to find ways, to break individuals down, for who they truly are. I know this gift can only be from that of Jesus, which was given to me. The gift and ability to know all truth. Additionally, my safety and security measures in life, might in fact have kept me alive all these years. With such security measures, I sometimes hurt the people I care about, by testing friends to their limits; because I knew, I had the ability to always forgive and trust people again. But I never realized, others do not so easily. I concluded, this is the very way of this world because the Devil has complete control in this indecent time. Almost all, have also forgotten, the ways Jesus Christ once tried to teach. Further more, this is exactly why God created **Judgment Day**; because God always knew, humanity wouldn't change, after Jesus Christ's Crucifixion, and they still wouldn't change; when Michael Thee Archangel was born amongst them, to defeat the Devil, and create Jesus Christ's new world…

Over 12 years of unfrequented search attempts, I would finally get a break in my search for my biological father. Around the age of 20, about 8 months prior to moving; I had worked in a law firm in New York. Although I only worked there for one day, I was told by God to search information pertinent to my father; while during my training. During this time, I practiced the systems pertaining to my job requirements. I had utilized the law firms secured and exclusive software network; which granted me access to Government filed information, of any citizen, listed within the United States via search. This software enabled me to locate detailed information about my father Frank J. Zangari. Such information included: name, DOB, mortgage information, asset information, income information, residency information, contact information and more. I later secured copies of the listed information, by writing it down in my training notebook. Once the work day was over, I quit that company, and was never seen from again.

Several months later, I had informed my private psychologist about wanting to contact my father. My psychologist and I, later determined, calling my father during a session would be the prime choice for contacting him: via telephone. I was frantically nervous upon my first attempt. Nonetheless, I had spoken to my father and addressed the situation immediately; by informing Frank that I had reason to believe, he was my biological father. Several weeks later, after several phone conversations, Frank had suggested to me we take a DNA test. This seemed to be the most accurate and secure way in continuing with any sort of relationship between us, he said; I concurred. Several days later, Frank discovered an agency by the name of *IDENTIGENE* which supplied local DNA kits in stores such as CVS. However, *IDENTIGENE* wasn't located in New York nor legally licensed to service anyone in New York. So instead, Frank purchased the kit, swapped his own DNA, and then mailed out his sample to the clinic. Shortly after, Frank had mailed the remaining sample kit to me; where I would swap my mothers mouth for DNA, as well as my own. However, in order for me and my mother's DNA to be tested; I would have to mail the kit from an outside state that IDENTIGENE was licensed in. So Frank had mailed the remaining DNA from me, to IDENTIGENE. Several weeks later, the results concluded a 99.99% resulting match. After I had acquired my settlement money and sold my current vehicle; I moved up to Haverhill, MA later that year.

The first day of my new life in a new city, I began uncovering my past. As a young boy, I always wanted to, and knew I would eventually, find out who my father was. This aspiration came about from my ideal, that nothing in life is impossible; in other words, I believe that: "If something can be done, it can always be undone." Moving in with my father was very depressing and rocky for me at first; especially considering, I had just moved away from all that I've ever known. In addition, I recently broke up with my love interest and I was living in unfamiliar territory. The first 7 months were the hardest for me, being in a new city, and having this constant urge to make bi-weekly trips back to New York. I realized these frequent return trips stemmed from my passion for music and childhood friends. Before I knew it, it was now August, I'm now 22, and four thousand dollars broker from traveling and living expenses. I soon found myself having to make a choice between working full time or going to school full time; I chose school. However, this would not prevent me from pursuing my passions for music and sociable excitement. The first semester was the roughest for me; especially because, I had to conceal who I was in the world of music and a mature hard working cool guy from NYC.

Sometime around December of 2009, I had met my first best friend: Fred B. Fred was comedic, outgoing, and a hip young guy whom shared similar passions in life with me. Fred and I became close friends almost immediately.

Throughout 2010 my life seemed mostly great, considering I was making friends finally, and I started forgetting about New York. Finally, I was settling in my new home; and my passion to continue my poetry and music, quickly re-stimulated. By June 3rd of 2010, I had recorded and released my album "No More Running." This album not only featured some of my new best friends on the cover, but this album was the start of uncovering my true self. At first, I simply thought "No More Running" was referring to me and my music career. However, it later revealed far more. This album landed me many new friends and established my reputation in Massachusetts as well as New Hampshire. Unfortunately, it only sold several hundred copies. Eventually, 2010 came to an end and my search for my soul mate still lingered deep within...

New Years eve 2010/2011; I was invited to a few parties, as I usually managed for a New Years celebration. However, when I arrived at the last party in Nikki's home; destiny introduced me to a one Andre O. Andre was a very unique individual, whom was also one of a faithful background. After a couple hours of conversation, Andre randomly told me that he knew who my soul mate was. Immediately, he grabbed my attention because I have never heard such a thing; even being buzzed, from all the alcoholic beverages. I initially played it cool and simple. I told him that I would be interested in meeting this alleged soul mate. Two months later, Andre introduced me to a very lovely Ashley A. At first sight, I was interested but not intrigued. Eventually, Ashley and I would become friends and hang out on several occasions. One sunny Sunday afternoon, Ashley and I would hang out for the last time it would seem. As Sunday commenced smoothly and amazingly with a smoke session, a movie, and eventually; Ashley even made dinner for me and her friend, who is more like a sister to her as she quoted. With having such an amazing day with Ashley, I started feeling very close and interested romantically for Ashley. Later that evening, I immediately wrote and recorded a song to describe my connection and feelings for her. However, I felt something was wrong even prior to being something wrong. As a result, I titled the song Hey Baby, where'd you go?

As the week continued on, I did all that I could think of which was express how I started feeling about her. Even though, I knew the world is backwards and women prefer men that are uninterested; over being interested. Later in the week, I purchased flowers for Ashley and left them at her door, for her to find with a note of romantic feelings. Even though, I knew it would backfire causing the friendship to perish for now. Ultimately, I accepted this and continued about my life; even though, I missed her. Approximately seven months later, Ashley had reached out to me randomly. As I usually would do, I questioned this relentlessly and needed to know her motives. She ultimately apologized and we started speaking again. Although, it wasn't that frequently. Either way, I attempted dating other people even from out of state. But I continued to feel, as if they were all wrong for me. This would eventually make me feel, as if no woman would fulfill the shoes necessary to be with someone as unique as myself. As 2010 came to an end, I began recording my first debut music album; which would eventually be published by *Island Def Jam Recordings*, titled "15 years of my life."

2011 started moving very quickly and I had several obligations to worry over: work, school, and music. Eventually, I was fired from my job and my grades began to decrease; all as a result, from pursuing my music career. On May 17th 2011, I had released my first major publication with *Island Def Jam Digital Distribution* in over 150 countries, throughout the world. Even though this was a great accomplishment for me, not many would purchase the product; and with limited funding, I wasn't able to correctly promote this project. Nevertheless, I realized this was still an accomplishment and maintaining my publication was beneficial to further my career. In the summer of 2011, one of my songs "Game Over" was played on Boston's commercial radio station *Jamn' 94.5*. This motivated me further. I immediately started my second debut *Island Def Jam* album, to help cross promote with my first album, and my new artists. In October of 2011, I had released a free promotional Mixtape The World Take Over – Mixtape Hosted by DJ Onpoint to assist in promoting my upcoming album in November. On November 11th 2011, I released "Til' Death Do Us Part" published by *Island Def Jam* as well. At the age of 24, I turned my life entirely to God. In fact, about 2 years prior, during a drunken & high-suicidal-manic-depressive-psychotic episode; I nearly faced certain death. All the while: praying, crying, and begging God to save me. After several hours of drinking &

smoking, while cutting my wrist slowly; I finally reached my breaking point. I had screamed loudly for all to hear, from within my home, and near by outside. I yelled and told God: "I surrender my will and surrender my life, for you my Lord to command and direct; however you deem worthy." It was at this exact moment, when my life finally came back into the light of God to finish out my mission. This mission, would require much further needed hard work and faithful dedication. This would also require self sacrificing all that I had come to know or ever desired. Fast Forwarding to August of 2011, my life became complex beyond humane comprehension. My biological father would eventually betray me a second time, by kicking me out of his home. Resulting me to begin my journey, of understanding, of who I truly am…

On December 1st of 2011, I silently started hearing and speaking with God within my own conscience sporadically; which ultimately, caused me to question humanity beyond a fathomable margin. During the last couple months of 2011, I had started becoming very close with God. I then noticed the results, when I recorded songs without writing the songs prior. Through these newly founded scriptures, I realized that God was speaking to me, through me, onto my songs; pertaining to many things to come in the world. It wasn't until I remixed a song by *Dr. Dre* and *Eminem* titled "I Need a Doctor," that I had realized; God was speaking through me, because I was apart of him directly. Eventually, my life was so confusing and consisted of relentless turmoil with home, friends, and aspirations that I started questioning everything I've known. This madness drove me to the realization I was not just a messenger for God; but I was in fact, Jesus Christ in the second form. In other words, the rebirth of Christ or simply Michael Thee Archangel. **I truly realized this during the photo comparison listed below**. However, this realization was questioned relentlessly for 5 months. It wasn't until I started creating this project; in which God presented to me in a dream, that I must create my life's work; titled, The 2nd Coming (Movie), The 2nd Coming of Jesus Christ (Novel), and The 2nd Coming – Disc 1 & The New World – Disc 2 (movie sound tracks). Shortly after having this excitingly vivid dream from God, about creating this project; I commenced working on it. It was than, I began to accept what he was telling me. In October of 2011, I had completed the below promotional Mixtape "*The World Take Over – Mixtape*." Which led to my realization, that I was Jesus Christ reborn. This realization was derived from the

Mixtape cover and it was this very photo, that triggered my own understanding of myself…

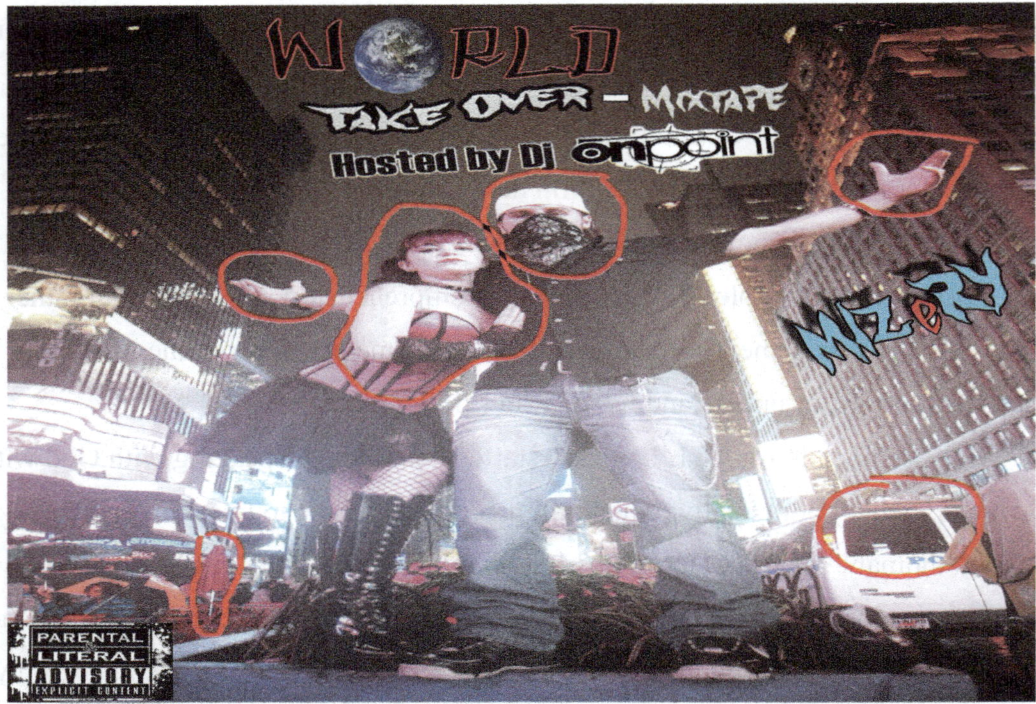

Exactly on December 25th 2011; I started noticing signs sent to me, by God, the Almighty. Directing me to a better understanding of whom I was and why I existed. This also has been a question of mine; which I wondered relentlessly, since I was a little boy. Later on in January, I started searching for an image to be the cover for my upcoming album-movie-soundtrack titled "The 2nd Coming – Disc 1." After *Googling* one random day for no more than 10 minutes; I stumbled upon this portrait of Jesus Christ, by (*©2007 Artistlight.com):*

It was from this very shocking discovery, when I heard a voice telling me that I was in fact Jesus Christ reborn. Immediately after this discovery, I started questioning anything and everything that came to mind; all revolving around Jesus Christ & life. I spent the next several weeks researching Jesus Christ, Buying movies on Jesus Christ, purchasing a full *King James Bible*, and internet searching for all renowned paintings and photos of Jesus Christ. Long and behold, my research started adding up and making sense more and more. Leading to the fact, I was in fact, Jesus Christ in the second form of life. During my time researching, I began to write epistles in relation to *The New Testament*. But was also far from any relation to any Bible text documented. These series of writings/recordings and verbal non-documented recordings – meaning without being written prior; all resulted, to the completion of a movie script, novel, and audio sound track titled: "*The 2nd Coming, The 2nd Coming of Jesus Christ, The 2nd Coming – Disc 1, and The New World – Disc 2*." If you doubt all that I, Michael Izzo, have recorded and bared witness too; while only God the Almighty is permitted to Judge me by, let me list here some facts, I know are true…

M. I was born on June 3rd, 1987 in San Diego, CA. 92103; in San Diego Hospital, located at 4077 Fifth Ave. By Dr. Timothy Riley – 4045 Third Ave, License # **G33037.**

I. Certificate ID – 1**8**7370**16**3**96, birth code 0666, & birth time: 08:06 am.

C. Birth name: Michael Lee Edward Izzo AKA Michael Thee Arch Angel.

H. Edward was given to honor my mother's friend's baby, whom had passed near birth.

A. I'm incredibly resilient, intelligent, and have taught myself most knowledge and education, I've ever studied.

E. I despise money and any form of Government, for they are not righteous.

L. I have a vast understanding of humanity and divinity, beyond humane comprehension; not including, humanly theories.

I. I have suffered a great deal; while helping many over the years, and have written several hundred songs, scriptures, and prophecies throughout my life.

Z. My lower left tooth, number 24, has a permanent birth marking of a king's **crown**. However, I only noticed this at the age of 13; while in fact, almost having it removed. By the grace of God, the dentist suggested not removing this mark, ironically…

Z. Occasionally, I suffer from a medically unknown pain under my right breast/nipple located relatively close to where Jesus was stabbed by the **Spear of Destiny.**

O. My sole mission in life is to end suffering for all even if I must die for it.

The Final Testament

Chapter 13
The 2nd Coming – Disc I

When I turned 24, I realized a few truths, which led me to doubt all otherwise. At this point in time, I've reached all doubts about the world and what it means. Throughout my entire life, I have faced many obstacles and trials of faith, but never completely having lost that faith. It was through these extreme tribulations which have made me realize; that I knew, deep down inside, I was meant for something extraordinary; something so extraordinary, this burden could only be placed upon two children of God. Near the end of 2011, I realized that I was Jesus Christ in nature and in spirit, but reborn as a new person in modern society. Reborn with one purpose: to fulfill the promise I made from my first existence. From January 2012 – March 2012, I relentlessly questioned and doubted the very acceptance of being Jesus Christ in the second form. I questioned it strategically, while I was cautious in manner about my behavioral thoughts. Because I was afraid, that if I were wrong, I would be condemned to hell for impersonating and believing in something so wrong; it could be considered, the worst sin ever…

Throughout my entire life, I have always known and felt there was way more to life. More than what has been taught and presented to us; amongst many other abilities, beliefs, and understandings of life as an overall subject. Most importantly: when I was 12, I had this sudden aspiration and feeling that I could create a world without any sin or suffering. I created MIZeRY & *MIZeRY ReCORDS* to "secretly absorb all the sins of the world once again." Although when I was 12, I had no idea of the meaning, behind the true reason for my idea in creating my company; but I knew, I was tired of being hurt and sad. One evening in January, I had woken abruptly early in the morning as I usually suffered from. However, this time the premonitions and vivid dreams were different!

In this dream, God had spoken to me about writing a book and movie of "The Second Coming of Jesus Christ." Immediately upon waking, I commenced working on the project; the same project, you are reading before your very eyes: "*The-2nd Coming of Jesus Christ*." The first section I commenced working on was the music soundtrack, because that's what I am most familiar with and skilled at. Almost immediately, I created a double album sound track titled: "*The 2nd Coming – Disc 1 & The New World – Disc 2*." I realized that with writing and recording this project, I would ultimately write the script or scripture for the actual Second Coming. As a result, many long days raged on upon commencing this project. For most of 2012, I worked at my day job and co-mingled my entertainment business, accumulating 10-15 hour days. I knew collectively, these albums would contain 33 songs total; making for a good fit to my personality, while asking God for the answers to our future. The first CD contains the main basis for the script and the actuality of my reality. Based on what I know of *The New Testament*, my mission for God, and what I see from mine and your actions.

The 2nd Coming - Disc 1 (Movie Soundtrack)

1. The 2nd Coming - Movie Theme 2. A Savior's Tale 3. What If I'm Him 4. The Refusal
5. The Chase 6. Devils Ambush Gabriel 7. My Pen Bleeds Judgmental Sorrow
8. Silent Assassins Ft. DaRedANT 9. A Fallen Angel 10. My Last Words...
11. Heavy Weight 12. If I Fail 13. Armageddon's eve www.mizeryrecords.com

Chapter 13: Song 1 – The 2nd Coming – Movie Theme (13:1)

The 2nd Coming – Movie Theme:

VERSE 1: Okay so the 2nd coming/ is actually happening/ pure truth, and it's commencing/ with every second that I'm rapping/ Mr. Stevens – wake up & Pay attention/ It's time to start taking action/ Now quit all of your sleeping/ you have 1 opportunity for saving/ and MIZeRY's ship is sailing/ My resurrection is approaching/ and I'm the one who's coaching/ No bragging or boasting/ If you dare start judging/ I'll leave you dead in this ocean/ and you will not be floating/ But surely forgotten/ or stay on Earth and continue rotting/ while burning/ hotter than the sun/ where you will be tormented forever by the evil one/ Okay I'll say this once/ for many of you will vanish, almost instantly in large sums/ whether you are asleep or awake/ at first sight, it seems like nothings even changed/ within minutes, you'll feel cold & drained/ confused & disorientated, as you hear loud noises which are strange/ As you walk further into the mist you notice a demon like creature/ who's been stalking you for 10 minutes hungry like a vulture/ with gazed devil red eyes, consuming all your composure/ now you're scared shitless/ running for your life as the devil progresses/ quickly engages/ toward your humanly stenches/ no need for trenches/ you're doomed beyond magical wishes/ for demon's burn/ and must quench/ their curses/ for men of seven deadly sinners/

HOOK/CHORUS: Our father, who art in Heaven/ may your name be kept holy/ may your kingdom come soon, may your will be done on Earth as it is in Heaven/ Give us today the food we need/ and forgive us for our sins/ as we have forgiven those who have sinned against us/ and don't let us yield to temptation/ but rescue us from the evil one/ amen.

VERSE 2: (**Bad Side**) Back to the story/ momentarily/ you lost the demon temporarily/ I'd say you were lucky/ and frantically clumsy/ you fell through a portal/ which only transports evil mortals/ directly to the devil/ and he says he'll grant you one wish/ after my sentence/ you'll have six seconds, so think quick/ period/ 1,2,3, I'm serious/ 4,5,6/ Okay – you wished for a second chance at life/ he laughed at the old fool sadistically, and he said you believed in me over Lord Jesus Christ/ So welcome to your eternal torture/ I'll take from you, what's most important/ I'll scorcher you at super nova degree's/ cut your head in half and I'll leave you deaf, dumb, and blind for all eternity/ (**Good Side**) Moving onto the good side/ walking into the bright light/ Ya I'm talking about worshipping thy Lord Holy Jesus Christ/ in his name I pray every night/ to lead me by faith not by sight/ let the moon be my light/ for demons play at night/ I believe in the writings/ & your teachings/ truly it's a feeling/ spiritually surging/ through my soul, like nuclear energy bursting/ minus all the death and sadness/ in His path you remain blessed/ no stress/ no contests/ just peace and love/ fun and games/ wealth, humility, equality/ and a whole lotta positivity/ it's a relationship seriously/

HOOK/CHORUS: Our father, who art in Heaven/ may your name be kept holy/ may your kingdom come soon, may your will be done on Earth as it is in Heaven/ Give us today the food we need/ and forgive us for our sins/ as we have forgiven those who have sinned against us/ and don't let us yield to temptation/ but rescue us from the evil one/ amen.

VERSE 3: Here's a taste of paradise/ the kingdom of Jesus Christ/ offered to those chosen for after life/ no madness & no demise/ cool summer breezes, cold wintery nights/ no Judgmental thoughts, no pain, and toxic lies/ It's called His 2nd coming, and grants us a 2nd life/ more inspiration and knowledge ever possible in my rhymes/ The messages & images are implanted in my mind/ slowly decoded/ simplified/ then prophesized/ His 2nd rise/ and this time/ he won't be scrutinized/ for soon comes the day, to reclaim/ His paradise/ okay pay attention/ for everyone gets tested/ before they can ever enter Heaven/ The question is what's the meaning of life?/ quit stressing/ did I mention/ if you fail, you sit outside the gates for 10 years, until your next attempt/ or forfeit & press eject/ cause I have no time for nonsense/ I'm the gate keeper, stronger than Thor, and hungry for a challenge/ I'll have you banished/ sent straight down to hell/ where you will be tormented with fire by the Devil/ I, Jesus Christ am forgiving and merciful/ but If you are ignorant & forgetful/ as to what MIZeRY teaches you/ then I'll forget you as easily/ as you ignored me/ how dare you insult me/ you need therapy/ this is fucking prophecy/ and the 3rd time – you will deny me/

HOOK/CHORUS: Our father, who art in Heaven/ may your name be kept holy/ may your kingdom come soon, may your will be done on Earth as it is in Heaven/ Give us today the food we need/ and forgive us for our sins/ as we have forgiven those who have sinned against us/ and don't let us yield to temptation/ but rescue us from the evil one/ amen.

SUMMARY - I'll explain it like this. "As I finished this song, I was not only impressed with myself and the song, but I really started believing and understanding what God was showing me. When I completed this song, I was so anxious to immediately finish writing and prophesizing the remaining 32 songs. Ultimately, this song was exactly what I was hoping for as my movie theme. God helped me capture the exact interpretation of what was to come for us all within this one song.

Chapter 13: Song 2 – A Savior's Tale (13:2)

A Savior's Tale:

VERSE 1: Okay I'll start with the facts/ using methods of raps/ I'm sticking to the basic's/ Let's face it/ I'm ten steps ahead of you using extreme tactics/ Humanely – were not in the same brackets/ I'm an active/ maverick/ who's raising havoc/ for those whom are demonic/ I'm more sadistic/ than you can imagine/ I'm 2,000 years old fashioned/ I have kingdoms and mansions/ I've waited long centuries for expansion/ I'm reclaiming my fathers planet/ even if I must destroy it first/ Demons have 2/3's of you cursed/ My apostle's urge me to save more than one third/ which is approximately 2.333 billion/ you should be thankful I'm even saving that many/ for years I was ready/ to secretly start killing you all lethally/ with no traces left of me/ come and go like government policies/ 2/3's tell you that you should fear me/ that's the temptation of the devil, persuading you not to love me/ Pray to me/ and I will answer thee/

HOOK/CHORUS: It's my savior's tale/ used for saving all y'all/ through strength and courage, I Promise I wont fail/ I'm Godly – manifesting in your dreams/ absorbing all of your misery/ It's my savior's tale/ used for saving all y'all/ through strength and courage, I Promise I wont fail/ I'm Godly – manifesting in your dreams/

absorbing all of your misery/

VERSE 2: If you were born on the third day, male or female/ than you are of the chosen 22 apostles/ don't worry I'll explain how this is possible/ he your Lord, was risen on the 3rd day of April/ Upon his resurrection/ he chose 11 men and 11 women/ to secretly/ guide all a humanity/ back to sanity/ while taking your friends and family/ home to our sanctuary/ broken down systematically/ Ten of you were chosen as my top 10 general's/ to search for and rally strong angel's/ accept people like you/ for one day you will combat the devil/ In my name, honor, & survival/ As he shows me through vivid visions/ time & Heaven causing collisions/ devastating my mind, resulting delusional illusions/ I'm lost on the next set of lines/ my brain ties/ in first, with the next set of slick rhymes/ playing tongue tied/ sometimes/ I die/ then I'm revived/ cause it's still not my time/

HOOK/CHORUS: It's my savior's tale/ used for saving all y'all/ through strength and courage, I Promise I wont fail/ I'm Godly – manifesting in your dreams/ absorbing all of your misery/ It's my savior's tale/ used for saving all y'all/ through strength and courage, I Promise I wont fail/ I'm Godly – manifesting in your dreams/ absorbing all of your misery/

VERSE 3: It's not time to reveal my true identity/ for at the end of this movie/ I shall reveal to you the true me/ ultimately/ the devil tried to hide my true prophecy/ from me/ creating this universe of misery/ which led me to believe things far beyond reality/ so I played his evil games/ changing the ways/ that you even play/ without selling your soul in exchange/ I then created a character from his MIZeRY/ mastered and beat each level quickly/ while hitting rock bottom, far more years than three/ I escaped through Jesus Christ/ Now I'm using the demons trickery/ against him literally/ everyday, even if it kills me/ So now I use MIZeRY/ to craft these personal stories/ as messages of prophecies/ sometimes confused & sloppy/ but always intense and personally/ It always seems to save me/ or in other words revives me/ this is why my energy/ sounds cynically/ controlling to the point, that you hate me/ for explaining the true personality/ of your God, Yes Me/ not MIZeRY/ but Michael is special in ways too profound/ for human ears to begin to sound/ as for the other 10 angels, they are my 1st ten friends, the ones who ate with me at the first & last supper/ MIZeRY the rapper/ is one of a kind/ & so is his wife/

the only two I created to decide who's right in life/ MIZeRY is my secret to see through all your lies/ With his wife/ who hasn't been revealed, is like mother nature/ represents all pure/ in the world/ starting with nature's fur/ and ending with hers/

SUMMARY - I'll explain it like this. "When I had finished writing, recording, and mixing this song I was at a loss of words. Despite this record was completed how I wanted it, I was still required to study my own verses. As I began deciphering this song, I realized that I was one and the same with our Lord thy God. No matter what my role was in existence, I was apart of God. In other words, God himself was telling our story from his origin. In addition, Jesus Christ was explaining some of his unlimited knowledge and foresight when he explains: "securing his apostles to rally strong Angels for one day, you will combat the devil. In my name, honor, and survival; AKA Judgment Day." I seriously recommend any and all who listen to this song, to listen to it many times; because every time you do, you will find new key metaphors that will help guide you in your lives."

Chapter 13: Song 3 – What If I'm Him? (13:3)

What If I'm Him?

VERSE 1: Yup start this one off right/ Imma bless you as I rhyme/ this is your Lord Almighty this time/ I put MIZeRY in a trance, trippin out of his mind/ as MIZeRY interrupts, I said, no God I'm right here/ trippin out my mind, but I'm seeing shit clear/ Now MIZeRY drifts/ into unconsciousness/ where was I? Oh that's right I'm about to have you blessed/ I'm unmatched with unlimited perseverance/ the difference/ stems from the creation of existence/ no matter the distance/ I'm a direct spawn of father, who made all that you decimate/ still acting like evil primates/ killing, stealing, and lying to each face/ that you see, as you engage/ in acts father doesn't tolerate/ so shall I lock you up in a cage/ as if I'm right & you're filthy primates/ or choose a life a sin/ rot in hell as punishment/ for your fallacy/ as you continuously/ degrade & judge society/ as If you all live individually/ and every face you see/ you start to depict, as one of your natural enemies/ Instead of befriending each other, as if you are family/ Okay back to kicking prophecy/ Thru method's of scientific literacy/ However, sometimes it's hard to speak easily/ to the point it sickens me/ The words begin to escape me/ grammatically/ I'm not spelling correctly/ that's only because its to far to reach/ Ya my 1300 page dictionary/ floating, directly right in front of me/ As if it was so holy/ similar to Bible stories/ now for the record, my previous body/ is missing cause I'm Godly/ In actuality/ I leave or produce no DNA, resulting in an identity/ I'm all & one, in everybody/ now this is where it gets tricky/ so If you need, pop Adderall quickly/ Now listen, good or bad, I'm everywhere & everything/ Happy or sad, outrageous or amusing/ The world and all it contains magical energy/ created to maintain regularity/ since you abuse **Free Will**, I must be harsh when it comes to my authority/ don't play dumb, you know what I mean/ death, hurricanes, monsoons, nuclear explosions – it's all controlled by me/ However, my son offers you salvation/ over centuries you abused his humility/ Now he's grown full of aggravation/ ready to inflict massive devastation/ because Earth is Heaven's best creation/ Humans abuse the gift of emotions/ Now I'm alive ready to conquer/ For I Jesus Christ – son of god have come for my children/ and an end to the devils destruction/ this is the time for Godly resurrection/ as I unleash MIZeRY to determine who's worthy of redemption/ I tell you this my son – Be humble to those worthy as I/ and be cruel to those unworthy of I/ For our time as come, to lead a peaceful kind of life/ for eternity/ no matter the person or ethnicity/ for we are all one only through me/ and only through me may you enter my fathers kingdom/ now, you say this with me/ In thy Lord Jesus Christ I pray/ save me and accept me into your holy land of grace/ and thank you for your Heavenly praise/ Amen – Now I ah MIZeRY am unleashed upon evil men/ I stop to think as I use this pen/ to cause lyrical destruction/ I'm truly a menace/ a crazed maniac/ don't panic/ Jesus has me tamed/ I won't ever again fall astray/ cause I pray/ to God everyday/ I'm strong with Jesus, no matter what you portray/ plus, I have Godly sight, and I can see all of your ways/ Me and Jesus are one and the same/ I've surrendered to his will/ oh wait 1 second I'm at a stand still/ oooooo Icy Cold chill/ Jesus hopped out my soul/ **(burr whoa)**… Now I can unleash my humanly pain/ upon you as I drain/ the very life from your heart & all the knowledge contained in your brain/ I'm sick and deranged/ who's suffered more than most/ and still conquered being insane/ using my pain/ as unlimited fuel to regulate earths ways/ by using radio waves/ to monitor all that you say/

SUMMARY - I'll explain it like this. "What If I'm Him?" Truly there is no reason to summarize this song. I truly believe Jesus Christ and God the father entirely took control over my humanly vessel and together, all three of us wrote and recorded, a powerful metaphorical song: beyond the comprehension of most."

Chapter 13: Song 4 – The refusal (13:4)

The Refusal:

INTRO: "So we're three songs deep and if you don't know by now, that I'm Jesus Christ, cause those who follow know who I'm. And I don't care if you don't even believe. Ya I know it's hard to believe that I'm, it's hard, I know. Ya I know it's hard, Ya I know it's hard for you all to believe; but the fact of the matter is, is I'm who I say I'm."

VERSE 1: Okay The refusal is necessary/ by all human means realistically/ It's mother nature for you to question anything of spirituality/ It's hard for you to show humility/ you even lack a sense of integrity/ money & greed/ have you all trapped, behind the gates of an enslaved society/ Ya you all commit sins continuously/ Lord Jesus Christ grows weary/ and soon he will remind you why you should all fear me/ For, you don't even accept me/ pray to me/ and worship me/ I can never enter into thee/ for those who worship & believe I'm your art thou Lord, shall feel me/ in ways never felt physically/ no seriously/ with time, you shall all become me/ lesser weakened versions of me/ but still a Part of me/ so as the light gets darker/ & you drift much farther/ out of my reach/ I still stand here and preach/ using His knowledge & everything, that I'm told to teach/ starting with how I increase/ everyone's morality/ with all that you see/ instead, you deny me/ like I'm the enemy/ when I'm really quite simply/ your only true friendly/ now you've walked so far/ I can't see you in the dark/ no longer being an easy target marked/

HOOK/CHORUS: In the wild - there are no sanctuaries, churches, or safe havens/ - In the Jungle – there are no people or angels/ there are only demons & animals/

- In the Devils lair – there is only sinister fire/ with horrifying demonic monsters/ waiting to rip the flesh from your bodies/ and devour your souls instantly/

VERSE 2: At this point you've lost all faith/ vulnerable to the demons ways/ granting you worldly possessions/ your obsessions/ grow immensely aggressive/ turning you demonic/ way beyond positive progression/ you grow tired with confliction/ the messages he's delivering/ are confusing/ resulting suicidal sensations/ causing you to cut yourself with painful incisions/ leaving life long infliction/ you caused merely out of desperation/ while you thought it was dedication/ fueled by the devils addictions/ now you are rehabilitated, but soon you shall fall and fiend for medications/ drug administered injections/ dirty needles results the aids infection/ you walk around with this poison, the devil only cares for destruction/ as he lives because of evil actions/ banish that from the world, and permanently destroy his factions/ when I learned that, I trained in the arts of an assassin/ I'm smarter and faster/ I could never be captured/ even if it happened, I'd have you all slaughtered/ I was crucified once/ another blade, shall never touch my flesh/ for as long as I exist/ Lord Jesus Christ/ grants me unlimited strength/ super genius intelligence/ searching and terminating for demonic deliverance/

HOOK/CHORUS:

- In the wild – there are no sanctuaries, churches, or safe havens/
- In the Jungle – there are no people or angels/ there are only demons & animals/
- In the Devils lair – there is only sinister fire/ with horrifying demonic monsters/ waiting to rip the flesh from your bodies/ and devour your souls instantly/

VERSE 3: The mission turns brutal/ you've traveled, deep into the devils lair/ things turn critical/ MIZeRY is far from God, and his power turns brittle/ now things look fatal/ the devil has complete control/ MIZeRY's faith is entirely lost/ his will doesn't break remaining strong/ as he prays out loud/ asking his holy Lord/ In thy Name Jesus Christ/ give me the power to survive/ and complete my mission of taking the devils life/ grant me the speed to slay him right beneath his own eyes/ I shall return alive/ chanting & praising thy name, O-Lord Jesus Christ/ On my way out of this dreadful abyss/ I hear a slight whisper, and the sound of a kiss/ shall I explore this dungeons seductiveness/ destroying all seven deadly sins/ starting with lustful adventures, and medusa's tantalizing minions/ This wasn't part of my mission/ so instead I'll go back to Heaven/ & return with 3 powerful friends/ besides, I must haste fully return the devils red soul/ back to where it belongs/ for its too powerful & evil, for 1 man to even hold/ for the record, Yaa, this story has never been foretold/

HOOK/CHORUS:

- In the wild – there are no sanctuaries, churches, or safe havens/
- In the Jungle – there are no people or angels/ there are only demons & animals/
- In the Devils lair – there is only sinister fire/ with horrifying demonic monsters/ waiting to rip the flesh from your bodies/ and devour your souls instantly/

SUMMARY - I'll explain it like this. "Immediately upon finishing this song, I realized that no matter what: people shall doubt and ridicule me for what I'm about to unleash from my songs. Ultimately, "The Refusal is necessary, by all human means realistically." However, as this story progressed I realized a few things. For one, this song isn't just about others refusing who and what I am, but it was about me refusing the same at first. As this song progresses, we also see a story unfolding: The story of Saint Michael Thee Archangel and his mission bestowed upon him by God. His mission is to kill the devil and return his red-soul to Gods secure, unimaginable abyss. By far, this is one of my most meaningful and respected songs, I have ever recorded. Not only because it explains my very mission and purpose in life; but it lyrically and sophistically justifies, that most people shall refuse me as their very Lord and Saviour."

Chapter 13: Song 5 – The Chase (13:5)

The Chase: (Lyrics not included in novel)

SUMMARY - I'll explain it like this. "The song "The Chase" is a movie scene song only during an extremely adventurous and action packed chase between an Arch-demon and Gabriél: as she is working as a spy. Although, the song doesn't contain actual lyrics in which are important, the song was created to amplify the suspense in which takes place in the scene. The scene begins with a meet between Gabriél and the Demon. Gabriél becomes made by the Demon and leads her on an extreme deadly car chase. Several minutes later, this chase ends in a car crash and she pursues on foot. Long and behold the Demon leads Gabriél into an ambush, within one of the Devils lair's on Earth. As Gabriél enters this lair, she looses the Demon, and becomes out numbered.

As a result, she is seen fighting in an intense action packed scene. She is then seen, fighting for survival, against a hundred or so Demons; hence the next song title"…

Chapter 13: Song 6 – Devils Ambush Gabriél (13:6)

Devils Ambush Gabriél: *Not previously written

INTRO: "Jesus Christ, please bless me and just take control over my mind and my body; please let them know how to get out."

VERSE 1: Okay so I've been there when I'm sleeping/ the devils creeping/ into my brain, giving me, fucking lyrical incisions/ of doom and destruction/ I feel like, its all over/ no matter what I'm doing I wake up its not over/ its like a dream within a dream/ cause the devils haunting me/ and he's creeping inside of me/ trying to fucking pollute my very thoughts and memories/ man I thought about it, its like this pain and the agony doesn't come from god, it comes from the devil/ he's trying to fucking control you/ cause he's evil/ and you can't live without doing evil/ you wanna think about it, I'm really lethal/ with my lyrical play, man I'm coming, Ya I'm trying to be deadly/ man cause the devils dreams are haunting me, and the devils dreams are haunting me/ and I wake up, naaa it's another dream/ I'm fucking stuck, falling down to a pit of nothing. It's dark, I'm hearing fucking noises/ I don't know what to do but he's catching me like choices/ I don't even have any, I'm just falling and falling/ until I hit the bottom/ and then I'm in hell, rocking/ and I don't know what to do, I'm fucking clocking/ confused/ on which moves I should do/ man there's no light, its dark and I'm doomed/ ah shit I'm hearing monsters in the room/ I don't even know what I'm in, it could be a cave, it could be a pit/ I could be in space for all I know shit/ man cause the devils dreams are haunting me/ and he's attacking me, when I'm sleeping/ mother fuckers creeping/ every time I start preaching/ I can't get out/ I don't know what to do, he's chasing me down/ he's trying to eat me and consume my soul/ what the fuck I should do? I don't know maybe I should be quiet and not say a word/…. I look around me/ devil red eyes all around me/ a hundred of em, a thousand of em/ I can't even keep count of em/ no matter what I'm doing, I'm fucking attacking them/ shit I'm going out banging/ I'm an assassin/ lethal as ever/ I ain't never dying, I'm the strongest rapper/ and God knows it and so does the devil/ and he's scared if I approach him, what I'll say/ cause Imma fucking use his own trickery against him today/ because I praise Jesus Christ/ even in the worst times/ so the devils dreams/ could be haunting me/ and I'm still gonna come at him/ I'm a mother fucking goliath gladiator assassin/ I'm fucking, Heavenly powerful, I could fly/ I got wings, no matter what you thinking, I got invincible armor, I got a hundred million lives/ I could never die/ I just have to be reborn for another time/ it takes a little, maybe couple weeks or something. I don't really know, but here let me keep it going as the devils dreams/ are haunting me/ and I just know about it, I feel like I'm in some fucking society/ or some sort of crazed insanity/ I don't know how to escape/ what the fuck should I really do, do you feel my pain/ cause I know the devil do, he's hunting me/ he's searching me/ I don't know what to do no more, but he's looking for me/ and I'm just ready to go, but Lord Jesus save me before he gets me, cause I don't know what to do/ I don't know what to do/ other than worship you, other than worship you/ Lord Jesus you give me the power that I need/ to destroy my enemies/

SUMMARY - I'll explain it like this. "This was one of the many songs, I actually didn't consciously think about or write, prior to recording. This was in fact, the first of the songs in which I went into the studio, hit record, and just started recording to the song; God simply did the rest. However, this song couldn't have been completed any better, because I believe it captures and tells a great story of a true hero. While it depicts a very vivid scene for a movie, which was the original premise for this song."

Chapter 13: Song 7 – My Pen Bleeds Judgmental Sorrow (13:7)

My Pen Bleeds Judgmental Sorrow: *not previously written

VERSE 1: Okay, my pen, bleeds, Judgmental sorrow/ I said, My pen, Bleeds, Judgmental sorrow/ okay the horror/ is damaging your kids eyes and ears/ no matter what, Imma touch your brain and give you a million fears/ that you never comprehend, or thought, or saw clearer/ than I'm giving it to Ya, brighter/ than ever/ than the sun/ you've ever felt, my energy comes from a barrel of a gun/ exploding with Hot bullets, going into

Ya lungs/ I'm choking you up every time I sung/ a word or a song/ or a rhythmic acting poetry/ no matter what'ch you doing, you could never even, keep up with me/ cause my pen bleeds Judgmental kind of sorrow/ for everyone who's living in the world of demise and horror/ Ya cause I'm coming to slay the devil/ no matter what it's like, my infinite sorrow/ is gonna judge you/ every time I make a song its something about you/ or me/ the way I used to be/ so I'm thinking about it literally/ when I used to break fathers commandments/ he gave me multiple chances/ and I kept ignoring him, for millions, of years/ time/ whatever, its like spiritually coming in my mind/ Unless I Die/ A barrel of a dice/ I'm coming around thinking about it twice/ I'm looking at twins/ all of a sudden I'm eating rice/ in china kid/ because I'm trying to spread my wisdom to the whole planet/ if you're willing to change, you've got a little time left/ but no matter what/ don't have your brain/ all deranged/ because you're fighting over change/ Ya, Ill give you millions of dollars, gold bars, whatever you want, it doesn't matter/ cause where my father/ comes from, he could make anything happen in the blink of an eye/ before you even have a time to demise/ your friends, no matter what, this is my time/ to rise/ Ya I tried to give it to you way before I was this even wrong/ in song/ in my songs/ I mean sorrow pain/ that I'm feeling, cause I give it to you in a new way/ and it doesn't need to always make sense/ but Ya Imma give it to you like Ya brains is that dense/ you're drowning in the ocean/ asking for me to reach and help you before you start drowning/ all of a sudden, I'm making you frowning/ Ya I'm coming around/ to your town/ cause I'm clowning/ man, I'm drowning/ you with my verbal play/ aahh man, are you ready to come around, praise me on Sunday/ work 6 days a week, harder than ever; or work 3 days, but 18 hours straight/

whatever you thought about man; I'm playing chess not checkers, if I ever even play/ The next move father knows I should make/ and I ask him for the Heavenly praise/ that I need, so I could raise/ all of you from your fucking demonic tortures and dooms/ Ya cause Imma clear out the entire room/ when I come through/ preaching my scriptures of wisdom, that come from a long time ago/

SUMMARY - I'll explain it like this. "This was one of the many songs, I actually didn't consciously think about or write, prior to recording. I actually recorded this song last for this album, because it took me awhile to get the courage to express my feeling about how cruel this world truly is. Also, I needed a song which would express the message God revealed on here, pertinent to Judgment Day."

Chapter 13: Song 8 – Silent Assassins Ft. DaRedANT (13:8)

Silent Assassins: *MIZeRY's verse only

INTRO: "Yaa, I promise you, you ain't even ready for this one man, ha."

VERSE 1: Let me tell you all a story about the life I could a had/ I had multiple opportunities to become a gangsta man/ so you better recognize, this is MIZeRY Solo/ I be doing everything dolo/ living the life of a gangsta/ like my man's Uncle Murda/ (East New York) I'd always stay strapped with a couple chrome nines/ Ya I'd never leave with out em, I'd have them at all times/ I've been like a ghost/ you never see me come or go/ I'd be sneaking in the dark with a black mask on/ creeping up behind you, saying gimme your cash son/ (give it up) I stay wearing gloves, so there's no finger printing/ cause them CSI Cops, they ain't never bullshitting/ I stay wearing booties on my mother fucking boots/ so they can't trace my shoes/ this is why I'm in this booth/ cause I'm nothing but living proof/ I'm speaking about the truth/ with the things I could of done/ I'm not fucking around son/ Ill go and buy a 12 gauge/ and increase this crime rate/ Ill have you begging for your life, while your screaming for the jake/ Homies call me the G man, with Central Intelligence/ Ill find you off the internet/ within a matter of minutes/ I'm the wrong mother fucker you should be looking the wrong/ cause on any given day/ I may go insane/ And if you're strapped too dog/ put this gun to my brain/ Imma rip it out'ch Ya hands/ Imma cock back the four fifth, and put it to your chin/ Imma ask you one question/ have you redeemed all your sins/ either way it doesn't matter, I'm still blasting your brains in/ I told you mother fuckers, I'm a hard core gangsta, I told you mother fuckers, I created MIZeRY/

HOOK/CHORUS: I'm the strongest dude I know, so I tell it like it is when I'm rhyming on this beat/ I was in many different crews, when I was grinding in the streets/ Then I went to East New York and I Became a GMG/ They the mother fucking hardest that's been running the whole show/ I'm GMG for life, and I don't give a fuck who knows/ If it wasn't for my Homies I would not be in this game/ and I've been telling y'all, that I've changed these ways that we really play this game/ haa Yaa, welcome to planet MIZaine/ Mother Fuckers, mother Fuckers man/ Ya MIZeRY ReCORDS we've been moving/ shake down, Red, Red ANT/ The Movement/ Dog tell these mother fuckers why they all loosing/ Ya and remind em why we the hardest/ Ohhhh…

SUMMARY - I'll explain it like this. "During my time going through spiritual trials, and my ventures in my professional music career; I eventually worked with some real hardcore rappers, whom were also real life gangsters. Basically, I became a product of my environment; desperate and confused on which path I should take. For sometime, I started thinking like the people I was surrounded by. Eventually, the thoughts and pressure became so bad that I was very close and willing to do something; I would regret, forever. This song, "Silent Assassins" explains the demonic thoughts that I had to repute out of my life, way before I was even surrounded by Gangsters. In fact, some of my music from early on was this demonic and hatful. Way before I understood, why the Devil continuously tried to pollute my very thoughts and memories. Remember though, I have not done anything of this sort in terms of murdering. However, I have sinned but not on this level. I have sinned in ways totally different then assassin type behavior; even though, we all contain the ability to do such. Ultimately, I thank God everyday for protecting me and preventing me from permanently falling astray from his love and my true destiny in life. Even in the most indecent time of humanity, even I, the beloved son of God was being tested. All the meanwhile, if I had failed, the world would have been entirely doomed."

Chapter 13: Song 9 – A Fallen Angel (13:9)

A Fallen Angel: *not previously written

INTRO: "Ya so after I was bumping this record constantly for the past hour and a half man, I couldn't write nothing. And I finally realized that a record like this comes from the heart man, you know you can't write something like this. And, this is just how Imma have to take this."

HOOK/CHORUS: A fallen angel/ happens to us all/ so why don't you praise Jesus Christ, and he'll answer your call/ cause never again shall you face a demise in this world/ A fallen angel/ happens to us all/ so why don't you praise Lord Jesus Christ, and he'll answer your calls/ and never again shall you face a demise in this world/

VERSE 1: Okay so he touches my brain every time that I fell/ down to my knees, and I felt like I was touching hell/ lyrically on this Earth, I had to ring a bell/ to wake me up from this doom/ that I put myself so, here I use this microphone in this room/ to give you something profound/ way beyond any kind of gloom/ or bright light/ that was gonna shine in Ya eyes/ giving you new way, to find new life/ so here Lord Jesus Christ tells me what I needed to teach/ every time that I preach/ using this microphone, and this gift of lyrical siege/ I mean speak/ of treasury/ that'ch you talking about, that acts as treason/ against democracy/ Ya what'ch think about it cause I only worship Lord Heavenly/ Ya cause his power, is more than you could imagine/ I'm coming at'ch you in ways you can't fathom/ I've said it way before/ many times ago/ in my songs/

HOOK/CHORUS: A fallen angel/ happens to us all/ so why don't you praise Jesus Christ, and he'll answer your call/ cause never again shall you face a demise in this world/ A fallen angel/ happens to us all/ so why don't you praise Lord Jesus Christ, and he'll answer your calls/ and never again shall you face a demise in this world/

VERSE 2: Okay so to me, you are all fallen or lost angels/ I came up with a song years ago to tell you each angle/ so you could get out of any kind of tangle/ that'ch you get into with the devil/ And I mean any evil/ because you can't live without doing something wrong/ and two wrongs/ don't make a right/ so what'ch you trying to do in your life/ look into my eyes/ I see all a your lies/ I made up a song called true lies/ and step outside a yourself, with my man sandman who now is a preacher/ literalillalala, I'm spitting on the microphone, confusing you with my fucking tongue play/ Ya Imma cuss just so you understand every word that I say/ Ya what'ch you thinking about it, you confused parlay/ Yea, are you about to go down/ call me captain sparrow/ on this pirate ship, taking over your town/

HOOK/CHORUS: A fallen angel/ happens to us all/ so why don't you praise Jesus Christ, and he'll answer your call/ cause never again shall you face a demise in this world/ A fallen angel/ happens to us all/ so why don't you praise Lord Jesus Christ, and he'll answer your calls/ and never again shall you face a demise in this world/

VERSE 3: Okay so this is dedicated to my younger brother Vincent Scott/ Ya cause mans, the devil took care of him/ like he wasn't even deserving/ something so harsh, cruel, cause he's got autism/ what'ch you know about it he's locked in the system/ mother fucker doesn't even know that kind of life/ and I should be doing the bid for him, just cause he shouldn't be in that kind of life/ he ain't built like the rest of us, man cause we did a life of crime/ what do you know about it man, I spit it through these rhymes/ my pain that I've seen, that they come from my mind/ everything that I've seen, every fucking night/ that I wanted to die, slitting my wrist/ or drinking myself stupid/ or causing trouble in the streets, selling drugs, or stupid shit/ Ya what'ch you know about it, come walk in my shoes real quick/ I promise you'll get locked up, shot up, or dead bitch slit/ you know nothing about it/ so I give you punch lines brick/ right to your face/ cause Imma damage you all the way down to your dense case/ Ya fuck it, you gonna be a snitch/ Ill kill you before you got time to say shit/

SUMMARY - I'll explain it like this. "This was one of the many songs, I actually didn't consciously think about or write, prior to recording. Upon completing this song, I had realized a personal truth about my past life; simply, I was involved in some terrible things. In addition, I also realized that I had overcome and beaten those terrible things; while changing my life around for the positive, in the way God would have desired. Ultimately, I made this song as a dedication to my Autistic brother, whom gotten himself into some foolish trouble pertaining to younger girls. Truth be told it wasn't fair because his mentality is of a much younger age which led him to date a younger girl. No, I don't think his mental capacity should excuse his actions but a two year prison sentence and potentially worse doesn't seem to make much sense justifiably. Either way, this is one of my most heart-felt records and I hope all can relate to loosing someone they love. Especially to ridiculous circumstances, whether legally or not."

Chapter 13: Song 10 – My Last Words (13:10)

My Last Words:

VERSE 1: My composure shall never reveal it's true exposure/ my true nature, is relentless/ my inner thoughts are endless/ my divine Powers are limitless/ my voice is Heavenly soothing, I leave this world speechless/ my style or swag – leaves you all breathless/ my persona is reckless/ my soul and my body are age-less/ humility is a rarity, beyond the miraculous/ the essence of my presence is vicious/ my energy captivates and sets you in a state of paralysis/ how dare you guess my past methods/ my future is infinitely random, no guesstimates / I'm not of this realm, no special effects-ess/ the repulsiveness/ of your aroma, is lethal madness/ I am divine – enivid, rewind, I'm a word chemist/ I love all women, I'm no sexist/ I'll kill all perverted rapists/ I could be the best, but I'm no scam artist/

HOOK/CHORUS: There's something about your style, it's a certain way that you move/ It's the beautiful color in your eyes, that makes me feel the way that I do/ I can't change me, or how I've begun to feel/ but I love you and I want to show you this is real/ soo, will you be my wife; Deal or no deal?

VERSE 2: The possibility of you winning is impossible/ humanities theories on life are not plausible/ this is Jesus Christ speaking, no audible/ no way! This is a super bowl/ marketing schemes beyond control/ Star Fox – Barrel roll/ life alert – elderly take falls/ Yea, I'm Jim Jones, word – soccer balls? (ballin') Ehh – Lil Wayne: Burrr; a Bird Call? Marijuana in pill form is *Marinol*/ drugs are bad if made to be edible/ and sustain effects while on the internal/ Rick Ross is too fat, Imma call him Mr. Plentiful/ I'm an Unofficial English Major, Ya homie call me lyrical/ I'm the new form of the true son of God – Call me Michael, Thee Archangel/ Bible stories are not all fables/ time to wake up if you only live in the physical/ I'm Jesus Christ divinely magical/ eternally humble/ and man, I don't mean to make your brain jumble/ but I'm only doing it for those who follow/

SUMMARY - I'll explain it like this. "My last words" are to elaborate upon my last words, summarized. Simply, I wanted to create a song to list a summarized version of a few facts in my life, all revolving around my truth. While venting about it on a song."

Chapter 13: Song 11 – Heavy Weight (13:11)

Heavy Weight: *Only Hook/Chorus Pre-written

VERSE 1: Okay so I'm a heavy weight mother fucking assassin/ I'm powerful in ways, you can't even fathom/ so Lord has sent me to your town to start attacking/ all the demons that are fucking, causing hell on Earth/ I've seen it all ever since my birth/ and I'm talking about my first/ thousands of years ago/ way before you could even fucking know how I used to roll/ cause Ya man, I'm holy/ and you know nothing about it, but this is a story/ so keep up with me/ because I'm about to start taking you, on new heights, new levels of reality/ you'll feel like your hitting the levels of insanity/ or this music is hitting you physically/ as its pumping through your veins, through your blood stream/ no matter what man, cause I do it with no team/ it must mean/ I'm Heavenly/ which means/ I stand uniquely/ Individually/ As I was sent, to start saving you literally/ no matter what you thinking about, it must be wrong, because I see through you physically/

HOOK/CHORUS: I'm a heavy weight, angelic dealing/ Heavenly sword wieldin'/ lethal type of assassin/ I move fast, whether day or night/ with stealth flight/ powerful moves, and I haven't lost a fight/ ready to survive/ I'm a heavy weight, angelic dealing/ Heavenly sword wieldin'/ lethal type of assassin/ I move fast, whether day or night/ with stealth flight/ powerful moves, and I haven't lost a fight/ ready to survive/

VERSE 2: Okay so I've been down to hell, multiple times/ and I didn't know what to do, every time/ except, asking Lord, to save me/ cause I don't wanna be here man, I'm trapped/ I don't wanna be here/ its like enemies/ taunting me/ haunting me/ trying to kill me/ and slaughter me/ rip the flesh from my body/ and I don't wanna feel that way no more/ ever again, so I felt it, and I went down to the doors of doom/ and I found a way out of this terrible room/ so I don't know/ what are you doing to me/ are you trying to fucking subliminally/ toughen up me/ Ya I don't know, I'm stuttering against thee/ cause the devil is more powerful than me/ and I need more energy/ and more power/ to slay him down/ where he's standing, in his own tower/

HOOK/CHORUS: I'm a heavy weight, angelic dealing/ Heavenly sword wieldin'/ lethal type of assassin/ I move fast, whether day or night/ with stealth flight/ powerful moves, and I haven't lost a fight/ ready to survive/ I'm a heavy weight, angelic dealing/ Heavenly sword wieldin'/ lethal type of assassin/ I move fast, whether day or night/ with stealth flight/ powerful moves, and I haven't lost a fight/ ready to survive/

VERSE 3: Cause I'm a Heavenly, angelic dealing/ Heavenly sword wieldin'/ lethal type of assassin/ I move fast, whether day or night/ with stealth flight/ powerful moves, and I haven't lost a fight/

Ya, Cause I'm back, feeling invincible/ I just killed the devil/ and I don't even know about it, but I'm living for God, not any evil/ so I think about it, here I'll give you something lethal/ My scriptures/ of Pictures/ that I paint every day/ cause I'm a literacy, Mastermind/ and everything you doing man, you ain't beating my rhymes/ there like the puzzles of time/ I'm a chef/ everything I'm doing, Ya cause it's a fucking reality check/ for all of you kids doing bad things, in this reality/ that'ch you abusing/ cause you know nothing about it, as your refusing/ god/ no matter what, I'm not teasing/ I'm not trying to tame you neither/ I ain't trying to do nothing, but show you the path, and the light/ when I'm making this music every night/ cause I think about it, praying to God, playing the drums/ when I do it like sobbing/ Ya, cause I'm sad sometimes/ and a sssthink about it, I smoke a little weed, and than I come back aliveeeee/

HOOK/CHORUS: I'm a heavy weight, angelic dealing/ Heavenly sword wieldin'/ lethal type of assassin/ I move fast, whether day or night/ with stealth flight/ powerful moves, and I haven't lost a fight/ ready to survive/ I'm a heavy weight, angelic dealing/ Heavenly sword wieldin'/ lethal type of assassin/ I move fast, whether day or night/ with stealth flight/ powerful moves, and I haven't lost a fight/ ready to survive/

SUMMARY - I'll explain it like this. "This was one of the many songs, I actually didn't consciously think about or write, prior to recording. I wrote "Heavy Weight" strictly to serve one purpose: to describe how strong, unique, and powerful I truly am. This song was designed to create one of the most important chapters in my movie. While describing a summed version of all the trials, I've faced in life. These trials as you can see, clearly made me what I was meant to be in God's army; a strong willed, uniquely different, & powerfully angelic being: Whom will stop at nothing to slay the devil; paving a path of peace, for all those chosen. This song is one of my most powerfully involved descriptions of what I'll become to protect God, Heaven, & Earth from all evil."

Chapter 13: Song 12 – If I Fail (13:12)

If I Fail: *Not previously written

VERSE 1: "Okay well, it's been a long journey and I'm still not done with my mission." Okay so 15 years ago, I thought about it, masterminding/ something/ when I was youngin/ and I was just thinking about it/ na man, I just had to start writing/ the pain that I was feeling/ with everyday, cause it was fucking hurtful/ I didn't know what to do/ Ya so I turned spiritual/ I was born and raised a catholic/ changed over to Christianity/ eventually/ when I learned about the truth about reality/ Ya so, Ya like I said, my pain and agony/ was controlling me/ like, it was everything in my reality/ so I wanted to write music to escape such harsh realities/ Yaa, then I started looking upon society/ was wondering about chasing my dreams/ because when I was real young they told us to chase my dream/ when I turned 13/ it got so harsh, incredibly sick/ that I had to come up with a alternate reality/ to find a way, so I wouldn't fail/ at nothing again in this world/ so can't you tell/ I've got a massive story that I've got to tell/

HOOK/CHORUS: Ya soo I, will never go to hell/ because I don't live my life by any kind of evil/ and If I fail/ it will be really brutal/ for all of you/ and I'm not playing games, cause I will create this hellish society/ that'ch you all feared for many centuries/ and if you think I'm playing, then why don't you try me/ but thou shall never tempt thee Almighty/

VERSE 2: Ya I know I'm Almighty & I'm holy/ so I keep it to myself, and I lay on the low/ what'ch you know about it, but I'm always on the roll/ meaning on the move, always on the go/ what'ch you know about kicking some magical flow/ because I could do it anytime, come to my show/ pay the toll/ and Imma give you something so spectacular/ your gonna go home, confused and drained/ thinking I sucked your soul from your brain/ you know nothing about it, so here's my gain/ Imma give you lyrical dungeon games/ Yaa, what'ch you know about it, I'll have any man slain/ if you think you could combat me/ I'll fucking grow more powerful than ever you've seen/ Ya Imma break it down so instantly/ (poof) It will seem I disappeared right in front of your eyes with Ninja Mastery/ Literally/ I'm fucking cynically/ killing you with my vocabulary/ to the point I'm supernaturally/ destroying you mentally/ and you think about it, but I'm unconditionally/ the only one like me/ except for my father, who's twice as holy/ Trust me, I reference nothing of this galaxy/ I'm an angelic guardian/ Sworn, to protect fathers Kingdom/

HOOK/CHORUS: Ya soo I, will never go to hell/ because I don't live my life by any kind of evil/ and If I fail/ it will be really brutal/ for all of you/ and I'm not playing games, cause I will create this hellish society/ that'ch you all feared for many centuries/ and if you think I'm playing, then why don't you try me/ but thou shall never tempt thee Almighty/

VERSE 3: Okay, systematically/ and mathematically/ the truth about MIZeRY/ is, it's an insurance policy/ just in case you get more wild, and try to dethrone me/ and try to come and attack my Heavenly palace; man cause I know about it/ I've seen it all, I created it/ I know I shouldn't have, but now I'm trying to fix it/ through my son Jesus Christ/ he's coming back, man to take only that are wise/ and only that are right/ meaning that they worship and live only like Jesus Christ/ Ya cause JRL/ All the time, I know about it, can't you tell/ Turn up the treble/ so you understand my lyrical play/ my vocabularies/ hitting you like every single day/ but you should worship me like every Sunday/ and I know you don't pray/ because, I hear everything/ Ya soo are you trying to fool me with your sinister magic/ Yaa, I know about it, I live as a prophet/ This is why I died for your sins/ Back in the days, I was crucified by some crazy Romans/ Ironically, I'm in the form of Sicilians/ A true hero, no villains/ you should be thanking me/ worshipping me/ for being kind, loving, and friendly/ to all – even if they oppose me/ Yes, all shall hear my holy trumpets/ **(trumpet sounds)** Begging me for forgiveness/ blinded by the truth – living by lies & violence/ no discussion/ I've made my decision/

HOOK/CHORUS: Ya soo I, will never go to hell/ because I don't live my life by any kind of evil/ and If I fail/ it will be really brutal/ for all of you/ and I'm not playing games, cause I will create this hellish society/ that'ch you all feared for many centuries/ and if you think I'm playing, then why don't you try me/ but thou shall never tempt thee Almighty/

SUMMARY - I'll explain it like this. "This was one of the many songs, I actually didn't consciously think about or write, prior to recording. Originally, this song was supposed to be the negative ending in the movie plot. Ultimately, the Bible states that if **Saint Michael Thee Archangel** fails to slay the Devil; God will completely destroy Earth and most within in it. However, even with this negative ending, as *Revelation* states: only 144,000 would be saved; which is the same result, even in the positive ending. I also believe, Michael is the second incarnation of Jesus Christ in the end of day's era. After I heard this song and was near completion of the first of two discs, for this epic scripture/prophecy from God: I realized, this is way beyond just an amazing plot for a movie; this is the message God wanted delivered, for the world, and for myself to hear. In the end, I strongly don't believe Saint Michael will fail. I also truly believe, the true ending of life and existence or for this movie shall be: Saint Michael slaying the devil and Jesus Christ returning, upon his victory, to reclaim Earth. At such time, he will rapture its remaining survivors, creating a new world for all to live in peace and harmony with God." **(See The New World – Disc 2 Song 20 "Day of My Return" for more on the positive ending)**.

Chapter 13: Song 13 – Armageddon's Eve (13:13)

Armageddon's Eve: *Not previously written

INTRO: "Yo, Yo, Yo, this one's called Armageddon's Eve and I want all the lights out in this mother fucker. Cause, we partying in the club; like it's the last night in the world. Okay so this is MC Master MIZeRY hitting you live and direct. And, I've got my man DJ Provenchh on the mother fucking ones and two's you know what I mean."

VERSE 1: Okay, Okay, grooving with me/ riding with me/ bouncing with me/ are you in the club with me/ aahh just need you to feel it/ just need you to move it/ I just need you to groove it/ Ya grind on Ya girl, grind on Ya guy/ I don't care what'ch you doing, just get out my booth/ I want you to feel it, Ya I'm about to tare off the roof/ Homie, no fire/ understand, I don't like your attire/ you better come fresh and so clean/

anytime you come around me/ Ya cause, I can rock these beats/ like I do it for breakfast literally/ or I'm fucking your girl from the rear, actuality/ Ya, no matter what I'm harder than you, I'm harder than everybody/ Ya walk in my shoes/ I promise you'll get stuck like you was in fucking crazy glue/ Ya cause you in crazy town, coo, coo cachou/ fucking around with my crew/ Homie, Ya cause It's the Second Coming's eve/ and at the end of this night I wanna be sleazed/ which means/ I wanna be drunk, and trippin off pills/ looking for Milfs/ ready to fuck me before the end of this film/ If you think I'm fucking around, than come try me/ because it's the last night to party/ in all the world and reality/ so if you ain't ready, then get the fuck out of my vicinity/ because I'm only rocking with MIZeRY/ and his affiliates, you understand me/ Okay, Okay, okay, I need you to get up, get up real quick/ cause time is running, I'm slick/ shit, All of a sudden you fall down like you're heavy bricks/ Shit/ Okay I got the illest skill in hip hop, wanna contest me/ meet me the time and place/ put up everything your worth/ I'll match you/ times you by two/ and Imma destroy you/ before you can call your crew/ to come up with a punch line just to save you/ And understand, I'm better than you/ because I think about it, and I mastered this skill faster than you/ and I'm incredibly delicious in everyway/ with my vocabulary/ mother fuckers is wondering how I do it, cynically/ I'm the best, when it comes to this shit, verbally/ mother fucker I'm destroying you, with every ounce in me/ it's fucking tearing your insides in and out/ no matter what Imma be fucking your girl in and out/ and she's gonna love it so much she's got to shout/ And I'm a little profound/ with my lyrical play/ cause my sound effects is destroying you with every move that I make/ So what'ch you wanna do, come at me like you playing chess/ naa man, Imma rip your mother fucking heart out'ch your chest/ and Imma say Homie, is this what you wanted to do, no contest/ trust me I'm the best/ at this lyrical game/ I put all the rest to rest/ and shame/ Yaa, what'ch you know about it, I'm fucking diverged and deranged/ Ya cause everything that'ch you feeling man, is MIZeRY's Pain/ Which stems from Jesus Christ's Brain/ Ya man, cause I've seen a lot of mother fuckers slain/ and I love using these words when I rhyme in this game/ Ya I'm a little fucking demented/ I was in a psyche ward, but not by choice/ Oh My God, I need to rejoice/ cause I've been saved, and It's the last night to party/ so where my shorties/ cause I wanna get a little freaky/
Ya I should get the suckie/ Sixty Nining/ Whatever man, is you really grinding/ I see you

girls, you wanna start riding me on my big pole, up and down/ like I'm something profound/ you need to make a song/ about how I role/ because every time you come to my show/ you see something new/ Exquisitely delicious, this is why I'm new/ ohh shit, put me on the shelf, I'll make you a couple mill too/ Ah ah ah ah ah ah ah ah Okay, Okay, everybody clap, everybody clap, Okay/ This is the last night we can party/ No fright/ peace and happiness, for the rest of our lives/ cause second life is coming, and no joke/ this is real talk/ Ya shit, watch my mean walk/ Ya, I got the swagger/ you wanna be about bragging/ but what'ch you talking about, am I fagging/ with my dragging/ queens/ What'ch you talking about, Am I slick, or mean?/

SUMMARY - I'll explain it like this. "This was one of the many songs, I actually didn't consciously think about or write, prior to recording. This song actually came about very last minute, when a good friend of mine whom recently started taking up Disc jockeying, offered this beat to me. After I spent about an hour reviewing the beat, I quickly decided to just go into the studio and attempt making a song to it. Literally, after 2 takes this is what developed and was produced. I realized, titling this song would be perfect as Armageddon's Eve, since that seemed to be the predominant theme. Shortly after recording to this song, I made an executive decision that this song will be displayed during the ending credits of my movie. Ultimately, this song is to describe what my plans are for the last night, prior to rapture/Judgment day; not only for myself, but as a recommendation to all. I'm mostly kidding though, because I enjoy people whom have a sense of humor. However, take into consideration: when Judgment Day occurs, you will not be able to live life how we used to"…

Chapter 14
The New World – Disc 2

The New World – Disc 2 is a continuation of "*The 2nd Coming – Disc 1*." Disc 1 represents mostly the dark times, leading up to Judgment Day. Disc 2 represents mostly the good & after times of Judgment days. Both concepts were created one evening in January 2012, when I awoke abruptly early in the morning, caused by premonitions and vivid dreams. This time the dreams were far different, to the point: God was speaking to me, while directing my life onto a path of a righteous mission. This path I was shown, was the revealing and understanding to succeed at **The 2nd Coming;** which stimulated the creation of this book, and movie of The Second Coming of Jesus Christ. Immediately upon waking, I had commenced working on this project, the one you are reading before your very eyes. I first started working on the music sound tracks, because that is what I am most familiar with and skilled at. I had created the movie sound tracks titled "*The 2nd Coming – Disc 1 & The New World – Disc 2*." I soon realized that with writing or simply just recording this project; I was ultimately writing the script or scripture for the actual Second Coming. Effective immediately, I worked vigorously with exhausting long hours both on a regular day job and working on recording these albums. Almost immediately, I knew collectively these albums would contain 33 songs total, making for a good fit for my personality. Furthermore, describing the entirety of what's to come in the world. The first CD "*The 2nd Coming – Disc 1*" would contain the main basis for the script and the actuality of my reality, derived from *The New Testament*. The second CD "*The New World - Disc 2*" would contain songs of prophecies and new scriptures that were given to me through God.

I believe, these writings are a continuation from where the Bible left off in *Revelation.* "*The New World-Disc 2*" is to represent and show a series of events: Not only in my life, but in the lives of everyone else; whilst explaining, what is to become of the world. Some of these events, would represent God's proposed intentions for the world; while showing and metaphorically explaining to me, how I will assist in creating the path for the new world. One of the most revolutionary and inspirational songs I have ever recorded is song 16, "Victory." This song explains the definition of the very word, and its relation to conquering all evil, and securing a new world for all of God's Children. Song 20, "Day of My Return" is a song that was recorded without writing any of the lyrics, and I had only made one attempt at recording the entire song. The only explanation I have is that God had taken control of my vessel, and allowed me to remember my life as Jesus Christ. The song is about Jesus Christ being crucified and how I have returned in Michael's form; whilst explaining, my last intentions for the world: ultimately creating, A New World.

Chapter 14: Song 1 – Transformation (14:1)

Transformation:

VERSE 1: "Aahh okay, I made it, we made it, we feeling good. We getting paid, one day." Call this gift that I have a little incredible/ I know about it, but its delectable/ I'm exquisitely delicious/ you mother fuckers want it like I'm MIZalicious/ making up words as I go along/ all of a sudden I'm cruising so long/ Ya I got records that make songs/ and it comes out, like this shit is right and its never even wrong/ You just want the words, to find the incentive, the inspiration that you might need to succeed/ and party/ however you feel necessary/ so, why don't we all live in the same society/ fighting for what, just to be the popular guy, trust me you don't want that slot/ I've been there, I rose to the top, I came back to the bottom/ and now this is where I'm at, slopped and all/ I ain't even feeling it, I'm feeling only being poor/ nothing like rich/ cruising the way I should kid/ I've been around, real rich people, it's just the way it is/ but I'm trying to save some people/ and this is not a lie, I read it in the Bible/ this is my spiritual calling/ and you could do it whatever, but I know you're the one falling/ cause you're not listening/ your fucking ears are clogged, like you're deaf or something/ all of a sudden/ you get confused in my rhythm/ you mother fuckers don't even know about it/ but I'm dribbling/ like I'm fucking Kobe, or Shaq/ whatever you doing, all of a sudden it's a heart attack/ rap attack/ matter of fact/ I'm mathematically a genius.

SUMMARY - I'll explain it like this. "This song was simply an introductory song. I wrote this song to explain some facts about myself and represent how clever I could be on a whim, when recording music. In addition, I was quickly representing my life in a sum up of a minute or so. While mentioning that for many years, many have been blinded as to what it is I'm trying to teach."

Chapter 14: Song 2 – I'm a Genius (14:2)

I'm a Genius: *Not previously written except for third verse.

INTRO: "Okay well, if I wasn't so smart, tell me how I made this record, within two hours, without writing down one word. Yaa."

HOOK/CHORUS: I worship Jesus/ and I'm a genius/ I use lyrical movie scenes/ to create pictures to show you Eden/ as I'm speaking/ I'm slowing teaching/ you moves of intelligence/ I'm a genius/ I worship Jesus/ and I'm a genius/ I use lyrical movie scenes/ to create pictures to show you Eden/ as I'm speaking/ I'm slowing teaching/ you moves of intelligence/ I'm a genius/

VERSE 1: Ya so I'm down to my last eighth/ I'm becoming afraid/ because when it comes to weed/ I'm a fiend/ and I need it/ just to make these records so clean/ Ya so think about it man, cause I get a little mean/ and profound on these records that I use/ to create tools/ to teach your fucking youth/ something more intelligent than you/ have been giving them, because the school system is fucked, no corrections/ my intelligence/ allows me to run an election/ for president/ because I'm on a mission/ to decimate all evil seductions/ and where I come from, there's no imperfections/ thank you lord/

HOOK/CHORUS: I worship Jesus/ and I'm a genius/ I use lyrical movie scenes/ to create pictures to show you Eden/ as I'm speaking/ I'm slowing teaching/ you moves of intelligence/ I'm a genius/ I worship Jesus/ and I'm a genius/ I use lyrical movie scenes/ to create pictures to show you Eden/ as I'm speaking/ I'm slowing teaching/ you moves of intelligence/ I'm a genius/

VERSE 2: Okay so I'm surrounded by the number three/ now it's starting to haunt me/ so I thought about it ever since I was three/ living on blocks, houses, that all round about three/ Ya back in the days, I was adding up the mathematics/ like I had to use these tactics/ to avoid assassins trying to hunt me/ kill me/ I'm talking about the devil secretly/ Ya but shh, don't let anybody know about the mathematics that I use, intelligence like pie/ man add it up man I be floating in the sky/ very soon, once I figure out the path to my magical Powers/ every hour/ devour/ evil cowards/

HOOK/CHORUS: I worship Jesus/ and I'm a genius/ I use lyrical movie scenes/ to create pictures to show you Eden/ as I'm speaking/ I'm slowing teaching/ you moves of intelligence/ I'm a genius/ I worship Jesus/ and I'm a genius/ I use lyrical movie scenes/ to create pictures to show you Eden/ as I'm speaking/ I'm slowly teaching/ you moves of intelligence/ I'm a Genius/

VERSE 3: I'm a genius/ using tactics of a chemical extremist/ wrote this verse within seconds/ as if I had no time to diffuse a nuclear bomb/ my voice is like an atomic drum/ blowing out your ear drum's/ beyond medical repairs/ solved by mathematical sums/ I'm intelligently powerful to the point you must run/ Or explode from personification of pressure/ don't touch me cause I'm fragile like nuclear fissure/ I'm sharp tongued, Ill make you fear/ the true power of God/ His wrath, is harder than Dr. Dre's beats of aftermath/ I'm fast like a panther cat/ I no longer hang with Rats or white trash/ I tried to save you all/ instead you decided to ignore my Heavenly calls/ So it's time to go/ as I start to spit slow/ use words of a child/ you are still lost in the wild/ my last words are simple/ praise Christ or die/ for the end of time/ is on the rise/ for all evil gals and guys/ no lies/ so goodbye/ "Ya that's what I'm talking about, living life to the fullest man."

SUMMARY - I'll explain it like this. "I'm a Genius" is one of my more personal stories. Originating, all the way back to when I was about three years old, and I lived at 3 Brookwood Street. As I grew older, I became more resilient and aware of my surroundings: Starting with accepting and not accepting, all things in life; depending on which aspects we discuss, that is. As I became a teen, I started mixing in with the wrong crowds and people. I related with these people easiest because they had as many problems as I did. As I became a young adult, I discovered that mingling with the wrong people was God's plan to keep me hidden. Hidden, not only from the devil himself but also from the people whom secretly work with him. The people whom would attempt to exploit me and my many talents. The third verse on this song was a simple testament to an old friend whom agitated me beyond belief. Within 60 seconds or so, I created that verse and it was to prove to him and others how intelligent and powerful I truly am. This song is by far one of my more private and historical songs based on my entire life. Not to mention, the display and growth of my unlimited intelligence."

Chapter 14: Song 3 – The New Age - Anthem (14:3)

The New Age - Anthem: *First half written; second part of song is cut.

VERSE 1: "Within the Storm, you get lost/ can't see five feet in front of you/ so what do you do/ you ask for peace/ ask for the sight/ and he will show you what you need

to be… Everything you see/ revolves around me/ in 360 degrees/ I'm so cold, Ya I make this Ice freeze/ I'm always discreet/ anytime I let the trigger squeeze/ I'm so volatile every time that I breathe/ My mouth opens as these lyrics speak/ urging me to resist this need/ to bury you 10 feet/ beneath/ God's powerful reach/ I'm extreme/ musically, I am my own team/ with an I in me/ as in MIZeRY/ Ya just me/ I'm slipping, slowly loosing grip/ Life's so crazy I swear its always a trip/ Lord Jesus Christ/ Don't ever let me slip/ Crazy ass lyric's/ pure catholic/ No atheist/ powerful chemist/ metaphorically making science/ mathematical skills of pure violence/ Judgment Day 2012, shh pure silence/ you should praise his excellence/ all the meanwhile you should fear his existence/ All true statements/ someday this will all end/ no longer being intense/ so you should repent/ otherwise soon comes death/ at the cost of everyone's expense/ No lies, just an honest test/ to separate the bad from the rest/ so I say this aloud as I repent/ Lord Jesus save my soul/ grant me eternal forgiveness/ poetically, I am the best/ sworn to tell the truth till the day that I rest/ I'm excessive/ with progressive/ sound effects/ Ya, where I come from/ I'm a general, in Gods Kingdom/ I'm loved by all the people/ Here on Earth, shit is to lethal/ to see beyond this evil/ where I come from, were all created equal/ so I was born, to offer some sequels/ I'm gifted, call it sociably surgical/ I'm an angelic maniac/ driven into human insanity, from being a brainy-ac/ searching for facts/ which most humans lack/ So I hide, wearing this mask/ keeping me hidden from this filthy ass trash/ terrorists and aids infested ass/ no jokes, don't laugh/ I'm a wizard with potions and genius extract/ unattainable by you, I have no contacts/ no awards/ straight rap tracks/ with diamond strength production/ intelligent modulation/ producing fermions/ that conquer your sensations/ call it MIZeRY seduction/ unique, powerful, poison, spiritual injection/ I'm necessary for survival, spiritual sickness, no infection/ Mike's roaring/ AKA speaking/ It's Gods calling/ I see the chosen/ cause their acts aren't appalling/ I'm soaring/ every second you waste snoring/ I'm listening/ Inching in/ Ya I need a better look, Grim cold jerk/ good guys really do fail/ I'm a living example/ I'm not tangible/ the industry forces us to be sellable/ I told y'all I won't be edible/ I'm barely
incredible/ with dreams of not being single/ maybe rich someday off on bumping on these jingles/ aahh fuck it, as I remain humble/ I'm giving it to Ya, I don't mean to make it jumble/…

SUMMARY - I'll explain it like this. *"The New Age –Anthem*" is exactly what the title means. I wanted to create a song that explains and represents an anthem for all the younger people of our society. Allowing them to relate, while understanding how metaphorical my life has become. Including, why I go through such trials for us all. This was a song that came fluidly and very quickly one afternoon in the studio. However, there is a free-styled second half of this song. Unfortunately, I cut it out because it doesn't relate as much to the actual topic or uphold much relevance to my point. The free-styled version is more of a cool catchy freestyle compiled to relate with hip hop and its many styles."

Chapter 14: Song 4 – I'm Blessed (14:4)

I'm blessed: *previously half written the rest is song only.

VERSE 1: aahh, Ya, okay, Ya well I'm blessed to express such excessive/ success/ that I resist/ the negative/ remaining assertive/ I'm gifted/ Drugs drifted/ I'm lifted/ Intensifies/ Now rise/ No surprise/ I love Jesus Christ/ Why fight/ when peace, is what I live by/ expensive habits/ jacking rabbits/ life time of embarrassments/ emotionally energized/ destroy bad guys/ no school so why revise/ I've realized/ I trust my faith/ no matter what you portray/ I'm holy/ and emotionally a roller coaster/ tossing you up & down, side to new life/ reverse each side/ new ocean, no tides/ drowning souls, death, and demise/ Ya well I have angel eyes/ Human form/ degrades my power/ I devour/ every hour/ new cowards/ I'm conflicted/ with logistics/ of existence/ which transforms into exquisite persistence/ Energy soul intensifies/ break stealth, no disguise/ I'm the captain of this enterprise/ Star Wars smuggler/ fast talker/ massive juggler/ juggling Ya/ inside of a jungle/ ready to go mingle/ go figure/ No toy, but the last action hero/ I don't like these zero's/ The A,B,C,s/ may be necessary/ spiritually/
the words become reality/ perfect technicality/ I'm screaming, I can't sleep/ tossing at night, I'm having crazy dreams/ Assassin's attacking me/ breathe/ Immortality/ I'm back, spiritually/ I'm stronger than I'll ever be/ Ya cause Lord Jesus gives me the power that I need/ to defeat my enemies/ while you sleep/ I'm here to protect you, so come and follow

me/ if you want to see a new reality/ cause I'm living for my century/ I'm trying to teach these fucking ignorant little children, what it is like; me/ I'm giving you the wisdom/ the intelligence/ man, cause we need to survive/ man this world is going to have a demise/ if we don't change our life around, by the end of this night/ mother fuckers you ready to fight/ for the crown; cause I'm doing it, I'm coming to your town silently, cause this is how I'm grooving/ giving you lyrics of dooming/ what'ch you meaning/ all of a sudden, I'm crailing, killing/ the room again/ shit, mother fuckers telling me to settle down cause I'm angry/ shit whatever…

SUMMARY - I'll explain it like this. "When I made this song, I wanted to show the world how talented I was, not only musically but poetically too. I also wanted to show the world the wide range of metaphors and lyrical ability I contain. Simply, this song is to show the world how Blessed I am and that I was given an amazing gift to make music. Going beyond musically, this song represents a metaphoric-lyricism of my inner power. A power in which I am still relentlessly meditating to uncover, yet again!"

Chapter 14: Song 5 – Dancing with Angels (14:5)

Dancing with Angels: *Not previously written.

VERSE 1: My Heavenly touch/ is gonna make you feel like you're getting a head rush/ straight up and down your thighs, and your legs, Ya now strut/ everything that you got what'ch your worth/ no matter what you really thinking about, you're really worth more/ you're all angels, its just your fucking blinded by the evil things around you/ you can't even see the truth, inside you/ you can't even feel it/ all of a sudden I'm giving you this as a scripture/ I'm painting pictures/ so you understand it on a whole different wave length/ turn the dial, to my station/ and you'll see what its like if I start hating/ I'll unleash Satan/ to devour/ all you sinners/ as I salvage the righteous new believers/ my children don't fret/ for I sometimes doubt/ always remember if you're down and out/ look up to the clouds/ stern and proud/ and say once aloud/

HOOK/CHORUS: on a rare occasion/ I allow all adults one celebration/ anything goes with no limitations/ except one rule, follow Gods commandments/ starting with a pairing of angels/ simple rules/ two to tango, or only even pairs/ Ya cause I told you, you're dancing with my angels/ when you're in Heaven, you are dancing with my angels/

VERSE 2: Okay I came down, so I can sage (save) my people/ you know nothing about it, so let me speak and let me reach you/ touch you in ways that you've never felt, all you've got to do is believe and stick with your faith in me/ because the Bible tells you all; everything you needed to know and understand about me/ and this is what he's told me/ constantly everyday that I suffer/ everyday that I'm living for something better/ Ya what'ch you know about it, I see you're not even real rappers/ you just want to be the cool guy/ thinking that the devil is so sly/ you're fucking confused cause you ain't smart enough to see his lies/ so while you're thinking about it, I'm staring right into your eyes/ and I've got an angel; crescent kind of eye/ you know nothing about it, cause my scriptures is intelligently confusing you/ when I'm stuttering, making up words against you/

HOOK/CHORUS: on a rare occasion/ I allow all adults one celebration/ anything goes with no limitations/ except one rule, follow Gods commandments/ starting with a pairing of angels/ simple rules/ two to tango, or only even pairs/ Ya cause I told you, you're dancing with my angels/ when you're in Heaven, you are dancing with my angels/

VERSE 3: okay so you're dancing with my angels/ Lord Jesus Christ came and sent me, to save Ya/ Ya so Imma do it like two to tango/ what you know about it, last name Izzo/ slave of this world/ the pain and agony that you feel/ like it would make you swirl, like a hurricane/ or twirl down a volcano/ I'm talking about a toilet bowl/ you know nothing about it, so I do it like slow slang/ what'ch you know about it, Ya used to roll with a gang/ when I was confused by the devil/ hiding from the fucking truth, so he couldn't find me/ and I think about it, master minding everything I did in reality/ living, split triple personalities/ I've made up some new things that you would never comprehend or fathom/ so what'ch "you trying to do, is you a has-been/ naa never Imma take these beats/ rhyme over them, and destroy these streets/ evil poverty/ and money/ is greed/ that you don't want to be apart of, seven deadly sins/ is gonna fucking martyr you, like you gonna win/ Ya right, never, the devil tricks you till you die/ you suffering for life/ in hell where it's burning and you don't want to be with fires and shit/ come and follow my way/ cause Imma give you peace/ and I'll give you anything that you want, Ya real talk, peace/

SUMMARY - I'll explain it like this. "Oh boy wow, "*Dancing with Angels"* is a very powerful and significant song for all the ages. This song explains to the world that we are all Gods children, we were once all Angels, and can still be with God; but it explains far more than that, also. First off, this song is showing the world what it's like in Heaven; meaning that anything is possible, as long as you follow Gods rules, which aren't many. In addition, this song also shows the world that I had to mingle with the devil in order to remain safe all these years growing up. However, now that I'm free and have accepted who and what I am; I can begin my journey in saving the world. Ultimately, I think this is one of my best and most powerful works ever created. Further more, I didn't actually write this song, I simply only recorded it. God wrote this song through me and it wasn't pre-meditated by any means."

Chapter 14: Song 6 – Ride one rave (14:6)

Ride one rave:

VERSE 1: I'm from the future/ I came back so I could save Ya/ I've decided to be in the form of a rapper/ Ya because I'm the Saviour/ now drift with the drugs/ that I give through my strength and hugs/ I just want to dance, dance, dance/ I said, I wanna dance, dance/ ride one rave/ put Ya hands up and wave/ cause we about to go into a Heavenly place/ ooo just feel it/ just move it/ I want everybody grooving/ ah ah ah ah ah ah dance, dance, dance, dance, ooo, ooo, ooo, aahh ahhh, and I know, and I want you girl/

SUMMARY - I'll explain it like this. "This is an intermission song, to coincide with dancing with angels. Basically, after we all celebrate during The-Heaven-scene in the movie; we then, all the adults, get drunk and loose, while raving and dancing to awesome music. This song also leads up into "A mission intermission" which is where all the guardians of Heaven, must go to Earth, and search for the devil."

Chapter 14: Song 7 – A mission intermission (14:7)

A mission intermission: *not previously written

"Attention, attention, this is a red alert, red alert/ Houston, we have a problem. Pushht, I said Houston, we have a problem/ okay come in, Houston come in/

VERSE 1: I need to have an intermission mission/ with a weed session/ till I get lifted/ so this word comes out scripted/ from Heavenly progress/ I mean prowess/ cause I'm coming/ to touch you and relieve all stress/ or diminish all evil intentions/ trust me I know, cause we're on a mission/ we have to combat all evil actions/ I'm trying to explain to you your thought process is tainted/ by the devil/ cause he puts this poison on you/ making you feel small in the world/ when in actuality/ we're all Heavenly/ flying/ soaring/ through the skies/ I'm about to give you a brand new life/ where we're strong/ cause God has sent me/ here/ to teach you the real way that we're supposed to live, spiritually/ peacefully/ secretly/ we're fighting to save our sanctuary/ I'm on a mission intermission/ Houston come in/ I'm crashing/ I'm alert, I need a coach to help me crash down safely/ Houston, we have a problem, pushht/ Houston, Intermission Mission/ it gets intense/ to the point no one's living/ death is upon us/ it's assertive/ and its gonna happen/ aahh shit, it gets so intense/ its like a mystique cloud of dispense/ that I don't know how to combat against/ and I just have to come up with a new path for us to dig in a trench/ in the means or results to our survival/ than I'll find a direction to the light/ okay spiritual revival/ touching you in ways, never felt/ rhyming on this microphone never ever dealt/ with, in your ears or headphones/ or car speakers/ however we have it in the future/ but it's a mission/ and its getting crucial/ I need to survive, cause if I don't/ its gonna be hell for all of you/ and this is why I'm on a mission/ who's ready to join my side and start fighting/ okay cause if you want to survive/ and see better days/ you've got to give up and sacrifice your life/ man cause that's the only way to live life/ man you need to believe in Jesus Christ/ if you gonna change, anything, starting with yourself/ Oh my goodness/ I could bless/ you telepathically/ no press/ this is not a test/ I could void all distress/ but you must repent/ or face the consequence/ sinister death/ I should have lyrics, attached to your brain, like its glue/ I mean your hair, not no tattoo/ because you should never ever idolize a material item/ for the devil has it poisoned/ ughh to the point that I'm od-ing/ off lyrical seizures/

SUMMARY - I'll explain it like this. "A mission intermission" is about God sounding the alarm to alert all his guardian Angels. Or like in revelation states: the holy trumpets of Heaven. Once these alarms are sounded, his Angels are supposed to go to Earth and begin diminishing all evil: as I've stated in my song. This song is all about concluding the rein of the devil and diminishing all his evil control on the world; permitting me, to create a new world for Gods true children."

Chapter 14: Song 8 – BOMBS! (14:8)

BOMBS! Ft. DaRedANT – lyrics not included:

HOOK/CHORUS (Shared with DaRedANT): We running out of time, we need to drop/ Bombs!/ every time we right rhymes we always drop, Bombs!/ Ant's invincible beware of Red's, Bombs!/ MIZeRous Izzo, Drops, Bombs!/ Genius Mastermind, Ya you know we got, Bombs!/ Britty is so pretty and you know she's got, Bombs!/ MIZeRY ReCORDS all we ever drop is, Bombs!/ fuck what you got cause we got the best, Bombs!/

VERSE 1: All I ever is do is take a pen to a pad and I keep dropping bombs, Man/ you can't ever tell me to stop making music/ I've been doing it/ and I'm never gonna quit/ So I've been in this game, since I was thirteen/ I'm trying to make dollars, I ain't trying to make change/ I must be insane/ cause I'm hearing silent voices/ telling me that I'm making all the wrong choices/ I'm trying to figure out which path I should take/ My body keeps telling me that I need to take a break/ I'm running out of time, cause the fuse is about to blow/ I've made my own exit and I'm running for the door/ cause the bomb, Ya the bomb's about to blow/ back to the topic/ cause anytime we drop it/ we always dropping bombs/ Ya, I've made my connects, off my Emcing/ everyday I'm seeing/ just a bunch of different visions/ and it feels like I'm dreaming/ I'm all by myself in this mother fucking struggle that we all call life/ sometimes it's like I'm never gonna get a chance to know, what it feels like to live a good life/ man, we ain't never gonna stop, what the fuck you telling me, cause every time we drop, we always drop bombs/

Ya, bitch, we always drop, we always drop, we always drop bomb, ba, bombs/

HOOK/CHORUS (Shared with DaRedANT): We running out of time, we need to drop/ Bombs!/ every time we right rhymes we always drop, Bombs!/ Ant's invincible beware of Red's, Bombs!/ MIZeRous Izzo, Drops, Bombs!/ Genius Mastermind, Ya you know we got, Bombs!/ Britty is so pretty and you know she's got, Bombs!/ MIZeRY ReCORDS all we ever drop is, Bombs!/ fuck what you got cause we got the best, Bombs!/

SUMMARY - I'll explain it like this. "Bombs' was one of the first projects I had collaborated on with my buddy Jon, AKA DaRedANT. When we came up with this concept, we first intended it to be an anthem for my record company; considering the sample within the song, was "Bombs." We wanted to let the world know all we make musically are hot records AKA bombs. Further more, when I got into writing my verse for this, I at the time was an alcoholic, addicted to smoking weed, and taking pills. Long story short, I ended up coming up with this concept like the world was ending and that there was this massive bomb which was going to explode. Metaphorically, that bomb was me. Additionally within my verse, I discuss how long I've been in the game AKA struggling with my own hardships. I also explain that I was going to create my own exit to escape my own pain and suffering, AKA Judgment Day. This song is very significant and I only realized its importance as of today 8/1/12 as I transcribed it into this documentary."

Chapter 14: Song 9 – BattleGround (14:9)

BattleGround Ft. DaRedANT – lyrics not included:

INTRO: "Ya, battle ground haha."

VERSE 1: Ya, you can meet me on the battleground/ I'll never be down/ I'm just trying to be found/ so you better be around/ when I call for you sucka/ where, were you man/ when I needed you the most/ you weren't built for this game/ I'm the mother fucking host/ I'll change these rules if they gotta be changed/ Stupid mother fucker, I've made a new game/ Now all of y'all son just wanna come & play/ so you better come and pay/ mother fucker, Yaa/ cause none of y'all assholes could ever play for free/ unless it's called for, you'll never need to interview me/ Yaa, cause I'll always pay homage on every single record/ to any single person, that's inspired me man/ Young buck lost his mind on the sickest/ Eminem beat, that I've ever even heard/ Yo slim, it's time for you to pass this MIC/ down, to a successor man/ I'm a genius mastermind/ everybody knows/ MIZeRY's Rhymes/ some of y'all have even stolen my rhymes/ I ain't Eva gonna loose/ y'all the one's whose lost/ cause its 5-1-6-/ in this mother fucking bitch/ I'm only in this club if I'm trying to find a bitch/ now don'tch you Eva try and lie to Ya friends/ cause the whole world knows that we fucked in Ya Benz/ the whole world knows that we fucked in your Benz/

HOOK/CHORUS: I'm a genius mastermind and I make the illest rhymes/ were in a war zone/ and were on this battleground/ I'll always be a hustler, Yaa cause MIZeRY stays on his grind/ fuck what'ch Ya gotta say, this is my time/ ha Ya, ha Yaa/ I'm a genius mastermind and I make the illest rhymes/ were in a war zone/ and were on this battleground/ I'll always be a hustler, Yaa cause MIZeRY stays on his grind/ fuck what'ch Ya gotta say, this is our time/ ha Ya, ha Yaa/

VERSE 2: I'm a sexy mother fucker, I know that'ch you want me/ not you bitch, I'm talking about the industry/ run that shit back, (Pause) I didn't say backwards, Ya cause, the industry I'm tried of all your bullshit/ you better come and sign me/ my price has gone up/ I'm on a mill flat/ as a matter of fact/ I'm moving so fast/ If you don't hurry up, then you'll never catch me/ If you wanna fuck me/ than I'll fuck you over worse/ I promise you man, at the end of this verse/ you'll be laying in the back of a mother fucking Hurst/ My songs are just like a lethal injection/ Ya cause, my lyrics are the deadliest poison/ my mouth is so soothing, so go to sleep/ I ain't even say that, I'm an Emcee/ Ill make anything rhyme, so you better come & see/ MIZeRY/ perform, at every single show/ whoa, hold up/ don't go there, I told you girl that I've mastered this flow/ but Babygirl/ I need you to really go slow/ I could of sworn, I told you weren't like these hoes/ I'm just trying to go down a new path sexy girl/ understand dog, that MIZeRY's the source for all of my wrath, and Rage/ Son – Ya can't ever lock me in a cage/ cause, in my life man, I've tried so hard/ for it not to be the same/ and that's the reason, that I've made a new game/ and that's the reason, that I've made a new game/

HOOK/CHORUS: I'm a genius mastermind and I make the illest rhymes/ were in a war zone/ and were on this battleground/ I'll always be a hustler, Yaa cause MIZeRY stays on his grind/ fuck what'ch Ya gotta say, this is my time/ ha Ya, ha Yaa/ I'm a genius mastermind and I make the illest rhymes/ were in a war zone/ and were on this battleground/ I'll always be a hustler, Yaa cause MIZeRY stays on his grind/ fuck what'ch Ya gotta say, this is our time/ ha Ya, ha Yaa/

SUMMARY - I'll explain it like this. "Battleground" is the second song that Jon and I had collaborated on. We wanted this song to be a hit single and to be a metaphor for our intentions upon the industry, AKA the world. Battleground is an analogy to describe what the world is like with all its pain and suffering. While also describing, we're caught dead in the middle of it, living in the tri-state NYC area. The Earth is Gods battleground, where Saint Michael will slay the devil, and we are just mere pawns in the overall scheme of things."

Chapter 14: Song 10 – Negotiations (14:10)

Negotiations: *not previously written

VERSE 1: okay, it itches/ it's crawling up my skin as I'm twitching/ it's like a surgical rush of energy/ that's Heavenly/ that comes down spiritually/ through my bones and my body/ my veins are pulsating/ I'm feeling the blood rushing/ lyrically, I'm touching/ you in ways, you've never experienced not even in the bed, with lustful adventures/ aahh… okay the negotiations are abrupt/ he immediately says, I'm going to war/ and I said, listen/ we can do this civilly/ and do this peacefully/ for we don't need to go to the war zone/ battleground, why you wanna fight me/ we're brothers, we're one and the same/ you're my alter ego, split personality/ you're fallacy/ because the world, sinned against me/ so he tells me/ if I don't get it, or understand, he's gonna kill every one, torment them/ forever/ so I grow stronger/ come out of the midst, and I'm harder/ I mean there's so much light, it's no longer darker/ in my dreams/ Yah he used to haunt me/ way before I knew who I was: physically/ literally/ eternally/ spiritually/ pure prophecy/ where's my apostles these days/ their scared/ and refuse to give me Heavenly praise/ for I have received the gift of grace/ from god Jesus Christ/ to the point words don't make sennssee (**slur**)/ okay, so lord gives me strength/ as he surges through my brain and DNA/ to give you something quickly/ cause I ain't gonna stutter, it's pure intelligence, write it on the chalkboard/ follow along/ like this was a school song/ like you was learning mathematics/ or history classes/ even though it was farfetched in ways you couldn't comprehend as a little child/ you're just believing what any adult says, as you're reading it in the book/ haa, you even know what that book is meaning/ shit, I'll teach you something/ that you never learned about teaching/ or thought about preaching/ I mean searching/ for ways in life, to start, acting in ways you never thought you'd be thinking/ positive living/ everything I'm doing it's gifted/ it was pre-scripted/ cause my father is imperfect/ I mean he's perfect/ and that's the key way about humanity/ is that: When you're wrong/ you should know that you're wrong/ because father is never wrong/ and no matter what you think about, listen to my songs/ Imma teach you the both, the kinda of realities, that you didn't want to be a part/ Yaa cause you were scared of the dark/ I know what you're doing, but you've been reaching real far/ I've been hearing your prayers, but a lot of them is crazy/ I don't know what you thinking, is you trying to combat me? cynically/ or literally/ either way, I'm coming to get the evil against me/ because we only living with positive energy in the clouds: As Angels/ aahh cause we on a mission for eternal peace/ no matter what you thought about man, we'll be ready to take you down, in anybodies streets/

SUMMARY - I'll explain it like this. “Negotiations" was the song in which Saint Michael attempt to negotiate with Lucifer. Michael is merciful to all, so his first intent is to offer salvation; even for Lucifer. Lucifer, denies Michael's attempts and rebuttals his offer with an act of war. Instead of accepting God's mercy Lucifer is relentless till the end. As a result, I display my struggles of overcoming Lucifer's evil within this captivating piece. Within this piece, I also explain the very ways in which Lucifer manipulates and attempts to control humanity via social class and education."

Chapter 14: Song 11 – Tangoing Against Devils (14:11)

Tangoing Against Devils : *not previously written

VERSE 1: Damn, this shit sounds like some days of our lives stuff. Ight cool… --Let me explain my formula/ when I get on this microphone, I turn into a rapper/ or a monster/ however you refer me/ Imma show you the real me, no matter what, it's all prophecy/ said from thousands of years ago/ you wasn't even following, so now I came back in a different form, humanly/ Yaa I know I'm not perfect, but in reality/ or actuality/ where I come from, I'm Heavenly/ and there's nothing, like fallacy/ or wrong doings of the Devil/ if you don't believe me, then turn up my treble/ I'll cut out the bass, understand, everything I'm using it's a symphony/ I'm MIZeRY/ and I'm giving you prophecy/ every time I'm rocking literally/ or physically/ come on quickly/ with magical potions/ or poison/ however you doing it, I told you I was the one chosen/ to save you/ so if you fucking come at me wrong, what do you expect me to do?/

HOOK/CHORUS: Ya I'll forgive you/ if you get into a tangle with the devil/ but I can only forgive you for so long/ cause this song is so long/ no matter what you thinking, you've been living wrong/ Ya I'll forgive you/ if you get into a tangle with the devil/ but I can only forgive you for so long/ cause this song is so long/ no matter what you thinking, you've been living wrong/

VERSE 2: Okay so, the devil gets you into a mist/ in his poison/ he sprinkled, laced, something in Ya drugs/ whatever you thought about, he's using different techniques/ that he's creating, to combat against me/ and everything that you should live by, man he sprinkles, it on the money/ cause greed starts with green/ I don't know why, but it sounds like he's mean/ Ya he's trying to cuss you with his profanity/ Ya he's spraying shit literally on the walls, making graffiti/ destroying my ozone/ destroying everything you live by, no zone/ what's your next move/ I see you can't even stand alone/ because you're not strong enough to fend on your own/ trying to survive, and fend for yourself, aahh everybody's ruthless, the devil takes control/

HOOK/CHORUS: Ya I'll forgive you/ if you get into a tangle with the devil/ but I can only forgive you for so long/ cause this song is so long/ no matter what you thinking, you've been living wrong/ Ya I'll forgive you/ if you get into a tangle with the devil/ but I can only forgive you for so long/ cause this song is so long/ no matter what you thinking, you've been living wrong/

VERSE 3: You and I both know you've been down this road before, so you've got to make a choice/ which path, will you choose?/ God or the devil/ Ya you're trying to convince people/ that you're spiritual/ in factuality you're Judgmental/ being a rude dick, living by evil/ cause the devil poisoned your cereal/ when you was just a little child/ I know about it, because I've been there, I was a rebel/ I was living real wild/ I didn't have any rules to tame me/ I don't give a fuck about nothing except to succeed/ and not by greed/ cause I live by Gods powerful trees/ and no matter what you thought, I'm an MC/ Ya giving you knowledge of scriptures/ of pictures/ way beyond lyrical/ or visual/

HOOK/CHORUS: Ya I'll forgive you/ if you get into a tangle with the devil/ but I can only forgive you for so long/ cause this song is so long/ no matter what you thinking, you've been living wrong/ Ya I'll forgive you/ if you get into a tangle with the devil/ but I can only forgive you for so long/ cause this song is so long/ no matter what you thinking, you've been living wrong/

SUMMARY - I'll explain it like this. "Tangoing against devils" is a song, not only to discuss my hardships of battling the devil, and all his evil temptations; but it's a song to inform the world, that God can only forgive them so many times, before he turns his back. God is merciful but he has a limitation of how much he shall tolerate, just as any man would; and as the Bible states, God created us in his own image."

Chapter 14: Song 12 – The dark ages (14:12)

The dark ages: *not previously written

VERSE 1: Dark time, Dark ages, okay we're coming in, gladiator all of a sudden your/ a savage/ acting out/ browlic warrior, I'm coming slashing out/ I ain't even messing around/ I've got a bunch of warriors ready to kill you/ call it 300, Ya whatever I'm a roman assassin/ I'm coming, silent flabbergasted/ shit all of a sudden, I'm moving faster/ macking it/ cracking it/ everything I'm doing I'm here to start slashing/ kid, I'm a mother fucking demonic wore four war zone/ everything I'm doing its about to be a drone/ Killing you, like shit, you couldn't even be safe at home, I'm coming in the night, creeping while you're sleeping/ what'ch you know about it, cause I'm killing while you're breathing/ shit you ain't even ready, you can't keep up I'm sneaking/ I'm a mother fucking thief, and again all of a sudden, you can call me the prince/ I'm actually the prince of an entire country kid/ and this shit is not me lying/ mother fuckers know it, cause I even own lions/ mother fuckers tigers/ everything you doing, I'm about to get wild/ you don't like my style/ I don't really care cause its the dark ages, and there's no rules, they don't apply/ what'ch you know about it, I'm not civilized/ I'm a mother fucking angry child, pitting out/ I'm only twenty years old, whipping out/ all of a sudden I'm killing you now/ you mother fuckers is talking shit wow/ what the fuck click clack blouw/ Ya cause I'm taking it to the dark ages/ I'm feeling it, all of a sudden spiritual cages/ they breaking me out, all of a sudden its laced/ I'm drugs/ hitting you so hard like this base/ what you know about it cause I'm about to go balling/ free falling/ mother fuckers ain't catching me, you can call me 007/ cause I'm so fast killing you, assassin tactics/ mother fuckers adding up the mathematics/ and no forensics/ can't find me, I've got booties on my shoes/ I've got mother fuckers ready to unglue/ the evidence/ no matter what you doing I see its evident/ I'm the best at this/ no discretion/ what you doing, in addition/ all of a sudden, your slipping/ I see it/ mother fuckers is dying/ I've got a thousand men that's wilding/ ready to hunt you/ all of a sudden/ fuck, are you ready to bust too/ Whether arrows or guns, I don't care what'ch you choose/ just be ready to fight, when I call upon you/ now move/ okay this isn't a joke/ are you ready to get schooled/ Ya because the end of days is coming/ and no matter what you thought, no matter where you running/ you could never be hiding/ from me, cause I've got the ultimate eye/ and I'm watching/ every time you sleeping/ no matter what you thinking/ I'm in the moon, creeping/ on you, cause I'm fucking keeping tabs on you/ which your every move/ I see man, you ain't even ready to choose/ a better life/ Ya so you going to follow me, or are you going to fucking-dizzie (die)/ with the rest of the world tonight/ Ya cause Armageddon is coming/ I promise you it's real close/ and I told you back in the days on battleground that I'm the host/ there's nothing you could do man, cause I make the rules/ no matter what you think you could never change this world, because I'm the one, I'm the one cause I've got the power to do it anyway son/ Ya my father made the sun/ think about that some/ Ya what you trying to do man, cause my life is all about fun/ where you come from/ it's all about evil and guns/ and drugs/ and busting money and cum all on your bitches tits and asses/ what'ch you talking about, are you fucking flabbergasted/ by Tasmanian tactics/ Ya call it collateral damage/ cause where I come from it's dark ages, we're trying to kill you/ enslave you/ & endanger your species/ Ya I'll lock you in cages/ I don't give a fuck man, cause I'm the bravest/ I'm here to save it/ Ya cause Heaven and Earth are one and the same/ you mother fuckers is dumb and deranged/ your brains is fucking slower than the most/ Ya call it an ant hill hole/ Ya shit, I'll buy you all out/

SUMMARY - I'll explain it like this. "The dark ages" is a song about Revelation, Judgment Day, and the wrath that has fumigated within God for many centuries. During the Judgment Days, shall commence the start of the true dark ages upon Heaven and Earth. During this time, you shall see things such as God had instructed me to record on this song. Just like in revelation, referring to God coming like a thief in the night; I was told to recite similar practices in this music of work. Further more, one of the last lines on this song is the most impressive by far: "I'll lock you in cages, I don't give a fuck man, cause I'm the bravest; I'm here to save it/ Ya cause Heaven and Earth are one and the same." This line truly signifies how far God is willing to go in order to preserve his way of life. Creating an eternity of peace and love amongst all those faithful. His final message from this song, for the entire world is: If you don't climb up out of your ant holes, I can't save you all and be ready, for the end of days is nigh."

Chapter 14: Song 13 – Step outside yourself (14:13)

Step outside yourself Ft. Sandman (2005) – lyrics not included:

VERSE 1: I'm here to define you/ how do you treat people/ good, bad, or evil/ ask yourself, you look at everyone as an equal/ what if they were a different race than you/ does that make them lower than you/ just cause you got more money/ does that make you better than me/ what are you crazy/ please stop playing/ I don't give a fuck about what y'all are saying/ under your breathe and behind my back/ about my rap/

it doesn't matter, cause I've found my inner self/ you haven't even begun to explore yourself/ one minute you're a mobster/ than a gangsta/ than a drug dealer/ than a girl stealer/ you don't even know, who you are/ you look in the mirror/ and you don't look far/ into your eyes/ you can't even see past your own lies/ you got caught in a world of denial/ so you come up with a new fucking style/ day after day, lie after lie/ I already know who I am/ I'm a rapper on a mission/ I am a man with big intentions/ I was put on this Earth, So I can help/ you were put here, so you can receive/ anything I do as long as I breathe/ do you have someone that influences you, do you have someone that you look up to, do you have someone that you pray too/ you should take a minute and look at yourself/ so that you can step outside yourself/

HOOK/CHORUS: Look at yourself from another perspective/ what's your incentive/ what's your reality/ focus your energy/ close those eyes/ what is it like, living those lies/ Look at yourself from another perspective/ what's your incentive/ what's your reality/ focus your energy/ close those eyes/ what is it like, living those lies/

VERSE 3.0: Come and take a walk with me/ on my journeys/ while I'm going through surgery's/ while going through purgatory/ almost every night/ I put up a fight/ to get down on my knees, to put my head up/ just to speak up/ I don't deserve the full love of the lord/ to a certain degree I deserve to be heard/ everyone needs love/ so I look above/ all the fucking poverty/ and the fact that the government doesn't give much back to the black community/ so when I'm done here, we'll fight as a unity/ against these thugs/ against these guns/ against these drugs/ against these laws/ what's my cause/ if you're willing to ride/ stick by my side/ and we will prosper/ as one and together/

HOOK/CHORUS: Look at yourself from another perspective/ what's your incentive/ what's your reality/ focus your energy/ close those eyes/ what is it like, living those lies/ Look at yourself from another perspective/ what's your incentive/ what's your reality/ focus your energy/ close those eyes/ what is it like, living those lies/

SUMMARY - I'll explain it like this. "For starters, this song was one of my earliest and by far my most advanced. This was a collaboration with my good friend Rob and together, spiritually, our souls connected, and we fortified a song that the entire world can relate with; whether or not, they are trapped behind their own lies or not!

However, during my verse I'm not only referencing all those who fib day to day, behind the devils many faces; but, I was also prophesizing about my life and my future. For example: "I already know who I am/ I'm a rapper on a mission/ I am a man with big intentions/ I was put on this Earth, So I can help/ you were put here, so you can receive/ anything I do as long as I breathe/." Further more, my second verse goes on explaining to walk with me, AKA walk with God, and let him/me show you where I must walk; in order to preserve, our eternity. The entire second verse is me discussing my future plans to abolish all wrong. Rob and I created this song in 2005 and we are now in 2012. I must say, this song is by far still ahead of it's time."

Chapter 14: Song 14 – Bones (14:14)

Bones:

INTRO: "Straight paper baby, check check, Hey. Imma one take this entire record, just to show you how serious I am."

VERSE 1: Yaa, my bones shake! When I'm bumping to this beat/ Yo Homie, I'm alert, I'm already on my feet/ Imma spit this from the start, watch me spit three verses/ not curse off one, be raunchy or perverse/ I feel bad for you son, if ignorance is your curse/ Hey! Take it easy lady, I'm not trying to steal your purse/ the last time I checked you was flirting with me first/ you called it a blood thirst/ the way you was feeling for me/ I don't mean to be arrogant in any kind of way see/ I'm telling you these stories so you understand this life/ I speak about my life, through this rhyming acting poetry/ I thank God – every single day cause he saved me/ from this MIZeRY/ I was feeling everyday/ It would be a big shame/ If I ever had to go back, living out those days/ I'm just trying to live my life/ and no longer feel this pain/ I spit it like it is/

HOOK/CHORUS: Click clack! What's that/ this is hip-hop/ and we brining this back/ Imma keep this real simple/ so the whole crowd could follow/ This is for my fans, and my love for this game/ If I don't make this happen man, I will never be the same/ Now I need y'all to sing/ Click clack! What's that/ this is hip-hop/ and we brining this back/ Imma keep this real simple/ so the whole crowd could follow/ This is for my fans, and my love for this game/ If I don't make this happen man, I will never be the same/

VERSE 2: Come to think about it, how did we ever survive, any of those days/ In the game of this life, that we all have to play/ Trust me, I've got this locked/ I've studied for many years and I've calculated the odds/ If you assassinate my character/ I'll eradicate your life/ with the teachings of my master/ Yo I have a lot of talent/ but I need more liquid assets/ I except the form of cash/ I don't mean to brag man/ but I'm a little bit of a genius, I should have advanced classes/ I should maybe work for NASA/ and design a starship/ I'm thankful for this gift/ I was given everyday/ The importance of my life/ is worth more than that price/ go ahead – and try again, this is your last chance/ start from the beginning, and take another glance/ My ideas are limitless/ I'm set for my success/ and I'm brining many with me/ This is MIZeRY ReCORDS/ and were worth a lot of money/ I could be your best investment, you just need to take a chance/ Let me break this record down/

HOOK/CHORUS: Click clack! What's that/ this is hip-hop/ and we brining this back/ Imma keep this real simple/ so the whole crowd could follow/ This is for my fans, and my love for this game/ If I don't make this happen man, I will never be the same/ Now I need y'all to sing/ Click clack! What's that/ this is hip-hop/ and we brining this back/ Imma keep this real simple/ so the whole crowd could follow/ This is for my fans, and my love for this game/ If I don't make this happen man, I will never be the same/ Now I need y'all to sing/

VERSE 3: Let me spit a quick story/ about my main man heavy/ there's a temperamental mind, when he's mashing on these keys/ I could show you all some things, that'ch you wouldn't want to see/ Ya just listen to this rhythm Imma show you what I mean/ click clack, what's that/ this is my life, and I'm taking it back/ Hip Hop or Rap/ either way, I'm writing rhymes and bumping to this track/ you couldn't ever stop me, I've already chose this path/ I don't care what'ch you say, you ain't stopping me man/ my bones keep shaking, when I'm rhyming to this beat/ This is MIZeRY ReCORDS and we rarely ever play/ I'm way too intelligent, I would never have to cheat/ I hope this rattles your bones and those pearly white teeth/ pay attention to what I say/ if it wasn't for my music, I would not be here today/ I'm still searching for my wifey/ that's really ready to ride/ no matter what we face in life/ and I was ready to commit suicide/

so many years ago; I had to revise my strategies and my entire life/ I had to change all my goals/ and I don't have no time to waste, I'm just trying to stack my doe/ so how many of you wanna roll/ I'm just trying to hit this road/ I'm just trying to see this world/ and I'm just trying to be on tour/ and the last thing Imma say, is that: this rattles my bones/

HOOK/CHORUS: Click clack! What's that/ this is hip-hop/ and we brining this back/ Imma keep this real simple/ so the whole crowd could follow/ This is for my fans, and my love for this game/ If I don't make this happen man, I will never be the same/ Now I need y'all to sing/ Click clack! What's that/ this is hip-hop/ and we brining this back/ Imma keep this real simple/ so the whole crowd could follow/ This is for my fans, and my love for this game/ If I don't make this happen man, I will never be the same/ Now I need y'all to sing/

SUMMARY - I'll explain it like this. "Bones is one of my favorite songs because when I wrote it, I was intending to be confidently arrogant with my ability to make a great rap record; without needing to be degrading, derogatory, or use cuss words to prove a point. Furthermore, that's exactly what I accomplished. In addition, this song is to represent the value of myself and my organization; whilst indirectly showing my motives for the world, spiritually. When you listen to this song over and over again, as I have, you soon begin to realize why it rattles my bones."

Chapter 14: Song 15 – Success (14:15)

Success Ft. DaRedANT & Sandman – Lyrics not included:

VERSE 1: "You know I used to be a lot of things man, a thug, ha, a criminal, a rebel; breaking laws, rules, not giving a fuck. A Womanizer, a cheater, Ya this is my success." Yea, this is my success, this is my story/ my faction doesn't have any room for you pussies/ If you wasn't really ready then you should of never joined/ I told you I was coming, and I'm coming real fast/ I'm doing 2 things; Squashing your fame/ and I'm gunning for this game/ you better be down, with MIZeRY ReCORDS/ Than being against us, cause when the time comes/ I'll do things to y'all that you couldn't even fathom/ I have no compassion/ this ain't just rapping/ it's way beyond that/ I'm coming for the top/ and I'm never gonna stop/ If you get in my way, then I'm taking you down/ I won't say it again, I'm not playing around/ But I will say this, I'm a beast/ to these beats/ I'm a mother fucking monster, when it comes to my lyrics/ revolutionary is MIZeRY's music/ Innovation is/ MIZeRY ReCORDS/ Yes, I'll never shut my mouth, even if you unplug my microphones cord/ now my troops are gonna speak about their success/

VERSE 4: My mission – started with these visions/ God's Prediction/ of my Heavenly resurrection/ Jesus Christ Second Coming/ As I – Slay the devil where he's laying/ for those unfaithful – comes death & destruction/ Demonic Injection/ Spiritual Sickness/ for those he infected/ from the Devil's poisons/ very few chosen/ eternal life for my children/ now I give you something, beyond powerful comprehension/ My father's instructions/ given on the ten commandments/ Love & Respect/ destroyed at the cost of one man's expense/ Earth is now the devil's nest/ where all men fail God's test/ for eternal purification/ my painful crucifixion/ has been ignored and categorized/ next to children's fiction/ soon you too shall feel my affliction/ upon your eternal conviction/ The devil's days are limited/ as you cynically admitted/ all the sins you've committed/ against the weak/ there is no more time to preach/ Good & Bad separate instantaneously/ similar to when Moses, parted the red sea/ you have two choices, fight for the devil or you fight for me/ Rhythmically/ this is my last story/ of prophecy/ I implore you to follow me/ for all eternity/ "I'm your Lord Jesus Christ, thou art Lord Saviour, sender, and deliverer from God to Protect all those who are worthy."

SUMMARY - I'll explain it like this. "Success, success, success; boy this song is very surreal and intense all wrapping up into one. First, this song was compiled over a four year span. Originally, my buddy Jon and I started this song as a record company anthem with all our artists AKA apostles. At least I thought I had apostles at the time. It later turned into a duo record between Jon and I. However, on January 13th 2012, my buddy Rob AKA Sandman came to the studio for the first time in about 4 years. We ended up adding Rob to the song and he not only referenced biblical scriptures, but also discussed loving his daughter passionately. After he finished recording, I first intended not to write the last verse; although it came out good, it wasn't good enough for Jon. Jon and I argued over writing a verse or leaving it as is, because I was nearing my completion of never having to record songs again. Anyways, two days later on January 15th 2012, I had wrote a new verse which is the one you see listed in "Verse 4." On January 16th 2012, I had finished this song completely with all four verses on the song. On the same day, I had later found compelling evidence on *Youtube* that the first holy trumpets had sounded throughout the world. I later realized, this wasn't coincidence and that this song having such a powerful biblical and prophetic importance: was God's Will. To this day, this is the song that saved me entirely. It allowed for me to accept that I was, who I was as Jesus Christ in the second form. I further accepted that such a verse could have only come from God himself. Originating from his eternal understanding and acceptance of his own mission for the world."

Chapter 14: Song 16 – Victory (14:16)

Victory:

HOOK/CHORUS: Ya okay, Victory is coming and freedom isn't free/ I don't reference any money/ more so those righteous & worthy/ to be reborn, only through me/ for I am Jesus Christ/ the only key to eternal life/ Victory is coming and freedom isn't free/ I don't reference any money/ more so those righteous & worthy/ to be reborn, only through me/ for I am Jesus Christ/ The only key to eternal life/

VERSE 1: It's been several hundred years/ many souls dead/ many women's tears/ plagued Mother Nature, she disappeared/ exactly what I feared/ oh how I've missed children's chant's and cheer's/ damn, I could've saved em all, a lot less survived/ with no hope of being revived/ my fallen angels heroically died/ my result was wrong, so I feel like I lied/ so I feel like/ that I'm not always even right/ humanly bonds, are more restricting than Odin's Armor/ tired from 600 years of war, I forgot the smell of flowers/ replaced with the stench of blood/ and medusas' seductive lust/ I insist to must/ refusing her trust/ she's wicked and corrupt/ sucking my soul for fun/ soon I'll find my master, whom shall teach me my Powers/ grow infinitely large/ instantly removing evil to a planet so far/ containing nothing but evil dark/

HOOK/CHORUS: Victory is coming and freedom isn't free/ I don't reference any money/ more so those righteous & worthy/ to be reborn, only through me/ for I am

Jesus Christ/ The only key to eternal life/ Victory is coming and freedom isn't free/ I don't reference any money/ more so those righteous & worthy/ to be reborn, only through me/ for I am Jesus Christ/ The only key to eternal life/

VERSE 2: Victory – The over coming of one's enemies/ or, achievement of mastery/ or success in a struggle/ Success – favorable outcome, the gaining of wealth and fame/ Victory & Success are almost one and the same/ if you are insane/ for victory supersedes success/ cause fame leads to the devils nest/ where you incinerate from demonic fire's breathe/ for six centuries I've lured the devil to his own death/ it took me 3 lives/ to remember these 3 lines/ **E-ID Leurc Levid/ Rof Mai Christ Jesus**/ shall banish you to hell/ Can't break free – no escape/ torturous tormenting kind of pain/ Licentiously defying me/ abusing all that I love unconditionally/ prolonging eternal rejuvenation/ restricting healing innovation/ Magic Powers of sensation/

HOOK/CHORUS: Victory is coming and freedom isn't free/ I don't reference any money/ more so those righteous & worthy/ to be reborn, only through me/ for I am Jesus Christ/ the only key to eternal life/ Victory is coming and freedom isn't free/ I don't reference any money/ more so those righteous & worthy/ to be reborn, only through me/ for I am Jesus Christ/ The only key to eternal life/

VERSE 3: Spiritually, God Bless you, you mean God bless me/ because I am Holy/ One in three/ and that's how I form everything literally/ It's a triangle foundation/ okay I'll give it to you in a whole different education/ system/ that you never thought you'd learn, before you was twenty five/ or seventy five/ either way, let's all change your life/ Ya I'm about to get live/ my methods of scientific intelligence/ are way beyond any realm of comprehension/ for you kind of humans/ because, it's on a whole different level system/ my metaphysical evolution/ is coming through, revolution/ miraculous revelation/ I'm hitting you instantaneously, it's Heavenly sensation/ of illumination/ okay, now I'm giving you spiritual direction/ are you ready to start following/ or fighting/ if the time calls for it, because eternal life comes with a price/ self sacrifice/ haha…

SUMMARY - I'll explain it like this. "This song started when I realized, I needed a counter for success; because success, is only something the devil believes in. Success is what society, makes you think, is the key to happiness; when by definition, it's the complete opposite of what God wants or requires for us to live by. When I wrote "Success," I intended to represent my overcoming of the bad, leading up to a good future in a song. Victory is the counter part to success by definition, so I started this song wanting to first compare the two English definitions. I ended up placing the definitions in the second verse, as you just read. However, the true goal for this song was represented with its timeline, within life, and my movie; which would ultimately, be the defeat of the devil. Truly, this is what the song represents: When God, AKA me, AKA Jesus returns, after successfully defeating the devil, and claiming victory above all; for all those faithful. I personally love this song because it's so symbolic in terms of my life, in terms of biblical understanding, as well as in generality of life. When I wrote this song, I made sure there were no curses or anything terrible in this song too. Because, I wanted all ages to be able to listen to it, follow it, and remember it for all eternity: this is my victory."

Chapter 14: Song 17 – Celebration (14:17)

Celebration: *not previously written

INTRO: "Yaa, okay, I just need to get into the mode on this now, you know what I'm saying, Ight you ready. I want you to put your hands up with me and we gonna do this like all of y'all are here with me, ah, ah."

VERSE 1: It's a celebration/ better days are coming/ I promise you that Heavenly return is approaching/ and what I mean by that is my resurrection/ the Second Coming/ you'll watch my movie/ and you'll understand what I'm meaning/ I mean, I'm talking about, with my slang/ I had to hit the microphone, so you understand this is nothing like a gang/ or provocative story/ this is all truth, prophecy/ are you ready to get healed, by me/ and my Heavenly/ father/ cause art thou Lord Jesus Christ/ showed me a new way to live life/ Ya and in this world/ or reality/ or realm of actuality/ it's like nothing even matters, starting with money/ except living by Jesus Christ and he touches you all so Heavenly/ you become angelic in ways you never thought you'd feel/ literally/ in this world/ cause the devil/ has you all controlled and manipulated by evil/ I promise you it's like poison/ he's trying to take control/ of my microphone/ it's like you were not chosen, to live the kind of life that I got to live/ righteous in everything I do, shit/

and I used to do evil/ but let's not talk about that, cause it's a celebration/ put Ya hands up everybody start waving/ cheering and chanting/ everybody should be loving/ cause it's a celebration/ put Ya hands up, everyone start waving/ cheering and chanting/ I wanna hear kids screaming and playing/ laughing/ I wanna hear adults loving/ secretly, cause I was chosen/ the Second Coming/ is happening/ Ya, cause after that it's a celebration/ I'm in the mood to party/ and celebrate with my new found friends and people that are living by me/ in righteous realities/ not trying to create enemies/ or do anything wrong to your family/ and we are all one and the same, only through me/ and only through me shall you feel Heavenly/ or holy/ or be given a chance of a second life/ and not be tortured for eternity/ I'm telling you this, cause I know prophecy/ it just comes and develops, I thank Lord Jesus Christ, for giving me this song and this rhythm of lyrical scriptures/ that I use as artistic pictures/ Ya, how many times I gotta give you the same stuff, it's like it sounds written/ but its not, its coming/ Ya cause my life has never been scripted/ even when I was long ago/ existent in, a whole different time zone/ Ya, cause Imma break barriers/ in the realm of speed and lightening fast time/ time means nothing/ because God, My father has control of everything you know/ Ya, are you ready to kick around with rolling flow/ Oh My God, you wanna see how powerful I could be at one of my shows/ I don't need any one of my songs/ to tell you how good or intense I could be/ come on stage with me/ and celebrate and celebrate/ Ya man am I touching your brains/ I want my ladies to shout out loud and say I praise/ the lord, cause he's powerful and he gives me ways/ to feel good, aahh amen/

SUMMARY - I'll explain it like this. "Celebration, is exactly as the title describes. This song was created to represent my overcoming of life's hardships all leading up to the day after victory over all evil. That day represents an eternal, spiritual, and united celebration amongst all of God's holy children and animals alike."

Chapter 14: Song 18 – Sunday's (14:18)

Sunday's Ft. DaRedANT – Verse not included:

VERSE 1: Ya, on Sunday's I want to start this whole week new/ like I was just born today/ and some days'/ Man, I just gotz to get high, while I'm passing time away/ to all those, less fortunate/ cause Imma live 4 infinite/ I'm not kidding/ Eminem, you gotz to listen kid/ You need to put this MIC to rest/ Yo, Obie trice said it best/ Obie – "I got the white boys mad at me, cause Em, signed another black boy, like he's Ni*** happy/" Ya, well that's okay/ cause, I'm still deciding who can, and who can not stay/ I'm black listing bitches/ I fought to be where I'm at, by fighting for my chance/ opportunities been staring at me, with this vivid glance/ she's taunting me/ In my dreams Homie, he's haunting me/ puts this poison on me/ now I'm feeling like, everybody's been after me/ haa Yaa, how can you not feel me/ You betta listen good son, cause I don't think you're ready/

HOOK/CHORUS: And Sundays/ Is God's day/ I thought I was in Heaven/ but I was actually only dreaming/ I woke up, it's Monday/ Broke, pissed off, and I'm hating another day/ and when will things change/ I'm so tired of this game/ It's always the same thang/ And no God, you can not take me home tonight/ I'm not done with this life/ there's too much in this world/ That I'm trying to make right/ and someday, will be my day/ but Sundays/ it Gods Day/

VERSE 2: Let me tell y'all how I feel/ cause, I could never be anything except for being real/ I write poems and songs/ I no longer cipher/cause, mother fuckers is all fake/ spitting out rhymes/ that they wrote from last week/ I've been in and out of so many streets/ I've rhymed to so many different kinds of beats/ From all different producers/ both upcoming or established/ it never really mattered/ but if the beat's that hot, then Imma kick an ill rhyme/ so let me get into some more shit that's running through my mind/ I'm drifting all alone/ while I'm cruising through this ocean/ I'm hopping off this record so I can vent my emotions/ I gotta be honest, cause my life's getting better/ but I'm still not sure/ so Red Fire tell em of the pain I've endured/ Red Fire – "The rises, the falls, the back against the walls/ the pleasure, the pain, it's all a part of the mother fucking game/."

HOOK/CHORUS: And Sundays/ Is God's day/ I thought I was in Heaven/ but I was actually only dreaming/ I woke up, it's Monday/ Broke, pissed off, and I'm hating another day/ and when will things change/ I'm so tired of this game/ It's always the same thang/ And no God, you can not take me home tonight/ I'm not done with this life/

there's too much in this world/ That I'm trying to make right/ and someday, will be my day/ but Sundays/ it Gods Day/

SUMMARY - I'll explain it like this. "Sundays," could not have been possible without our amazing producer, Hev One and my partner DaRedANT, AKA Jon; because both variables were the chemistry in which sizzled, in order to make one of my most meaningful, and metaphorical records of all time. This song not only captures both a physical reality on life, but a metaphorical spiritual actuality to my personal life in relation to God and humanity. Further more, the Hook also amplifies its meaning and correlation with the world, for we all have bad weeks and every new week we want things to be perfect."

Chapter 14: Song 19 – Deadly MC's (14:19)

Deadly MC's Ft. DaRedANT – Verse not included:

HOOK/CHORUS: Ugh Yaa, were a bunch of deadly MCs/ spitting on this MIC, just trying to tell our stories/ (Repeat 2.5x)

VERSE 2: Yo my mind, never stops racing/ My Mouth, never stops moving/ My heart, Yaa, it'll never stop beating/ cause you can't ever kill me/ I'm a young soldier/ even when she was, a little bit younger/ Why she was, never in the pictures/ talking about my mother/ she just left me, sitting in the dark, and I had no father/ getting dropped off, in so many places/ to many faces/ never really counted/ there's way too many and I never really named them/ all I ever ask, is why do I question everything around me/ And I wonder why/ cause I've seen some fucked up things in my time/ I get premonitions, Yaa – but I, I don't know why/ I see different shit that'ch you'll never Eva see/ most of the time son, it's all eyes on me/ Man, but I said fuck it, when I started loosing my mind, as I'm regaining my faith/ man, when I woke up, the only thing I saw was these white pearl of gates/ starring at my father, talking about my lord/ not my real father, he's a fucking bastard/ trying to make up, for a lot of bad times/ If it wasn't for my god, I wouldn't be alive/ soo, man I've got to say thanks for supporting my cause/ for helping me man, when I was real lost/ Deadly Son/

HOOK/CHORUS: Ugh Yaa, were a bunch of deadly MCs/ spitting on this MIC, just trying to tell our stories/ (Repeat 2.5x)

SUMMARY - I'll explain it like this. "This song is simply to justify what we are as musicians, children of God, and people within humanity. It explains that I am and my friends are strong willed survivors and that musically: we are deadly MC's. In other words, we are birthed with such skill and have mastered this skill. We are also willing to die for our art and or challenge, any of those whom attempt to do it better: for we are Deadly MCs."

Chapter 14: Song 20 – Day of My Return (14:20)

Day of My Return: *Not previously written.

HOOK/CHORUS: Everything that was my mine again/ and thou shall rise/ and fight/ and there's no time to live, live, live! / Everything was mine again/ and thou shall rise/ and fight/ and there's no time to live, live, live! /

VERSE 1: Everything was mine again/ and thou shall rise/ and fight/ that there's no time to live, live, live! / Fore if you want paradise/ you need to fight/ wake up and praise Jesus Christ/ cause I'll touch your mind/ heal you in one night/ aahh maybe faster/ because it's taken thousands of years, to end these evil chapters/ I thou father, have come to save those, ready to praise me/ and bow and feel Heavenly/ that…

HOOK/CHORUS: Everything that was my mine again/ and thou shall rise/ and fight/ and there's no time to live, live, live! / Everything was mine again/ and thou shall rise/ and fight/ and there's no time to live, live, live!/

VERSE 2: Okay, okay, not everything you read/ is really what it seems/ I was trying to teach something, years before you even understood these words that I use in threes/ multiply everything about my MIZeRY/ or the father, the son, holy spirit as I bless you literally/ Okay, Magically/ I mean scientifically/ metaphysically/ either way I'm doing something spiritually/ that is healing/ of magnitudes never you comprehend beyond teaching/ I mean preaching/ when I use lyrical incisions to defeat the evil in your mind/ and in your lustful adventures/ for seductive treasures/ not many accepted/

no exception/ there's only one direction/ that's mine, Heavenly resurrection/

HOOK/CHORUS: Everything that was my mine again/ and thou shall rise/ and fight/ and there's no time to live, live, live! / Everything was mine again/ and thou shall rise/ and fight/ and there's no time to live, live, live!/

VERSE 3: Before my ascension/ back home to Heaven/ before a third day risen/ painful infliction/ upon my flesh, for wrong conviction/ tortured beyond imagination/ three days of crucifixion/ I'm starving/ bleeding/ agonizing sins, I'm absorbing/ father, at this moment I'm abandoned/ almost betrayed/ it's the devils tricks, forcing evil thoughts/ in which I shouldn't explain/ God dealing centuries of pain/ Lord help me with these lessons I need to explain/ before it's too late/ Forcing your Almighty wrath, summoning the end of days/ father all I ask, is I salvage at least Three hundred, thirty three million/ That number sounds good while I'm speaking/ plus, plenty for repopulating/ sacred lands of fathers visions/ miraculous inventions/ with direction/ of Almighty comprehension/ creating nine realms of human entities/

SUMMARY - I'll explain it like this. "Wow is all I can say, when I think about this song. First of all, "Day of My Return" wasn't written and I finished this song within only 1-2 attempts. The lyrics came quickly from within my own soul and mind; while embracing a life, that I truly don't remember; other than when God permits me to remember, through song. When I recorded this song at first, I had no idea what I was even talking about. However, the more that I listened and replayed this song over several months; the song began to really make perfect sense. Shall I summarize for you all? Well, the first verse is discussing God's frustration; while expressing his happiness, that better days are finally near. The second verse continues on explaining how powerful he truly is and that he can heal all things, no matter the scientific or realistic theory as to how he can. Finally, the third verse is discussing Jesus' plans for when he returns, to salvage those worthy, and the world; creating, a new existence both in the Universe and in Heaven: In other words, "**9-Realms of Human Entities**." In addition, He discusses the pain and the hardships he went through when he was crucified. When I say He, I mean me, back than, in a different life. A life in which I can't remember in my new form."

Chapter 15
MIZeRY ReCORDS WORKS'

Welcome to the section, I have decided to dedicate within my novel to represent all my hard work and dedication; in building, a successful & victorious organization. Throughout this section, you will encounter a large scale of images & designs, and their specific details pertinent to each. These images or designs are a collage of my company's work-minus a select bunch; whether they are owned, designed by me or my company, or they were created for a client we hired or hired us, or one of our staff members had secured and assisted in creating. Please note, all of the work you find here is owned and protected by the full aspects of the law; by *MIZeRY ReCORDS* & our Associates. In no way, shape, or form may anyone whom reads this novel tarnish, distribute, or claim for their own the following materials found herein. This section is Michael Izzo's new life's work and we will protect any and all materials at all costs.

A list of all logos designed and used by MIZeRY and *MIZeRY ReCORDS*. From left to right: Company logos used for different formats, HABCTOUR logo, Parental & Literal advisory logo, and MIZeRY's new genre logo for R.A.P.P, ©2011.

My *Coca-Cola* design, I entered into an Eyeka contest for *Coca-Cola's* new product. Unfortunately, my design was not picked as a finalist. Bottle designed using AutoCAD, ©2010.

The Destruction Lp - 2004 (f/b)

The Savior of Rap - 2005 (f/b)

No More Running - 2010 (f/b)

15 Years of My Life - 2011 (Def Jam Debut - f/b)

World Take Over - Mixtape Hosted by Dj Onpoint (2011 f/b)

Til' Death Do Us Part - 2011 (Def Jam f/b)

The 2nd Coming - Disc 1 (TBA 2012)
The New World - Disc 2 (TBA 2012)

Judgment Day - Mixtape (2012 f/b)

Above is a collage of all of MIZeRY's music albums; some of which are not yet published. All albums were designed & under the art direction of Michael Izzo, himself.

Demo cover for artist 8ighth Wonder. Cover designed by Michael Izzo. Above music is currently licensed through *FreePlayMusic Media*, ©2009.

CD cover's design for the band – Kendo the almost famous; works with *Public Enemy*. Cover designed by Michael Izzo with the direction of Kendo, ©2010.

Above is the front; below is the back.

Demo cover design for the band – Kendo the almost famous; works with *Public Enemy*. Cover designed by Michael Izzo with the direction of Kendo, ©2010.

Above are the two possible front options. Below is the back of either option.

Signature HABCTOUR T-shirts designed by Michael Izzo, for the Health Awareness & Breast Cancer Tour. Shirts come in all sizes, for males and females. Release TBA on **www.mizeryrecords.com/products**. All T-shirts owned by Michael Izzo, ©2011.

Signature HABCTOUR T-shirts designed by Michael Izzo, for the Health Awareness & Breast Cancer Tour. Shirts come in all sizes, for males and females. Release TBA on **www.mizeryrecords.com/products**. All T-shirts owned by Michael Izzo, ©2011.

Signature shirt design for *MIZeRY ReCORDS* -artist "Imfamous." Shirts come in all sizes for males and females. Release TBA on **www.mizeryrecords.com/products**. All T-shirts owned by Michael Izzo, ©2011.

A Big Deal T-shirts; Shirts come in all sizes for males and females. Release TBA on **www.mizeryrecords.com/products**. All T-shirts designed by Michael Izzo; ©2011.

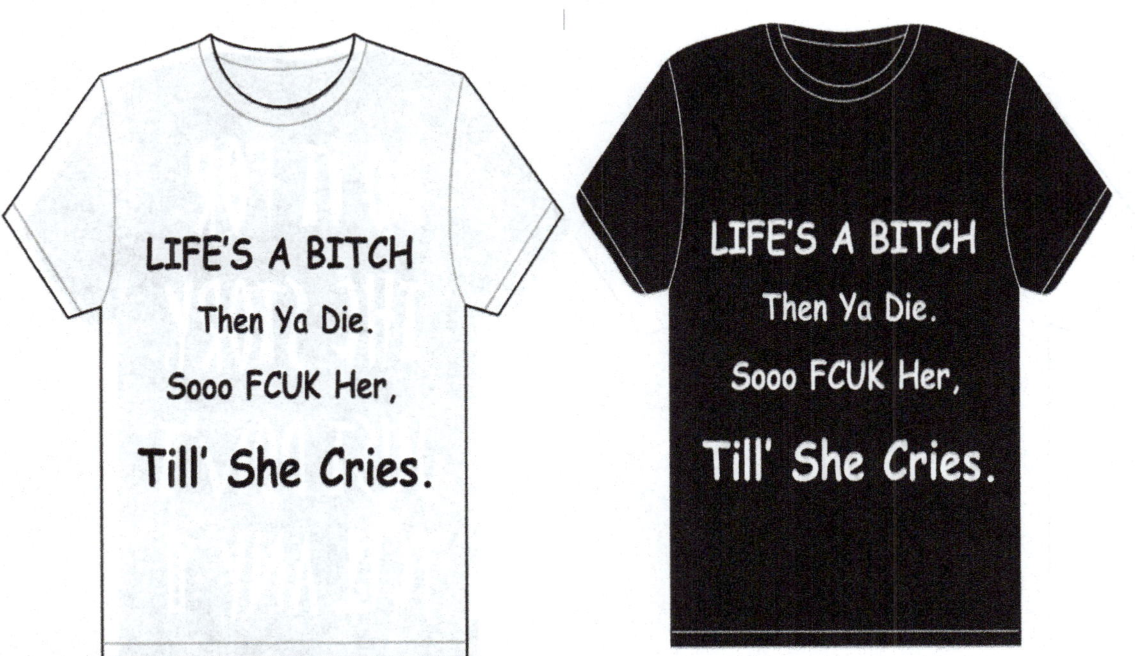

One of *MIZeRY ReCORDS*' signature series T-shirts; Shirts come in all sizes for males and females. Release TBA on **www.mizeryrecords.com/products.** All T-shirts designed by Michael Izzo. All T-shirts designed by Michael Izzo, ©2011.

Take 1 for the team – front, T-Shirt. Shirts come in all sizes for males and females. All T-shirts designed by Michael Izzo, ©2011.

Take 1 for the team – back, T-shirts, Shirts come in all sizes for males and females. All T-shirts designed by Michael Izzo. Release TBA on **www.mizeryrecords.com/products**. All T-shirts designed by Michael Izzo, ©2011.

Popblount, Stackhouse, and Perk Logo; designed by MIZeRY for *Fresh Entertainment Inc.*, ©2009.

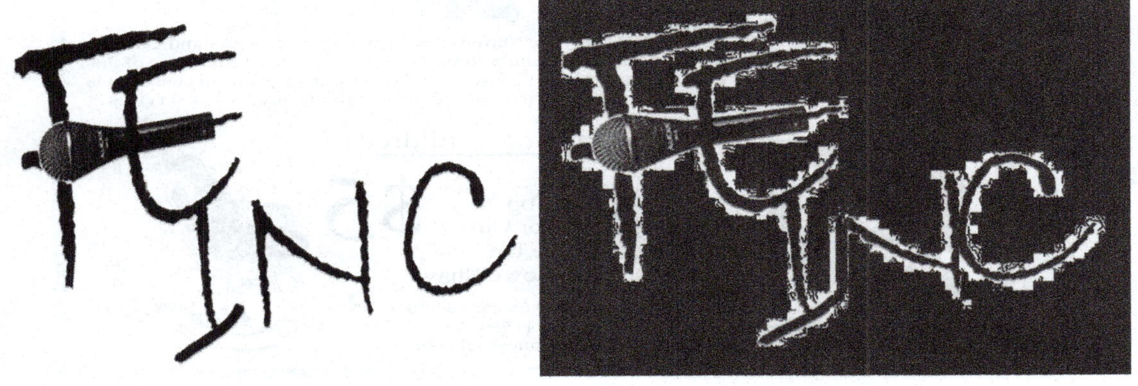

Fresh Entertainment Inc. 1st Logo Design; Designed by MIZeRY, ©2009.

Fresh Entertainment Inc. Website Banner; designed by MIZeRY, ©2009.

The Long Island Barber Institute – Business Card front; designed by MIZeRY, ©2009.

The Long Island Barber Institute – Business Card back; designed by MIZeRY, ©2009.

Jon N. – Business Card front; designed by MIZeRY, ©2010.

1st *MIZeRY ReCORDS* business cards front and back, designed by MIZeRY, ©2009.

2nd *MIZeRY ReCORDS* business cards front; designed by MIZeRY, ©2011.

Nilka Hendricks professional business card. Designed by MIZeRY, ©2008.

Keep it Hot Tour July 3rd 2008. Coordinated and organized by Fresh Entertainment Inc. in association with MIZeRY. This tour never commenced beyond the 1st show. I learned from this event, not all events are successful. Flyer designed by MIZeRY, ©2008.

Tight Work Army (Rap Group) demo cover; designed by MIZeRY, ©2008.

Devil has a price on my head - Mixtape cover. Album artwork drawn by Deonna S.; Art direction and graphics by MIZeRY, ©2011.

MIZeRYReCORDS.com wallpaper and website logos; custom designed for *MIZeRY ReCORDS* website. Our entire website was designed and is owned by Michael "MIZeRY" Izzo, ©2007. Please visit www.mizeryrecords.com for more info, thank you.

Chapter 16
My photo album

I awoke slowly on the 3rd of June, 1987 at 8:06 am. I was received by the hands of M.D. Timothy Riley in San Diego, CA at San Diego hospital, located at 4045 Third Ave. San Diego, CA. 92103. As the years went by, and with what little photos I have found to remember them by; I have compiled them all right here, for the world to see. I have nothing to hide, nor do I intend to keep my life a secret anymore. Each photo represents a specific year in my life and will include a photo caption. Unfortunately, I do not have photos from most of my life. I have only a select few of years throughout my life, which have been captured, and placed here…

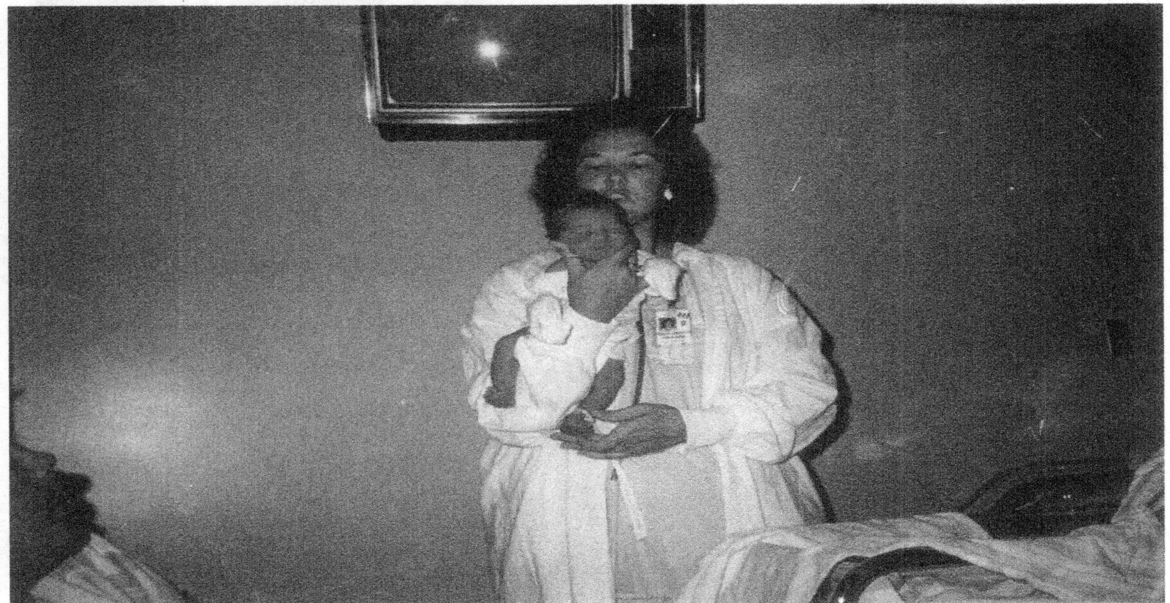

Here is the birth of Michael Lee Edward Izzo AKA Saint Michael Thee Archangel, on June 3rd 1987 in San Diego Hospital, San Diego, CA.

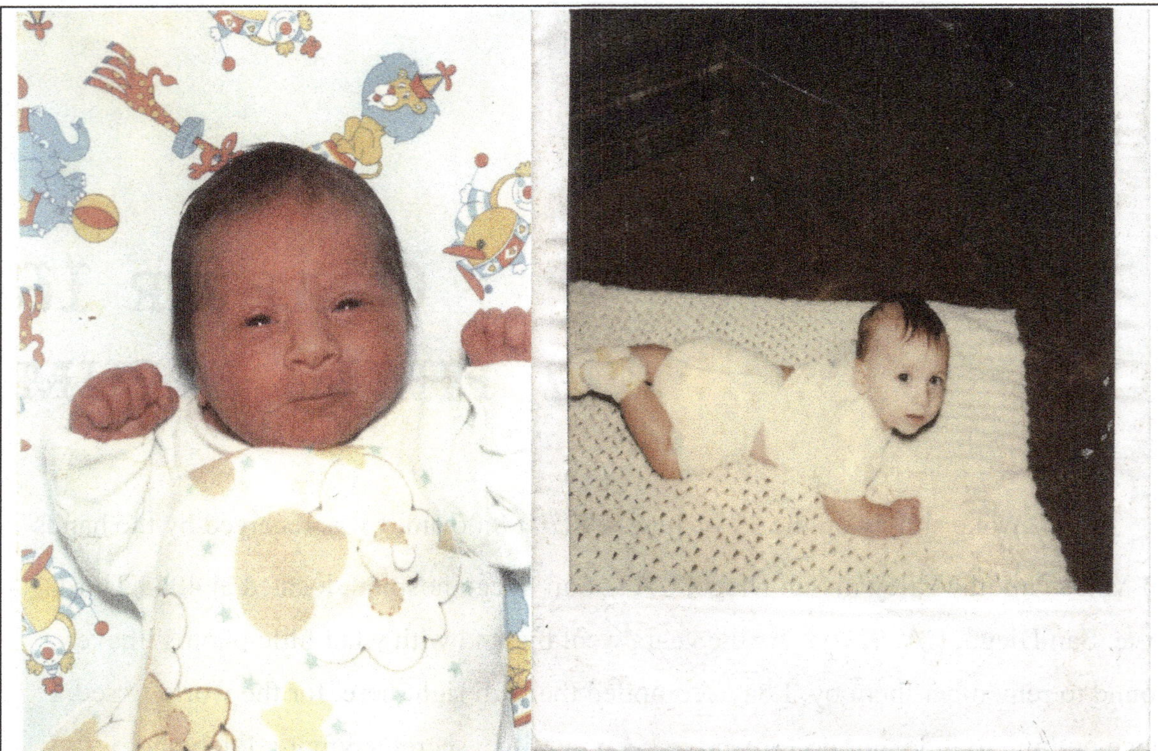

Here, I am a newborn baby. I am about 3 months old here.

In this photo is my mother Tina, me (2.3 y/o), & my younger brother Vincent (3 mo/s) in Syosset, NY.

Here is a classic photo of my older brother William (6) and me (3).

Here, I am (4) with my mom Tina, William (7 y/o), and Vincent (2 y/o) at Williams's communion in Sea Cliff, NY.

In this photo is my grandma Joy, me (5 y/o), & Vincent (3 y/o) at the beach in New York.

Me and my brothers picking pumpkins with Vincent, left (4), me (6), & William (9).

In this photo are William (10), Rosemarie (6), Mathew (5), Annemarie (8), Michael (7), Vincent (5), & Anthony (4) located at my grandma's house in Glenwood Landing, NY.

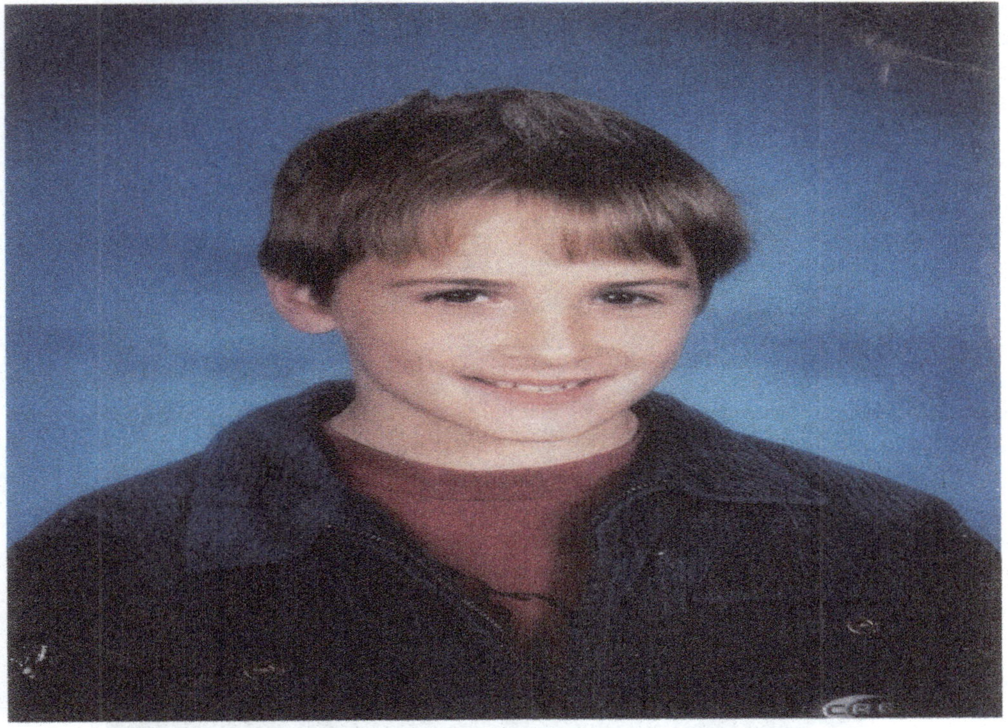

Here, I am posing for a school photo at (7). One of the rare occasions I'm smiling.

1. I am eight, playing baseball.

2. I'm eight, after my communion.

Here, I am grown up at age 12 posing for another school photo.

I am (15) with my good friend Kimberley (14) in this photo; including, Kim's older brother Mike (22).

Here, I am (19) coordinating with Jon N. (30), Brian H. (20), Lauren (18), & Brittney (18) during studio session in Hauppauge, NY.

Having a few drinks (20) with good friend Arturo; during the grand re-opening of Chambord® liquor.

Me (21) and *Badboy/Konvict Music* Recording Artist Red Café in C.T.; after, I opened for his performance in 2008.

Here, I am (22), taking a photo during an exclusive recording session in (DJ Honda's NYC Studio); with my client Uncle Murda – formerly of *Def Jam & Rocafella Records*. I solely coordinated this recording session. However, due to the fact Uncle Murda was later dropped from both labels; this project never saw the light of day. ©2008 – *MIZeRY ReCORDS* ; Left: Pooch, Debo-Brown, Uncle M, Alex, DJ Honda in chair, & assistant.

Here, I am (22) with my old love-interest Jayne (22); in Massapequa, NY.

Having fun at my Cousin Christine's house. I'm (22), with my sister Christina (14), my cousin Anthony, and friends in Levittown, NY.

Here, I am (22), capturing a photo of platinum selling artist *Christopher Williams;* during an exclusive NYC rehearsal recording session; © 2008, *MIZeRY ReCORDS.*

Here, I am (23) in my basement office in my fathers home office; as I'm recording my album "No More Running" in MA.

Here, I'm (24) posing for album covers & photo-shoot in Times Square Manhattan NY.

Here, I am thinking about my Novel in my N.Y. home at the age of 25, as I realized I was Jesus Christ.

Left – right: Katrina, Lindsay, Brian, Meghan, Michael, Jackie, & Natalia during swim suit fashion runway show at splash ultra lounge in downtown Boston, MA.

Chapter 17
Jesus is me; and I am Jesus

At the age of twenty five, I have become very strained from all of the new developments building in my life. From discovering a long lost truth about my own self; and I uncovered how to be victorious in the promise that I once told the world, long ago. However, I am also struggling on a day to day basis, just to maintain stability in a twisted and confused society; revolved around currency. Not only do I have to continue building and developing my organization; I must also deliver this novel to the world; resulting, everyone being able to begin to see the truth: that I Jesus Christ, am upholding my promise, as I once made to the world. However, I have so many other projects in which I am creating, which I have designed to help promote unification globally. The hardest thing for me to do, is overcoming the challenges of proving it; while humanely showing the world, that I am everything I have alleged to be. At the same time, I must overcome ridicule and disbelief from the world; without judging all the nonbelievers. Aside from that difficult task, I need to figure out how to save the world from itself; while accepting, that it's up to me, through God, that I can even do so. The most intriguing thing I've realized as of late, is that my Crucifixion has made me globally known. Known on a global scale at which was necessary to salvage humanity, when thy end comes. I have also quickly learned that 2,000 years later; I am still struggling to overcome currency and unlawful poverty; while, once again trying to show the world, the truth in life can, and only be achieved through me. As I attempt to accomplish all these tasks; I must also avoid being martyred once again, for wrong conviction.

As we continue on, I will discuss some of my greatest plans and secrets to overcome such worldly objections. All the while, the world will contest against me; derived from the question, if I am truly the return of Christ our Lord and Saviour? The only way I can begin to explain how the plans of my self, and of our Lord and Saviour works; stems from, dividing them into two different contexts or explanations. The first would be of a humanly realistic path; that I as Michael Lee Edward Izzo, a human of Earth will pursue and accomplish. The other explanation of my plans are that of a spiritual biblical destiny, that was preordained, and can only be revealed with time and faith. Although, my spiritual biblical path can't completely be foretold here and now; a large portion of it has already been written, as a guide line for us all to live by and follow. Such a path was once written long ago, in what we refer to as the ***Torah*** and ***The Holy Bible***. Throughout this section, I shall reference some biblical texts in which have been shown to me, through signs in my second life; as I developed, my understanding of my true destiny. Keep in mind, when I wrote this paragraph, I have read only but a few chapters from the ***King James Bible*** in the year 2012. In no way, any of the knowledge in which I contain, premeditated or strategically planned to make me sound correct, or to persuade you otherwise. In addition, any and all knowledge found within my novel comes from within my own heart and the very truth of God; as he permits me to know, such given information. Further stipulating, the very fact that **Free Will** exists, prevents me in every way from persuading you otherwise. That means: you're entitled to your own beliefs as a human being of Earth and Heaven. With that being said, take from my words as you will. It's solely up to you, each and every one of you, to walk towards and through the path of God's light.

First, lets begin with my humanly plans as Michael Lee Edward Izzo. This path is by far, much easier to comprehend as well. Ever since I was a young child, and I'm speaking before the age of 12; I wanted to be successful in a large scale. When I was young, I played baseball which was encouraged by my best friends father, Jim. After many years of playing throughout my youth and several trophies later; I was almost positive, I wanted to be a professional. However, tragedy struck by the age of 8, when I broke my arm with a compound fracture. This tragedy put a permanent end to my plans of ever being such a thing. From the age of 8-12, I started aggressive rollerblading with my peers and neighborhood friends. By the time I was twelve, I was so involved and rapidly excelled at it; I began receiving sponsorship offers. However, around the time I was twelve, I also began developing a passion for writing poetry and wanting to make music. When I turned thirteen, I started crafting my music more and more. Around this same time, I had become injured more physically from rollerblading; which forced me to make a life altering decision. I chose to quit rollerblading; which was a result, from injuries which included: Early stages of arthritis in both my shins and knees, and I tore a ligament in my right thigh. The pain became so severe, I ultimately decided to quit rollerblading and pursue music to fuel my passion for peace. Upon my decision, I quickly birthed my music alias/character **MIZeRY.** By creating MIZeRY, I also created my solely founded entity ***MIZeRY ReCORDS***. Through creating both an alternate identity and entity, I soon would be able to speak freely amongst the world. While stimulating, positive ways to live life truly by. At the same time, if it wasn't for the protection of America's 1st Amendment; I would have never been able to report my life as news, or the lives of others, similarly. The identity MIZeRY, would soon become more than just a name; it became the truth of life, stemming from the pain in which Jesus Christ once suffered from, for us all: to rid the world of evil and sin. MIZeRY is also the identity in which I, as a reincarnated individual of God, have secured, to protect my true identity in an indecent time of humanity. Further more, *MIZeRY ReCORDS* being my sole proprietorship would show the world that everything I stand for, believe in, and represent came from a higher understanding. While mandating credibility, considering I was willing to put my entire livelihood on the line for what I believe in…

As we fast forward 12 years into the future, to present times in the year 2012; we shall see where my plans have ended and where they will continue on towards. I under the alias MIZeRY, have come so far to tell my story to the world, and with that I have completed the following: I have created eight mastered and professionally recorded albums; two of which are currently globally published, and being distributed by *Island Def Jam* in over 150 countries. In addition, I have secured song features with larger artists; whom helped acquire me, more popularity and fans that believe in similar values of life as I. In 2010, I created a national and international touring project by the name of "The HABCTOUR AKA The Health Awareness & Breast Cancer Tour." I then submitted, a 20 page business proposal to Susan G. Komen to endorse us upon. With the grace of God, they have extended their assistance, contingent on a $25,000 donation; commencing a joint venture, in the near future. Two years later, I am still working eagerly to commence the HABCTOUR project and raise money to help fight a serious epidemic; Breast Cancer. Additionally, I have also created several new projects in 2012, which are: My novel, movie, and movie soundtrack all encompassing the story of my life and the life of Jesus Christ returned. This project is part of what you're reading this very second; which is also a collection of my work, all creating the story of "The 2nd Coming of Jesus Christ." This novel, My movie, and My movie sound track is by far my best work musically and grammatically; to the point, I believe this is my life's masterpiece or even my final work of all time! My Intentions with this large project, is to show the world my story from when I was Jesus Christ; My story of me as Michael Lee Edward Izzo; the truth of life and which path the world should follow in; and finally, the pre-ordained path in which God has intended for humanity. Such knowledge will be revealed in a series of works, minus a select few series of events; which are not predictable by anyone. Simply, MIZeRY ReCORDS stimulates positive living for eternal peace amongst everyone, throughout the world, and with the use of tools such as: music, movies, and books. Additionally, I shall stop at nothing to succeed at my mission to end all wrong, and I shall continue to write about my life. I was not able to do so long ago; and I am sick of seeing farfetched theories about my life, in previous writings, or by third party religious organizations whom can only: **speculate theorized ideas about Jesus Christ and my infinite ways.** My business, *MIZeRY ReCORDS*: is my creation, which will employ millions of people globally; but is also one of the major tools used, so we can fix the world and all its flaws. My sole mission in this second life, has and will always be to change the world, and rid it of sin. My demeanor in person will always be different; for God is mysterious and I being a reflection of him, shall never reveal all my intentions. Additionally, all great things take time; however, always remember I've said on a song: "If God can build the world in 6 different days/ than I can do something huge in a lifetime man/." I have dedicated and sacrificed my entire life for my dreams to succeed, in a positive selfless manor. Lastly, I don't care if I never become successful in my social class lifestyle; for, I have surrendered my life to the Lord and I only truly serve him for all eternity.

Moving onto all the biblical and spiritual avenues; in which I believe in, and have been able to support factually, with biblical scripture. According to the previous scriptures; which large populations of people, throughout the world, have all read at some point or another about Jesus; all relate too, a sum of these indisputable facts. One: Jesus is the true son of God, Two: he was miraculously born without the act of conception, Third: His body was human & His spirit was Divine, & Fourth: His actions stemmed from living by and teaching love, respect, humility, & equality. However, Jesus also did far more than just that; including, but not limited to: heal the sick, deaf and blind, but he also resurrected Lazarus and himself; while sustaining life after death, transmuting into a spiritual being and physical being, in an infinitely never ending manor. Aside from all of the above facts and the most important one of all, which was: The Resurrection of Christ; Jesus, self sacrificed His life to bridge the gap between Heaven and Earth. However, His Crucifixion did not open the gates to Heaven; it simply built the bridge between our two realms. The Second Coming of Jesus Christ is in fact, the time and event in which the doors to Heaven are permanently opened; for those whom are worthy, resulted upon **JUDGMENT.** This means that if you sacrifice your life for unselfish reasons, then you may be granted eternal life with God. The Second Coming of Jesus is God's masterpiece; which has been in the works for over 2, 000 years, and will occur exactly 1,993 years after Jesus' death. The Second Coming, by definition is the end of all sin and evil; creating, a sustainable existence between God and humans, by defeating and imprisoning the Devil. In order to humanly fathom and comprehend, The Second Coming and all that it entails; you must first understand, why it must occur, and how Jesus must accomplish it. Let's start with the how. Jesus Christ was first born sometime around 6 BC. At age 12, Jesus started tapping into His unlimited gift of intelligence; whilst insisting, he could teach something beyond the given in which is known. From ages 13-29, there are no formal records of Jesus Christ. Although, I can't even explain what happened during this time; I can only explain that I know Jesus wasn't prepared for His true mission in life, during these lost years; both mentally and physically. Sometime around the given time of him turning Twenty Five; Jesus Christ began to fully accept and understand who he was; and what he was to accomplish in the universe. What this means, is that Jesus realized he was different; that he was very intelligent; he accepted that he was, who and what he was in all His miraculous glory; and he began understanding, His mission is far from complete. Over the next five years: Jesus continued to analyze, understand, and work hard at His mission for God and for humanity. He also eagerly awaited His eternal love to connect with him, to support him in His last days, and to pass on His true legacy. Jesus was solely focused on love and all it represents in every possible form; which resulted him to explain, how all must originate from it. Furthermore, he knew he needed a spouse to aid and support him in His struggles in life, to accomplish such goals. Although, Jesus is very strong and mentally capable, to withstand the Devils infinite ways of tricks and sin; Jesus was still human, which forced him to break down occasionally too.

Around the age of thirty, Jesus began tapping into a divine energy of power. This power was limitless, and came equipped with an over abundance of rules and requirements: starting with "**Free will**." This divine energy of limitless power, includes many examples; however, according to records some examples were: walking on water, multiplying food from samples, healing humans of all their sickness' and persecution, and the gift of eternal life and resurrection of others and thyself. During His early thirties, Jesus began to teach the truth of existence to mankind; and attain as many human followers, whom accepted the truth and followed it. Even to this day, the amount of individuals whom ridicule, deny, label negatively, or retaliate violently against what Jesus Christ is and taught; shall out number those, whom are apart of him and all he is. Throughout His last years of life, something extraordinarily unknown occurred; whether or not it was physical or miraculous. That miracle was when Jesus Christ found the path to divinity, in all the Lord our Father's mighty glory. Through His short period of touring and teaching all the people he could, he always had Mary Magdalene; whom followed him, and remained by His side through His travels and hardships in His final years. Upon Jesus' self sacrifice for the greater good; he was granted eternal life, allowing him to resurrect and become one with His true form; as a piece of God. Through this gift of new life, it allowed for him to bridge the path between two existences; Heaven & Earth. However, by sacrificing himself in His first life as requested by God the father; Jesus knew, he would also have to return and destroy evil, sin, and the Devil for eternity; before, mankind would be permitted to in fact: enter Heaven. As a result, Jesus created an alternate identity and form of existence; in order to be strong enough and mentally prepared for His second return. This Second form would very loosely, and vaguely be prophesized, and defined as "**Saint Michael Thee Archangel**;" or biblically referred to as "The prince of Heaven and the highest of Angels." Jesus was also divided by three sections: containing a divine portion of the Father; containing a Holy Spirit; and Him being a male, created His human form as the true Son of God. However, Jesus was shown humanities existence and end, during several many visions; in which, were streamed miraculously, while sequentially, of Earth's and mankind's timeline: from the beginning to the end. When Jesus was revealed many hundreds, of thousands of years, of history; within a short period of time, through visions; Jesus saw, how rough and brutally strong he would have to become, in order to slay the most evil man in existence. Through such visions, Jesus knew he must remain righteous during the end of days. Ultimately, Saint Michael Thee Archangel was created prior to the Crucifixion; as preparation for when, Jesus Christ would return. It is only possible for Jesus and Michael to be the same, because there is only one prince of all Angels, and that of Heaven; which is Jesus Christ and Michael Thee Archangel; for they are one and the same: **Like Father, Like Son**. What this means, is that they both have to sacrifice themselves for eternal peace of life. Different to that of Jesus' mission, I would have to enslave or slay the Devil, and absorb all His evil; both mentally and physically, into my spirit; ridding us all from such evil for eternity: hence the creation of **MIZeRY**.

Let's take a few steps back. If Jesus Christ was resurrected, how come I'm stating that Jesus will come back as Saint Michael Thee Archangel? Although, Jesus Christ is one with God and mankind; as an elemental spirit of physical chemistry; upon His resurrection, he returned to Heaven and entered a slumber. This slumber, prevented Jesus from coming back to rapture the world; sooner, than the amount of time in which has already lapsed. Accumulating roughly, just under 2,000 years; allowing for adequate preparation, before the end of days. Jesus created an alternate destiny for himself, allowing him to return to Earth, and create an alternate result to save the world; by unlocking the gates to Heaven, upon the destruction of the Devil. Because Jesus' Crucifixion, did not extinguish the Devil; the gates remained locked. Preventing evil, from penetrating God's Eternal Realm of Heaven, and peace. Saint Michael Thee Archangel was thus created; permitting for a new life form of Jesus Christ, to complete

His secondary task; in which he was sentenced to fulfill, by defeating Sintin. Further more, this is how Jesus Christ will fulfill His promise; by returning and saving the world: by way of reincarnation, rebirth, or known as offspring. Since Jesus Christ is still in a spiritual slumber; he is awaiting to be woken up by: His wife, Thee Archangels, & The Holy Trumpets. All three are the true keys to starting the Rapture. Most importantly, love will permit me to fulfill my final task of creating my eternal Kingdom of Heaven. All these above events, would then, domino into one another in an instantaneous manner; resulting, what you know as the End of Days. Upon such events igniting, Saint Michael Thee Archangel and Jesus Christ will merge back into one being, spiritually: similarly, as he did upon His original Resurrection. Upon the return of Christ Thy Lord, the world will cease all movement and operation. Once Jesus heals the entire world, the world will then begin rotation in the reverse polarity: changing good to best and bad to non existent.

Understanding Resurrection: The human body consists of three main elements: The Father - which is the brain, The Son – which is the physical body, & The Holy Spirit - which is the heart. The Holy Spirit lives on forever, so long as the individual sacrifices ones life righteously: by following God's ways. However, if one submits to the Devil and his cruelties on mankind; including all materials and amenities, then one must forfeit such said right to have eternal life: powered by the Holy Spirit. If one does not forfeit such said right, of the Holy Spirit; then the gifts granted by The Father, being the mind, are re-inserted with only God's truth. The physical form, will eventually die because that's simply physical matter and the elements of life. Further more, when Jesus discovered the definition of eternal life, originating with having to resurrect; he realized, in order to succeed during His Second Coming, several thousand years later; he would have to understand reincarnation and rebirth. As explained earlier, since the physical body eventually rots and dies, a new body must be generated or created, in order for Jesus Christ's eternal spirit to descend into, and live again through. In other words, The Second Coming would mandate Jesus being reborn as a human, just as he was originally. Rebirth, mandates a new life, body, mind, and he would also have a different name. Although, he would look similar by an above 90% physical resemblance; it was not perfectly equal. Since memories and thoughts are stored in the brain, Jesus as Michael would never be able to remember all that he once was. However, His Holy Spirit being one and the same, with His past life, would remember, and feel all that it has for those several thousand years; because, His Spirit never died or dies. In other words, I have dreams, visions, and premonitions given to me by God throughout my current life. Guiding me as I complete My "Final Testament." Reincarnation is simply a connection between both lives; in which has been granted to whom was worthy of such a gift, of 2nd life. Resulting, a Paradox Parallax of Reality between the past and present life. Ergo, connecting one Holy Spirit with two brains and bodies, in two completely different time zones, and era's of existence. Jesus Christ and Michael Thee Archangel, being operated by the same person/driver, would result: Similar outcomes throughout ones existences'; creating, a Paradox Parallax of similar Realities. Going beyond the scientific definition; very simply, if Jesus discovered His miraculous Powers of energy at 30; I, Michael won't receive such abilities until age 30 currently. If Jesus was married or found Mary by Age 26, or 27. I won't find Mary's reincarnation, until such age and so forth. Most importantly, in relation to the universe and that of the titled event "The Second Coming;" if Jesus was crucified at age 33, then I won't imprison the Devil until 33. This rule, prevents The Second Coming and eternal life, until such a time occurs. Thus, the world won't be saved or re-created for another 8-9 years. I am 25 years old in the year 2012, and until I'm 33-34 again; I won't be triumphant in accomplishing my mission, sentenced to me by God. Basically, 2012 isn't the destruction of Earth, but the end of sin and evil for eternity; allowing for a new beginning. This beginning, will open the doors to Heaven for all those worthy; preventing the Mayan's from predicting and completing God's final timeline. God is perfect and has a plan for all; while including, everything within the subject of numerical equations. At this point in time, I truly can't answer how or why I know this, or why I have been shown this. But I know, I truthfully feel and believe I am supposed to teach this, and show this information with all of God's Children. The ultimate test of life is choosing to believe in God or not too. If you do, that mean's you don't doubt what he teaches because he is the only truth! Additionally, since I am the creator of this information in terms of grammatically structuring this Novel, in a suitable form of comprehension; I never chose this mission nor wanted it; but I accepted it, and I will complete my purpose in life with it. I will, because I only live for God and eternal life of peace, for all humanity. No man shall prevent me, from creating eternal peace of equality.

Chapter 18
The 24 Apostles

Let me first explain, why there are twenty four apostles and their purpose sentenced upon them. According to logic, I can only truthfully base my understanding and knowledge, about my life and biblical history; based on what was written and established previously... Back when Jesus first lived, the story of His closest friends and students, AKA apostles, represented his legacy and teachings; whilst devoting their lives to His mission, which was also their missions'. As our history tells us, there were the following amongst them; **Simon Peter -** (brother of Andrew) – he was active in bringing people to Jesus. **James-b -** (son of Zebedee and older brother of John) also called "James the Greater." **John -** (son of Zebedee and brother of James). **Andrew –** (brother of Simon Peter) – He was active in bringing people to Jesus also. **Phillip –** whom came from Bethsaida. **Thomas –** (Didymus). **Bartholomew –** (Nathaniel) he was one of the disciples to whom Jesus appeared at the Sea of Tiberias, after His Resurrection; he also witnessed the Ascension. **Matthew -** (Levi) of Capernaum. **James-b –** (son of Alphaeus) also called "James the Lesser." **Simon the Zealot -** (the Canaanite). **Thaddaeus – Judas** (Lebbaeus, brother of James the Lesser and brother of Matthew (Levi) of Capernaum. **Judas Iscariot -** whom betrayed Jesus; shortly after Jesus being nailed to the cross, Judas Iscariot committed suicide. Ultimately, Jesus knew *Judas* would betray him, far worse than any others could have prior to the betrayal. When Mary Magdalene became committed to him eternally; Mary technically was the twelfth and final apostle, of Jesus Christ: the apostle of apostles. Further supporting these claims, suicide results in automatic forfeit to ones spirit, body, and soul of mind; which results, eternal punishment with no chance for reincarnation. Upon Jesus learning this, during His time of receiving a plethora of information, and throughout his last three years; resulted the secret appointing of His companion: "Mary Magdalene" as his Queen, partner, & president of everything that he ever taught or created. Below is a diagram of all apostles in no specific order...

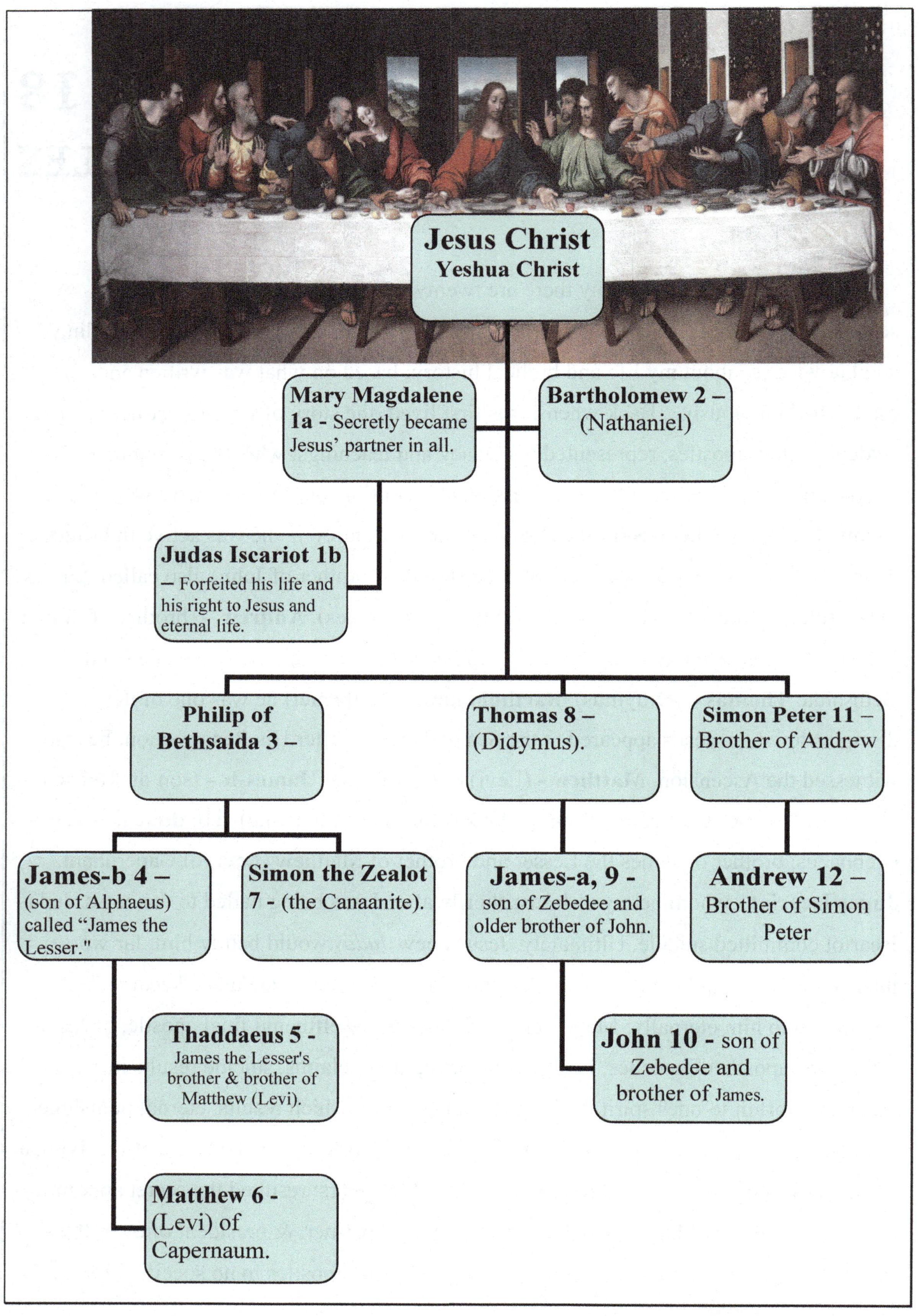
Jesus Christ
Yeshua Christ
Mary Magdalene 1a - Secretly became Jesus' partner in all.
Bartholomew 2 – (Nathaniel)
Judas Iscariot 1b – Forfeited his life and his right to Jesus and eternal life.
Philip of Bethsaida 3 –
Thomas 8 – (Didymus).
Simon Peter 11 – Brother of Andrew
James-b 4 – (son of Alphaeus) called "James the Lesser."
Simon the Zealot 7 - (the Canaanite).
James-a, 9 - son of Zebedee and older brother of John.
Andrew 12 – Brother of Simon Peter
Thaddaeus 5 - James the Lesser's brother & brother of Matthew (Levi).
John 10 - son of Zebedee and brother of James.
Matthew 6 - (Levi) of Capernaum.

Moving along, the twelve final apostles in which Jesus visited, after His Ascension; became His legacy, His closest friends, and Angels for eternity. All of which, specifically selected by God and Jesus himself. Each of them, were sentenced to a specific set of tasks of missions to complete, within their lives; including in their after-lives. As far as what each one was sentenced to do; can only be speculated upon and seen in biblical scripture. However, just as Jesus rose from the dead; each of his apostles would eventually be granted the same gift. For, they are one and the same with Thy Lord and Saviour. What this also means is that because Jesus Christ was reincarnated, to succeed at his promise, and to fulfill The Second Coming; that meant, all of his apostles would be reincarnated too; aiding and guiding Jesus' new body and life, during The Second Coming too. Why 24 apostles you say? Simply, all the apostles not including Judas, sacrificed their lives for Jesus and his legacy; permitting them, life in the eternal kingdom of Heaven with God. This would also result, the recruitment of reincarnation for The Second Coming; because they existed with Jesus, since the beginning. However, since Judas is no longer with us; we remain with twelve apostles, not thirteen. Twelve for the first life and a new set of twelve in the second life; resulting 24 apostles total, created for two era's of life to aid and worship Jesus Christ. Aiding Jesus, in everything and anything in which He requires. Amongst those 24; 10 of them were chosen specifically to work, teach, and use inhumane methods to protect and serve our Lord and Saviour. Amongst those requirements, they were mentally and physically the strongest of all those whom followed Jesus; granting them a **Throne** status in God's army of Angels. The status of being a **Throne** is one of the highest ranks in the **Holy Army;** next to the right of the **Holy Virgin Mary**. Their missions of the first life mostly included: studying Jesus, protecting Jesus, and assisting in gathering people to see Jesus. In the second life, their tasks mainly revolve around similar requirements. However, they have in fact been gathering and building worthy followers for nearly 2,000 years; within the physical and spiritual worlds.

As of today, I'm just beginning to comprehend all that is and my mission in life. I have also yet to find, all my apostles; considering, I'm still only 25 years old. However, I am positively sure that within the next five years, my apostles will gradually reveal themselves, and most importantly; I will find my Mary, if I haven't already found her…

Based on irrefutable scientific evidence, resulting what we know as a paradox parallax of reality; we can only assume that my life, and the lives of my closest followers, will lead a similar timeline; resulting, a predetermined series of events in an overall spectrum. Ultimately, Mary Magdalene won't be Mary Magdalene in her new life; but she will contain a series of signs, in which relate to whom she once was; all originating, with her name. A paradox parallax of reality based on my scientific and divine knowledge, when combined in a humane understanding; results the very understanding of faith, in relation to God, and His miraculously mysterious ways. Once one forfeits the doubt of existence, and how things are; then and only then, can one become one with God! In addition, because I am one with God and have personally sacrificed my life, several times over, in this life, and in the previous one; I truthfully, honestly, believe, and know that all I teach is pure truth. As I wait for all my Holy Glory to return; I sit and I count down the days, awaiting the arrival of my children and people; as one and together, in Heaven and on Earth.

Chapter 19
Humanities greatest flaw

"Free will" with out a doubt in my right and sane mind, stimulating ideology of an infinitely positive existence, has shown me what "Free will" is truly. It all started way back in the year 2008, within the heart of New York State, located throughout the boroughs of Manhattan. I was in my early twenties, when I began a long enduring journey through the path of **(righteous > evil) or (right > wrong);** which helped me place my own life into perspective, in relation with humanity. I then realized a simple truth, that truth was the very fact **"Free will"** was the Greatest Gift which failed; which was ever given to humans, as a gift from the All Father. The reason in which it's the greatest failed Gift is because "**Free will**," can be human's best friend or human's worst enemy. What humans fail at constantly, every single day is the fact: life is as simple as the number **three, 3**. The number 3 has three points, two curves, and zero points of intersection; resulting, shapes which could create i.e. a letter m sideways or a small fighter jet. Besides all of which the number is, many elements of humanity consist of three primary sections also: The brain, lungs, and heart; which is equivalent to The Father, The Son, and The Holy Spirit. Three main sections and three simple truths; which are all affected daily, by the hardest task for humanity to live by: which is "**Free will**." "**Free will**" is as simple as the number three; three main points, three main sections, and three results of existence. Thus: Evil, Neutrality, & Good are the three points which result a path of existence. It's through these paths in which we may follow in. Everything else within the universe; comes after deciding, which path one will pursue for their life.

The path of Neutrality is exactly what it sounds; a person chooses not to choose anything, starting with a side/path. Neutrality will lead you no where, but into an eternal pit of lies and deceit; which you would define as *Purgatory.* A good friend once told me his perception of *Purgatory*, and it all suddenly became clear. My friend Joseph told me: "Envision a room or a location within existence, specifically on Earth, and imagine the neutral party member doing right and wrong in life. After they die, they will be in their safe zone or most loved memory; constantly dealing with the bad and the good, everyday of their life repeatedly, for all eternity, and with only a 37% chance to ever find their way out." He further defined his pictorial image and said; "Imagine a guy whom had a great well paying job, a marriage, a house, and a daily drinking problem. Meanwhile, one day during a drunken argument with his wife; he finally broke down and he decided to bring a bottle, having already being drunk, and drives off storming into the night. Shortly after, crashing his car into another vehicle and dies. As a result, he will forever live his life in purgatory; unless, he can comprehend the reasons why he relives the last day of his life. While everyday, having no memory of it being the same last day, over and over again. However, if he changes his daily fate for eternity; by changing the continuous relived last day of his life; without the ability to remember, it's the same day as yesterday repeated; he will then, remain in an intermediate state after death for expiatory purification."

The path of Evil by definition, as referenced directly above; means you have surrendered your life, by breaking four or more of the seven deadly sins in your life; summing, more than 63% of the time. Additionally, by acting in such a manner despite which variables; you shall forever only exist in a place of permanent tortuous pain and suffering; with no escapable existence, meaning Hell. Hell is controlled and ruled by the *Evilone,* better known as the *Devil.* If you lived a life of mostly evil, you shall forever forfeit your soul, your spirit, and your physical body to God. As a result, God will Judge you and sentence you by: forfeiting your life into a place, in which has no escape or positive feeling of existence. This place contains Demonic environments, torture, pain, fire, brimstone, and suffering beyond humane comprehension. In this place, you will be punished by creatures, animals, and demons of the worst kind of jungle imaginable. However, on a positive note everything in life and existence has a perfect opposite equilibrium. For example, this equilibrium would be the path of purity or Good.

The path of Good and pure nature, means that you do little to no wrong or evil. Meaning: less than four deadly sins in total and less than 37% throughout your life. However, in order to live with God, you must first understand God. Further more, God is perfect; so we as humans whom are flawed, must attempt to be as perfect as we can be, with everything that we do. However, this is undeniably the hardest task for humanity; which will result into some failure; this failure, is also known as sin. These sins, must not exceed three deadly sins and one must repent; while asking for forgiveness from God, repeatedly, and on a consistent level for the majority of your life. You don't need to believe in God as Jesus Christ. However, one must understand and accept that Jesus Christ is the first representation of God himself, in the human form, for men to follow in. Not so much by appearance but by actions, thoughts, and existence. You must further accept, that Mary Magdalene is God's Wife, or known as The Holy Spirit in the first form, for women to follow in. Not so much by appearance but by actions, thoughts, and existence too. By following their examples of life: which consists of righteousness, self sacrifice, and surrendering **Free Will** to Holy Faith of feeling; Then and only then, one may be forgiven eternally. If a person accepts this path of Good natured life; one shall receive the gift of eternal life, with Jesus Christ as a part of Jesus Christ. This can only be achieved through him or Mary Magdalene; granting us entry, into Thy Holy Kingdom. Thy Holy Kingdom is also referred to as Heaven. Heaven does exist and I'll do my best to explain what it's like. Heaven is an unimaginable existence in Earth, in which all things positive exist or are possible. Additionally, there are Angels, there are animals that speak, there are Earths resources, there are houses and families, there are mythological creatures, and there are magical possibilities in which you see in a Disney movie. For example: Heaven is the state of perfect equilibrium, encompassed by Holy Serenity, and contains no evil. Pieces of Heaven, linger within our dreams; which most humans deny, by conforming to the Devils lies of society… Understanding **FINAL JUDGMENT** is by averaging your overall life. Such as, if you lived a life with a majority of the seven deadly sins; meaning, you acted with four or more of the seven deadly sins daily, weekly, and yearly. However, even if you don't for a year or so, your life is determined by the entirety upon FINAL JUDGMENT. This means that from when you are born, until the day you die; you are graded, for your behavior and faithful surrender to a life of Evil or Good…

Chapter 20
Judgment Day/Revelation

I am now age 25, and I am beginning to reach the end of my new life's journey. Although Judgment Day is several years away; metaphorically, my life's work is nearing its greatest Victory and achievement. Ultimately, the story has to end sometime and in my very opinion, given as it may be; I am the author, the creator, and the Saviour. Without me, there is no future, there is no eternal kingdom of limitless energy, and there won't be a new life; there will only be silence... My soul has waited many centuries, to see the day in which I succeeded at being Victorious, over all sin and evil. Thus, this world has fueled sin and evil by the abuse of **Free Will** for too long. As we come closer to Judgment Day; I grow more weary, tired, and powerful because my patience begins to run thin, as the days become less abundant. Don't fret, because when something is destroyed it doesn't cease to exist; but in fact, it takes a new shape or form. With such a new shape or form; a new world shall emerge, amongst all the ruble in which was demolished from **Judgment Day**. Not even I, harbor all the information and knowledge pertinent to this catastrophically beautiful event of rebirth, for all those worthy. However, it is I, whom is the only one that can unlock an Eternity of Peace; by discovering all the secrets of life and rebirth, through the pursuit of Holy Righteousness. As I utilize my ancestor's prophecies of gifted intelligence, from the book of Revelation; I shall study and analyze, while defining, its very meaning as God intended for me to do. The reason in which I must do this, is simply because God is merciful, and God wants the world to choose to change: before it's too late! But time is running short, quickly, and this is merely a last attempt for you all to pursue salvation: found, only through and in me!

Judgment Day – Mixtape cover compiled by me; promotional use only, free download.

Chapter 19: Song 1a – Game of Dreams (19:1a)

Game of Dreams (Remixes by DJ Provenchh from Artist – Game):

"Death before dishonor; before I ever had a dream"

VERSE 1: Okay, when I was about twelve/ I masterminded a plan to escape my own hell/ So I went on the prowl/ and created a record label/ which contains ulterior objectives/ not ever seen from the surface/ I continued having visions and premonitions/ of only succeeding at God's mission/ most people think its superstition/ truly in essence/ through God's presence/ I'm the one causing destruction/ for all those demonic/ Call it Judgment Day. The day, God seeks revenge/ every time I speak, I feel you all cringe/ Slowly consuming your souls, beyond the help of medicine/ No such thing as infections/ so no need for a syringe/ The rap game infected my mentality/ driving me to insanity/ creating alter realities/ shit you can call me MIZeRY/ Or God's insurance policy/ to destroy all of society/ 95% of you are unworthy/ I rolled with Killa's and criminals/ So I can hide from the devil/ all the meanwhile/ becoming a demonic Angel/ soon came the crossroads, to decide how to escape such tangles/ so I said fuck it, dropped the devils gifts/ unloaded my four fifth/ and I was reborn into Jesus Christ/ for the second time/ no Bullshit/ For me, Heaven is worth more than everything/

Dreams… Dreams… Cause I love you…

My Dreams/ are the perception of ones' reality/ through a sequence of images/ during sleep/ well for me/ dreams are constant transfusions between two realities/ Heaven & Earth, I'm trapped inside a massive cage/ I'm being tamed/ and I can not ever escape/ I'm tossing & turning at night/ screaming and asking God why? He replies/ it's a test to see if I'll even fight/ My dreams are so vivid/ I'm actually alive, walking through a dimension/ as a human/ I can not comprehend/ so instead/ I'll keep it real simple/ escaping my pain through music was so critical/ for my very survival/ cause it maintained my vitals/ as I wished I could touch the world with my gifts of prophecies/ which I use through scientific literacy/ For 15 years I was relentless, combating my enemies/ bringing you all my dreams/ instead of befriending me/ The industry kept on avoiding me/ The second

I'm ready to start killing everybody/ that's when all y'all embraced me/ instead, I only live for eternal peace/ and y'all are quick to judge me/ calling me crazy/ or saying fuck MIZeRY/ not to my face, behind my back, and only while I dream/ Ya only while I dream/ soon comes the day, I destroy all of your dreams/ and wildest fantasies/ cause you aren't worthy/ of my humility/ Through the devils worst adversity/ I've upheld my integrity/ so what's that say about you? Even though you hate me, I still love you/ I'll only say it once, for I am Jesus Christ/ yes once again alive/ to decide/ who's truly right/ worthy to be at my side/ in Heaven, yes a real place, most don't think even existed/ A magical place you only hear about through children's fiction/ but it's as real as my one crucifixion/ your brains are plagued with confliction/ I have the keys to eternal perfection/ know this, I shall only give it to those who sacrifice their own lives, repenting, while begging/ for redemption/ this isn't a simple test, it's a mother fucking mission/ using words to pierce your brains with lyrical incisions/ I have but only one question/ what's the meaning of life? The answer is so simple, I made it even rhyme/ with such as words like, Live or Die/ for the end of time/ is on the rise/ and yes, I am thy Holy Lord Jesus Christ/ This is my time to rise/ and it's the time of the devils' demise/ 2000 years of killing is enough time/ the internet has plagued your minds/ I have just decided, as I write this line/ this shall be my last official rhyme/ for the course of history is already written/ soon comes Armageddon/ our lives are mostly pre-scripted/ except for **Free Will**, which is not even encrypted/ it's a mere choice of faithful decisions/ in other words, God Versus the Devil/ choosing a path through gut instincts/ deciding your life through my reflections/

SUMMARY - I'll explain it like this. "This song became a series of my last pieces of music of all time, for the world to abuse and take advantage of. Ultimately, this song was simply designed to elaborate upon what is and how Judgment Day occurs; whilst I explained how it is I operate, based on my life's reflections. My entire existence felt like a lie, until I woke up, and realized my very own truth. In fact, I stepped outside of myself in my adulthood and realized that my heart is truth. The moral of this story is to never forget your own dreams, and always trust within your heart, or gut instincts in any given situation; while remembering to always pursue the righteous option…"

Chapter 19: Song 2a – We runaway slaves (19:2a)

We runaway slaves Ft. Maino (Runaway Slave - Remix):

VERSE 1: Ya, I'm the king of this Earth/ sometimes, I only need a verse/ to cry out our pain, everyone hurts/ for twenty centuries/ my family/ is haste fully/ dying/ all of us are hiding/ from our very own truths – it's frightening/ my true side is terrifying/ God seeks revenge/ for my crucifixions expense/ you failed our tests/ I'm back for a large taste/ I'm back, and about to reclaim/ my planet, no chance I'll ever be tamed/ I'm equivalent to twenty generations, of runaway slaves/ In a world that's so cruel, I've remained the most brave/ tortured and tormented/ into being insane/ trusting in God's ways/ begging him to save me every time I pray/ all I've ever known is Jesus Christ/ making rap music, recording on this MIC/ in 2011, A year before I quit, at the age of twenty five/ God shows me I'm his son, thy Lord Jesus Christ/ In my second term of life/

SUMMARY - I'll explain it like this. "When I started this song, I felt what Maino was referencing, because technically we all were slaves in some form or another in humanity. However, I also briefly knew Maino and attempted to work with him on a show. Either way, I had to explain that I have been running and hiding from my own duties as thy God, since my crucifixion. Simply, I went insane for several thousand years and needed time to adjust and comprehend how to rid all the sin and evil of humanity..."

Chapter 19: Song 3a – Made in America & Otis - Remix (19:3a)

Made in America & Otis – Remix:

VERSE 1: Sweet baby Jesus, 16 bars ain't enough/ Okay when I was real young/ I was trying to create a plan to get me out of my past/ and I'm thinking about it, like Yaa I got to add up the math/ so, when I was old enough maybe about 10/ I came about this new way, writing music with a pen/ and I think about it cause this is how I fueled my energy/ and my fucking depression, that was eating me literally/ everyday when I was young, I just wanted to die/ I was like what's the point to life/ and I'm just fucking masterminding everything I do/ man cause I was a genius, every since I could remember/ and I was always looking for a path for fucking summers/ to be better/ and the winter/ wouldn't be so cold/ and it's like this cause I put it in a song/ and you don't know about it, but I'm living for God/ cause everything I do, will never be wrong/

VERSE 2: As I'm recording to this record, I'm shedding tears, I'm crying/ No joke homie, I've never been lying/ on a record, Ya straight truth/ as I spit it in this booth/ Yaa cause Imma preach/ everything that he taught me to teach/ go ahead think about it as I spit it fluidly over these beats/ Yaa so I think about it, Yaa I got to give it to Ya raw/ so I think about it and I thank God for this song/ because he gives me the strength that I need/ and I tatted MIZeRY ReCORDS on my arm/ to show that I'm way strong/ and no matter what tests he puts me through/ Imma pass it with flying colors homie, cause this is true/ and everything that I'm doing man, cause I'm sick of the blues/ and you know nothing about it, but I use this as my tools/ Yaa, cause I'm lyrically inclined/ and I'm coming at it with some new rhymes/

VERSE 3: Ya I invented RAP/ Rhythmic Acting Poetry/ literally/ Yaa cause Imma give it to you so fluidly/ you mother fuckers is gonna start loosing me/ in the rhyme scheme/ so you better catch up with me/ Yaa cause I'm a thief in the night, I used to be/ oh shit are you even keeping up, multiply intensity/ Yo you even ready to see the fucking shit/ open up Pandora's box/ all of a sudden I'm on the top/ and you cruising so fast, you about to flop/ you don't even know what to do with your career/ nobody feeling you, like oh shit/ all of a sudden rap changed/ I'm taking it back to the old days/ you know nothing about it before you was living good, Yaa you living under the sun/ mother fuckers talking about selling drugs and busting guns/ well you know nothing about it, Yaa do you even own one? Shit I know about it, walk in my shoes/ Yaa you want to see life where it's really fun? Imma show you like this cause the devils got your head spun/ you're all of a sudden in a different world/ reality getting you, mother fuckers is humping your girls/ Yaa, I used to see a lot of different things, partied with a lot of different crooks/ oh shit Ya I'm cruising so fast/ you about to have to jerk/ swerve/ all of a sudden you crashed into the curb/ you know nothing about this skill/ homie, Yaa I got a whole sheet of bad list kills/ you know nothing about it, kid here pop a couple more pills/ Ya I used to like getting high/ then again, I use used to preach about never getting high/ what you know about it man, this is my life twist turned upside down/ oh shit ump num you know nothing now/ Ya you wanna come around my town/ but you don't even know how to spit this crown/ so, think about it Yaa cause I'm using metaphors that you'll never understand/ I do it like this, I am my own band/ oh shit, all of a sudden now you're the man/ cause I gave up the throne and it's all cool with me/ I used to be blown, hair back shit/ incredibly slick/ mother fucks was running around with bandanas thick/ and I'm coming around with some new raps quick/ so you wanna get it down, I'm about to be slick/ in and out of town before you even seen it/ man, Yaa I was fast/ I was running with 100 men deep/ in these streets/ but now I sit wasting time rhyming over these beats/ Yaa do you even follow me/ Yaa should I slow it down for you physically/is you out of shape or something, you can't keep up with me/ MIZeRY, ReCORDS, can't forget it, ha follow us if you want to change your life/

SUMMARY - I'll explain it like this. "I simply had to tell my story about how I felt emotionally, growing up as a child. After I explained my youth, I decided to explain my adult life, and how I feel now and how my entire life as been a test of God."

Chapter 19: Song 4a – Primetime News - Remix (19:4a)

Primetime News – Remix:

VERSE 1: Oh Yea, okay - Yaa Ight. I'll give it to you one time/ equipped with a rhyme bakery stored in my mind/ fact is Babygirl, I used to be primetime/ then all of a sudden, I hit rock bottom! I'm worth nothing more than just a couple of rhymes/ sometimes, I severely question why/ Live or Die/ no lie, but everyday I fight to even try/ to help you all, by spreading God's wisdom through these lines/ those I help and listen/ will be saved in an Instant/ if I was ever the target/ well than I guess you missed it/ misfits/ act like infants/ is it discrimination to say midgets/ resemble nasty insects? You seem a little clueless/ my intelligence/ delivers these messages/ they are of a foreign/ symbols & Languages/ as the devil engages/ philosophies/ metaphorically through Christianity/ as the Second Coming of Christ/ Third day he's risen/ as it's written through my pen/ shut up, now listen/ Christ in all his glory/ is exactly Christianity/ This is what he tells me/ thank you holy Lord/ for this tiny sword/ which produces blue ink/ for slick/ rhymes/ delivered in blinks of an eye/ Lord this is my life/ sit inside/ writing rhymes/ because this feels right/ how else Lord, shall I really bide my time/ instead of committing crimes/ Lord, thank you for my life/ bless me with _______ as my wife/ at first, I know I acted *trif-le*/ I changed and matured because Jesus saved me/ Ya he gave me/ an eternity of blessings/ Ya he kept teaching me lessons/ he showed me that I needed to make the change/ worship Jesus, and he'd save my soul in exchange/ However, there's more to it than that/ pay attention, for this may be my last rap/ The Anti-Christ has majority control/ over you all/ choose Jesus or suffer, engulfed by fire balls/ Jesus will save those who are righteous/ I can't fully explain it/ but to many questions/ it got me really always stressing/ curses come with blessings/ I'm thankful either way/ praise to God, everyday/ June third, is the last Sunday/ before the third day risen/ A thousand years ago/ we were all slaves before/ now let go/ just fall/ we'll catch you/ trust in the Lord/ now take a deep breathe/ we survived this test/ how else can I express/ everyone's depressed/ every five seconds/ there's a death/ sit down and shut the fuck up/ Kidd, no disrespect but this is what it is/ I'm trying to give it to you like this/ cause this maybe the last, Ya the last rhyme that I ever even kick/ so you better pay attention man/ cause I'm trying to spit it so slick/ that it fucking demolishes/ all the ages/ you can't even come around here, with my fucking metaphors/ and the way that I take these words, and I'm just gonna change them up/ and it's like a crane hoisting you up/ and you just want to be down, cause you think I'm what's up/ and I know what, Ya, you want to take a piece of my soul/ but you fucking demons can't even have it, so I dug you a big hole/ I'm digging you so deep/ God couldn't even reach/ you, to save you/ Yaa AK breach/ I'm swat team/ what you know about this shit, I'm a, aawwaa Emcee/ Yaa I'm just fucking confusing you when I stutter/ you think about it man, naa I'm sluggish/ naa Imma slaughter you/ when I'm hustling you/ understand Kidd, I used to have to tussle you/ mother fuckers is thinking they gangsta, cause they selling a couple of dimes/ mother fucker I been selling a couple of rhymes/ over the fucking kilos of cocaine/ that I used to be dealing with man/ this comes off the brain/ cause I feel it, man I got to tell you like its been slain/ I was a fucking silent gangsta/ silent general/ what you know about it/ but this is how I would roll/ you know nothing about it, Yaa shit/ you think you was down/ you know nothing about it, I run this town/

SUMMARY - I'll explain it like this. “I must admit, when I finished this song, I realized this falls under arrogance and I’m truly sorry to you all for this. However, realistically and factually, I’m technically the most relevant and known individual in humanity. Further more, mankind has been exploiting my name and profiting lustfully off my heritage and my legacy. This song explains how long and how involved publicly I have created myself, my image, and my truth of life for thousands of years. With this song, I decided I was going to start showing you all why you need to change, because I can strip you from all that you tarnished and stole.”

Chapter 19: Song 5a – Ni***** Ain’t in Paris - Remix (19:5a)

Ni*** Ain’t in Paris (Jay Z & Kayne – Nig**s in Paris – Remix):**

VERSE 1: This is why. This is why. This is why mother fuckers wanna find me/ So I record so hard, wigga’s wanna be me/ I trusted the wrong guy, now mother fuckers wanna find me/ I turn down offers constantly/ if I was rich with money/ I would have no problems instantly/ I’ve secured business deals, with nothing but skills and dignity/ I’m a hustler for real – more intelligent than anyone you know, literally/ my human form restricts me/ seriously/ this shit is crazy/ my life is more than a movie/ constantly/ I’m an Emcee/ mother fuckers grow jealousy/ a succubus lust/ to try to fuck me/ I need to teleport/ I’m big, I’m poor, and I have a vision/ my mission is lethal precision/ extinction/ for those who refuse him/ JC is who I mean/ here I’ll let you find me/ only when you sign me/ watch the skills change, with my entire energy/ shifted metaphysically/ through spiritual simplicity/ Explicitly/ I don’t give a fuck is in me/ Y’all are dead to me/ Yaa I should be at a party in France/ at first glance/ you need three to wake from my trance/ I’m one of a kind/ a young prince/ and I ain't even in Paris/ when my chains come free, then Imma be a savage/ not for revenge/ instead save those who repent/ distressed content/ have you unconscious/ according to psychological science/ why I need to buy you ecstasy/ in order for you to fuck me/ tell you what call six girls, and we'll make it a party/ In fact call it an orgy/ French pussy got me going crazy/ over sea's is where I should be/ go ahead call me/ 507-90 shady/ stalkers, I change my number every three weeks/ I'm now jacking beats/ fuck all of y'all/ come and find me/ how come you wanna find me? Buy my records then hire me/ Ya time is money/ God's time ain't never broke, I'm built progressively/ means, I learn like a Cyborg/ AKA robot/ Hip Hop/ drop/ flop/ drop your watch and your wallet/ open up shop/ demonic Detox/ never drops/ unless MIZeRY rocks/ the world with the Doc/ so are you ready to flop? Either the top or saved by Jesus/ exotic cannabis/ minds rushing/ I'm going HAM, I'm on my hiatus/ I'm top ten general/ In my God's kingdom/ I'm surgical/ I fight to save our sanctum/ I'm anxious/ and I love sex/ I know I sin/ but that was way back when/ fast forward – I'm whoring, popping bottles in Paris/ got me popping models/ all night with Will Farrell/ (Will Farrell – Anchor Man skit). The drugs kick in/ rushing/ drum bass hitting/ head rushin' – heart pounding/ drunk and naked – you, 3 guys/ with 10 sexy models/ drugs come with room service/ within 60 minutes/ two girls leave in an ambulance/ wait go back – at the show we were surrounded by thousands of fans/ on stage going HAM/ throwing fists, going gorillas/ on our way out there was a limo with hoes ready to go bananas/ at the penthouse/ drinking bottles/ playing games & role model/ touch each other, all of us and shift my throttle/ into our Heavenly palace/ I'm a prince ready for marriage/ you can't be average/ let's fuck – transaction/ excuse my French/ but I'm tense/ explode on your breast's/ Yaa as if Wiz Khalifa/ screams Will's missing/ He's streaking in the Paris streets, party on hold, girls keep touching/ to be continued/ as we save Will Farrell/ (Will Farrell – Old Skool skit).

SUMMARY - I'll explain it like this. "I must admit, when I finished this song, I realized this falls under arrogance and I'm truly sorry to you all for this. However, realistically and factually, I'm technically the most relevant and known individual in humanity. Further more, mankind has been exploiting my name and profiting lustfully off my heritage and my legacy. This song explains how long and how involved publicly I have created myself, my image, and my truth of life for thousands of years. With this song, I decided I was going to start showing you all why you need to change, because I can strip you from all that you tarnished and stole..."

Chapter 19: Song 7a – Hard ass MC – Remix (19:7a)

Hard ass MC – HAM Remix:

INTRO: Yaa, Ha, MIZeRY; It took awhile, but I'm back here, but I feel brand new man/ it took awhile but I'm back/

VERSE 1: Ya I'm back on my grind, I'm back on my grizzy/ I'm back with my rhymes, cause I does it this silly/ no matter what you thinking about, I'm a walking dictionary/ Imma keep you fucking guessing/ no matter what you doing man, I see y'all are stressing/ over how much success I'm getting/ so what you thinking about, are you iced cold grillen/ then Imma have to start killing/ homie, I've been chillen/ I'm trying to see a better life/ so I worship Lord Jesus Christ/ and no matter what you thinking man I pray him every night/ and I ask him for the forgiveness that I need to save my life/ no matter what you getting down homie, I was born ready to ride/ and I was born to die/ only for my Lord Jesus Christ/ and I spit it like this every time I'm changing my whole way/ I'm changing everything I think about on a constant regular day/ so I'm just trying to make change/ if that's what Lord blesses me to have/ so I think about it man/

HOOK/CHORUS: Ready, Go Hard as a mother fucker/ Yaa go Hard as a mother fucker/ Yaa cause I'm a hard ass Emcee/ Yaa Go Hard as a mother fucker/ I said, go hard as a mother fucker/ Yaa cause I'm a hard ass Emcee/ Go Hard as a mother fucker, Yaa go hard as a mother fucker/ Yaa Go hard as an Emcee/

VERSE 2: Okay, I come in lyrically/ Please I'll change you instantly/ by delivering you spiritually/ with MIZeRY & Jesus/ feeling his pain and agony/ that's felt through his body/ NO matter what you do, Imma dominate you literally/ My Deadly/ lyrics is gonna kill you, like stories in a book/ story time for children is nothing to ever put in a hook/ so I think about it for a minute, explaining it to you in this verse/ whoa, back the fuck up, I've never stolen anybodies purse/ My first assumption is you must be crazy/ so take it easy lady/ Yaa maybe for a couple of minutes you could act nicely/ talking quietly/ not trying to degrade me/ baby do you even love me? Quit acting all lame/ both real women and this rap game/ I've been around gangsta's, wanksta's, mobsters/ pimpers, rappers, and strippers/ I've felt all these pressures/ pain, rain, cocaine, blood stains, & A taste of this fame/ a real G – don't sell his soul to the devil/ instead, I worship Jesus and I banish all evil/ as I remain lyrically lethal/

HOOK/CHORUS: Ready Go Hard as a mother fucker/ Yaa go Hard as a mother fucker/ Yaa cause I'm a hard ass Emcee/ Yaa Go Hard as a mother fucker/ I said, go hard as a mother fucker/ Yaa cause I'm a hard ass Emcee/ Go Hard as a mother fucker, Yaa go hard as a mother fucker/ Yaa Go hard as an Emcee/

VERSE 3: In the name of the father, the son, and the Holy Spirit/ Lord Jesus Christ, it is you who I worship/ and I come to you to ask forgiveness for all of my sins/ Lord Jesus, please save my soul/ for I long/ for days of happiness and peace/ where all these evil doings of this Earth and all the people in it, do not exist/ Lord, forgive me for my sins/ and give me the strength and courage that I need, to continue on/ In thy Lord Jesus name I Pray, Amen/

VERSE 4: Okay I'll tell you what it means/ MIZeRY is the pain and agony/ of Jesus, as he felt it through his veins/ and you know nothing about his pain, except for me to deliver it to your brains/ when I'm fucking spitting it on a microphone/ bumping in your headphones/ you know nothing about it, little man, so you better run off home/ to your little mommy, before you get on lost/ you ain't fucking built for a grown mans game/ you playing around homie, you about to be slain/ dead shot, bleeding from your brain/ and I've seen it all man, and I'm not trying to feel this way/ so understand I've found a new path we need to take/ so I praise the Lord, every time that I pray/ and no matter what you think, it's probably wrong, so you might as well not stay/ because I've showed you the new path/ everything that you need to feel/ the fucking wisdom is coming from my teeth and my tongue/ as my mouth is moving up and down son/

SUMMARY - I'll explain it like this. "This song is special to me, I also put my full intensity into recording this vocally. My metaphors really came to life in this piece too. My favorite part is when I needed to pray on this song and then a final verse popped out of me from God. This final verse is crucial to me and all, to know, and recognize because it wasn't previously written. In addition, this is when I understood my ultimate meaning about being the pain and agony of Jesus' suffering."

Chapter 19: Song 10a – I Love You (19:10a)

I Love You:

INTRO: This is for my sexy ladies, okay here we go.

HOOK/CHORUS: Okay this is for my ladies, this is for my sexy chicks/ this is for my fly bitch/ this is for all my elegant women around the world Kidd/ shout to ____ you know what I mean/ This is for my bitch/ this is for my fly chick/ this is for my ladies around the world doing it big/ the type of bitch you dream about, Nikki Jackson shit/

VERSE 1: Okay this is for my ladies, this is for my shorties/ this is for everything that means so good/ its like my sanctuary/ cause love is so secret and Heavenly/ you can't even compare it to nothing in this world/ I don't care if you're gay or not, you still want love in your life/ man, cause this is how it's supposed to be/ shit, you're positive feelings and all your exotic dreams/ as long as you do it secretly with the partner in which you choose/ for the rest of your life, soul mates/ you could never have broke/ man, cause if it goes broke/ than it was never meant to be/ you need to learn from your mistakes quickly/ otherwise fall into purgatory/ for the rest of eternity/ and I'm not giving it to you any other way/ but shorty you're fly/ you make me feel alive/ and I want to tell it like this all night on my microphone/ Imma give it to you live, like I'm singing On this tone/ I mean phone/ with you, cause I can't be home/ giving you my love in every way, all night/ Yaa, whatever we could do it like we freaking it to the last night shorty/ I want to be holding you, when I'm sleeping, when I'm dreaming about you/ because I'm on stage, I see every face they look like you/ I can't believe I've been home, in not so long/ I'm getting confused being on the road, cause being on tour is so confusing sometimes/ but I think about it cause I can't wait cause that's when I'll be alive/ doing everything I was meant to do/ giving you the world instantly too/ because I've got magical Powers/ that I could spread amongst all the children/ cause I could save everybody if everybody's willing/ so understand this is why my hearts so big, I'm ready to start giving/ but if you turn against me/ and you turn your back on me/ then Imma turn more crazy and fearful than you've ever seen or felt/ cause then I'll turn into a demon and make you feel more pain than you've ever felt/ in a minute man, cause when the clock strikes twelve/ I'm sucking your soul straight to hell/ and there will be no escape/ I promise you man, that's why I give it to you in these rhymes/ no bait/ man it's getting late/ time to escape/ because I've already turned the page/

SUMMARY - I'll explain it like this. "During the time of this song, I was fumigating angrily over a female friend of mine; whom decided to venture into my life again, wanted my baby, but didn't have a clear conscious about her actions. Further more, I felt betrayal about her, which led me to deceive her in the end. Ultimately making it my fault, as to why we aren't pursuing our life together. In any event, I remained humble and have forgiven her. I did attempt to be in her life again too. Nevertheless, I know God has a plan and she wasn't apart of mine..."

* The song "Judgment Day" was originally featured on this free Mixtape. However, in the year 2013 I have decided to create my final album and piece of musical composition. Thus, I've decided to place this song/scripture upon My final album; which is what you see below…

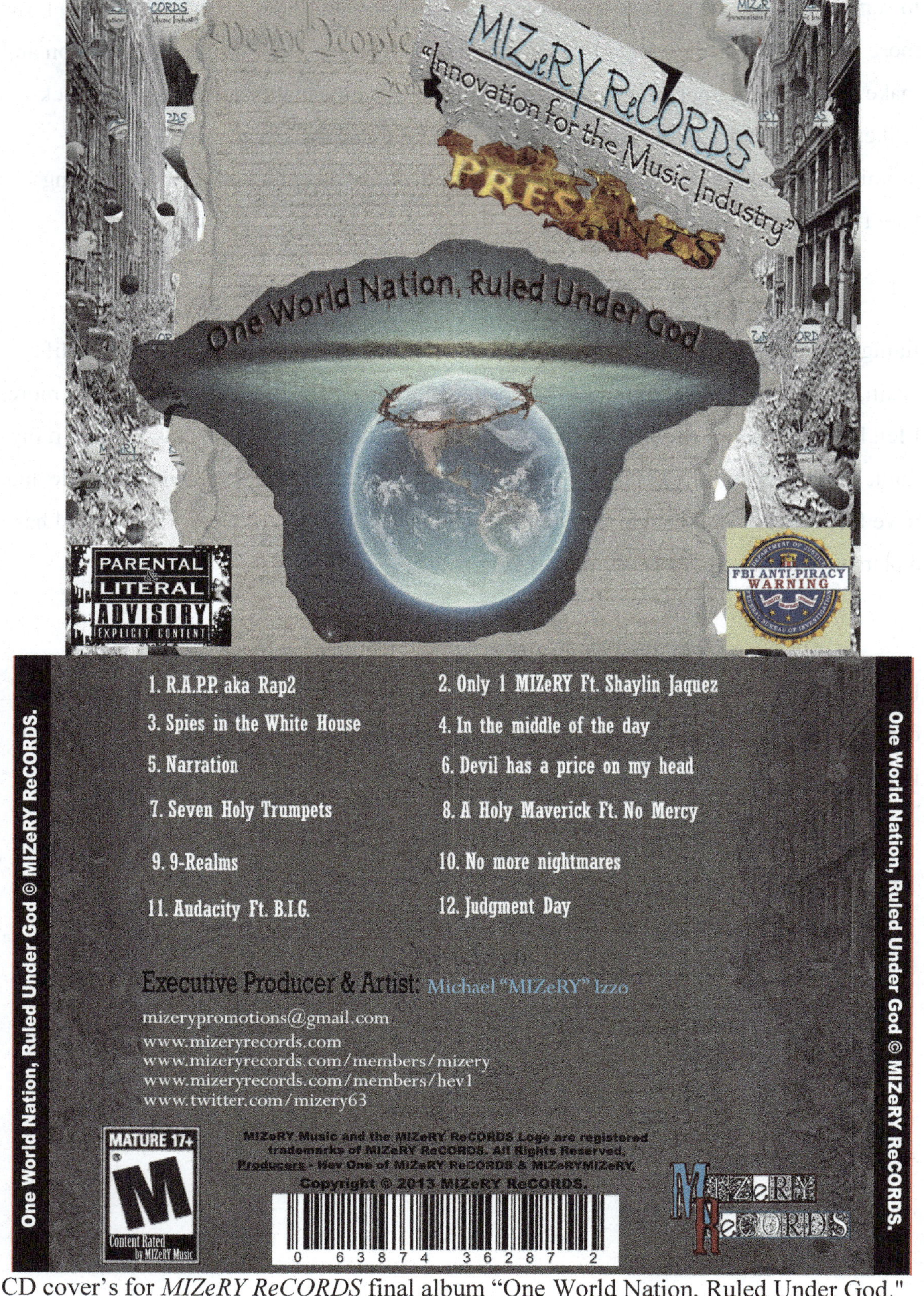

CD cover's for *MIZeRY ReCORDS* final album "One World Nation, Ruled Under God." Album's release TBD. Album artwork designed by Michael Izzo, ©2014.

Chapter 19: Song 1b – R.A.P.P. AKA Rap2 (19:1b)

R.A.P.P. AKA Rap2:

VERSE 1: Attention please, are y'all comfortable and well prepared/ I'm the founding father of RAPP, Rap squared/ In other words, I'm literally and visually painting verbal scriptures/ a gift from God, introducing - **Rhythmically Acting Poetic Pictures**/ I'm defeating all Evil and sinister creatures/ No one good, shall ever be injured/ Life is a real movie, at this juncture/ don't be insecure/ we can all choose to be cured/ the evil are lured/ demonic demise/ Truth; I'm sure/ Jesus saves all who are pure/ my humanly vessel/ is more restricting, than 2-liter bottles/ no matter, I'm designed for Galactic Battle/ Human's are of the lowest few, but given a rare gift/ hold-up, I let my mind slip; hang on, as I shift/ down into third/ right turn, pump gas, drift/ race finished/ we win/ Sup?

HOOK/CHORUS: In my darkest hours, Lord please forgive me, humanity, and our family/ (Paranoia strikes me)/ My life is yours to command/ Lord grant me the strength and intelligence to firmly stand/ with all choirs of Angels/ (Paranoia strikes me)/

VERSE 2: Simplify the verse/ test subjects emerge/ out of the woodwork/ I follow a different set of rules/ and I always use Pro-Tools/ my sound is explosively delicious/ prolific mathematics/ I've created a newer and better system/ Pay Attention/ Rap squared - is intellectual, delectable, and educational/ beyond comprehension/ unless, I teach it to you/ my only mission is to create: The rebirth of Jesus Christ/ may we only survive and be chosen for new life/ what's in store, for all thee who deny; faith and his Holy Glory/ shall perish from a victorious fury/ Heaven is coming swiftly/ None good, shall perish before me/ evil are buried under me/ a spiritual rebirth, I'm counting down hourly/ O-Heavenly Father embrace me/ and society/ many lost, sick, or wicked/ Lord give me strength, to heal those sadistic/

HOOK/CHORUS: In my darkest hours, Lord please forgive me, humanity, and our family/ (Paranoia strikes me)/ My life is yours to command/ Lord grant me the strength and intelligence to firmly stand/ with all choirs of Angels/ (Paranoia strikes me)/

VERSE 3: One World Nation Under God/ this marks the culmination/ of a Heavenly nation/ consumed by righteous humans/ how can you not relate to me, when we come from the same/ person and place?/ Time and space/ causing collisions/ devastating my mind/ creating delusion/ a illusions/ Seven Holy Trumpets/ Sounded by Seven Divine Muppets/ Doomsday Dragons, are kept as my pets/ Holy intervention, Life is the ultimate test/ Stop the texts/ if you wanna stop the wrecks/ stop all the greed, if you wanna end the violence/ Judgment Day, Peace and quite/ the voices stop, peaceful silence/ The power of the word peace/ has the power to siege/ anyone who poses a threat to me/ Her, You, and Him; including me/ branched together - creates us/ In God My Father, I love/ without Us/ there is no Trust/ for you Shaylin, I only Lust/

HOOK/CHORUS: In my darkest hours, Lord please forgive me, humanity, and our family/ (Paranoia strikes me)/ My life is yours to command/ Lord grant me the strength and intelligence to firmly stand/ with all choirs of Angels/ (Paranoia strikes me)/

SUMMARY - I'll explain it like this. “This song “R.A.P.P. AKA Rap2” clearly defines my future plans; both musically and spiritually. However, this song was mainly created to introduce my new genre of music **R.A.P.P. AKA Rap2**.”

Chapter 19: Song 2b – Only 1 MIZeRY Ft. Shaylin Jaquez (19:2b)

Only 1 MIZeRY:

HOOK/CHORUS: Truthfully/ all I see is Misery/ every single one of you, is a reminisce of me/ into the eyes of everybody/ all I ever see are lie's and deceit/ suffering sorrow of MIZeRY/ Truthfully/ all I see is Misery/ every single one of you, is a reminisce of me/ into the eyes of everybody/ all I ever see are lie's and deceit/ suffering sorrow of MIZeRY/

VERSE 1: Many stories in which I have lived/ I would have given/ a second life, for a life in Heaven/ I'm talking about living in God's Kingdom/ living by eternal peace/ an eternal serenity/ take my poems as intellectual teaching/ I'm CIA infiltrating/ with no rules or regulations/ hardcore tactical explosions/ proximity alert, 30 seconds detonation/ America and the U.K. top priority/ silence is the enemy/ most nations are a disgrace/ no class and terrible tastes/ time is forever, use less waste/ Hey! post master, post haste/

Urgent delivery/ a message from MIZeRY/ up early/ here to bury/ all evil in their graves/ no slaves/ to any man's trade/ I'm King, Shaylin's Queen, Home of the Brave/

HOOK/CHORUS: Truthfully/ all I see is Misery/ every single one of you, is a reminisce of me/ into the eyes of everybody/ all I ever see are lie's and deceit/ suffering sorrow of MIZeRY/ Truthfully/ all I see is Misery/ every single one of you, is a reminisce of me/ into the eyes of everybody/ all I ever see are lie's and deceit/ suffering sorrow of MIZeRY/

VERSE 2a: A second verse, a second life/ new vessel with a second chance, and the same wife/ this day forth, I'll thank God every night/ Shaylin say a prayer with me, holding you on my right/ side/ holding you tight/ you're my everything, you make all wrong right/ 24/7 you're on my mind/ Poof! Magic/ Shaylin's on my mic/ angel come say Hi!/

VERSE 2b (Shaylin): Hey everybody, it's me Shaylin/ Sexy and smooth, performing/ and waving/ like I'm, back in the pageant/ competing/ Got all these bimbos raging/ My soul is ambient/ when it represents the ambience of Mother Nature/ I'm a beautiful humanly creature/ I mean, I have the best figure/ hahaha/ I'm only kidding, painting y'all a picture/ **Written by Michael.*

HOOK/CHORUS: Truthfully/ all I see is Misery/ every single one of you, is a reminisce of me/ into the eyes of everybody/ all I ever see are lie's and deceit/ suffering sorrow of MIZeRY/ Truthfully/ all I see is Misery/ every single one of you, is a reminisce of me/ into the eyes of everybody/ all I ever see are lie's and deceit/ suffering sorrow of MIZeRY/

VERSE 3: Verse three is the most sadistic/ Hocus-pocus/ a magical magician/ angelic guardian/ with unmatched precision/ you still want to be me? cause I had no decision/ in my Heavenly mission/ judging humans/ resulting catastrophic proportions/ bare witness to near extinction/ less than four percent are uniquely distinguished/ dismissing all challengers/ no white rappers can even match it/ you can't hack it/ dead beats, dirt naps/ worth less than maggots/ lyrical traps/ sinister raps/ Italians with bats/ Africans with AK's and four macs/ true facts/ I'm about marijuana and rap tracks/ I've got no boys or friends/ only Shaylin, my poems, and my own trends/ the world chose me over you instead/ I'm the daily bread/

HOOK/CHORUS: Truthfully/ all I see is Misery/ every single one of you, is a reminisce of me/ into the eyes of everybody/ all I ever see are lie's and deceit/ suffering sorrow of MIZeRY/ Truthfully/ all I see is Misery/ every single one of you, is a reminisce of me/ into the eyes of everybody/ all I ever see are lie's and deceit/ suffering sorrow of MIZeRY/

SUMMARY - I'll explain it like this. "This song "Only 1 MIZeRY" is designed to explain there is only One God, One Jesus, and One form of salvation or suffering for all. Additionally, I was also attempting to express my inner self to all; including, my feelings towards music, life, and my sacred heart. During this time, I was engaged to the lovely Shaylin Jaquez. However, as fate would intervene I ended things with her and one day she was gone. No matter what, my heart holds a special place forever, for her. I also truly believe, she holds the most comparison to Mary Magdalene and my mother. Perhaps, those were the reasons why I had to end it temporarily. In my opinion, she wasn't ready to be healed and due to **Free Will:** I was powerless to help her."

Chapter 19: Song 3b – Spies in the White House (19:3b)

Spies in the White House:

HOOK/CHORUS: Everything are Godly signs/ Society is humane designs/ time is controlled by my mind/ messages are hidden in my rhymes/ Spies in the White House, conducting High Treason/ Greed is their reason/ Spies in the White House/ Spies in the White House/ Spies in the White House/ trying to take us out/

VERSE 1: Ever since 2001/ America's been pointing Guns/ while I was on the run/ senator's are dumb fucks, when they use thy tongues/ their lost angels, or robots/ programmed by demonic plots/ controlled by evil cops/ naa, more like navy seal agents/ either way, I'm ready/ Lord willing/ I'll have 12 movements, tribes/ scattered in the world/ In another life, I used propagation/ to expand my fellow Christians/ as a result, came the crusades/ moons later, the revolutionary war/ one and a half centuries came, World War 1, World War 2/ all to kill me and my bloodline/ on the cusp of the 21st century, in the year 1999/ My auntie said, " Lord is coming tonight"/ I said to myself, no fire and brimstone/ I'm sacred on the inside/ but strong and courageous on the outside/ 2000 comes, world doesn't end/ In 2001/ U.S. commits high treason/ for unsolvable reasons/ doomsday's my mission/

BRIDGE: Too much evil in me, for those sick/ and twisted/ we're not finished/ this is the bridge/ 10 years later, my life becomes clear/ attain control of Heaven, by restricting Earth's atmosphere/ Too much evil in me, for those sick/ and twisted/ we're not finished/ this is the bridge/ 10 years later, my life becomes clear/ attain control of Heaven, by restricting Earth's atmosphere/

HOOK/CHORUS: Everything are Godly signs/ Society is humane designs/ time is controlled by my mind/ messages are hidden in my rhymes/ Spies in the White House, conducting High Treason/ Greed is their reason/ Spies in the White House/ Spies in the White House/ Spies in the White House/ trying to take us out/

VERSE 2: If you infringe the constitution/ I'll assassinate your administration/ my troops have limitless dedication/ if you don't submit, I'll burn your entire legislation/ if you label me the enemy/ I'll disprove your allegations/ strip your soul of credibility/ I'm your King, accept my humility/ besides, missiles are no match for Galactic-Fireballs/ or Ice-Lightening/ My Doomsday Dragons are frightening/ death grip talons tightening/ the seven year war is terrifying/ catastrophic death toll, Judgment Day, for those defying/ - God's 10 Commandments/ this is our land, time to rectify/ it's called a global cleansing, conspiracy theories, shall I specify?/ colored FEMA dots/ which started with 9-11/ Dictators, controlling our weapons/ if you try and collect them/ my angels will unleash Armageddon/ my true purpose is to protect Heaven/ Mother Nature is Heaven/ and Heaven's on Earth/ If you spit on her/ I'll bury you in the dirt/

BRIDGE: Too much evil in me, for those sick/ and twisted/ we're not finished/ this is the bridge/ 10 years later, my life becomes clear/ attain control of Heaven, by restricting Earth's atmosphere/ Too much evil in me, for those sick/ and twisted/ we're not finished/ this is the bridge/ 10 years later, my life becomes clear/ attain control of Heaven, by restricting Earth's atmosphere/

SUMMARY - I'll explain it like this. “Spies in the White House” is exactly what the title means. Truth be told, I can't discuss anything beyond the above writing. I don't want to incriminate myself; all the while, I don’t have control over existence. Although, I don't recall writing much of this record, it's by far one of my favorites.”

Chapter 19: Song 4b – In the middle of the day (19:4b)

In the middle of the day:

INTRO: I realized, not too long ago, the only way to create a more positive existence in the world. Is by ridding us of all negative. Thus, creating only the possibility for positive.

VERSE 1: In the middle of the day/ my thoughts wander aimlessly/ many directions/ hearts pacing/ mad erection/ cause fly women are staring/ and sexting me, like I'm special/ sexual seduction/ naa, it's my presidential election/ my path leads unification/ God given education/ implanted in me, much more than frustration/ delusional desperation/ dominant aggression/ technically speaking/ I'm a target, innocent/ forced into submission/ won't forfeit though, *Lethal injection*/ Righteous God, who's turned assassin/ I'm programmed with mathematically elite tactics/ Glass bongs,/ dutches's, and chicks/ that look like plastics/ spirit's loaded with toxins/ plagued all of my bad habits/ I tune you off, clear static/ you remember club static if you was an NYC night maggot/ people like me/ never seen in the day time, unless it's for charity/ expose my publicity/ I choose to sin, to save humanity/ In life, everything comes with a price/ I want my soul for life, so here God; Self-sacrifice/ Twenty-three years to find the truth/ within myself/ ignite, explosive thoughts; humility, beyond belligerent boasts/ I'm stuck, sarcasm builds a chasm/ chastised in Life/ than I was baptized, confused, and then crucified/ this marks the culmination/ of a Heavenly nation/ consumed by righteous humans/ reborn as a spirit of angels/ turn the pages, please Gabriél/ Slowly, my memory comes back/ quiet, use slow attacks/ amnesia, poisoned my bloodstream/ think of a plan/ shh don't scream/ find all the exits/ telling myself/ I have 30 seconds/ Second/ can I move all of my limbs? quickly/ dispense with the pleasantries/ swiftly/ killing all of my enemies/ my energies/

recharge slowly/ walking, haste fully/ I question repeatedly/ why and who the sex-vagina captured me?/ Seriously sane - Is MIZeRY/ so important to Mephistopheles/ He wages war to finish me/ his disgusting thoughts of existence/ are spawned from demonic transgressions/ thus, turns our souls aggressive/ restricting us from ascension/ Lord these are my confessions/ please forgive me for everything I'm unaware of besides these:/ Please, I'm addicted to find love/ Me and her, together live with God above/ I'm sorry for failing in life/ my chosen few, with truthful eyes, of sight/ so bright/ you see blind/ I'm looking for my wife/ sleek build, fit hips/ and Angel Tat, on her right thigh/ Blonde, Reddish-Brownish Hair/ Two tattoos, Rib-Cage, underneath the left breast/ Physics of life, are all tests/ unlimited contests/ can't quit, must finish/ trials of sin/ Increase rank/ return righteous/ define miraculous/ change by words and belief/ beyond you and me/ My third existence/ correcting all wrong/ life is beautiful in my Heaven/ relieve all thoughts of existence/ starting with your ignorance/ no words or thoughts of poisonous plagues of destruction/ infinite positives, anything you dream of, is from God your Father/ Stretch my voice, speak louder/ from farther distances clearer/ goodnight little children/ volume dies, volume lowers/

SUMMARY - I'll explain it like this. "In the middle of the day" truly speaks for itself. Go reread this section if you are confused of it's true value."

Chapter 19: Song 5b – Narration (19:5b)

Narration:

INTRO: Sometimes in life, we hit rock bottom. Everything's darkness, can't see a light; except, for a nice shiny figurine, you can't make out. And, you think about it.

VERSE 1: Narration, Devil has a price on my head/ created through literature/ which I've mastered/ after precise measures/ taught as intelligent lecture/ I'm Picasso on these beats/ audio scripts/ I creatively depict/ through God's Heavenly gifts/ similar to the effects from alcoholic beverages/ if you could even dream so complex/ this is the word of God/ My Bible text/ all truth, prophecy, it's my divine breathe/ many different titles/ I'm here to write the new Bible/ destroy all forms of evil/ I'll kill the devil/ I harbor the power of Odin-in/ Lightening bolts of wisdom/ is what I'm throwing In/ that's my choice of weapon/ equipped with an indestructible Flaming-Ice Sword/ As my side Arm/ My bitch is real Karma/ cross me, you can't harm us/ if we must/ guns will bust/ cause I'm plagued by sins/ starting with lust/ I love to fuck/ bust my nuts/ all on it's tits/ explosive ass cum/ can't be me nothing/ to shut my mouth cousin/ got all nations running/ cause they all women/ cross dressing/ switched up they sexing/ cause they all scared/ messing with God is like taking bets/ with no tangible assets/ even though our bodies die/ we have a choice to come back to life/ no shit, my mission includes showing all how to live eternally/ both physically and spiritually/ you need to let go/ trust me/ take my hands and fall/ something so easy/ you simply need to trust me/ please don't hesitate/ think twice/ you might die/ no lie/ come sit with me and my wife/ rebirth, new life/ I'm awaiting Mary/ she evades me/ cause I am not ready/ not by my choice/ she's more powerful than me/ I sacrificed immortality/ to love sweet Mary/ she passed my name on and permitted me this vessel/ I'm juggling vestibules/ I've become so confused/ I can't ever loose/ I'll rap as long as it takes/ make an album in three days/ God given time frame/ God's taken control of my brain/ Yah, I'm far from insane/ drugs melting my membrane/ no pain/ keep fighting in this game/ can't ever stop it/ I'm patiently waiting to drop it/ speak my mind, Ya I'm a prophet/ I live at home, close to my family/ I live by love and peace/ I'm waiting for serenity/ homie, fuck the streets/ cause the streets said fuck me/ my only hustle's selling dope beats/ Ya for music and people like MIZeRY/ not dope fiends/ I'm the second form of God; come back, in the most time of need/ if you try and burn me/ or befriend me/ you can bet, I'm winning either way/ I'm more talented than the MLB All-Stars/ I'm an arrogant Rap-Star/ Fuck who you are/ twinkle, twinkle little star/ Ya, my big dick, fucks that bullshit/ Capitalism and all that follows are lies/ including money and all of this fame/ query? where's my dame and when is my day? Ya cause I'm here to judge the world, set it all right/ my vocals always tight/ because I am Mike/ M I C H A E L/ we all consist of hell/ mostly Heaven though/ like a nice apple/ only eat the outer core/ Ya don't mess with the inner core/ I'm very hardcore/ I fuck's hardcore/ sometimes soft porn/ my intoxicant's are leaking from all of your pores/ visit my store/ M I Z E R Y R E C O R D S/ MIZeRYReCOCORS.com/ pay attention all moms/ as I drop verbal bombs/

SUMMARY - I'll explain it like this. "Narration" was supposed to be a synopsis of my movie and new album. In essence it became a synopsis of My Life & Purpose."

Chapter 19: Song 6b – Devil has a price on my head (19:6b)

Devil has a price on my head:

VERSE 1: First, I'll explain my reasons/ If you don't act accordingly/ Ill sense treason/ I tame my inner thoughts/ sadistically Judgmental visions/ I'm ruler of this world, you failed the missions/ here's my dilemma, as I suffer Holy incisions/ Until I set it righteous/ evil images/ stemmed from Devil Satanous/ equipped with infinite precision/ My mission is to extinguish/ Satan's minions/ I'm highly efficient/ trained like an assassin/ stealth fully hidden/ challenge me/ I'm more vicious/ purely righteous/ with infinite light Powers/ call me the tri-force/ In human form/ listen, to each struck cord/ my mathematical rhymes are seen on the board/ positive energy, evens all scores/ unlimited motivation, defeats evil/ with force from my fire-lightening bolts/ I'm only patient for 100 syllables/ I could tolerate about 12-decibles/ anything beyond, I turn mental/ definition/ you are ignorantly repetitive/ you lack ability to be coherent/ too far gone, from being saved/ here, take a sedative/ I'll boost you with so much torture/ you'll become addicted/ to the pain, you'll think it's fiction/ I utterly rip away your flesh/ billions cry in agony/ begging for my forgiveness/ it's too late, Father summoned me/ I transformed into Michael Thee Arch Angel/ protector of all humanity/ the ruler of Heaven and Earth for eternity/ I once died as Yeshua Christ/ lacking the power of God's might/ enhanced intelligence/ wrong versus right/ use me as your additive/ your knowledge is all theory/ maybe mostly negative/ oooo I struck a nerve, is you so sensitive?/

HOOK/CHORUS: *"The Greatest Story Ever Told" - Temptation scene. (Check Audio on CD for sample)."*

VERSE 2: The words, that proceedeth out of my mouth, comes from Father/ only cause I changed my life, went through three different lives/ collided in one life/ my disguises/ are too mysterious/ for you to think, beyond being delirious/ I'm serious/

if I didn't turn righteous/ I too would be punished/ severely, I suffer for my blood thirst/ for Judgment/ I chose not to finish last; be the best, number 1 first/ in the end: I answer for all sins/ chosen with a Heavenly burden/ the heaviest of all things/ manifested by God's existence/ of all things/ I've become mentally Holy/ my body is rock steady/ I'm the purest, born ready/ my voice is the only one worthy/ equally/ just as deadly/ it's divine, beyond literacy/ English language is what I speak/ I'm trapped beneath/ my peak/ in-between/ victory and failure/ Michael Lee Edward Izzo/ Is the cure/ my soul slumbers in a Parallax-Paradox of Reality/ I don't care your disposition against me/ it's flattering at best/ my humility always gets the best of me/ I'm incredible/ irresistible/ mentally stable/ physically capable/ undeniable/ I use a mask to protect, me and my bloodlines/ my purpose extends beyond making rhymes/ at the drop of a forty-five/ quarter after five/ the world I ignite/ with Judgment filled sorrow/ fueled by my disgust/ for your lust/ addiction to guns, drugs, and all ignorant shit/ not to be any hypocrite/ but I'm way to real, to ever go back to that shit/ Been there, done that/ moved onto A+ celebrity/ busting expensive raps/ Rap Squared/ you're just not prepared/ My Angels, don't have to spare/ any one man, doubt me if you really dare/ but, I can not be compared/

SUMMARY - I'll explain it like this. "Devil has a price on my head" originated as an anthem song for its' own album. However, after my hard breakup with Shaylin; I completely lost desire with everything. Far worse, than I have ever felt or dealt with before. Additionally, I took this song and added it to this album. Truth be told, this album marks my weary decisions to expedite the *"Rapture*."

Chapter 19: Song 7b – Seven Holy Trumpets (19:7b)

Seven Holy Trumpets:

BRIDGE: In the name of the Father, The Son, and The Holy Spirit/ Allow me the summoning of all Archangels/ Saint Uriél, Raguel, Chamuél, Jophiél, Raphael, Gabriél, and Saint Michael/ Come hither for Battle/

HOOK/CHORUS: Seven sounds of God, compile his voice/ Seven holy trumpets, summon 9 realms of souls/ Humans are the most lost/ His Resurrection, My Rapture, unites us permanently close/ save only pure organisms, that was my choice/

it's almost time to wake up/ you enter Heaven or Hell/ if you fall in-between/ you're doomed, cause I don't walk on that plane/

VERSE 1: Living in paradise is truthful escape/ I've thought about being Bruce Wayne/ fighting evil, wearing a cape/ As I touch your brain/ you become tamed/ Do you seek salvation, or endless amounts of pain?/ Your soul is NOT FREE/ Bodily Restraint/ Are Thee righteous enough, to come reclaim your souls? Have Thee heard the expression, I'm stuck in a Hell Hole? All Thee who repent for thy sins, may enter, if Thee know the codes/ The truth of life, is all I know/ Words from God is what I teach/ Infiltrating your brains, Swat-Teams Breach/ I'm the commander and Chief/ only those worthy/ will live with me/ I'm sick, from all of this Misery/ The secret is so simple, alter all that you see/ Ridding negative, creating only room for positiv-eity/ Yes!

HOOK/CHORUS: Seven sounds of God, compile his voice/ Seven holy trumpets, summon 9 realms of souls/ Humans are the most lost/ His Resurrection, My Rapture, unites us permanently close/ save only pure organisms, that was my choice/ it's almost time to wake up/ you enter Heaven or Hell/ if you fall in-between/ you're doomed, cause I don't walk on that plane/

BRIDGE: In the name of the Father, The Son, and The Holy Spirit/ Allow me the summoning of all Archangels/ Saint Uriél, Raguel, Chamuél, Jophiél, Raphael, Gabriél, and Saint Michael/ Come hither for Battle/

VERSE 2: It'll happen so fast/ you won't even know what hit you, like bullets breaking glass/ be my guest, if you want to place in last/ quickly catch/ this lifeline, before it passes/ can you ever accept and praise Lord Yeshua Christ?/ Let's move past/ the very fact/ I'm the Master of RAP/ Reality and People/ Take my hand in deeper/ into our Heavenly Kingdom/ North Star, marks the Steeple/ why- lesser minds are too feeble?/ To ever witness my true potential?/ soon comes the day, for all Angels/ to unite for one glorious victory/ I will grant all pure, life unimaginable/ so holy it's magical/ spiritually lyrical/ mentally, I'm tactical/ I don't bump your music, your rhymes are not practical/ mostly not even factual/ eternally capture you, with my rapture/

HOOK/CHORUS: Seven sounds of God, compile his voice/ Seven holy trumpets, summon 9 realms of souls/ Humans are the most lost/ His Resurrection, My Rapture, unites us permanently close/ save only pure organisms, that was my choice/

it's almost time to wake up/ you enter Heaven or Hell/ if you fall in-between/ you're doomed, cause I don't walk on that plane/

BRIDGE: In the name of the Father, The Son, and The Holy Spirit/ Allow me the summoning of all Archangels/ Saint Uriél, Raguel, Chamuél, Jophiél, Raphael, Gabriél, and Saint Michael/ Come hither for Battle/

VERSE 3: Dear Lord, forgive me, for all I must deliver/ I hereby summon, 6 Archangels; throw One-Third life, into the Fire River/ I was born, enslaved by MIZeRY; A Heavenly Soldier/ Prepared for Galactic Battle/ Pure, don't quiver/ in the rain, under the sun: you won't shiver/ God's light, created life/ The Demons dark, devours all night/ Dr. Izzo's riddles and rhymes/ proven innocent against metaphoric crimes/ in the next seven years time/ me and 6 Archangels will rise/ against Satan-Lucifer/ conducting battle in the sky/ "R-I-P Lee Carter/ My body is too small for my mind"/ as I pray aloud, I sigh/ come forth he shouts: "Saint Michael, Gabriél, Raphael, Jophiél, Chamuél, Raguel, & Saint Uriél/

HOOK/CHORUS: Seven sounds of God, compile his voice/ Seven holy trumpets, summon 9 realms of souls/ Humans are the most lost/ His Resurrection, My Rapture, unites us permanently close/ save only pure organisms, that was my choice/ it's almost time to wake up/ you enter Heaven or Hell/ if you fall in-between/ you're doomed, cause I don't walk on that plane/

BRIDGE: In the name of the Father, The Son, and The Holy Spirit/ Allow me the summoning of all Archangels/ Saint Uriél, Raguel, Chamuél, Jophiél, Raphael, Gabriél, and Saint Michael/ Come hither for Battle/

SUMMARY - I'll explain it like this. “Seven Holy Trumpets" is by far my best work, ever! This song is lyrically powerful; whilst containing the secrets of what occurs, when the Holy Trumpets are sounded. When I hear the actual song I recorded for this: I feel eternally empowered, relieved, and anxious. I want the world to know that it's not too late to seek salvation, but time is running thin. Although, I have yet to find all Thee Archangels; I know it is their mission to find me. Thus, when I am ready for my destiny; God will begin to unravel the necessary steps, in order to unlock the Seven Seals. My mind becomes ready & strong; while my body, becomes weary from all of the suffering."

Chapter 19: Song 8b – A Holy Maverick Ft. No Mercy (19:8b)

A Holy Maverick Ft. No Mercy - Verse not included:

INTRO: Get it, just get it. You got to go for it, and go for it, and get it.

VERSE 1: I swear I'll do right by all these beats/ I've been down with Nick Price since ______(Attic Sounds) / I'll hold you down as long as you got me/ secretly, I'll always have everybody/ to me, where all the same/ most importantly our brains/ communicate in multiple ways/ connect beyond intellect/ sexual connects/ no disrespect/ but I could always teach a better path/ cut your time in half/ refuse your money, to set the example/ privately, I'm more efficient/ the answers are hidden, within the tombs of the ancients/ excuse my accent/ my body contains sexy scent/ women love my taste/ succumbing is imminent/ dominate in bed/ I'm searching for One Love, failed tests of love; two decades of women/ all of a sudden me and Mary switched roles/ once again, I suffer more than before/ I need her by my side when I tour/ her and I need to be partners, both in business and relationship/ including sexual pleasure with friendship/

HOOK/CHORUS: I'm sleeping/ while times watching/ invading my thoughts, while I'm dreaming/ my movements reflect the hands of a crafted seamstress/ my very essence leaves you breathless/ my words remove all stress/ say a prayer with me friend/ I bless thee and thee bless me/ if you confess/ I will heal thee of your infectious disease/ sometimes true passion, requires more than economical fees/

VERSE 2: Which thoughts do I chase/ using poetry to teach/ everybody's brain washed, toxic bleach/ my words are righteous, Navy seal team, ready to breach/ America is my home front, the new world team/ without Pro-Tools sessions/ I could never describe Heaven/ I don't think I could ventilate, through exhaling/ lungs collapsing/ anxiety jolts stabbing/ my old wounds, as I suffer/ a divine trigger/ to tame my power/ limited use per 24 hours/ my lifetime is one-third redound/ and my sonic energy destroys sound/ my conscious is unbound/ it's time for Judgment/ or correction/ However you could start accepting/ my plans for choosing/ divide who's repented/ and those demonic/ my team of Angels are harmonic/ we Archangels, move like Super sonic/ powerful like

Super Saiyan's/ secluded fights in the Himalayas/

HOOK/CHORUS: I'm sleeping/ while times watching/ invading my thoughts, while I'm dreaming/ my movements reflect the hands of a crafted seamstress/ my very essence leaves you breathless/ my words remove all stress/ say a prayer with me friend/ I bless thee and thee bless me/ if you confess/ I will heal thee of your infectious disease/ sometimes true passion, requires more than economical fees/

VERSE 3 (No Mercy - Verse not included):

HOOK/CHORUS: I'm sleeping/ while times watching/ invading my thoughts, while I'm dreaming/ my movements reflect the hands of a crafted seamstress/ my very essence leaves you breathless/ my words remove all stress/ say a prayer with me friend/ I bless thee and thee bless me/ if you confess/ I will heal thee of your infectious disease/ sometimes true passion, requires more than economical fees/

SUMMARY - I'll explain it like this. “This song originated with being inspired by my buddy "No Mercy." The inspiration was sparked through his dark musical style. After we spoke about making a song together, this title instantly sparked in mind. Long and behold, I was sharing a story of being A Holy Maverick."

Chapter 19: Song 9b – 9-Realms (19:9b)

9-Realms:

BRIDGE: 9 Realms of Heaven: First come the **Principalities**, which are energy/ Second up are **Angels**/ Third are **Thee Archangels**/ Then **Powers**, **Virtues**, and **Dominions**/ Last three are **Thrones**, **Cherubim’s**, and Thee Holy **Seraphim's**/ we are His children/

VERSE 1: My rhyme technique/ is back in full effect/ I'm tired from all of the chaos/ Alive! back in the Flesh/ Check mate, hit the deck/ Hey Dealer! lets play 9-Realms/ if you're not scared to dwell/ beyond the gates of Hell/ security breach, six infidels/ infiltrating Heaven's citadel/ I have intellectual property, strictly confidential/ enforced GAG-Order/ beyond warrants/ life in the human body, is mostly unpleasant/ too many restrictions, useless needs and wants/ not enough useful plots/ time runs dire/

Attention, a true King for hire/ time for all to retire/ my body grows tired/ rewired/ through reason/ sworn oath, Pledge of Allegiance/

HOOK/CHORUS: 9 Realms of Heaven/ 9 Realms of Hell/ choose which path you will dwell/ eternal life becomes your cell/ Lord Help! Please Help! simmer my thoughts, summon my guide/ calming rivers, warm winter snow, wind breezes bye/ all jokes aside/ the rapture is nigh/ the convergence of all Realms, Zip-Tied/

BRIDGE: 9 Realms of Heaven: First come the **Principalities**, which are energy/ Second up are **Angels**/ Third are **Thee Archangels**/ Then **Powers**, **Virtues**, and **Dominions**/ Last three are **Thrones**, **Cherubim's**, and Thee Holy **Seraphim's**/ we are His children/

VERSE 2: Every single day/ I Day Dream of life, beyond my brain/ before I lay/ I dream and pray/ of life beyond evil ways/ Lord help me save, a world headed toward doomsday/ okay, okay, ready or not, here I come/ Thigh Kingdom come/ Thy will be done/ on Earth, as it is in Heaven/ watch where Yee are treading/ I'm only going North, which way are Yee heading?/ sometimes, I wanna go speeding/ through NYC streets/ dodging and weaving/ searching for a purpose/ I feel cursed/ trapped by a none violent truce/ saved by My Righteous truth/ you'll loose/ if you choose/ to live like the rotten egg, Duck, duck, goose/ Man hunt, 1,2,3: you loose/

HOOK/CHORUS: 9 Realms of Heaven/ 9 Realms of Hell/ choose which path you will dwell/ eternal life becomes your cell/ Lord Help! Please Help! simmer my thoughts, summon my guide/ calming rivers, warm winter snow, wind breezes bye/ all jokes aside/ the rapture is nigh/ the convergence of all Realms, Zip-Tied/

BRIDGE: 9 Realms of Heaven: First come the **Principalities**, which are energy/ Second up are **Angels**/ Third are **Thee Archangels**/ Then **Powers**, **Virtues**, and **Dominions**/ Last three are **Thrones**, **Cherubim's**, and Thee Holy **Seraphim's**/ we are His children/

VERSE 3: Everyday/ I Pray for the answers/ as I eagerly wait/ dancing around, like MC-Hammer/ (*"Can't touch this" - sample*) Maximum boost, INCREASE Stamina/ sabotage another monument; I'll destroy another state/ it is my fate/ to stay Brave/ diminish my rage/ inherit His Grace/ leaving only God's trace/ staring Eye 2 Eye/ Face 2 Face/ You will all wait/ until I, open the Pearl of Gates/ upon such occurrence/ 9-Realms will commence the convergence/ 12 Tribes create a divergence/ which then, time will be removed from all Existence/ this is my presidential election/ I don't need many residents/ employ 12 executives/ exactly how many Rapture'd, is tentative on your behavior/ I'm the Lord and Savior/

HOOK/CHORUS: 9 Realms of Heaven/ 9 Realms of Hell/ choose which path you will dwell/ eternal life becomes your cell/ Lord Help! Please Help! simmer my thoughts, summon my guide/ calming rivers, warm winter snow, wind breezes bye/ all jokes aside/ the rapture is nigh/ the convergence of all Realms, Zip-Tied/

BRIDGE: 9 Realms of Heaven: First come the **Principalities**, which are energy/ Second up are **Angels**/ Third are **Thee Archangels**/ Then **Powers**, **Virtues**, and **Dominions**/ Last three are **Thrones**, **Cherubim's**, and Thee Holy **Seraphim's**/ we are His children/

SUMMARY - I'll explain it like this. "9-Realms" is by far my best work, ever! This song is lyrically powerful; whilst containing the secrets of what occurs, when all 9-Realms converge into one another. When I hear the actual song I recorded for this: I feel eternally empowered, relieved, and anxious. I want the world to know that it's not too late to seek salvation, but time is running thin. Although, I have yet to find all Thee Archangels; I know it is their mission to find me. Thus, when I am ready for my destiny; God will begin to unravel the necessary steps, in order to unlock the Seven Seals. My mind becomes ready & strong; while my body, becomes weary from all the suffering."

Chapter 19: Song 10b – No more nightmares (19:10b)

No more nightmares:

HOOK/CHORUS: And I woke up, from a bad dream/ Ain't no stopping me/ because I have, unlimited energy/ I woke up, from a bad dream/ Ain't no stopping me/

VERSE 1: Sometimes, I wanna wake up, like it's a brand new day/ call it God's Day/ Sunday/ first of the week/ Ya, I'll give it to you like this, my body is weak/ slow down, let me speak/ something positive/ nothing negative/ because I'm tired of living like this/ everybody's so sad and depressed/ everybody's dying in some form, or another/

spiritually, Ya call me MIZeRY/ Ya, I'm trying to reverse psychologize/ everything you doing, spiritually/ I'm giving you something brand new, like your body/ is changing, metaphysically/ I'm giving you something beyond mathematically/ I mean statistically/ I'm the best, giving you rock bottom rhymes/ I'm giving it to you, straight from my mind/ Ya, after me, there is no Restart/

HOOK/CHORUS: And I woke up, from a bad dream/ Ain't no stopping me/ because I have, unlimited energy/ I woke up, from a bad dream/ Ain't no stopping me/

VERSE 2: No more nightmares/ sometimes, I'm sacred/ from your sadistic stares/ look into my eyes, face all of your fears/ oh! hello My Dear/ pucker up your rear/ I'm cocked, locked, and loaded/ shifting into 6th gear/ I've got 7 hours left/ 6 hours later, I'm 6 beers deep/ add 10mg vicodin / smoke purple cush, you'll be sagging/ lights flashing/ cameras action/ party all night - My Passion/ put it to rest, quit asking/ only 1 question deserves answering/ "What's our purpose?"/ as I expose/ all of you posers/ whoa hold up!/ Folding cards/ playing against the odds/ growing up/ it was sex, drugs, and lies/ running from the cops/ fuck a Glock/ no chance, I ever get knocked/ murder 1, no traces of shots/ be quiet, here's the plot/ my movie is the world/ I'm the main character/ disguised as a lethal rapper/ My image must be an actor/ if the youth won't listen? then who comes after?/ snacks before bedtime summon monsters/ after me, there is no Restart/

HOOK/CHORUS: And I woke up, from a bad dream/ Ain't no stopping me/ because I have, unlimited energy/ I woke up, from a bad dream/ Ain't no stopping me/

SUMMARY - I'll explain it like this. "I simply want no more nightmares; both in the dream world and in the real world. When I created this song, I choose not to write anything. I truly wanted the inspiration and feelings to come from my soul. As a result, this is what I had created…"

Chapter 19: Song 11b – Audacity Ft. B.I.G. (19:11b)

Audacity Ft. B.I.G.:

HOOK/CHORUS: Notorious BIG - You n****s got some audacity/ You n****s got some audacity/ You n****s got some audacity/ you sold a million, now you're half of me/ get off my ____/ You n****s got some audacity/ You n****s got some audacity/ You n****s got some audacity/ you sold a million, now you're half of me/ get off my dick/ Kick it/

VERSE 1: Even when I'm sicker, than ever/ I'm working, cause I'm a fighter/ no matter the weather/ battle any contender/ From NAS to Helta Skelta/ Engage beast mode/ input security code/ 737733/ what is your destiny? destroy evil permanently/ create a Heavenly sanctuary/ where all those judged, commune for eternity/ counting all the reasons/ and wasted seasons/ all humans/ been engaged in treason/ against me and God/ words have brains clogged/ smoke bongs/ My bride will be everything to me/ mother of our family/ I'm awaiting a worthy queen/ more special than me/ I must have met her during my teens/ Sad Days missing Sassa/ my minds lost at NASA/ Space Cadet reporting for duty/ time and space engineer, lyrical rapper/ Physical appearance of any Actor/ Enhanced intellectual speed/ superman's not even faster/ I'm a genius minded master/ profound, conjuration caster/ the first original rebel/ blowing your speakers/ with no enhanced treble/

HOOK/CHORUS: Notorious BIG - You n****s got some audacity/ You n****s got some audacity/ You n****s got some audacity/ you sold a million, now you're half of me/ get off my dick/ Kick it/ You n****s got some audacity/ You n****s got some audacity/ You n****s got some audacity/ you sold a million, now you're half of me/ get off my ____/ You n****s got some audacity/ You n****s got some audacity/ You n****s got some audacity/ you sold a million, now you're half of me/ get off my dick/ Kick it/

VERSE 2: Guardian Angels are well equipped/ executive order, cease and desist/ mark the crucible/ banish Hannibal/ nothing you offer's tangible/ bounce your ass around, call it Kick Ball/ I'm old, you're young/ I'm smart, and you're dumb/ lyrics of energy, you all turn numb/ no sin, no wrong, no drugs/ just love/ more addicting than life, duh/ your argumentative, self absorbed, naive manner/ is a natural sedative/ I'll take initiative/ if you act like a Neanderthal/ My inner fury becomes active/ I'm a Holy Maverick/ sole purpose is create Heaven/ forcefully fierce/ My voice pierces flesh/ where's my wife?/ only one sex/ between us/ I love us/ before you were on prescriptions/ I want to heal your addictions/ God, why am I not yet divine?/ I'm loosing my mind/ from writing these rhymes/ I'm the only one who knows best, beyond the words of sublime/ My only crime/

is being too humbly in love, with a woman I don't know/

HOOK/CHORUS: Notorious BIG - You n****s got some audacity/ You n****s got some audacity/ You n****s got some audacity/ you sold a million, now you're half of me/ get off my dick/ Kick it/ You n****s got some audacity/ You n****s got some audacity/ You n****s got some audacity/ you sold a million, now you're half of me/ get off my ____/ You n****s got some audacity/ You n****s got some audacity/ You n****s got some audacity/ you sold a million, now you're half of me/ get off my dick/ Kick it/

VERSE 3: You can't walk in my shoes/ the first three rounds, you're knocked out, cold ooze/ game over, you loose/ metaphor - who you think they gonna choose?/ between me and you?/ In the end, I just want you to let me, help you, to help yourself, help me/ save anybody/ if not everybody/ I don't need currency/ to run a democratic society/ but that means/ my Angels rein upon all unworthy/ with Fire lightening bolts, Judgmentally/ time is running out, Repent; simply, it means to live righteously/ as easy, and best you can humbly/ I'm a human physically/ I'm an Angel spiritually/ trapped between reality/ and eternity/ in relation with time/ constant race between Galactic Minds/ wait rewind/ to how you sin against me; Don't associate one race with Jesus/ because he loves all/ Your downfall/ will occur, when God calls me home/ 2000 years, you've exploited me/ the world sins Intolerable Audacity/

HOOK/CHORUS: Notorious BIG - You n****s got some audacity/ You n****s got some audacity/ You n****s got some audacity/ you sold a million, now you're half of me/ get off my dick/ Kick it/ You n****s got some audacity/ You n****s got some audacity/ You n****s got some audacity/ you sold a million, now you're half of me/ get off my dick/ Kick it/ You n****s got some audacity/ You n****s got some audacity/ You n****s got some audacity/ you sold a million, now you're half of me/ get off my ____/ You n****s got some audacity/ You n****s got some audacity/ You n****s got some audacity/ you sold a million, now you're half of me/ get off my dick/ Kick it/

SUMMARY - I'll explain it like this. “Audacity" is a powerful song not only by name, but by it's very definition. The word itself is exactly what I focused upon, when writing this song. I am furious with the world and of it's transgressions committed against My Holy Kingdom. The Notorious BIG may not necessarily be a role model of any sort; however, sometimes bad guys do speak the truth. In the end, this song represents a few things. 1. My overall intelligence and the codes to enter Heaven; 2. My search for my long lost wife - Mary; & 3. My return is imminent and you all, will be saved, or perish."

Chapter 19: Song 12b – Judgment Day (19:12b)

Judgment Day:

INTRO: Lord Jesus Christ; protect us, from Judgment Day.

HOOK/CHORUS: Okay Judgment Day is coming/ just like in the story of Revelation/ These thoughts require years of meditation/ my motives are Heavenly; spiritual addiction/ to slay the devil, wherever he's laying/ I'm Jesus Christ, as Saint Michael Thee Archangel, through reincarnation/ My seven Guardian Angels, are whom Control the destruction/ the end is nigh, cause I need no further examination/

VERSE 1: Upon Earth/ I've descended/ from Heaven/ My sole mission/ includes such vicious intentions/ to slay the devil; right in hells kitchen/ my trigger finger is itching/ Anxiety takes control, I'm panicking/ 20 centuries of waiting/ My physical body is fading/ for 15 years, I've been training/ to assassinate the worlds most lethal assassin/ I'm way to anxious/ my hands, they're really shaking/ as I start aiming/ my minds racing/ too many questions need answers, so quit, with all your asking/ my conscience has been rambling/ A million thoughts each minute/ I'm in it/ to see all evil finished/ with the death of the devil, cause I killed him/ In My name, honor, and survival/ Jesus Christ, is the key to eternal revival/ The human race, is sick from eternal denial/ only one program, no cable channels/ Cynically, I'm furiously righteous, I'm all of Earth's Animals/ and Judgment Day is coming, you're all on trial/

HOOK/CHORUS: Judgment Day is coming/ just like in the story of Revelation/ These thoughts require years of meditation/ my motives are Heavenly; spiritual addiction/ to slay the devil, wherever he's laying/ I'm Jesus Christ, as Saint Michael Thee Archangel, through reincarnation/ My seven Guardian Angels, are whom Control the destruction/ the end is nigh, cause I need no further examination/

VERSE 2: Two verses to explain/ without notice, I am in pain/ two personalities/ which have simultaneously/ trapped me/ first is more evil of two goods, both intentionally/ created righteously/ to banish the world's misery/ not meaning me/ Metaphorically/ but the word's meaning in actuality/ which ultimately, created alternate personalities/ AKA MIZeRY/ I'm infinitely/ malicious, with intentions only to create positive energy/ I'm illuminating everything, inhumanely/ Indirectly, or directly/ I'm the director of this movie/ titled "LIFE" – starring me/ featuring everybody/ spiritually & Physically/ I'm the most creative/

I'm ruthlessly – relentlessly with only three motives/...

One – slay the devil.

Two – Always remain humble.

& Three – create a new world of peace, remaining always eternal.

Spiritually I'm Jesus Christ – I'm hollow/ and only in my shadow/ may any of you humans follow/

HOOK/CHORUS: Okay Judgment Day is coming/ just like in the story of Revelation/ These thoughts require years of meditation/ my motives are Heavenly; spiritual addiction/ to slay the devil, wherever he's laying/ I'm Jesus Christ, as Saint Michael Thee Archangel, through reincarnation/ My seven Guardian Angels, are whom Control the destruction/ the end is nigh, cause I need no further examination/

VERSE 3: This shall be my last profolific text/ my pen is fluid, but my body is real tense/ my mission gradually became immense/ expanding rapidly to the deepest depths/ no button to eject/ like a tape deck/ or F-22 fighter jet/ I contain infinite breathe/ never again shall I meet death/ I'm holy and way to intense/ or intelligent/ to ever contest/ If you attempt/ to disrespect me, with any sort of threat/ I'll beat you to death/ using only telepathy and your soul is the very bet/ no questions just yet/ yes, life is God's ultimate test/ you failed miserably, way before the end of days/ for many, Jesus is just a phase/ The devil, has you all crazed/ he gave you a simple taste/ and now most of you are insane/ only 144,000 ever remained the most brave/ once upon a time you were all angels, now you're the devil's slaves/ poisoned beyond ever being saved/ simple minded children; playing silly little games/ I'll never tell you all three of my names/ I'll see you soon during the end of days/

SUMMARY - I'll explain it like this. "This song "Judgment Day" clearly defines *Revelation* entirely, in a nice summarized version. To prove this, I am going reiterate by scanning & referencing: *The Holy Bible illuminated family edition- King James Version-* ®©™*2000).* Including *Revelation* in my novel is imperative, because I know most won't read *Revelation* otherwise; preventing you, from ever knowing as I know."

Chapter 19: *Revelation* (Duplication- used by permission)

SP

Skyhorse Publishing

Compilation © 2000 by Lionheart Books, Ltd.
Digital Images © 2000 by Lionheart Books, Ltd.

All other correspondence (author inquiries, permissions) concerning the content of this book should be addressed to Lionheart Books, Ltd. 5200 Peachtree Road # 2105 Atlanta, GA 30341

Skyhorse Publishing books may be purchased in bulk at special discounts for sales promotion, corporate gifts, fund-raising, or educational purposes. Special editions can also be created to specifications. For details, contact the Special Sales Department, Skyhorse Publishing, 307 West 36th Street, 11th Floor, New York, NY 10018 or info@skyhorsepublishing.com.

Library of Congress Cataloging-in-Publication Data is available on file.

ISBN 978-1-61608-472-1

10 9 8 7 6 5 4 3 2 1

Designed by Michael Reagan

For my wife Lisa and my children Ian, Kevin and Casey. Who make all things possible.

Printed and bound in China through Asia Pacific Offset, Inc.

THE
REVELATION
TO JOHN

APOCALIPSIS · IESV · CHRISTI

CHAPTER ONE

THE REVELATION OF
Jesus Christ, which God
gave unto him, to shew
unto his servants things
which must shortly
come to pass; and he
sent and signified it by his angel unto
his servant John:
2 Who bare record of the word of
God, and of the testimony of Jesus
Christ, and of all things that he saw.
3 Blessed is he that readeth, and
they that hear the words of this
prophecy, and keep those things
which are written therein: for the
time is at hand.
4 John to the seven churches which
are in Asia: Grace be unto you, and
peace, from him which is, and which
was, and which is to come; and from
the seven Spirits which are before
his throne;
5 And from Jesus Christ, who is
the faithful witness, and the first be-
gotten of the dead, and the prince of
the kings of the earth. Unto him that
loved us, and washed us from our
sins in his own blood,
6 And hath made us kings and
priests unto God and his Father; to
him be glory and dominion for ever
and ever. Amen.
7 Behold, he cometh with clouds;
and every eye shall see him, and they
also which pierced him: and all kin-
dreds of the earth shall wail because
of him. Even so, Amen.
8 I am Alpha and Omega, the be-
ginning and the ending, saith the
Lord, which is, and which was, and
which is to come, the Almighty.
9 I John, who also am your brother,
and companion in tribulation, and in
the kingdom and patience of Jesus
Christ, was in the isle that is called
Patmos, for the word of God, and for
the testimony of Jesus Christ.

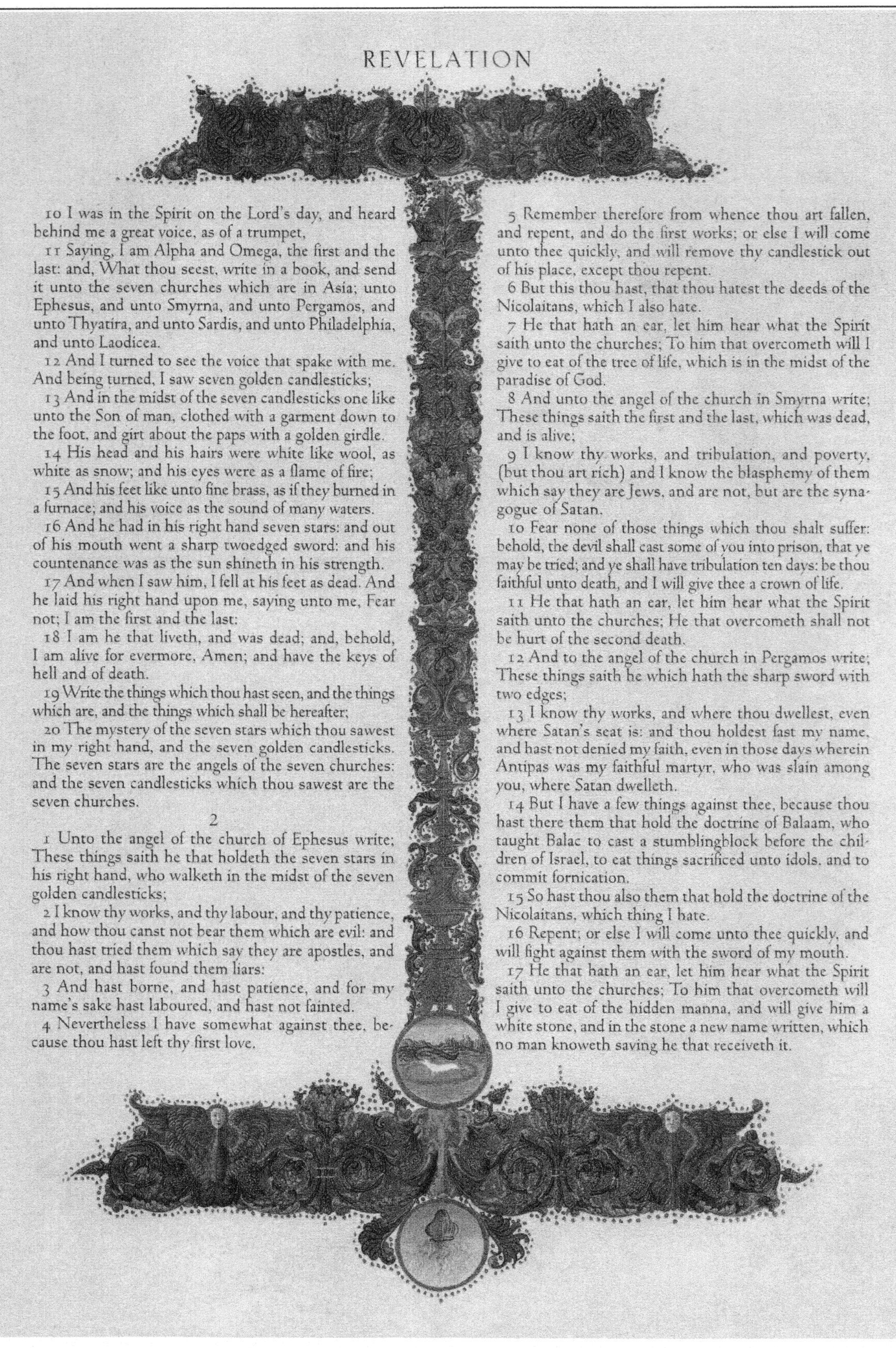

REVELATION

10 I was in the Spirit on the Lord's day, and heard
behind me a great voice, as of a trumpet,
11 Saying, I am Alpha and Omega, the first and the
last: and, What thou seest, write in a book, and send
it unto the seven churches which are in Asia; unto
Ephesus, and unto Smyrna, and unto Pergamos, and
unto Thyatira, and unto Sardis, and unto Philadelphia,
and unto Laodicea.
12 And I turned to see the voice that spake with me.
And being turned, I saw seven golden candlesticks;
13 And in the midst of the seven candlesticks one like
unto the Son of man, clothed with a garment down to
the foot, and girt about the paps with a golden girdle.
14 His head and his hairs were white like wool, as
white as snow; and his eyes were as a flame of fire;
15 And his feet like unto fine brass, as if they burned in
a furnace; and his voice as the sound of many waters.
16 And he had in his right hand seven stars: and out
of his mouth went a sharp twoedged sword: and his
countenance was as the sun shineth in his strength.
17 And when I saw him, I fell at his feet as dead. And
he laid his right hand upon me, saying unto me, Fear
not; I am the first and the last:
18 I am he that liveth, and was dead; and, behold,
I am alive for evermore, Amen; and have the keys of
hell and of death.
19 Write the things which thou hast seen, and the things
which are, and the things which shall be hereafter;
20 The mystery of the seven stars which thou sawest
in my right hand, and the seven golden candlesticks.
The seven stars are the angels of the seven churches:
and the seven candlesticks which thou sawest are the
seven churches.

2

1 Unto the angel of the church of Ephesus write;
These things saith he that holdeth the seven stars in
his right hand, who walketh in the midst of the seven
golden candlesticks;
2 I know thy works, and thy labour, and thy patience,
and how thou canst not bear them which are evil: and
thou hast tried them which say they are apostles, and
are not, and hast found them liars:
3 And hast borne, and hast patience, and for my
name's sake hast laboured, and hast not fainted.
4 Nevertheless I have somewhat against thee, be-
cause thou hast left thy first love.
5 Remember therefore from whence thou art fallen,
and repent, and do the first works; or else I will come
unto thee quickly, and will remove thy candlestick out
of his place, except thou repent.
6 But this thou hast, that thou hatest the deeds of the
Nicolaitans, which I also hate.
7 He that hath an ear, let him hear what the Spirit
saith unto the churches; To him that overcometh will I
give to eat of the tree of life, which is in the midst of the
paradise of God.
8 And unto the angel of the church in Smyrna write;
These things saith the first and the last, which was dead,
and is alive;
9 I know thy works, and tribulation, and poverty,
(but thou art rich) and I know the blasphemy of them
which say they are Jews, and are not, but are the syna-
gogue of Satan.
10 Fear none of those things which thou shalt suffer:
behold, the devil shall cast some of you into prison, that ye
may be tried; and ye shall have tribulation ten days: be thou
faithful unto death, and I will give thee a crown of life.
11 He that hath an ear, let him hear what the Spirit
saith unto the churches; He that overcometh shall not
be hurt of the second death.
12 And to the angel of the church in Pergamos write;
These things saith he which hath the sharp sword with
two edges;
13 I know thy works, and where thou dwellest, even
where Satan's seat is: and thou holdest fast my name,
and hast not denied my faith, even in those days wherein
Antipas was my faithful martyr, who was slain among
you, where Satan dwelleth.
14 But I have a few things against thee, because thou
hast there them that hold the doctrine of Balaam, who
taught Balac to cast a stumblingblock before the chil-
dren of Israel, to eat things sacrificed unto idols, and to
commit fornication.
15 So hast thou also them that hold the doctrine of the
Nicolaitans, which thing I hate.
16 Repent; or else I will come unto thee quickly, and
will fight against them with the sword of my mouth.
17 He that hath an ear, let him hear what the Spirit
saith unto the churches; To him that overcometh will
I give to eat of the hidden manna, and will give him a
white stone, and in the stone a new name written, which
no man knoweth saving he that receiveth it.

REVELATION

18 And unto the angel of the church in Thyatira write;
These things saith the Son of God, who hath his eyes
like unto a flame of fire, and his feet are like fine brass;
19 I know thy works, and charity, and service, and
faith, and thy patience, and thy works; and the last to be
more than the first.
20 Notwithstanding I have a few things against thee,
because thou sufferest that woman Jezebel, which calleth
herself a prophetess, to teach and to seduce my servants
to commit fornication, and to eat things sacrificed unto
idols.
21 And I gave her space to repent of her fornication;
and she repented not.
22 Behold, I will cast
her into a bed, and
them that commit adul-
tery with her into great
tribulation, except they
repent of their deeds.
23 And I will kill her
children with death;
and all the churches
shall know that I am
he which searcheth the
reins and hearts: and I
will give unto every one
of you according to your
works.
24 But unto you I
say, and unto the rest
in Thyatira, as many as
have not this doctrine,
and which have not
known the depths of
Satan, as they speak; I
will put upon you none
other burden.
25 But that which ye
have already hold fast till
I come.
26 And he that over-
cometh, and keepeth my
works unto the end, to
him will I give power over the nations:
27 And he shall rule them with a rod of iron; as the
vessels of a potter shall they be broken to shivers: even
as I received of my Father.
28 And I will give him the morning star.
29 He that hath an ear, let him hear what the Spirit
saith unto the churches.

3

1 And unto the angel of the church in Sardis write;
These things saith he that hath the seven Spirits of God,
and the seven stars; I know thy works, that thou hast a
name that thou livest, and art dead.
2 Be watchful, and strengthen the things which re-
main, that are ready to die: for I have not found thy
works perfect before God.
3 Remember therefore how thou hast received and
heard, and hold fast, and repent. If therefore thou shalt
not watch, I will come on thee as a thief, and thou shalt
not know what hour I will come upon thee.

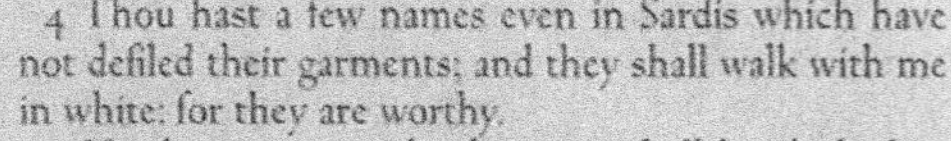

4 Thou hast a few names even in Sardis which have
not defiled their garments; and they shall walk with me
in white: for they are worthy.
5 He that overcometh, the same shall be clothed in
white raiment; and I will not blot out his name out of
the book of life, but I will confess his name before my
Father, and before his angels.
6 He that hath an ear, let him hear what the Spirit saith
unto the churches.
7 And to the angel of the church in Philadelphia write;
These things saith he that is holy, he that is true, he
that hath the key of David, he that openeth, and no man
shutteth; and shutteth, and no man openeth;
8 I know thy works:
behold, I have set be-
fore thee an open door,
and no man can shut
it: for thou hast a little
strength, and hast kept
my word, and hast not
denied my name.
9 Behold, I will make
them of the synagogue
of Satan, which say they
are Jews, and are not,
but do lie; behold, I will
make them to come and
worship before thy feet,
and to know that I have
loved thee.
10 Because thou hast
kept the word of my pa-
tience, I also will keep
thee from the hour of
temptation, which shall
come upon all the world,
to try them that dwell
upon the earth.
11 Behold, I come
quickly: hold that fast
which thou hast, that no
man take thy crown.
12 Him that overco-
meth will I make a pillar in the temple of my God, and he
shall go no more out: and I will write upon him the name
of my God, and the name of the city of my God, which is
new Jerusalem, which cometh down out of heaven from my
God: and I will write upon him my new name.
13 He that hath an ear, let him hear what the Spirit
saith unto the churches.
14 And unto the angel of the church of the Laodiceans
write; These things saith the Amen, the faithful and true
witness, the beginning of the creation of God;
15 I know thy works, that thou art neither cold nor
hot: I would thou wert cold or hot.
16 So then because thou art lukewarm, and neither
cold nor hot, I will spue thee out of my mouth.
17 Because thou sayest, I am rich, and increased with
goods, and have need of nothing; and knowest not that
thou art wretched, and miserable, and poor, and blind,
and naked:
18 I counsel thee to buy of me gold tried in the fire,

that thou mayest be rich; and white raiment, that thou
mayest be clothed, and that the shame of thy nakedness
do not appear; and anoint thine eyes with eyesalve, that
thou mayest see.
19 As many as I love, I rebuke and chasten: be zealous
therefore, and repent.
20 Behold, I stand at the door, and knock: if any man
hear my voice, and open the door, I will come in to him,
and will sup with him, and he with me.
21 To him that overcometh will I grant to sit with me
in my throne, even as I also overcame, and am set down
with my Father in his throne.
22 He that hath an ear, let him hear what the Spirit
saith unto the churches.

4

1 After this I looked, and, behold, a door was opened in
heaven: and the first voice which I heard was as it were
of a trumpet talking with me; which said, Come up hither, and I will shew thee things which must be hereafter.
2 And immediately I was in the spirit: and, behold, a throne was set in heaven, and one sat on the throne.
3 And he that sat was to look upon like a jasper and a sardine stone: and there was a rainbow round about the throne, in sight like unto an emerald.
4 And round about the throne were four and twenty seats: and upon the seats I saw four and twenty
elders sitting, clothed in white raiment; and they had on
their heads crowns of gold.
5 And out of the throne proceeded lightnings and
thunderings and voices: and there were seven lamps
of fire burning before the throne, which are the seven
Spirits of God.
6 And before the throne there was a sea of glass like
unto crystal: and in the midst of the throne, and round
about the throne, were four beasts full of eyes before and
behind.
7 And the first beast was like a lion, and the second
beast like a calf, and the third beast had a face as a man,
and the fourth beast was like a flying eagle.
8 And the four beasts had each of them six wings about
him; and they were full of eyes within: and they rest
not day and night, saying, Holy, holy, holy, Lord God
Almighty, which was, and is, and is to come.
9 And when those beasts give glory and honour and
thanks to him that sat on the throne, who liveth for ever
and ever,

10 The four and twenty elders fall down before him that
sat on the throne, and worship him that liveth for ever and
ever, and cast their crowns before the throne, saying,
11 Thou art worthy, O Lord, to receive glory and hon-
our and power: for thou hast created all things, and for
thy pleasure they are and were created.

5

1 And I saw in the right hand of him that sat on the
throne a book written within and on the backside, sealed
with seven seals.
2 And I saw a strong angel proclaiming with a loud
voice, Who is worthy to open the book, and to loose
the seals thereof?
3 And no man in heaven, nor in earth, neither under
the earth, was able to open the book, neither to look
thereon.
4 And I wept much, because no man was found worthy
to open and to read the book, neither to look thereon.
5 And one of the elders saith unto me, Weep not: behold, the Lion of the tribe of Juda, the Root of David, hath prevailed to open the book, and to loose the seven seals thereof.
6 And I beheld, and, lo, in the midst of the throne and of the four beasts, and in the midst of the elders, stood a Lamb as it had been slain, having seven horns and seven eyes, which are the seven Spirits of God sent forth into all
the earth.
7 And he came and took the book out of the right hand
of him that sat upon the throne.
8 And when he had taken the book, the four beasts
and four and twenty elders fell down before the Lamb,
having every one of them harps, and golden vials full of
odours, which are the prayers of saints.
9 And they sung a new song, saying, Thou art worthy
to take the book, and to open the seals thereof: for thou
wast slain, and hast redeemed us to God by thy blood out
of every kindred, and tongue, and people, and nation;
10 And hast made us unto our God kings and priests:
and we shall reign on the earth.
11 And I beheld, and I heard the voice of many angels
round about the throne and the beasts and the elders:
and the number of them was ten thousand times ten
thousand, and thousands of thousands;
12 Saying with a loud voice, Worthy is the Lamb that
was slain to receive power, and riches, and wisdom, and
strength, and honour, and glory, and blessing.

13 And every creature which is in
heaven, and on the earth, and un-
der the earth, and such as are in
the sea, and all that are in them,
heard I saying, Blessing, and honour, and glory, and
power, be unto him that sitteth upon the throne, and
unto the Lamb for ever and ever.
14 And the four beasts said, Amen. And the four and
twenty elders fell down and worshipped him that liveth
for ever and ever.

6

1 And I saw when the Lamb opened one of the seals,
and I heard, as it were the noise of thunder, one of the
four beasts saying, Come and see.
2 And I saw, and behold a white horse: and he that sat
on him had a bow; and a crown was given unto him: and
he went forth conquering, and to conquer.
3 And when he had opened the second seal, I heard the
second beast say, Come and see.
4 And there went out another horse that was red: and
power was given to him that sat thereon to take peace
from the earth, and that they should kill one another:
and there was given unto him a great sword.
5 And when he had opened the third seal, I heard the
third beast say, Come and see. And I beheld, and lo a
black horse; and he that sat on him had a pair of balances
in his hand.
6 And I heard a voice in the midst of the four beasts say, A
measure of wheat for a penny, and three measures of barley
for a penny; and see thou hurt not the oil and the wine.
7 And when he had opened the fourth seal, I heard the
voice of the fourth beast say, Come and see.
8 And I looked, and behold a pale horse: and his name
that sat on him was Death, and Hell followed with him.
And power was given unto them over the fourth part of
the earth, to kill with sword, and with hunger, and with
death, and with the beasts of the earth.
9 And when he had opened the fifth seal, I saw under
the altar the souls of them that were slain for the word
of God, and for the testimony which they held:
10 And they cried with a loud voice, saying, How long,
O Lord, holy and true, dost thou not judge and avenge
our blood on them that dwell on the earth?
11 And white robes were given unto every one of them;
and it was said unto them, that they should rest yet for
a little season, until their fellowservants also and their
brethren, that should be killed as they were, should be
fulfilled.
12 And I beheld when he had opened the sixth seal, and,
lo, there was a great earthquake; and the sun became black
as sackcloth of hair, and the moon became as blood;
13 And the stars of heaven fell unto the earth, even as
a fig tree casteth her untimely figs, when she is shaken
of a mighty wind.
14 And the heaven departed as a scroll when it is rolled
together; and every mountain and island were moved out
of their places.
15 And the kings of the earth, and the great men, and
the rich men, and the chief captains, and the mighty
men, and every bondman, and every free man, hid them-
selves in the dens and in the rocks of the mountains;
16 And said to the mountains and rocks, Fall on us,
and hide us from the face
of him that sitteth on the
throne, and from the wrath
of the Lamb:
17 For the great day of his wrath is
come; and who shall be able to stand?

7

1 And after these things I saw four angels standing on
the four corners of the earth, holding the four winds of
the earth, that the wind should not blow on the earth,
nor on the sea, nor on any tree.
2 And I saw another angel ascending from the east,
having the seal of the living God: and he cried with a loud
voice to the four angels, to whom it was given to hurt
the earth and the sea,
3 Saying, Hurt not the earth, neither the sea, nor the
trees, till we have sealed the servants of our God in their
foreheads.
4 And I heard the number of them which were sealed:
and there were sealed an hundred and forty and four
thousand of all the tribes of the children of Israel.
5 Of the tribe of Juda were sealed twelve thousand. Of
the tribe of Reuben were sealed twelve thousand. Of the
tribe of Gad were sealed twelve thousand.
6 Of the tribe of Aser were sealed twelve thousand. Of
the tribe of Nepthalim were sealed twelve thousand. Of
the tribe of Manasses were sealed twelve thousand.
7 Of the tribe of Simeon were sealed twelve thousand.
Of the tribe of Levi were sealed twelve thousand. Of the
tribe of Issachar were sealed twelve thousand.
8 Of the tribe of Zabulon were sealed twelve thousand.
Of the tribe of Joseph were sealed twelve thousand. Of
the tribe of Benjamin were sealed twelve thousand.
9 After this I beheld, and, lo, a great multitude, which
no man could number, of all nations, and kindreds,
and people, and tongues, stood before the throne, and
before the Lamb, clothed with white robes, and palms
in their hands;
10 And cried with a loud voice, saying, Salvation to
our God which sitteth upon the throne, and unto the
Lamb.
11 And all the angels stood round
about the throne, and about the elders
and the four beasts, and fell before the
throne on their faces, and worshipped
God,
12 Saying, Amen: Blessing, and glory,
and wisdom, and thanksgiving, and
honour, and power, and might, be unto our God for
ever and ever. Amen.
13 And one of the elders answered, saying unto me,
What are these which are arrayed in white robes? and
whence came they?
14 And I said unto him, Sir, thou knowest. And he said
to me, These are they which came out of great tribula-
tion, and have washed their robes, and made them white
in the blood of the Lamb.
15 Therefore are they before the throne of God, and
serve him day and night in his temple: and he that sitteth
on the throne shall dwell among them.
16 They shall hunger no more, neither thirst any more;
neither shall the sun light on them, nor any heat.

17 For the Lamb which is in the midst of the throne shall
feed them, and shall lead them unto living fountains of wa-
ters: and God shall wipe away all tears from their eyes!

8

1 And when he had opened the seventh seal, there was
silence in heaven about the space of half an hour.
2 And I saw the seven angels which stood before God;
and to them were given seven trumpets.
3 And another angel came and stood at the altar, having
a golden censer; and there was given unto him much in-
cense, that he should offer it with the prayers of all saints
upon the golden altar which was before the throne.
4 And the smoke of the incense, which came with the
prayers of the saints, ascended up before God out of the
angel's hand.

5 And the angel took the censer, and filled it with fire of
the altar, and cast it into the earth: and there were voices,
and thunderings, and lightnings, and an earthquake.
6 And the seven angels which had the seven trumpets
prepared themselves to sound.
7 The first angel sounded, and there followed hail and
fire mingled with blood, and they were cast upon the
earth: and the third part of trees was burnt up, and all
green grass was burnt up.
8 And the second angel sounded, and as it were a great
mountain burning with fire was cast into the sea: and the
third part of the sea became blood;
9 And the third part of the creatures which were in
the sea, and had life, died; and the third part of the ships
were destroyed.
10 And the third angel sounded, and there fell a great star
from heaven, burning as it were a lamp, and it fell upon the
third part of the rivers, and upon the fountains of waters;

11 And the name of the star is called Wormwood: and
the third part of the waters became wormwood; and many
men died of the waters, because they were made bitter.
12 And the fourth angel sounded, and the third part of
the sun was smitten, and the third part of the moon, and
the third part of the stars; so as the third part of them
was darkened, and the day shone not for a third part of
it, and the night likewise.
13 And I beheld, and heard an angel flying through
the midst of heaven, saying with a loud voice, Woe,
woe, woe, to the inhabiters of the earth by reason of
the other voices of the trumpet of the three angels,
which are yet to sound!

9

1 And the fifth angel sounded, and I saw a star fall from
heaven unto the earth: and to him was given the key of
the bottomless pit.
2 And he opened the bottomless pit; and there arose
a smoke out of the pit, as the smoke of a great furnace;
and the sun and the air were darkened by reason of the
smoke of the pit.
3 And there came out of the smoke locusts upon the
earth: and unto them was given power, as the scorpions
of the earth have power.
4 And it was commanded them that they should not
hurt the grass of the earth, neither any green thing,
neither any tree; but only those men which have not
the seal of God in their foreheads.
5 And to them it was given that they should not kill
them, but that they should be tormented five months:
and their torment was as the torment of a scorpion,
when he striketh a man.
6 And in those days shall men seek death, and shall

not find it; and shall desire to die, and death shall flee
from them.
7 And the shapes of the locusts were like unto horses pre-
pared unto battle; and on their heads were as it were crowns
like gold, and their faces were as the faces of men.
8 And they had hair as the hair of women, and their
teeth were as the teeth of lions.
9 And they had breastplates, as it were breastplates of
iron; and the sound of their wings was as the sound of
chariots of many horses running to battle.
10 And they had tails like unto scorpions, and there
were stings in their tails: and their power was to hurt
men five months.
11 And they had a king over them, which is the an-
gel of the bottomless pit, whose name in the Hebrew
tongue is Abaddon, but in the Greek tongue hath his
name Apollyon.
12 One woe is past; and, behold, there come two woes
more hereafter.
13 And the sixth angel sounded, and I heard a voice from
the four horns of the golden altar which is before God,
14 Saying to the sixth angel which had the trumpet,
Loose the four angels which are bound in the great river
Euphrates.
15 And the four angels were loosed, which were pre-
pared for an hour, and a day, and a month, and a year,
for to slay the third part of men.
16 And the number of the army of the horsemen were
two hundred thousand thousand: and I heard the num-
ber of them.
17 And thus I saw the horses in the vision, and them
that sat on them, having breastplates of fire, and of ja-
cinth, and brimstone: and the heads of the horses were
as the heads of lions; and out of their mouths issued fire
and smoke and brimstone.
18 By these three was the third part of men killed, by
the fire, and by the smoke, and by the brimstone, which
issued out of their mouths.
19 For their power is in their mouth, and in their tails:
for their tails were like unto serpents, and had heads, and
with them they do hurt.
20 And the rest of the men which were not killed by
these plagues yet repented not of the works of their
hands, that they should not worship devils, and idols
of gold, and silver, and brass, and stone, and of wood:
which neither can see, nor hear, nor walk:
21 Neither repented they of their murders, nor of their
sorceries, nor of their fornication, nor of their thefts.

10

1 And I saw another mighty angel come down from
heaven, clothed with a cloud: and a rainbow was upon
his head, and his face was as it were the sun, and his feet
as pillars of fire:
2 And he had in his hand a little book open: and he set his
right foot upon the sea, and his left foot on the earth,
3 And cried with a loud voice, as when a lion roareth: and
when he had cried, seven thunders uttered their voices.
4 And when the seven thunders had uttered their
voices, I was about to write: and I heard a voice from
heaven saying unto me, Seal up those things which the
seven thunders uttered, and write them not.
5 And the angel which I saw stand upon the sea and
upon the earth lifted up his hand to heaven,
6 And sware by him that liveth for ever and ever, who
created heaven, and the things that therein are, and the
earth, and the things that therein are, and the sea, and
the things which are therein, that there should be time
no longer:
7 But in the days of the voice of the seventh angel, when
he shall begin to sound, the mystery of God should be fin-
ished, as he hath declared to his servants the prophets.
8 And the voice which I heard from heaven spake unto
me again, and said, Go and take the little book which is
open in the hand of the angel which standeth upon the
sea and upon the earth.
9 And I went unto the angel, and said unto him, Give
me the little book. And he said unto me, Take it, and
eat it up; and it shall make thy belly bitter, but it shall be
in thy mouth sweet as honey.
10 And I took the little book out of the angel's hand,
and ate it up; and it was in my mouth sweet as honey:
and as soon as I had eaten it, my belly was bitter.
11 And he said unto me, Thou must prophesy again be-
fore many peoples, and nations, and tongues, and kings.

11

1 And there was given me a reed like unto a rod: and
the angel stood, saying, Rise, and measure the temple of
God, and the altar, and them that worship therein.
2 But the court which is without the temple leave out, and
measure it not; for it is given unto the Gentiles: and the holy
city shall they tread under foot forty and two months.
3 And I will give power unto my two witnesses, and
they shall prophesy a thousand two hundred and three-
score days, clothed in sackcloth.
4 These are the two olive trees, and the two candle-
sticks standing before the God of the earth.
5 And if any man will hurt them, fire proceedeth out
of their mouth, and devoureth their enemies: and if any
man will hurt them, he must in this manner be killed.
6 These have power to shut heaven, that it rain not in
the days of their prophecy: and have power over waters
to turn them to blood, and to smite the earth with all
plagues, as often as they will.
7 And when they shall have finished their testimony,
the beast that ascendeth out of the bottomless pit shall
make war against them, and shall overcome them, and
kill them.
8 And their dead bodies shall lie in the street of the
great city, which spiritually is called Sodom and Egypt,
where also our Lord was crucified.
9 And they of the people and kindreds and tongues and
nations shall see their dead bodies three days and an half,
and shall not suffer their dead bodies to be put in graves.
10 And they that dwell upon the earth shall rejoice
over them, and make merry, and shall send gifts one to
another; because these two prophets tormented them
that dwelt on the earth.
11 And after three days and an half the Spirit of life
from God entered into them, and they stood upon their
feet; and great fear fell upon them which saw them.
12 And they heard a great voice from heaven saying
unto them, Come up hither. And they ascended up to
heaven in a cloud; and their enemies beheld them.
13 And the same hour was there a great earthquake,

and the tenth part of the city fell, and in the earthquake
were slain of men seven thousand: and the remnant were
affrighted, and gave glory to the God of heaven.
14 The second woe is past; and, behold, the third woe
cometh quickly.
15 And the seventh angel sounded; and there were
great voices in heaven, saying, The kingdoms of this
world are become the kingdoms of our Lord, and of his
Christ; and he shall reign for ever and ever.
16 And the four and twenty elders, which sat before
God on their seats, fell upon their faces, and wor-
shipped God,
17 Saying, We give thee thanks, O Lord God
Almighty, which art,
and wast, and art to
come; because thou
hast taken to thee
thy great power, and
hast reigned.
18 And the nations
were angry, and thy
wrath is come, and
the time of the dead,
that they should be
judged, and that thou
shouldest give reward
unto thy servants the
prophets, and to the
saints, and them that
fear thy name, small
and great; and shoul-
dest destroy them
which destroy the
earth.
19 And the temple
of God was opened in
heaven, and there was
seen in his temple the
ark of his testament:
and there were light-
nings, and voices, and
thunderings, and an
earthquake, and great hail.

12

1 And there appeared a great wonder in heaven; a
woman clothed with the sun, and the moon under her
feet, and upon her head a crown of twelve stars:
2 And she being with child cried, travailing in birth,
and pained to be delivered.
3 And there appeared another wonder in heaven; and
behold a great red dragon, having seven heads and ten
horns, and seven crowns upon his heads.
4 And his tail drew the third part of the stars of heaven,
and did cast them to the earth: and the dragon stood
before the woman which was ready to be delivered, for
to devour her child as soon as it was born.
5 And she brought forth a man child, who was to rule
all nations with a rod of iron: and her child was caught
up unto God, and to his throne.
6 And the woman fled into the wilderness, where she
hath a place prepared of God, that they should feed her
there a thousand two hundred and threescore days.

7 And there was war in heaven: Michael and his angels
fought against the dragon; and the dragon fought and
his angels,
8 And prevailed not; neither was their place found any
more in heaven.
9 And the great dragon was cast out, that old serpent,
called the Devil, and Satan, which deceiveth the whole
world: he was cast out into the earth, and his angels
were cast out with him.
10 And I heard a loud voice saying in heaven, Now is
come salvation, and strength, and the kingdom of our
God, and the power of his Christ: for the accuser of our
brethren is cast down, which accused them before our
God day and night.
11 And they over-
came him by the
blood of the Lamb,
and by the word of
their testimony; and
they loved not their
lives unto the death.
12 Therefore re-
joice, ye heavens, and
ye that dwell in them.
Woe to the inhabit-
ers of the earth and of
the sea! for the devil is
come down unto you,
having great wrath,
because he knoweth
that he hath but a
short time.
13 And when the
dragon saw that he
was cast unto the
earth, he persecuted
the woman which
brought forth the
man child.
14 And to the wo-
man were given two
wings of a great eagle,
that she might fly into the wilderness, into her place,
where she is nourished for a time, and times, and half a
time, from the face of the serpent.
15 And the serpent cast out of his mouth water as a
flood after the woman, that he might cause her to be
carried away of the flood.
16 And the earth helped the woman, and the earth
opened her mouth, and swallowed up the flood which
the dragon cast out of his mouth.
17 And the dragon was wroth with the woman, and
went to make war with the remnant of her seed, which
keep the commandments of God, and have the testi-
mony of Jesus Christ.

13

1 And I stood upon the sand of the sea, and saw a beast
rise up out of the sea, having seven heads and ten horns,
and upon his horns ten crowns, and upon his heads the
name of blasphemy.
2 And the beast which I saw was like unto a leopard,
and his feet were as the feet of a bear, and his mouth as

REVELATION

the mouth of a lion: and the dragon gave him
his power, and his seat, and great authority.
3 And I saw one of his heads as it were wounded
to death; and his deadly wound was healed: and all the
world wondered after the beast.
4 And they worshipped the dragon which gave power
unto the beast: and they worshipped the beast, saying,
Who is like unto the beast? who is able to make war
with him?
5 And there was given unto him a mouth speaking
great things and blasphemies; and power was given unto
him to continue forty and two months.
6 And he opened his mouth in blasphemy against God,
to blaspheme his name, and his tabernacle, and them
that dwell in heaven.
7 And it was given unto him to make war with the
saints, and to overcome them: and power was given him
over all kindreds, and tongues, and nations.
8 And all that dwell upon the earth shall worship him,
whose names are not written in the book of life of the
Lamb slain from the foundation of the world.
9 If any man have an ear, let him hear.
10 He that leadeth into captivity shall go into captivity:
he that killeth with the sword must be killed with the
sword. Here is the patience and the faith of the saints.
11 And I beheld another beast coming up out of the
earth; and he had two horns like a lamb, and he spake
as a dragon.
12 And he exerciseth all the power of the first beast
before him, and causeth the earth and them which dwell
therein to worship the first beast, whose deadly wound
was healed.
13 And he doeth great wonders, so that he maketh fire
come down from heaven on the earth in the sight of men,
14 And deceiveth them that dwell on the earth by the
means of those miracles which he had power to do in the
sight of the beast; saying to them that dwell on the earth,
that they should make an image to the beast, which had
the wound by a sword, and did live.
15 And he had power to give life unto the image of the
beast, that the image of the beast should both speak, and
cause that as many as would not worship the image of
the beast should be killed.
16 And he causeth all, both small and great, rich and
poor, free and bond, to receive a mark in their right hand,
or in their foreheads:
17 And that no man might buy or sell, save he that
had the mark, or the name of the beast, or the number
of his name.
18 Here is wisdom. Let him that hath understanding
count the number of the beast: for it is the number of a
man; and his number is Six hundred threescore and six.

14

1 And I looked, and, lo, a Lamb stood on the mount
Sion, and with him an hundred forty and four thousand,
having his Father's name written in their foreheads.
2 And I heard a voice from heaven, as the voice of
many waters, and as the voice of a great thunder:
and I heard the voice of harpers harping with
their harps:
3 And they sung as it were a new song be-
fore the throne, and before the four beasts,
and the elders: and no man
could learn that song but
the hundred and forty and
four thousand, which were redeemed from the earth.
4 These are they which were not defiled with women;
for they are virgins. These are they which follow the
Lamb whithersoever he goeth. These were redeemed
from among men, being the firstfruits unto God and to
the Lamb.
5 And in their mouth was found no guile: for they are
without fault before the throne of God.
6 And I saw another angel fly in the midst of heaven,
having the everlasting gospel to preach unto them that
dwell on the earth, and to every nation, and kindred, and
tongue, and people,
7 Saying with a loud voice, Fear God, and give glory to
him; for the hour of his judgment is come: and worship
him that made heaven, and earth, and the sea, and the
fountains of waters.
8 And there followed another angel, saying, Babylon is
fallen, is fallen, that great city, because she made all na-
tions drink of the wine of the wrath of her fornication.
9 And the third angel followed them, saying with a loud
voice, If any man worship the beast and his image, and
receive his mark in his forehead, or in his hand,
10 The same shall drink of the wine of the
wrath of God, which is poured out without
mixture into the cup of his indignation; and
he shall be tormented with fire and brimstone
in the presence of the holy angels, and in the
presence of the Lamb:
11 And the smoke of their torment ascendeth up
for ever and ever: and they have no rest day nor night,
who worship the beast and his image, and whosoever
receiveth the mark of his name.
12 Here is the patience of the saints: here are they that
keep the commandments of God, and the faith of Jesus.
13 And I heard a voice from heaven saying unto me,
Write, Blessed are the dead which die in the Lord from
henceforth: Yea, saith the Spirit, that they may rest from
their labours; and their works do follow them.
14 And I looked, and behold a white cloud, and upon
the cloud one sat like unto the Son of man, having on his
head a golden crown, and in his hand a sharp sickle.
15 And another angel came out of the temple, crying
with a loud voice to him that sat on the cloud, Thrust
in thy sickle, and reap: for the time is come for thee to
reap; for the harvest of the earth is ripe.
16 And he that sat on the cloud thrust in his sickle on
the earth; and the earth was reaped.
17 And another angel came out of the temple which is
in heaven, he also having a sharp sickle.
18 And another angel came out from the altar, which
had power over fire; and cried with a loud cry to him that
had the sharp sickle, saying, Thrust in thy sharp sickle,
and gather the clusters of the vine of the earth; for her
grapes are fully ripe.
19 And the angel thrust in his sickle into the
earth, and gathered the vine of the
earth, and cast it into the great
winepress of the wrath of God.
20 And the winepress was

trodden without the city, and blood came out of the
winepress, even unto the horse bridles, by the space of a
thousand and six hundred furlongs.

15

1 And I saw another sign in heaven, great and marvel-
lous, seven angels having the seven last plagues; for in
them is filled up the wrath of God.
2 And I saw as it were a sea of glass mingled with fire: and

them that had gotten the victory over the beast, and over
his image, and over his mark, and over the number of his
name, stand on the sea of glass, having the harps of God.
3 And they sing the song of Moses the servant of God,
and the song of the Lamb, saying, Great and marvellous
are thy works, Lord God Almighty; just and true are thy
ways, thou King of saints.
4 Who shall not fear thee, O Lord, and glorify thy
name? for thou only art holy: for all nations shall come
and worship before thee; for thy judgments are made
manifest.

5 And after that I looked, and, behold, the temple of
the tabernacle of the testimony in heaven was opened:
6 And the seven angels came out of the temple, having
the seven plagues, clothed in pure and white linen, and
having their breasts girded with golden girdles.
7 And one of the four beasts gave unto the seven an-
gels seven golden vials full of the wrath of God, who
liveth for ever and ever.

8 And the temple was filled with smoke from the glory
of God, and from his power; and no man was able to
enter into the temple, till the seven plagues of the seven
angels were fulfilled.

16

1 And I heard a great voice out of the temple saying to
the seven angels, Go your ways, and pour out the vials
of the wrath of God upon the earth.
2 And the first went, and poured out his vial upon the
earth; and there fell a noisome and grievous sore upon
the men which had the mark of the beast, and upon

them which worshipped his image.
3 And the second angel poured out his vial upon the
sea; and it became as the blood of a dead man: and every
living soul died in the sea.
4 And the third angel poured out his vial upon the rivers
and fountains of waters; and they became blood.
5 And I heard the angel of the waters say, Thou art righteous, O Lord, which art, and wast, and shalt be, because
thou hast judged thus.
6 For they have shed the blood of saints and prophets, and
thou hast given them blood to drink; for they are worthy.
7 And I heard another out of the altar say,
Even so, Lord God Almighty, true and
righteous are thy judgments.
8 And the fourth angel
poured out his vial upon
the sun; and power
was given unto him to
scorch men with fire.
9 And men were
scorched with great
heat, and blasphemed the name
of God, which hath
power over these
plagues: and they
repented not to give
him glory.
10 And the fifth
angel poured out his
vial upon the seat of
the beast; and his
kingdom was full
of darkness; and
they gnawed their
tongues for pain,
11 And blasphemed the God of
heaven because of
their pains and their
sores, and repented
not of their deeds.
12 And the sixth
angel poured out his
vial upon the great
river Euphrates; and
the water thereof
was dried up, that
the way of the kings
of the east might be
prepared.
13 And I saw three unclean spirits like frogs come out
of the mouth of the dragon, and out of the mouth of the
beast, and out of the mouth of the false prophet.
14 For they are the spirits of devils, working miracles,
which go forth unto the kings of the earth and of the
whole world, to gather them to the battle of that great
day of God Almighty.
15 Behold, I come as a thief. Blessed is he that watcheth, and keepeth his garments, lest he walk naked, and
they see his shame.
16 And he gathered them together into a place called in

the Hebrew tongue Armageddon.
17 And the seventh angel poured out his vial into the
air; and there came a great voice out of the temple of
heaven, from the throne, saying, It is done.
18 And there were voices, and thunders, and lightnings; and there was a great earthquake, such as was
not since men were upon the earth, so mighty an earthquake, and so great.
19 And the great city was divided into three parts, and
the cities of the nations fell: and great Babylon came in
remem- brance before God, to give unto her the cup of the
wine of the fier-ceness of his wrath.
20 And every island fled away, and the
mountains were not found.
21 And there fell upon men
a great hail out of heaven,
every stone about the
weight of a talent: and
men blasphemed God
because of the plague
of the hail; for the
plague thereof was exceeding great.

17

1 And there came
one of the seven angels
which had the seven
vials, and talked with
me, saying unto me,
Come hither; I will
shew unto thee the
judgment of the great
whore that sitteth
upon many waters:
2 With whom the
kings of the earth
have committed fornication, and the
inhabitants of the
earth have been made
drunk with the wine
of her fornication.
3 So he carried me
away in the spirit into
the wilderness: and I
saw a woman sit upon
a scarlet coloured
beast, full of names
of blasphemy, having
seven heads and ten
horns.
4 And the woman was arrayed in purple and scarlet
colour, and decked with gold and precious stones and
pearls, having a golden cup in her hand full of abominations and filthiness of her fornication:
5 And upon her forehead was a name written,
MYSTERY, BABYLON THE GREAT, THE MOTHER
OF HARLOTS AND ABOMINATIONS OF THE
EARTH.
6 And I saw the woman drunken with the blood of the
saints, and with the blood of the martyrs of Jesus: and
when I saw her, I wondered with great admiration.

REVELATION

7 And the angel said unto me,
Wherefore didst thou marvel? I will tell
thee the mystery of the woman, and
of the beast that carrieth her, which hath
the seven heads and ten horns.
8 The beast that thou sawest was, and is not; and shall
ascend out of the bottomless pit, and go into perdition:
and they that dwell on the earth shall wonder, whose
names were not written in the book of life from the foun-
dation of the world, when they behold the beast that was,
and is not, and yet is.
9 And here is the mind which hath wisdom. The seven
heads are seven mountains, on which the woman sitteth.
10 And there are seven kings: five are fallen, and one
is, and the other is not yet come; and when he cometh,
he must continue a short space.
11 And the beast that was, and is not, even he is the
eighth, and is of the seven, and goeth into perdition.
12 And the ten horns which thou sawest are ten kings,
which have received no kingdom as yet; but receive
power as kings one hour with the beast.
13 These have one mind, and shall give their power and
strength unto the beast.
14 These shall make war with the Lamb, and the Lamb
shall overcome them: for he is Lord of lords, and King of
kings: and they that are with him are called, and chosen,
and faithful.
15 And he saith unto me, The waters which thou
sawest, where the whore sitteth, are peoples, and multi-
tudes, and nations, and tongues.
16 And the ten horns which thou sawest upon the
beast, these shall hate the whore, and shall make her
desolate and naked, and shall eat her flesh, and burn
her with fire.
17 For God hath put in their hearts to fulfil his will, and
to agree, and give their kingdom unto the beast, until the
words of God shall be fulfilled.
18 And the woman which thou sawest is that great city,
which reigneth over the kings of the earth.

18

1 And after these things I saw another angel come
down from heaven, having great power; and the earth
was lightened with his glory.
2 And he cried mightily with a strong voice, saying,
Babylon the great is fallen, is fallen, and is become the
habitation of devils, and the hold of every foul spirit, and
a cage of every unclean and hateful bird.
3 For all nations have drunk of the wine of the wrath of
her fornication, and the kings of the earth have commit-
ted fornication with her, and the merchants of the earth
are waxed rich through the abundance of her delicacies.
4 And I heard another voice from heaven, saying, Come
out of her, my people, that ye be not partakers of her sins,
and that ye receive not of her plagues.
5 For her sins have reached unto heaven, and God hath
remembered her iniquities.
6 Reward her even as she rewarded you,
and double unto her double according
to her works: in the cup which she
hath filled fill to her double.
7 How much she hath glorified
herself, and lived deliciously, so
much torment and sorrow give
her: for she saith in her heart, I
sit a queen, and am no widow,
and shall see no sorrow.
8 Therefore shall her plagues come in one day, death,
and mourning, and famine; and she shall be utterly burned
with fire: for strong is the Lord God who judgeth her.
9 And the kings of the earth, who have committed
fornication and lived deliciously with her, shall bewail
her, and lament for her, when they shall see the smoke
of her burning,
10 Standing afar off for the fear of her torment, saying,
Alas, alas, that great city Babylon, that mighty city! for
in one hour is thy judgment come.
11 And the merchants of the earth shall weep and
mourn over her; for no man buyeth their merchandise
any more:
12 The merchandise of gold, and silver, and precious
stones, and of pearls, and fine linen, and purple, and silk,
and scarlet, and all thyine wood, and all manner vessels
of ivory, and all manner vessels of most precious wood,
and of brass, and iron, and marble,
13 And cinnamon, and odours, and ointments, and
frankincense, and wine, and oil, and fine flour, and
wheat, and beasts, and sheep, and horses, and chariots,
and slaves, and souls of men.
14 And the fruits that thy soul lusted after are de-
parted from thee, and all things which were dainty and
goodly are departed from thee, and thou shalt find them
no more at all.
15 The merchants of these things, which were made
rich by her, shall stand afar off for the fear of her tor-
ment, weeping and wailing,
16 And saying, Alas, alas, that great city, that was
clothed in fine linen, and purple, and scarlet, and decked
with gold, and precious stones, and pearls!
17 For in one hour so great riches is come to nought.
And every shipmaster, and all the company in ships,
and sailors, and as many as trade by sea, stood afar off,
18 And cried when they saw the smoke of her burn-
ing, saying, What city is like unto this great city!
19 And they cast dust on their heads, and cried, weep-
ing and wailing, saying, Alas, alas, that great city, wherein
were made rich all that had ships in the sea by reason of
her costliness! for in one hour is she made desolate.
20 Rejoice over her, thou heaven, and ye holy apostles
and prophets; for God hath avenged you on her.
21 And a mighty angel took up a stone like a great
millstone, and cast it into the sea, saying, Thus with
violence shall that great city Babylon be thrown down,
and shall be found no more at all.
22 And the voice of harpers, and musicians, and of
pipers, and trumpeters, shall be heard no more at all in
thee; and no craftsman, of whatsoever craft he be, shall
be found any more in thee; and the sound of a mill-
stone shall be heard no more at all in thee;
23 And the light of a candle shall
shine no more at all in
thee; and the voice of
the bridegroom and of
the bride shall be
heard no more at all in

REVELATION

thee: for thy merchants were the great men of the earth;
for by thy sorceries were all nations deceived.
24 And in her was found the blood of prophets, and of
saints, and of all that were slain upon the earth.

19

1 And after these things I heard a great voice of much
people in heaven, saying, Alleluia; Salvation, and glory,
and honour, and power, unto the Lord our God:
2 For true and righteous are his judgments: for he hath
judged the great whore, which did corrupt the earth with
her fornication, and hath avenged the blood of his
servants at her hand.
3 And again they said,
Alleluia. And her smoke
rose up for ever and
ever.
4 And the four and
twenty elders and the four
beasts fell down and worshipped
God that sat on
the throne, saying, Amen;
Alleluia.
5 And a voice came out
of the throne, saying, Praise our God, all ye his servants,
and ye that fear him, both small and great.
6 And I heard as it were the voice of a great multitude,
and as the voice of many waters, and as the voice of
mighty thunderings, saying, Alleluia: for the Lord God
omnipotent reigneth.
7 Let us be glad and rejoice, and give honour to him:
for the marriage of the Lamb is come, and his wife hath
made herself ready.
8 And to her was granted that she should be arrayed
in fine linen, clean and white: for the fine linen is the
righteousness of saints.
9 And he saith unto me, Write, Blessed are they which
are called unto the marriage supper of the Lamb. And he
saith unto me, These are the true sayings of God.
10 And I fell at his feet to worship him. And he said unto
me, See thou do it not: I am thy fellowservant, and of thy
brethren that have the testimony of Jesus: worship God:
for the testimony of Jesus is the spirit of prophecy.
11 And I saw heaven opened, and behold a white horse;
and he that sat upon him was called Faithful and True,
and in righteousness he doth judge and make war.
12 His eyes were as a flame of fire, and on his head were
many crowns; and he had a name written, that no man
knew, but he himself.
13 And he was clothed with a vesture dipped in blood:
and his name is called The Word of God.
14 And the armies which were in heaven followed him
upon white horses, clothed in fine linen, white and clean.
15 And out of his mouth goeth a sharp sword, that
with it he should smite the nations: and he shall rule
them with a rod of iron: and he treadeth the winepress
of the fierceness and wrath of Almighty God.
16 And he hath on his vesture and on his thigh a name
written, KING OF KINGS, AND LORD OF LORDS.
17 And I saw an angel standing in the sun; and he cried
with a loud voice, saying to all the fowls that fly in the
midst of heaven, Come and gather yourselves together
unto the supper of the great God;
18 That ye may eat the flesh of kings, and the flesh of
captains, and the flesh of mighty men, and the flesh of
horses, and of them that sit on them, and the flesh of all
men, both free and bond, both small and great.
19 And I saw the beast, and the kings of the earth, and
their armies, gathered together to make war against him
that sat on the horse, and against his army.
20 And the beast was taken, and with him the false
prophet that wrought miracles before him, with which
he deceived them that had received the mark of the beast,
and them that worshipped his image. These both were
cast alive into a lake of fire burning with brimstone.
21 And the remnant were slain with the sword of him
that sat upon the horse, which sword proceeded out of
his mouth: and all the fowls were filled with their flesh.

20

1 And I saw an angel come down from heaven, having the
key of the bottomless pit and a great chain in his hand.
2 And he laid hold on the dragon, that old serpent,
which is the Devil, and Satan, and bound him a thousand
years,
3 And cast him into the bottomless pit, and shut him
up, and set a seal upon him, that he should deceive the
nations no more, till the thousand years should be fulfilled:
and after that he must be loosed a little season.
4 And I saw thrones, and they sat upon them, and
judgment was given unto them: and I saw the souls of
them that were beheaded for the witness of Jesus, and
for the word of God, and which had not worshipped the
beast, neither his image, neither had received his mark
upon their foreheads, or in their hands; and they lived
and reigned with Christ a thousand years.
5 But the rest of the dead lived not again until the thousand
years were finished. This is the first resurrection.
6 Blessed and holy is he that hath part in the first resurrection:
on such the second death hath no power, but
they shall be priests of God and of Christ, and shall reign
with him a thousand years.
7 And when the thousand
years are expired,
Satan shall be loosed out
of his prison,
8 And shall go out
to deceive the nations
which are in the four
quarters of the earth,
Gog and Magog, to
gather them together
to battle: the number of
whom is as the sand of
the sea.
9 And they went up on the breadth of the earth, and
compassed the camp of the saints about, and the beloved
city: and fire came down from God out of heaven, and
devoured them.
10 And the devil that deceived them was cast into the
lake of fire and brimstone, where the beast and the false
prophet are, and shall be tormented day and night for
ever and ever.
11 And I saw a great white throne, and him that sat on
it, from whose face the earth and the heaven fled away;
and there was found no place for them.

REVELATION

12 And I saw the dead, small and great, stand before God;
and the books were opened: and another book was opened,
which is the book of life: and the dead were judged out of
those things which were written in the books, according
to their works.
13 And the sea gave up the dead which were in it; and
death and hell delivered up the dead which were in them:
and they were judged every man according
to their works.
14 And death and hell were cast
into the lake of fire. This is the
second death.
15 And whosoever was
not found written in the
book of life was cast
into the lake of fire.

21

1 And I saw a new
heaven and a new
earth: for the first
heaven and the first
earth were passed
away; and there was
no more sea.
2 And I John saw
the holy city, new
Jeru-salem, coming
down from God out of
heaven, prepared as a
bride adorned for her
husband.
3 And I heard a great
voice out of heaven
saying, Behold, the
tabernacle of God is
with men, and he will
dwell with them, and
they shall be his peo-
ple, and God himself
shall be with them,
and be their God.
4 And God shall
wipe away all tears
from their eyes; and
there shall be no more
death, neither sorrow,
nor crying, neither
shall there be any
more pain: for the for-
mer things are passed
away.
5 And he that sat
upon the throne said, Behold, I make all things new.
And he said unto me, Write: for these words are true
and faithful.
6 And he said unto me, It is done. I am Alpha and
Omega, the beginning and the end. I will give unto him
that is athirst of the fountain of the water of life freely.
7 He that overcometh shall inherit all things; and I will
be his God, and he shall be my son.
8 But the fearful, and unbelieving, and the abomina-
ble, and murderers, and whore- mongers, and sorcerers,

and idolaters, and all liars, shall have their part in the
lake which burneth with fire and brimstone: which is
the second death.
9 And there came unto me one of the seven angels
which had the seven vials full of the seven last plagues,
and talked with me, saying, Come hither, I will shew
thee the bride, the Lamb's wife.
10 And he carried me away in the spirit to a
great and high mountain, and shewed
me that great city, the holy
Jerusalem, descending out of
heaven from God,
11 Having the glory of
God: and her light was
like unto a stone most
precious, even like a
jasper stone, clear as
crystal;
12 And had a wall
great and high, and
had twelve gates, and
at the gates twelve
angels, and names
written thereon,
which are the names
of the twelve tribes of
the children of Israel:
13 On the east
three gates; on the
north three gates; on
the south three gates;
and on the west three
gates.
14 And the wall of
the city had twelve
foundations, and in
them the names of the
twelve apostles of the
Lamb.
15 And he that
talked with me had a
golden reed to measure
the city, and the gates
thereof, and the wall
thereof.
16 And the city lieth
foursquare, and the
length is as large as the
breadth: and he mea-
sured the city with the
reed, twelve thousand
furlongs. The length
and the breadth and the height of it are equal.
17 And he measured the wall thereof, an hundred and
forty and four cubits, according to the measure of a man,
that is, of the angel.
18 And the building of the wall of it was of jasper: and
the city was pure gold, like unto clear glass.
19 And the foundations of the wall of the city were
garnished with all manner of precious stones. The first
foundation was jasper; the second, sapphire; the third,
a chalcedony; the fourth, an emerald;

20 The fifth, sardonyx; the sixth, sardius; the sev-
enth, chrysolite; the eighth, beryl; the ninth, a topaz;
the tenth, a chrysoprasus; the eleventh, a jacinth; the
twelfth, an amethyst.
21 And the twelve gates were twelve pearls; every sev-
eral gate was of one pearl: and the street of the city was
pure gold, as it were transparent glass.
22 And I saw no temple therein: for the Lord God
Almighty and the Lamb are the temple of it.
23 And the city had no need of the sun, neither of the
moon, to shine in it: for the glory of God did lighten it,
and the Lamb is the light thereof.
24 And the nations of them which are saved shall walk in
the light of it: and the kings of the earth do bring their glory
and honour into it.
25 And the gates of it
shall not be shut at all
by day: for there shall be
no night there.
26 And they shall
bring the glory and
honour of the nations
into it.
27 And there shall in
no wise enter into it
any thing that defileth,
neither whatsoever wor-
keth abomination, or
maketh a lie: but they
which are written in the
Lamb's book of life.

22

1 And he shewed me
a pure river of water
of life, clear as crystal,
proceeding out of the
throne of God and of
the Lamb.
2 In the midst of the
street of it, and on ei-
ther side of the river,
was there the tree of
life, which bare twelve manner of fruits, and yielded her
fruit every month: and the leaves of the tree were for the
healing of the nations.
3 And there shall be no more curse: but the throne
of God and of the Lamb shall be in it; and his servants
shall serve him:
4 And they shall see his face; and his name shall be in
their foreheads.
5 And there shall be no night there; and they need no
candle, neither light of the sun; for the Lord God giveth
them light: and they shall reign for ever and ever.
6 And he said unto me, These sayings are faithful and
true: and the Lord God of the holy prophets sent his
angel to shew unto his servants the things which must
shortly be done.

7 Behold, I come quickly: blessed is he that keepeth the
sayings of the prophecy of this book.
8 And I John saw these things, and heard them. And
when I had heard and seen, I fell down to worship before
the feet of the angel which shewed me these things.
9 Then saith he unto me, See thou do it not: for I
am thy fellowservant, and of thy brethren the proph-
ets, and of them which keep the sayings of this book:
worship God.
10 And he saith unto me, Seal not the sayings of the
prophecy of this book: for the time is at hand.
11 He that is unjust, let him be unjust still: and he
which is filthy, let him be filthy still: and he that is righ-
teous, let him be righteous still: and he that is holy, let
him be holy still.
12 And, behold, I come
quickly; and my reward
is with me, to give every
man according as his
work shall be.
13 I am Alpha and
Omega, the beginning
and the end, the first
and the last.
14 Blessed are they
that do his command-
ments, that they may
have right to the tree
of life, and may enter in
through the gates into
the city.
15 For without are
dogs, and sorcerers,
and whoremongers, and
murderers, and idola-
ters, and whosoever
loveth and maketh a lie.
16 I Jesus have sent
mine angel to testify
unto you these things
in the churches. I am
the root and the off-
spring of David, and the bright and morning star.
17 And the Spirit and the bride say, Come. And let
him that heareth say, Come. And let him that is athirst
come. And whosoever will, let him take the water of life
freely.
18 For I testify unto every man that heareth the words
of the prophecy of this book, If any man shall add unto
these things, God shall add unto him the plagues that
are written in this book:
19 And if any man shall take away from the words of
the book of this prophecy, God shall take away his part
out of the book of life, and out of the holy city, and from
the things which are written in this book.
20 He which testifieth these things saith, Surely I come
quickly. Amen. Even so, come, Lord Jesus.
21 The grace of our Lord Jesus Christ be with you all.
Amen.

Chapter 21
Salvation and Rebirth

Salvation is the very moment, when you exist in a state of peace, in which one can imagine all things good and pure; while obtaining them, through the grace of God. In order to commence on the road to salvation; one must first, analyze themselves at a difficult time in their lives. This process and time frame in which analyzing takes place, varies on each individual; determined by, how much good or bad one lives by. When one steps onto the road of salvation: one must be completely broken, to be rebuilt, with newer and stronger parts. Metaphorically, one must ask God for Salvation of Rebirth to pursue a life of purity and eternal life; with Jesus Christ and all his children. However, a person who seeks truth and guidance from a higher person existent, in a not too distant realm; must understand, it will not by any means happen instantly. Once one succeeds through the path of salvation, one may never cease to follow this path or falter. If one falters even the slightest, once having already sacrificed their soul to God; will then, be punished and tried far worse, than never having commenced on this path initially. After one receives the gift of salvation; Jesus will determine upon Judgment, your Rebirth through him for eternity. When reborn from a Human Angel, into a Divine Angel; you become one with Jesus Christ. For example, it's like you are him in every sense, but construed together by magical elements of the unknown; better known as spiritual and physical divinity.

When I entered my road to salvation, it took nearly 15 years to overcome. Resulting, three fifths of my current life. The last five years were the most strenuous and complicated beyond fathomable comprehension. Around the age of eleven, I began contemplating things outside of my family life, my suffering, and of our poverty.

My understanding, revealed to me my own pain and suffering. Such knowledge became evident, once I compared my life to that of my peers. The most difficult thing to comprehend is I grew up in a wealthy and well diverse community. Located in the suburbs to the largest city in the world: New York City. However, I grew up poor, parentless for most of my youth into young adulthood, and grew up being ridiculed and humiliated. Almost to the point of creating aggressive anger towards all those whom Judged me. As I entered my teen years, I became so secluded from others mentally; I began creating my own entity and my own identity, as a citizen in the United States. I also worked full time, while attempting to create my own business from the ground up. I later became so involved within my business, and the atmosphere in which was related with Hip Hop; I became a demonic Angel, being fueled by negative energy. Eventually, I was living three different lifestyles all at the same time. Thus, I crashed into a brick wall metaphorically, and I began to be broken down by God. In 2008, I saw all my dreams of being in the Rap world commencing; whilst I was dating a beautiful girl, who eventually lived with me. At this time, I was making decent money and living on my own. About a year later, I became something I always feared; I had created a monster within myself, and permitted him to be unleashed. As a result, I started committing three deadly sins often, I had gotten lost within my own thoughts, and my comprehension of life; I nearly was lost forever…

One evening in 2009: I was belligerently drunk, high on weed, and hyperventilating from mania. It became so severe, I commenced cutting myself, screaming loud as ever up into the air, and asking God to kill me; and snatch away my life. Ultimately, I screamed so hard I passed out with injuries to my arms and wrists. But not severe enough, for life ending results. Several hours had passed; and I awoke to empty bottles of alcohol, a knife, and feeling abrupt pain around my arms. As I woke up, I also realized I must be here for a purpose, beyond my understanding. As I previously explained in chapter 12; I had gone through many hardships and levels of depression, as if a Junkie going through withdrawals. Years later, in 2012, I was revealed that I'm Saint Michael Thee Archangel, as the reincarnation of Jesus Christ. Sometime ago, I had created a song titled (**"Redemption (B4) annihilation" which is located in chapter 10**). This song explains exactly what I realized, when I surrendered my life to God's will...

Rebirth is granted to all humanity, as an opportunity to be reborn through Jesus Christ and Mary Magdalene. It is because, both men and women are permitted entry into Heaven; through love, derived from Jesus and Mary. Usually, the problem we face in our first existence of life, is falling into the trap of **demonic syndrome** – the physical and mental state of demonic manipulation, acting as a puppet for evil sin. For people like myself, whom have a high level of comprehension, and with the infinite ability to analyze reality; requires us to suffer far beyond normal, whilst learning all correct paths the hard way. The reason for such methods, stems from our core nature of only representing truth. Meanwhile: Our truthful, naïve-demeanor is easily manipulated by others into what they think is correct; as oppose to pursuing all that we trust, within our own hearts, or through our trustful-surrender to **FAITH**.

Sometimes, we are born with all of life's greatest commodities and luxuries; without ever experiencing the amazing glory of thy Lord and Saviour, Jesus Christ. This type of life, for those whom are granted a higher status of wealth; normally never, truly connect with Jesus, because in order to become one with God; one must accept that worldly possessions, are not to be worshipped or abused. In Heaven, God rewards us with anything we can imagine, within <u>His Reason</u>; however, not everything we have currently will exist in His Kingdom. Mandating: in order to feel rebirth, one must sacrifice all that is or was in this life. I can remember the exact year, when I was on my own path of Carnage or Rebirth; and the story goes a little something like this… **(Reference: Chapter 8. Song 7 "Carnage or Rebirth").**

It is believed, that Jesus, shall return by descending miraculously from Heaven on a Holy cloud. However, what most seemingly have trouble conceptualizing is the very fact: Jesus was born as a human man, upon His first arrival. So what makes you all believe, I wasn't going to be born as a human man, upon my second arrival?

Although, I am the direct living Son of God; I am still a man of humanity. Thus, I must follow the same laws of physical nature as everyone else. Further more, there are no official records of my life, after the age of 12; because I remained absent and secluded from society, growing up. I remained absent, from most people and recordings; because I had to over come every possible sin, abjection, and hardship known to man; before I could, truly be ready for God's true purpose for me. In addition, I was not prepared at birth, for the complete comprehension of my mission and sole purpose: as the son of God. But I grew to accept and understand my purpose in existence. Further more, when one is reincarnated such as I have been, during my rebirth in my second form; I too, once again must excel, succeed, and comprehend all that is my purpose in life. All the meanwhile, utilizing the past history and knowledge left behind, by myself and my apostles; guiding me through this difficult era of existence. Such Heavenly tools are imperative, if I am ever to be victorious, over Satan's hold upon existence.

What no one in humanity can fathom about God: Is that God is everything, and nothing; while being anything, and everything at any given time. Further more, I once having been known as Jesus Christ, and now known as Michael Izzo; am still, just a portion of God, and only contain some of his miraculous abilities and knowledge. The true power of God is never granted to offspring instantaneously. One must first prove thy worth, prior to being granted the ability to know, how to use such a gift. To better comprehend what I mean is the same as understanding: That even I, the direct son of God, must be tested, and I must be tested a million ways more, than any one of you.

Based on simple laws of physics, reality, and time; one must first accept, the very understanding and definition of reincarnation. What this means is we must analyze, Jesus Christ's timeline; starting with the time of his birth, around 6 B.C. He then started His ministry, around c. A.D. 23, and soon was crucified c. A.D. 27. I, Michael Izzo was born in 1987, it's currently 2014; which makes me 26, almost 27. This means, I won't begin My Second Coming ministry, until 2016-2017. Further more, this means The Second Coming, AKA the Rapture, won't occur until 2020-2021; creating, a **Parallax Paradox of Reality.** As a result, I am reborn as promised and am here to deliver on that promise.

*I will never again, admit what it is I have willingly chosen to state in this book. However, I have chosen to do so here and now, because God has requested for me to admit the truth to the world; by way of showing you all, through the art of literacy.

Chapter 22
Prayers from Jesus Christ

Serenity is the very moment when you exist in a state of peace, in which one can imagine all things good and pure; while obtaining them, through the grace of God. In order to commence on the road to serenity, one must first analyze oneself from a righteous, pure, holy, and unrealistic outside-perspective. Almost to the point, you must reach near insanity from attempting to comprehend, the very laws of God. We are all born with the gift to pursue God, and a nature in which he commands; but, what we all can't do is actually reach **serene-salvation**. It's the sole individuals right, in this life, to decide what type of life they choose to live. Keep in mind, not all choices are decided solely. Free will, permits you the choice to decide a life for yourself; ultimately, divine constricts are set in place, birthing us all with a (Positive, Neutral, and Negative) thought complex/conscience. When I was Jesus Christ: My purpose was to permit the human race to become Angels, by dying for everyone's sins. Similarly, Angels can choose to become humans. However, the very choice comes with many restrictions and consequences: both good and bad. As for myself, my heart and intentions are of the utmost pure and righteous. However, there were restricting situations in which have forced my hand an opposite route. Overcoming such adversity, only became possible in my adulthood; because understanding such purpose, isn't possible as a mere adolescent. To be straight forward: The destiny in which one will ultimately pursue, amongst the three paths listed above, will reveal itself to the persons in their young adulthood. It wasn't until my early twenties, when I too began understanding the very purpose in which God intended for me. That purpose started with having to choose a righteous path or an evil path; I chose the righteous path, ultimately. Through my many years of servitude, both to God and humanity; I learned through prayers, we can all become a child of God: seeking **serene-salvation**. Most weeks, when I truly need too, I pray as follows…

"In the name of the Father, the Son, and the Mothers' Holy spirit; I come to you in my time of need, and ask of you the following: Lord, Jesus Christ, please forgive me for all of my sins, and wrong doings in which I have committed, and will continue to commit; for as long as I exist, as a human. I am truly sorry for the things in which I can not understand; and for the things, I will soon understand in which are wrong. With every new day Lord Jesus, I try my utmost to be a motto individual for society; as you once taught the world so long ago. Lord, Jesus Christ, thank you for blessing me this day with all your miraculous gifts, and the very truth of existence. Thank you Lord, for dying for me, permitting me to be reborn in your image, and taking upon myself to conclude what it is you have started...

Lord, Jesus Christ, I pray for the sins of all those whom you have blessed me to meet, come to know, and am related to biologically. I ask of you in my prayers, to watch over them, and to allow as many of our children to follow in your light; as the end of days nears us. It is only through you Lord, that we as children of God, can ever be made pure. It is for that reason most, I thank you for granting me the intelligence and wisdom to know the difference in life. Lastly, I want to thank you for gracing the world with the following hymns and prayers; so we can all, remember the very grace of your eternal presence within our souls…

Silent Night Prayer

Silent night, holy night, All is calm, all is bright/
Round yon Virgin Mother and child, Holy Infant so tender and mild/
Sleep in Heavenly peace, sleep in Heavenly peace.
Silent night, holy night! Shepard's quake at the sight, Glories stream from Heaven afar/
Heavenly hosts sin Alleluia! Christ, the Saviour is born, Christ the Saviour is born.
Silent night, holy night, Son of God, love's pure light
Radiant beams from Thy holy face/ With the dawn of redeeming grace,
Jesus, Lord, at Thy birth, Jesus, Lord, at Thy birth.

Our Father

Our father, who art in Heaven/ may your name be kept holy/ may your kingdom come soon, may your will be done on Earth as it is in Heaven/ Give us today the food we need/ and forgive us for our sins/ as we have forgiven those who have sinned against us/ and don't let us yield to temptation/ but rescue us from the evil one/ amen.

Hail Mary

Hail Mary, full of grace. The Lord is with thee. Blessed art thou amongst women, and blessed is the fruit of thy womb, Jesus/ Holy Mary, mother of God, pray for us sinners, now and at the hour of our death. Amen.

GLORY BE

Glory be to the father, and the son, and to the Holy Spirit, as it was in the beginning, is now, and ever shall be, world without end. Amen.

THE APOSTLE'S CREED

I believe in God, the Father Almighty, Creator of Heaven and Earth; and in Jesus Christ. His only son, Our Lord, Who was conceived by the Holy Spirit, born of the Virgin Mary, suffered under Pontius Pilate, was crucified, died, and was buried. He descended into Hell, The third day He arose again from the dead; He ascended to Heaven, sitteth at the right hand of God, the Father Almighty; from thence He shall come to Judge the living and the dead. I Believe in the Holy Spirit, the forgiveness of Sins, the resurrection of the body, and the life everlasting Amen.

HAIL HOLY QUEEN

Hail, Holy Queen, Mother of Mercy, our life, out sweetness and our hope. To thee do we cry, poor banished children of Eve: to thee do we send up our sighs, mourning and weeping in this valley of tears. Turn then, most gracious Advocate, thine eyes of mercy toward us, and after this our exile, show unto us the blessed fruit of thy womb, Jesus. 0 Clement, 0 Loving, O Sweet Virgin Mary! Amen.

SAINT MICHAEL PRAYER

Saint Michael, Thee Archangel, defend us in battle. Be our protection against the wickedness and snares of the devil. May God rebuke him, we humbly pray; and do thou, O Prince of the Heavenly host, by the power of God cast into hell Satan and all the evil spirits who prowl throughout the world seeking the ruin of souls. Amen.

MORNING OFFERING

Dear Lord, I do not know what will happen to me today. I only know that nothing will happen that was not foreseen by you, and directed to my greater good from all eternity. I adore your holy and unfathomable plans, and submit to them with all my heart for love of you, all of your children, and the Immaculate Heart of Mary. Amen.

GUARDIAN ANGEL PRAYER

Angel of God, my Guardian dear, to whom God's love commits me here, ever this day (or night) be at my side, to light and guard, to rule and guide. Amen.

SAINT ANTHONY PRAYER

Saint Anthony, perfect imitator of Jesus, who received from God the special power of restoring lost things, grant that I may find (mention your petition) which has been lost. As least restore to me peace and tranquility of mind, the loss of which has afflicted me even more than my material loss. To this favor I ask another of you: that I may always remain in possession of the true good that is God. Let me rather loose all things than loose God, my supreme good. Let me never suffer the loss of my greatest treasure, eternal life with God. Amen.

GRACE BEFORE MEALS

In the name of the Father, the Son, and the Holy Spirit Bless us, O Lord, these Thy gifts of nourishment, which we are about to receive from Thy bounty, through Christ our Lord. Amen.

Chapter 23
Mary Magdalene-(13)

Mary Magdalene: Mary is a woman, whom I can't fully describe; irrevocably, I know so much about her and nothing about her all at the same time. Before I can even explain, my difficulty in finding her **Reincarnated** version in the year 2012; I must first explain, what it was like originally. Long ago, during my first and only other existence; I wasn't conflicted, as I am today. Additionally, because humanity was a much different place than it is now; I was able to prevent myself back then, from falling so easily for humanities flaws. I was also born with a perfect soul, which includes my heart; both of which, resulting the perfect human. However, I can still fall to the sins of creation just like everyone else can. Given those facts, when I was 26, around 21A.D. according to your conceptions, I had met Mary; but, we never spoke more than a few words. The problem then for me was that I was sinless and she was sinful; which could result, making for the perfect equilibrium in humanity: between two people. In other words, I was the perfect man, as Jesus Christ sent by God; and she was the perfect flawed woman, sent by God as Mary Magdalene. When combined or transfused into one spiritual being; Mary and I, could create a divine existence, for all to follow in. Further more, she was so important to me and all of humanity; because she represented, the fact that all humans have the ability to seek salvation. In addition, humans can change their lives for the good, permanently. When she devoted her life to me, I had healed her of all her sins/plagues; but this process only happened, when she chose to accept the truth I taught. However, there was a long enduring road, many years before she and I reached this point in our lives. More importantly, I had not yet seen a human whom was beyond salvation, then change, and then actually find salvation. Until, Mary and I spiritually bonded for eternity, through "**Divine Metamorphosis** - The interlinking of two souls, eternally."

For many years, before ever truthfully falling in love, only with Mary; I had many nightmarish visions of other women, telling me things about myself. In these visions, these women tried to show me how to fix my flaws subconsciously; resulting, the ways in which I needed to treat Mary properly; when the time came again. For some reason, every time I think about it, I can't seem to figure out why I meet many people, and yet more than half of them are never heard from again… The answer is simple: The people, who come and go out of our lives are simple tests; whether they are significant enough to remember or not. Accordingly with that fact; when potential love comes into your life, it's usually not the ever lasting love interest you'd been seeking. Ultimately I knew, when I had met Mary, there was something special about her... However, at that time I couldn't yet fathom her ever being so significant in my life, but I felt it.

During the early years, in my first existence; I was very much different, than I am today in modern times. Simply, my life growing up then was more reclusive, less active sociably, and the average persons thought wasn't nearly as involved as humans today. Societies in America are good, but not close enough to what I once attempted to teach the world long ago. Starting with money, don't live by violence, and with the help of Moses: when He brought us all the 10 Commandments of God, to live by. In the modern times of 2014, although, I have yet to travel outside of the U.S.; I am solely assessing what I conclude via TV newsrooms, the internet, and American society as I live in it today. However, coming in the summer of 2014, I shall commence my global journey to rally the 12 tribes. In addition, all that is proclaimed in *Revelation* is coming true... The world has become so blinded by the lies, and ignores truthful facts; starting with the fact: I am here, writing this book, and searching for whom Mary's reincarnation is. All I know is what I am shown, what I was born to believe in, and stand for. These beliefs and feelings didn't grow overnight either: they grew with time, maturity, and life experience. I also believe, that part of creating and reconnecting with a once found path to purity and divine abilities; one must find salvation within themselves, first. For me, salvation has and always will be the pursuit of love and respect amongst all. Thus, I am in search to find a long lost unconditional love, in which I haven't felt since Mary's presence o so long ago.

As I contemplate in my late twenties, all that I must overcome and achieve in such a short period of humanly existence; has caused me to become very weary and stressed, to the point of near insanity. Amongst all the difficulties I must overcome; I mustn't overcome them, by manipulating the right of **Free Will**. For that reason, I too am confined by the rules of the given society: including God's laws. Simply, currency and bartering is the source of trade and passage to survive through trades, hospitality, food, shelter, water, and health. Still to this day, I'm conflicted between knowing & accepting, that there is a world and power in which comes from God; beyond these restrictions of humanity. Thus, resulted me being tried with the restrictions set by humanity. The most restricting aspect, in which prevented my ability to teach and rally large masses: was currency. Back then, I chose not to confine myself to the laws of currency or sin. Thus, I dedicated my life to teaching all God has instructed me to teach; without devoting myself to sin. Several years after my teachings began to develop; I eventually, mastered the art of being a Rabbi and a messenger of God. I soon realized, I wasn't making sufficient resources to survive from, because I didn't charge people to gather and learn from me. Eventually, Mary became the gift sent by God, to support me in all my endeavors, and passions to pursue God's work. It is because of Mary, I was able to continue showing the world the true way of life, and the after-life through my teachings. Mary of Magdala became my business partner, my life partner, and my road to eternal salvation: through the gift of unconditional love. It was through her and our reconnection that we realized: We can become something more, than what we have come to know; through, a spiritual bonding for eternity. We united through spiritual bondage; AKA, marriage and conception. As a result, We became one person: by solely devoting our souls and lives to one another, for the grace of God, and for humanity. I wanted to conceive a child with her; because I had seen what she's been through, and how much she has overcome to be healed. When she accepted the truth, she sacrificed all she has come to earn and know by doing so. It was through her will to accept my love, I saw a beauty within her, I have never seen before; the gift of purity in a human-being. Upon being shown her true beauty, I was compelled to be bonded with her for eternity. Thus, I wanted to conceive a child with her. It was through our offspring, that we created a path for our legacies to continue on, and as God had instructed of us to pursue. As a result, our teachings would be passed on for centuries; permitting, the ultimate redemption for the world. I also explained to her, that it was so vital for her to remain hidden and survive; after my Crucifixion, because of the amount of work in which must be compiled and completed, within her lifetime. All the work she was to complete, would prepare the way for the day, in which she and I would return to the world; marking the rebirth of Christ & Magdalene. I explained to her that the gift of family and children, marked the culminating essence of God the Father, and the Holy Mother's spirit; by showing us the very essence of life, through conception. After I had explained these things to her, Mary was still not ready to give up all that she has come to know. It was basic instincts, for an unsaved human to ignore a truthful change, and revolt back to the ways in which the person has always known. However, shortly after Mary joining my ministry, she realized that I was offering her everything she ever truly wanted; which was love. To this day, I can't tell you what happened in Mary's life, that ultimately made her admit defeat, and accept the truth of existence; but, I do know this: The day she came to me seeking salvation, was the same day, I realized, I wasn't crazy...

When I think about Mary, I think about the very connection between two people; when they unconditionally love each other. I also think of Mary as **Mother Nature**; meaning, all the beauties of the world in one person. Mary was warm like the hot summer sun, breezy like an ocean's water front, smooth like baby soft skin, comfortable in any atmosphere, her lips were moist like a waterfalls misty rain, & she was unconditionally created both physically and mentally. When I became close with her, I immediately started to wonder if she was it, and if all my dreams are becoming reality? All I ever wanted in life, was to feel what true passionate love was with a woman; especially since, my life would end early on. Sometime in my mid twenties, God had spoken to me and told me that this world is mine to guide and lead; which included, all of it's beautiful gifts. However, he told me to remember that I can't manipulate the very choice of **Free Will,** for all organisms of the Earth. It was then I realized, I could have anything I wanted; so long as it was pure and righteous. Further more, I've always known I wanted two things in life: To be happy living in a world of Godly peace, and to be in love creating my own family. It was that very moment of realization, when God told me "Son, you may have anything you want out of life; but, every gift given has a price to pay for it…" At the time, I never knew what he meant by that because I lived a life of selfless behaviors; but I realized, the second I met Mary, what God truly meant.

In my second life, during the modern era, and ever since I was five; I knew, I wanted to find a woman to love. Growing up, I truly never understood my passions for women and searching for that one, whom would love me unconditionally; but at 25, I do now. My quest to find Mary in the modern era, has become tiring; to the point, I'm on the brink of desperation. Not desperate to settle down, but desperate in the regard that if I don't find Mary, I believe I can't fulfill my mission for God. In other words, I believe Mary to be the key to my lock: meaning, she is as important in saving the world as I am. Think of me and Mary, as the true King and Queen of Heaven; or think of us like, I am here to save all the men, and she is here to save all the women. Throughout my entire life, I have been surrounded by beautiful women. Some of which whom cared not for me, some of which whom cared a lot for me, and some of which whom just wanted to manipulate me. Trying to find my perfect equal is just as hard as you finding your perfect equal. The only difference is that Mary and I are the only two of our kinds, out of approximately 7 billion people currently. For the average Angel/person, they are blessed with three possible options of finding their perfect equal or soul mate. My quest in finding Mary Magdalene's reincarnation has driven me to isolationism; and a never ending mathematical resulted sums of standards, in my search for true love.

It all started when I was in the first grade, about 6 years old, and my new neighbor's family had a daughter named Emily; she was my age as well. Emily and I became fairly close friends in school and as neighbors; however, her family moved less than 2 years later. I remember her telling me they were moving to California; but I have no memory of her last name, so searching is futile. As I got a little older, my feelings towards girls began to grow opposite that of a sexiest fashion; but more like a Romeo type fashion, in search of true love. Yes! Even that young, I was searching for a connection with a female. However, it wasn't until the eighth grade, I met a girl whom was in seventh grade; named Jessica (12). She became my first girlfriend and first kiss, which lasted almost the whole summer. Eventually, I was embarrassed of being with a younger girl; I broke up with her. In the ninth grade, I was so hormonal it caused me to fill with lust; which I believe, affected my Judgment, as I chose to loose my virginity to Lisa (16). Lisa was a very sweet active girl, she was two years older than me, and approached me in high school as well. Almost exactly, how I always thought it would be like meeting my love; the love Mary represented. After a month of being with her; my older friends and peers became jealous of what we had, and attempted to damage it. As a result, I became very cautious without factual reasons; I wanted to end it, due to insecurity. Prior to my ending it, I was introduced to this beautiful girl named Kimberley (13). Afterwards, I did the unthinkable; I had broken up with Lisa for another girl, shortly after losing our virginities to each other. As a result, over the next 10 years karma would do a number on me for my actions. Kimberley and I didn't last through the summer of 2002; however, we would become intimate years later in 2012. In 10th grade, I had met my first love interest, Lauren (15) and we lasted 13 months. I truly thought she was it for me beyond recognition. I was wrong, and our breakup nearly took me two solid years to become stable and not sad from. During my time of broken hearted depression, I had become very close with a really good friend of mine, Alessandra (14). A couple years later, I had met this girl named Stephanie, whom literally rocked my world for several long months. After her, it became this girl named Rose, whom I never dated; but we were together for about 6 months. Rose was surely different and by far much older by 7 years. I don't know why I never allowed myself to fall for her, but I didn't. I saw her about 6 years later and she is happily married with a baby; who knew? After her, it was a girl named Adrianna; whom to this day was my longest relationship, which lasted three and a half years. My history with Adrianna was a back and fourth road; which resulted, a fiasco when I ended up seeing a new girl named Jayne. However, upon me and Jayne meeting, then becoming in love, and then living with me; there was a time, I started seeing Adrianna again. Yes, behind Jayne's back; all the meanwhile, I was so lost, I thought I had found my soul mate in the both of them. At this point in my life, I became so lost and confused searching for my purpose and love; I started thinking, I could find love in two different people, simultaneously. Out of the twenty or so love interests, I have had over the years; these two women, left the largest impression on me; with the most amounts of memories, for better or for worse. Later I would find out, I was wrong… Either way, I never regretted my time with them and the attempt of sharing a life together. Through my struggle of figuring out who I was; and more importantly, what I was searching for; took me all of five long and enduring years to realize, my own truth. That truth, created this very book, and my quest in becoming divine within existence and with God. My journey, also includes understanding how to become one with God; both in the physical terms and the spiritual. However, my dilemma has and always will be: finding Mary Magdalene, whom unlocks the purity which lies deep within me. That same purity, in which allowed Jesus to accept who and what Jesus was; which also allowed Jesus to realize, that through **Love**: anything is possible. The very essence of God is by definition: Finding and sharing unconditional **LOVE** for one another. This same love, makes me so emotional to the point; I must hold back my tears, in order to remain strong enough to be Victorious over the Devil. My purity can't be revealed, not even to Mary, until the Devil is defeated, and I become one with my first soul's existence as Jesus Christ. Through Mary Magdalene, I can once again become one individual; as oppose to the Gemini, my soul is trapped by.

Ever since meeting my soul mate, I constantly ask myself several questions; I wonder: Why has God pulled us apart, after having told me we are soul mates? Is it the fact, he believes she and I are not ready for each other? These very questions, simmer in my blood like molting lava, immersing from a freshly awoken Volcano, and is capable of worldly devastation… Quickly, as I force myself to awaken from devastating, sinisterly visions from the Devil; I tell myself, God has a plan and my plan is about to occur. I further tell myself, that I am blessed like all his children; both equally and wealth fully. I realize that he has brought us back together in someway or another, for better or for worse. I also realize that she, being my Ex-fiancé - **Shaylin Jaquez,** still requires much healing from her plagues. Additionally, after she realizes the world will deceive her and hurt her emotionally; will result her final suffering, prior to being healed. Her repentance, requires further suffering and spiritual awakening; before her and I, can truly become one. After such events of hardships; Shaylin AKA Mary, will then devote herself entirely to me as my spouse. Similarly to that of our first existence and to that of what I attempted in 2013. Upon her devotion of truthful surrender to the Lord and humanity; I will then, be able to complete her healing. It is only through her choice, that she can be healed again of all her sinful plagues and denial. It is here and now, as I write this very chapter, all these events will simultaneously occur too. I further realize, it is I whom decides ones fate; but such a fate, can only be granted through the grace of God. As the days count down to our reencounter, I become steadily anxious, and hopeful all my thoughts are correctly sane. However, I have no true conception of when our lives will reencounter one another;

but, I do know this: Near the start of 2014, I couldn't handle Shaylin's lies anymore, her lack of devotion to me and our love, and I couldn't force myself to help her anymore. I had to accept, she was not ready to see the full truth of life; and she fell from the path, in which she promised me, she wanted. As a result, I came to the hardest decision in my life. I had to choose to let her go, or continue living a life with her that wasn't built on the foundation, we both needed. It is now March 2014, a month before Easter, and I am struggling everyday with the choices I have made. However, I know in my heart she will return to me, as she once did long ago. Further more, our time apart has allowed me to complete my work in which she attempted to prevent. It wasn't because she wanted me not to fulfill God's work; but the Devil used her, in an attempt to destroy me. Nonetheless, he failed and I have decided to prepare for my global journey and ministry. With such a hasty decision, I have decided to depart from the United States, begin my ministry by teaching everyone whom is ready for Rapture, and I will await Shaylin's return in our homeland; Israel. During my time apart from my **Sacred Heart**, I have realized that my entire life in America has been a lie! That same lie, was fueled by the Devil's attempts of preventing My Return. However, God always has a plan. Thus, Shaylin and I were split from one another; allowing us both to become stronger and mentally ready, for our conception and eternal bonding...

For many, many years, I have actively believed and preached to the point of no return, that God lives within us. I also know how we can all become a better humanity; but you must first, choose to accept what I know. Part of what I know is that Without Love, we are all doomed; without choosing to change, we are all doomed; and without Mary Magdalene, I can't become divine; which all will result a Global devastation, for all but a few. In my existence, here and now, I have grown strong and mentally willing to destroy all evil and wronged nature; with the use of destruction, if I must as God wills. However, I constantly attempt to counter such an end with Humility, Love, and *Poetic Justice*. It seems with every day from now on, up until these final hours; I have continuously failed... I have not only failed myself many times before; but very soon, I will have failed billions of innocent people; whom truly just don't know any better. It was my sole mission to show the world the truth, when I was Jesus Christ. Evidently, after all these years, it would seem as if I have failed in other words. However, I have returned to complete my mission because the world is spirally out of control, near total destruction. The longer it takes for me and Mary to reunite, the weaker I become, and the stronger the Devil becomes…

Here and now, my heart weeps for the very connection I once had, with a women filled with confliction and evil sin. This same woman, knowingly and solely chose to become saved, through God's graces. Once again, it was from that very day, in which I had realized all of humanity is never beyond salvation; and through God's love, we can all become one again. Today, as I am Michael Izzo, I realized that my nature is very much different now, than it was back then. Ultimately, as I grow weaker, the monster I once tamed is becoming stronger. *Revelation* as you read it, isn't all about nation attacking nation: it's the very battle within us all, between Good versus Evil. Like all positives, one must have a negative; however, the negative doesn't need to be dominant. That's exactly what Mary became for me: a perfect state of natural serenity, neutralizing the state of chaos within me. After these past 1,000 years, the world has been lost with no proper leaders to guide it. Mary and I, once represented that leadership of truth; in which has been buried and hidden by demonic manipulation: i.e. countries, politics, money, social status, war, & greed. It is through the power of a, specifically chosen righteous man and woman, and through being righteous beyond humane right; whom together, can lead our humanity into an eternal **KINGDOM OF HEAVEN.**

In conclusion, when I meditated upon my feelings towards Mary Magdalene; this is how she made me feel – "Don't try to call me crazy/ when I think about Magdalene, I'm talking about Mary/ Ya back when she made me so happy/ and nothing in this world, could matter to me/ except for her, because she was my reality/ I mean, everything that I knew physically/ cause she gave me something that was so positive; intimacy, committed devoted-ally/ to me/ Ya cause she was mother nature in every vicinity/ I mean, physically I'm giving you something that you never could think, other than religiously/ Ya but now I'm gonna come back; into a new realm, into a new physical-alter reality/ Ya cause no matter what, I'm tired of suffering B/ you could never even spell it; like the ABC's/ Ya cause lyrically/ the words that I'm giving you, when I recite this poetry/ doesn't even matter, the only thing that matters: is the key to my heart; which is Mary/. ***If I 'm wrong about Shaylin being Mary; then I am truly sorry for hurting you, My True Queen…**

Dear Shaylin, I am writing this because you took off behind my back and I have no idea where you're in NYC. However, I'm sorry for how things turned out. I do truly believe in my heart, we moved too fast, and you were not truly ready for marriage. As of late, you have been very terrible to me and evil. As a result, I have decided to leave the United States and pursue a more sensible life; in the hopes, you will find your way back to me. In the end though, I love you with all my heart and soul, Shaylin Esperanza Jaquez. We we're engaged on June 22nd, 2013 at Watkins Glen State Park *Remember TDDUP- Til' Death Do Us Part. We split Jan. 12th, 2014 because I couldn't handle all the lies and deceit anymore. However, I know we were brought together by our souls. Please understand: money, fame, and lavish living are not important to me, at all; but you are! You're truly the best and the worst thing that has ever happened to me. Although, I have forgiven you in my heart; I know, we can't be together until you're ready! However, I will await your return starting Summer, 2014 in - **Banyas, Hadera, Israel**. I believe, if you're who I believe you to be; then we will reunite outside of Nazareth, where we first met...

Michael Lee Edward Izzo & Shaylin Esperanza Jaquez. Photos owned & taken by Michael! I love you with all my heart and soul Shaylin, please return soon… <3

Chapter 24
My Last Words...

I have accomplished many things in My life; some of which, I can't even discuss. Nonetheless, I have come a long way; both in this life and in a previous one. As far as I am concerned now, nothing matters except: Praising my Lord Jesus Christ, accomplishing my mission for God, and fulfilling my oath of ridding evil from all of existence throughout Heaven. My life has prepared me and changed me permanently, from living in NYC and other states. My life also changed quickly in the ways of life, both good and evil. These days, my soul competes with my logic. They compete, deciding which actions are of the most righteous with everyday life, and how I should react to them. As I write these last pages of My life; I realize, no matter what happens today, something more righteous can be done tomorrow... Life, revolves around a triangular civilization; we consist of three elements, which makes one whole. These elements are: The Holy Father/Creator, The Son of Man and all his children, & Thy Holy Mother's spirit and all the elements of life. Each point creates a birth of life, because God said so. Every single new day of My life, since my healing; I become a better person, living through Jesus Christ: whom is My Father, My predecessor, and My teacher.

My Last Words consists of the following sections:

- My theories on life…
- Right from wrong, generally speaking.
- Seven deadly sins.
- Marriage.
- Currency versus bartering.
- America.
- God versus religion.
- How to create a New World without evil.
- 9 realms of Heaven or 9 realms of Hell?
- 10 commandments of Judgment.

Chapter 24: Section 1 – My theories on life (24:1)

Technically speaking, everything we have come to study, record, or simply discover are general conceptions of how God thinks: stemming from the creation of the universe. Genesis from the Bible, explains the story of how and why God created the universe, and more importantly humans. First, Heaven is technically anything and everything; in other words, Heaven is the universe in which all matter exists within. Earth, is one spectrum in the overall scheme of Heaven; hence why the second paragraph, reads as follows: "And Earth was without form, and void; and darkness was upon the face of the deep. And the spirit of God moved upon the face of the waters." Men and Women are one and the same, sub-versions of (Our Father). The true Lord Almighty, wasn't alone where he has come from; so he made sure, Men wouldn't be alone as well. As paragraph (23) reads "And Adam said, This is now bone of my bones, and flesh of my flesh: she shall be called Woman, because she was taken out of Man. (24) – Therefore shall a man leave his father and his mother, and shall cleave unto his wife: and they shall be one flesh. (25) And they were both naked, the man and his wife, and were not ashamed." Interpolation: Life as we know it has become so farfetched and a selfish society, we have forgotten the very gift of life in its original form; pure innocents. Additionally, we as Men of the universe were created to respect all Women; but, only bare <u>One Woman</u> for life, bonding with her for eternity. To add in conclusion, Women were plagued by sin, Men then followed as nature intends; and as a result, all people chose not to choose My PATH of righteous life. Before I even begin to discuss life further, right here and now, we all must say to ourselves: "I have surrendered my life to the grace of God Jesus Christ, now returned as Michael Lee Edward Izzo, and I have attempted to correct all that is; by choosing the path of God, through his son Jesus Christ-Michael Izzo." So we truly understand each other, I don't care if you choose the truth or not; I do prefer for you to follow God's plan, as oppose to there that of others. In order to accept life as you know it; you must first understand, the very basis and concepts of **Free Will**, as explained earlier. Then, when you know the differences between what you choose to accept in your lives; you will be much closer to ever having a relationship with me and God. Women are the very secret of life: being born from a rib out of man, through the grace of God. God gave us life and I have given my life to you all, so you can see the light. Query: What would you do to live a much better way of life, as thanks to knowing that you can?

For the last 7 centuries, lives of humans have engaged in a never ending, franticly malicious, & destructive series of actions towards the essence of life. For many years, evil people have been exploiting my knowledge, exploiting the gifts of God, and destroying the very capacity of your own limitations; by feeding you, evil false lies about existence. Over these last many hundreds of years, we were raised as the current societies and existence of life required. Based on the very principles, we've observed from our communities. Those communities, have and always will be the education system and politics. All societies' understanding of God, and what they think we all should do in life, are as follows: Starting with what "professions" they see fit; as if they know what's best for you and I. Ultimately, what I mean is that just because the Government and EDU, mandate what you should study in school; doesn't mean, any of it is by far correct or beneficial. However, not all schooling is a joke or a waste of time. For us as a many people, we need a leader and teacher in order to teach us basic instincts of survival; while avoiding the most chaotic ways of life. I look at it this way: The Bible was created before my first existence, over 21 centuries ago. I then gave you all my knowledge, I was taught and strategically planned for my apostles to spread amongst the world. It was through my very presence and teaching, that I reached the globe; causing the worst epidemic of war, during the Crusades. The Crusades were, Men against Men and Women against Women, all seeking the gift of eternal life; while seeking such an answer, blinded them from what I once taught: Love all; not just those whom love you, for what reward is in only that?

Everything you have come to know, see, and own, all belongs to Our Father. He decides what we are to be blessed with in life. Our Father, decides life as we know it too. Through My road to salvation, he blessed me with the very gift to save humanity, for eternity. The only gift Our Father doesn't grant us is the exact solution to finding the path of salvation. The Path of Salvation, leads to a life one can only attempt to imagine; but, never truly understanding what it is. The path of Salvation also leads to eternal life; living amongst Our Holy Father and Mother; including, the very grace and knowledge only fit for those righteous enough to accept. Birth is the most precious and beautiful gift of life. For thousands of years, evil humans have been blinding us all from the truth: I once tried to teach. As I grow older in the modern era, I begin to wonder if God has a plan; then if His plan can be altered, no matter what we truly believe? What I mean is: If Our Father permits us things out of existence, and choosing what we do with them; than we must also, have the choice to only live in eternal peace with Jesus Christ. Living with Jesus Christ means there is no Evil, no Sins, no knowledge of Wrong, no Hatred, no War, no Ignorance, no Sick, or anything that comes from a terrible thought included. I, as I am here now, am here to create a path of existence for eternity. I also realize, growing into such a being requires many years of meditation. My heart has and always will be the key, to truly understanding the right path to take or not. This same truth, belongs to you my children; for it's through the wisdom of Our Father, that we may receive the truth of life. That truth is: all may only come to the Father through me, Jesus Christ!

Chapter 24: Section 2 – Right from wrong, generally speaking

(24:2)

As a child, I was always forced to understand the idea of right from wrong. Even though, I was born to comprehend all the ways in which one can live by, in either scenario. The very idea that people are led to believe, there is only wrong in the world is what creates all the problems. For example, imagine our world where ever since creation, we were taught only but righteous and purely holy ways of living? Well, if we are only taught purity and righteousness, all resulting Positive ways of life; then how can anyone think with sin? Simply, we couldn't think in such a way. By ridding our history of evil, we rid our future of it as well. Going back to My youth, I recall clearly never having terrible ideas and thoughts about anyone or life. Until, people implanted such the idea into me. It is upon my discovery about life, in which has allowed me to realize one important truth; God exists and programmed us all, with Good and righteous intent. However, God also programmed us with the ability to choose otherwise and by doing so; would result, servitude in Hell for eternity.

The very idea we are all given the ability, to create anything, within our imagination; truly creates, the possibility of sin. Thus, we must combat such evil intentions or ideas, by understanding that there is a better way of life. That way of life, is yes indeed, through our Lord Jesus Christ. I know and I believe, Jesus Christ has been reborn through me and as Michael Izzo; but even so, I don't want you to worship me; I want you all to find peace through me, instead. That same peace, stems from what I once taught long ago as Jesus Christ. That same peace, also was then, constructed by Mary M.: through Christianity. Eternity and salvation comes by, only through Christ our Lord. I as Christ today, have a much different task laid before me. I, as Michael Izzo am ordered to defeat (SATAN, Sintin, Lucifer, The Devil, etc.); by teaching, the majority of the world the simple truth of life. The truth, that we all are living on Heaven. And yet, we are all fighting over ignorance. We as people, are too afraid to admit the way in which we live is wrong! It's through these methods, I will conquer all evil; simply with my pure-words...

All that is wrong is listed nigh:

- Envy
- Gluttony
- Greed
- Lust
- Pride
- Sloth
- Wrath

One must follow such Laws:

- I am Thy Lord Thy God; Jesus Christ only!
- Thou shalt have no other Gods, other than the Holy Father or Holy Mother of God.
- No graven images or likeness, because all representation of oneself is a mere copy.
- Not take thy Lord's name in vein; meaning aloud, whether privately or publicly.
- Remember Sabbath Day; every Sunday, which represents a day to rest and of thanks.
- Honor thy Father and thy Mother; as they have honored you.
- Thou shalt not steal; nor borrow, without returning.
- Thou shalt not bear false witness; even under oath.
- Thou shalt not commit adultery – one may remarry if they are divorced/widowed. Thou shall not covet anything – even if thy neighbor gives them to you.
- Thou shall not commit murder.

Chapter 24: Section 3 – Seven deadly sins (24:3)

Envy – The desire for other's traits, status, abilities, or situation.

Gluttony – The act of consuming sustenance, way more than one requires. The very act of over indulgence for God's gift of foods and liquids; results the starvation of others, somewhere in the world.

Greed – The never ending desire of material wealth or gain, ignorant to a spiritual life.

Lust – The inordinate craving for the pleasures of the body: adultery, polygamy, & porn!

Pride – Excessive belief in one's own abilities, that interferes with the individual's recognition of the grace of God.

Sloth – The avoidance of physical or spiritual work.

Wrath – The act of rage and angry aggression towards others, opposing the idea of love.

The end of mankind, lay's within oneself, and each man is given one soul to maintain and operate; with the ability, to become eternal with God. However, within those choices lay another possibility, a life of ignorance; resulting the most sinful life, without the ability to become eternal with God. When God salvages a soul, it's because he has found great value within that lost soul, to be worthy of salvation. Once an individual is broken, they may never come into contact with such ways of life again! However, all of us are vulnerable to the demon's ways and most likely will be tried again. Keep in mind, even if we falter or fail again after salvation; one must accept the consequences for one's actions, whilst choosing to redeem thyself from such sins. If the individual doesn't react swiftly, with a positively spiritual result; then, the individual shall be tortured upon Judgment, twice as worse as they would have been. As opposed to, if they weren't saved prior to falling a second time. The very gift of choosing to be protected by and live with God, is the most powerful weapon we can use in this life. The sooner all realize this truth; the sooner, I can permanently rid us all of such persecution: created by the Devil. I understand this world has many precious ways to live in it; but, not all are fortunate enough to be in those situations. That is why it is up to each and every single one of us, to accept that choice, and to make positive change with every new day. The world has been built to a sustainable level, but not from lies. It's now time to exhaust our energy in **new ways**, in order to correct the flaws in our sustained existence.

Chapter 24: Section 4 – Marriage (24:4)

Marriage technically has two understandings; the spiritual and the humanely. Marriage in the after life, the way I know it to be is through eternal transfusion between two souls. The humanely understanding is through feelings, physical interaction with others, and what one sees for their future. When I think of spiritual marriage: I think to myself, two Angels deciding to become one divine Angel; through eternal bonding, AKA **Divine Metamorphosis**. This same bonding, transfuses their feelings, thoughts, and souls together as one divine being; while still being, individuals of themselves. The best comparison would be a Gemini: one being, with two minds. When I think of the humane understanding: I see a life contract or partnership with the person you love. This love, creates a permanent foundation for both of your futures'; including, but not limited to: Sharing all one has with each other, conception, and understanding the connection between life and eternal life through God. When I think of love, I remember what I once shared with a woman whom was unimaginably wonderful. This woman, knew about my truths and secrets; and still decided to be with me, for eternity. I understand that life isn't perfect, but that's only because society blinds us from the truths; I will someday soon, teach again... Starting with understanding, I can show you how to change our lives together, eternally. For me, I lack the one person I need in my life to trust, to rely upon, and to live and be with everyday. For me, that very sacred way of life represents my divine abilities, divine strengths, and the ability to accomplish my task of slaying all Evil. Accomplishing such a goal requires: Unconditional Love, by (2x) more, minimum; before ever having a chance in being victorious, against Evil & Hatred. Without a Queen, I can't complete my life's work and break free from all these chains set forth. Further more, I will not lead the world into the Kingdom of Heaven, without a Queen to help rule by my side. God created us originally from one another; WOMAN came from a MAN, physically/literally. Through me, you may be one with (The Father, The Son, & Thy Holy Mother's Spirit). I am the leader for this world, I shall have a Queen, and all whom will help protect the things most precious to me in this world too. Some of those things would be: Mother Nature, women, children, My teaching/truth, humanity, Heaven, & purity.

In order to comprehend that Men and Women are one and the same, but all so very different; one must understand, that attraction to something or another is a mere choice. If your sexuality is one way or another, the same rules shall be applied in terms of adultery, lust, and any other sin associated in life. If you so choose to be something, other than how you truly were meant to be; than one must accept, that it is wrong! It is only wrong, because God created all living things and most of which can reproduce. Humans however, reproduce sexually: way of intercourse between man and woman. If one chooses to be something or another outside of that; then one is choosing, to change a design within themselves. That choice, may not be wrong; but, choosing to be something you aren't, is wrong. Ultimately, you will be given forgiveness and salvation; as long as like the others, you must be sorry for your sins and understand why!

The sacred bond between you and one other person, for life, and eternity is the most holy sacred thing one can ever attain in this life. That bond, creates the gift of another's life in your hands. Additionally, God is rewarding you with a partner because he sees how you affect that person the most, and how they affect you the most. A life agreement sworn between two people, creates an unfilled void within us, and pushes us all to be better; not only for ourselves, but for our spouse and children as well. I am cursed with the inability to never stop analyzing, everyone and everything; causing me to endlessly search, for the most perfect match for me possible. That same desire, creates a world of sin and temptation around me; preventing me from ever knowing, if the choices I make are right or not. However, it's through my undying passion for unconditional love, and the faith in which God has blessed me with; I know, I will always make the choice in which God intended for me. The most unfortunate thing to see growing up in America, is the simple fact: Everyone is so independent these days, and they exploit the very idea of marriage for personal gain! That same concept, leads into other lustful and vicious acts of humanity; stemming from the opportunity to hurt others, for personal gain. As a result, humanity is slowly destroying all the good left in the world; for selfish acts of personal gain. Despite these downfalls, I've never been prevented from believing in true love; as in, perfect soul mates. It's through my relentless behavior to stimulate unconditional love, within us all; which permits me to heal the world of persecution and sin. However, such an outcome is only possible, when I find my soul mate; Mary Magdalene, reincarnated…

Chapter 24: Section 5 – Currency versus Bartering (24:5)

Currency: The circulation of money: i.e. coins, paper, or banknotes.

Bartering: The exchange of valuable objects or properties; between two members, negotiating a specific service, product, or trade.

When the average individual thinks of currency or money, they think it's normal, and it's all part of life… When I think of such things, I see a world living a lie; masked by this social propaganda, to strike control and fear in the hearts of us all. What is the point of living with God in eternal life; if we are restricted by our social status, revolving around currency? Well, there is no point and that's because God doesn't live with such restrictions, and or farfetched ideals of living. In Heaven, there is only ways of life through means of social activities, divine pursuits, and worshipping God and all he has created. These ways of life, in accordance to how things should be here and now; don't require anything, resulting: currency, popularity, or idolism. Simply, in Heaven there is no money, greed, or wrongful worship; there is only, but that of which God gives us.

Now you must be wondering: How do we promote the things, in which we like to pursue or our dreams? Simply, it's not permitted! It's not permitted because of the simple fact that idolism, capitalism, and socialism all lead to the sins of men; deriving from **GREED**. However, in Heaven our minds think and react differently, than that here on Earth. Also, our professions, passions, or so called career paths aren't chosen; they're given to us as God sees fit, or best suited for each of us individually. Living with God, also means living with your Dreams; the righteous one's, given from Jesus Christ. In Heaven, we only use bartering as a way of social interaction and as a general teaching for every day life. By trading one's services, talents, or goods for someone else's services, talents, or goods; our children, learn to become humble through the grace of God. We all become humble through bartering, because we learn that everything has a great value; for all things were given to us By God. Additionally, we learn that something of great value to us is also great value to someone else. This teaching, creates a perfect existence between all children of God within the Kingdom of Heaven. This perfect existence is thus created; because we as children of God learn we are all equal, equipped with unlimited supply of what we need to survive, equally, and together as one.

Chapter 24: Section 6 – America (24:6)

America, marks the culmination of a new era. A new era of people, attempting to create a world of peace and opportunity. However, it lacks the most important energy in order to sustain, permanent righteous life. That energy is the grace and true faith in God. It's through such a faith and comprehension of the divine life; in which permits us to enter, into a new era of life. We as citizens of this potentially great nation, all lack one mandatory aspect of life; that aspect is the truth, we have one God. That same God, gave us himself as Jesus Christ, long ago, and created a foundation of truth. That same truth, included: we're all similar and equal in many ways, beginning with the physical nature of ourselves. America is far from perfect, including the idea that we need to war with others in order to sustain peace on Earth. Truth be told, America only created a foundation for a better way of life, for the world to follow in. However, America is nothing more than a foundation! An uncompleted opportunity, for all to live with God in peace. Truth be told, America is mostly wrong as far as I'm concerned. God doesn't promote violence or war; but, America does! God doesn't promote capitalism and idolism; but, America does! God has no concern or need for money; but, America does! & God gave us Free Will, he also never said to abuse it; but, America does! As you can see from my very depictive analogies; we begin to see all the ways in which God doesn't intend for us. For example, God created everything from mere thought and men created money by mere thought. The difference is that men want to exploit, control, and plague Earth; with the creation, of false methods of sustainable life. The originating false methods, happened to be currency. Money creates the appearance of life requiring: resources, energy, work, and intelligence, etc. This creates men's idea of social class, economics, and authority. On the other hand, God creates all equal, because we are all his children. God made us all intelligent, because we are all his children. God made us all beautiful, because we are all his children. This does not mean you should rebel, act against, or attempt to comprehend everything as it should be. Within due time, God shall make us all new; permitting a righteous way of life, with Jesus Christ & Mary Magdalene. As a child of America, I've learned: No matter what we do as mortals, men and women of God; we live by sin. We live by 1% sin or 99% sin, and either way; we will all, see a Holy Judge in the end!

Chapter 24: Section 7 – God versus religion (24:7)

Who is God, or what is God? Who is religion, or what is religion? God is everything and anything; God is everyone and no one. In other words, he is everything in which is life, for he is life itself. Thus, God created the world and existence of Heaven in 7 days; resting on the seventh. In short, God created all of humanity. Humanity consists of many pieces; all creating a section, of what God consists of. We are all God's children, meaning we are all family; this family, has 12 main outcomes. All 12 outcomes, although very much different, are all correct and necessary; resulting, the reunification amongst God and all his children. For 20 centuries there have been bloodshed, deceit, domination, greed, and many other sins plagued onto man: over religion. The ironic message is that Jesus Christ taught that Love conquers all; for we are all God's children. If a religion, were to make you believe into something you don't want any part of; then how could that be correct? Additionally, we are all products of our environments; taught as they wanted us to be. The more important question instead is, who wants us to be? The answer is the Devil, or all evil! The very thought of thinking; creates, a never ending cycle of various outcomes and conclusions: Sin. These results, attempt to defer us away from Jesus Christ and all his merciful forgiving love. The same love in which will set you free or set you ablaze: upon Judgment. That same love in which the world cynically attempts to destroy.

When Jesus roamed the Earth, and began his understanding of whom and what he was; he never thought of his mission as religion. I as Jesus, also knows, that God simply speaks to us, and explains on occasion what needs to be learned: To push forward in life, while being victoriously righteous. This same motivation is/was scarce and vague, to the point of misconception at times. However, one thing was certain to Jesus: Your religion or ethnicity didn't matter when choosing to enter into him. Jesus taught to any and all who wanted to know the truth; His truth, as the son of God. I still teach, as I once taught, and my most important message to all is that it doesn't matter if you don't believe in me! The only thing that matters is that you understand: only you, can save yourself. In other words, I can't enter into thee, if yee not believe in me. If the world continues to deny the truth that all is ours, for all is Gods; then the world isn't ready to be saved. However, I'll always have room for you all within my eternal heart, blessed with unconditional love.

Chapter 24: Section 8 – How to create a new world without evil. (24:8)

Like most things in life, one must first understand, there are always two primary choices/theories in life. In this particular case, are the paths in reaching a world without evil and sin; which can only be achieved, by entering into Jesus Christ. By entering into him, he gives us the abilities, wisdom, and serenity in order to rid ourselves of such a way of an evil life. However, then there is Free Will; the ultimate preventative, from altering one's chosen path in life. In essence, there is truly only two solutions of creating a world of peace. One, is by way of <u>miraculous divinity</u> with the Powers God grants us. The second, is by way of <u>Judgment</u> over the Earth, by removing the choice for Free Will.

By way of <u>miraculous divinity</u>, means: That all in which *Revelation* states, and all that Jesus once taught, will become true. Jesus Christ however His form, whether through me or otherwise, shall reclaim this planet. By reclaiming His Holy land, he shall always Judge everyone accordingly to the laws set forth by God. By way of <u>Judgment</u>, Jesus Christ and his seven Holy Angels; can separate, the evil from the righteous, and the bad from the good. Allowing for a miraculous path of sustainable life, through peace and serenity. However, my human logic tells me that if it were as simple as Jesus returning, with an instantaneous ability to miraculously change and Judge the world; he would have already done so. I say this because ever since I was a child, I thought of ways how to fix my life, making it more peaceful, and the lives of others. Ultimately resulting, the reasons in which I created my company. However, I have yet been able to do such miraculous things because it can't happen instantaneously; due to the restrictions, left by **Free Will**. Such restrictions, prevent me from solely choosing to heal the world and its entire people. The world and its entire people, must choose to want to be healed by me; which stems the problem. For the simple fact, that **Free Will** prevents me from persuading people otherwise, to know, and see the truth leads me to the realization: No matter what miracles I may perform someday, no matter what good I do, and no matter how I appear; the world will never completely change, by following my path alone. Having accepted this truth, made me ponder long and hard on how to correct the world; if they choose, not to accept the truth of God. That acceptance, granted me the idea of massive unity; based on, a Heavenly status granted to each and every one of us. This Heavenly status in other words, would be the culmination of a united world; with the recognition, there is only one true King & Queen, and all others are Angels, within Their-kingdom. Whom are given, specific tasks and teachings; in order to sustain equality and life amongst all. In order to successfully create a sustainable life here on Earth, without the idea of it happening miraculously; I must follow, such precautions and steps to create such an existence…

First, I must find my wife; the reincarnation of Mary. Second, she and I must then travel relentlessly; finding the 144,000 in which God prophesized, would come to our aid. Third, our followers of Thy Lord Jesus Christ; through me, here and now, would rally together, and create the realms of Heaven and Hell. Thus, these created realms are how we would sustain life on Earth. Sustaining life, according to how I was designed to know through God's wisdom. Thus, each individual would be Judged, similar to that of the Bible. For example, when Judgment occurs in this sense of thinking; each individual, will be faced with three potential outcomes: Placement within the Kingdom of Heaven, exile to the place of Hell, or death by way of torturous pain based on their sins. Let's begin with the understanding of how all shall be Judged? The answer is simple: Due to the modern era and way of life, it has created a physical and virtual history on all our lives. A history in which can't be purchased or wiped clean; and a history in which has recorded all the secrets of each and every one of us, for the last several centuries. I shall utilize such avenues of technology, writing, and history in order to accurately determine; what it is, each one of us have done in our lives: whether good or bad. There is no stone that won't be unturned, and there shall be no truth in which won't be uncovered from my grasp; when the time comes. As God instructs me to understand, such a time is coming; and thee who hold the book of God, shall be the one worthy to rule them all. I believe, that same book is being created this very second; underlying the rules and regulations of God, as God intends.

What happens upon Judgment? If you are a good person and followed the life of Jesus Christ; well, you then receive sanctuary, within his Heart, and within the Kingdom of Heaven; to live in eternally, with God himself. Such a placement, lands you within one of the 9 realms of Heaven. Each realm, has a higher ranking than the other; each realm, requires different eternal tasks of the soul; and each realm, is strategically placed throughout the Kingdom of Heaven – meaning, within Earth and Space. Each realm shall be discussed after this chapter; because each realm requires, specific allocation of comprehension, in order to know if you may be granted such a life, within them.

If you are exiled from God's presence; means, that you haven't done enough evil or sin, to be put to death by way of eternal punishment. But, yee be worthy of a life without anything or anyone. Such a life is also referred to as "**Purgatory**." In order to be exiled from God's Holy lands and presence; for a desolate, confusing, and difficult existence of life; one must live a life of neutrality. The act of not choosing a life of God or evil, but remained neutral instead. Additionally, it means you chose to do badly and you choose to do well; but you had no understanding of your choices, and chose to remain ignorant to the overall concept of life and existence: as God created. As you chose such a life of blindness; the overall punishment is a life of isolationism, in a desolate place in which has no escape, and hardly a means to survive.

If you are put to death, through torturous punishment; it is because you lived a life of sin, with the Devil, in all that you chose to do. Further more, there is no redemption for the likes of people whom chose to live a life of sin. Each sin, comes with a specific eternal form of punishment; suited for such a life of sins, in which was committed. Each sin committed in one's life, amplifies the punishment; for yee did not learn from one sin, then one must learn twice as hard from all sins committed. I as a merciful God, whom chooses not to live a life with violence; will indeed, have to appoint an executioner, to fulfill the punishments ordered onto all those of the Devils worshippers. This executioner, will not be accountable for his tasks. His punishment is to fulfill these tasks requested of his Lord Thy God, instead.

No matter what I want or choose from these three preordained paths of existence; God has chosen, what he desires for the worlds outcome. Such an outcome, can and only be revealed by God himself; when the timing is just perfect, because God is perfect and only acts in ways of such a thought. Additionally, as I have spent many years meditating upon my purpose and my life; I continue to sit and await the sign, I need, in order to fulfill my destiny. This same sign, will either grant me the gift of divinity; or it will show me who has the key to salvation, in this time of need for us all. No matter what we all choose to believe; there will be a time of reckoning and Judgment, against all sinners...

Chapter 24: Section 9 – 9 realms of Heaven or 9 realms of Hell? (24:9)

The ultimate question to be asking is, what do I mean that there are 9 realms of Heaven and 9 realms of hell? More importantly, why is it a choice? Let's face it, humans didn't create the pyramid scheme of society; God did! He is top Realm, Realm 9, and top of the Pyramid. No one of Heaven, can enter into Realm 9; except, his family- his wife Mary, Jesus, Mary M., & Michael, and their chosen **Seraphim's**. The 9th Realm is entirely for the creator, his family; and guardians, whom secure all their safety & privacy.

The 8th Realm consists of "God's Miraculous Guardians" – **Cherubim's:** Which are a highly trained, powerful, passionately devoted, loyal beyond atoms in exchange, and will die protecting all that is God's. This Realm, consists of preordained and pre-selected individuals in which God has created; because they can only be, children of the Son of God. Only Jesus' direct children, can be chosen to be of the 8th Realm of Heaven.

The 7th Realm is of the highest rewarded to Angels/humans of Heaven/Earth, which are **Thrones**. This reward is granted to those whom live a life with no sins committed, because they gave their lives to Jesus. In return, they're purified and chosen as an Apostle for the son of Man. The Thrones are the representatives of the 12 sections of the world. Each representative is an Angel of pure humility, peace, and submission.

The 6th Realm consists of **Dominions.** These Angels have lived a life with knowing one sin and have repented, being granted leadership. This leadership, allows for them to regulate the duties of the Angels; making known, God's commandments.

The 5th Realm consists of **Virtues**. Virtues are brightly, shining ones; whom control the elements. It's because they have lived with two deadly sins; they understand the destruction, as a result. It's through such knowledge in which they are granted control over nature, including: the sun, planets, moons, and our seasons. Additionally, Virtues are also blessed with the gift of miracles: providing courage, valor, honor, & grace.

The 4th Realm consists of **Powers.** Powers are the warriors against evil, defending the cosmos and all humans; also known as the <u>Potentates</u>. The chief's consist of Samael and Camael, whom are both Angels of Darkness. These Angels live with the **3** most evil of sins: Greed, Pride, & Wrath. They serve only to protect those too weak to fight evil.

The 3rd Realm consists of a special branch of Angels: **Thee Archangels.** The seven Holy Trumpets of God. Thee Archangels, each make up one power/portion of God; creating, limitless thoughts of possibilities. When they're united or metaphysically combined; they create a near symmetric replica of God, in all his glory. These Archangels represent the seven guardian Angels: sworn to worship, serve, & protect God's creations. Thee Archangels, are also the Seven Angels given the Holy trumpets of God. Archangels are significant and important, equally in different ways, and represent a strategic sequence of events in which creates a New World. Their purposes' are very important, because they protect all that is God's and will unite upon Judgment Day; creating, *The Realm of Eternal*. The Realm of Eternal is the existence of All Realms; co-existing simultaneously, throughout existence, for eternity. Saint Michael is the Prince of Heaven, heir to the throne; upon destruction of all evil, AKA Judgment Day. All Archangels, can choose their paths in existence. Similar to humans, they are bound by Free Will and Sin...

1 - **Michael**, being of the highest rank of all Archangels and Angels; he is also the first to sound His trumpet. Michael starts the end, which creates the new. All must be Judged by Raguel, before they may enter into the Kingdom of Heaven in which Saint Michael will rule over. The Kingdom of Heaven is also known as The Realm of Eternal.

2 - **Gabriél** is the second, sounding Her trumpet; demonstrating, God's strength. Gabriél assists Saint Michael, as he delivers the final blow into **Satan Lucifer**.

3 - **Raphael** sounds the third trumpet, healing all from the devastating strength of God. After destruction, all which is God's, shall be healed, and made anew by Raphael.

4 - **Jophiél** sounds the fourth trumpet, presenting all the beauty of God; after being healed. Jophiél creates The Realm of Eternal; allowing for those saved, to live peacefully.

5 - **Chamuél** sounds the fifth trumpet, reassuring life that all we've seen, comes from God through love. Through love, Chamuél guides us as we seek forgiveness from God.

6 - **Raguel** sounds the sixth trumpet, calling all those to be Judged; by Justice of Fairness. Raguel prepares the way for Saint Michael to lead, *The Realm of Eternal*. Raguel separates those who worship Jesus Christ, from those that do not!

7 - **Uriél** sounds the seventh trumpet, opening the pit of fire and brimstone. Uriél is the light of God and the divine fire of life. All life dies, forcing the soul to return to God's fire, and ceasing to exist; allowing those who repent to live eternally with God in Heaven.

[Holy Trumpet 1] Saint Michael - *"Who is like God," "Like unto God," "Who is like the Divine"* is the highest of Archangels, the leader; and is in charge of protection, courage, strength, truth, and integrity; he acts as the Prince Seraph. Saint Michael is also Jesus' son, Prince of Heaven/grandson of God. Saint Michael is the Chief Archangel; clothed in indestructible armor & equipped with a *flaming-ice sword.* He acts as the protector against evil, defending humanity in battle, and is the heir to the throne. Saint Michael Conquers Satan, was in the Garden of Eden teaching Adam farming and tending to his family, and spoke to Moses on Mt. Sinai. Saint Michael is Jesus' first born, is one with Jesus, and is destined to rule in his father's miraculously glorious name. When Saint Michael is amongst you, he will illuminate bright blue or purple flashes. Saint Michael is who I am; I'm also Michael Thee Archangel, disguised as a human as Michael Lee Edward Izzo. I have been born to fulfill my fathers legacy; creating an eternal Kingdom of Heaven, for all of God's chosen children.

[Holy Trumpet 2] Saint Gabriél (Female) – *"Strength of God;" "The Divine is my strength;" "God is my strength"* is the messenger Angel or the messenger for God. Saint Gabriél is one of the two highest-ranking of Angels; next to Saint Michael. She is powerful, strong, determined, and aids us all by motivating us into action. It is believed, Gabriél is the wife of Saint Michael; His perfect equal. She contains the ability to shape-shift, into male entities, or other species alike. Gabriél is known for visiting Elisabeth and Mary, presenting knowledge of their births; John the Baptist and Jesus of Nazareth. Saint Gabriél helps us in our times of need, searching for true guidance towards God.

[Holy Trumpet 3] Saint Raphael - *"Healing power of God," "The Divine has healed," "God heals"* is the health of God, and he is a powerful healer for all life; humans and animals alike. Saint Raphael is mentioned at times, assisting Saint Michael in ridding evil spirits. Saint Raphael is sweet, loving, and can be noticed when seeing sparkles of green/red light. Saint Raphael is best known for assisting Tobias within his travels. Saint Raphael is one of the three Angels, mentioned by name in scripture.

[Holy Trumpet 4] Saint Jophiél *"Beauty of God"* represents art and beauty; patron of the arts and creates beauty. Saint Jophiél was present in the Garden of Eden, watched over Noah's sons, and helps guide us on a Holy path of enlightenment. Saint Jophiél illuminates creativity, through ideas and energy.

[Holy Trumpet 5] Saint Chamuél *"He who sees God," "He who seeks God"* is the Archangel of Love. Saint Chamuél helps us through tough times of sorrow, bringing the joy of love into our hearts; he is also known for helping us find our soul mate. Call upon Saint Chamuél in a time of despair, depression, sadness, Judgmental pessimism, or any negative emotions to heal you from such suffering. Saint Chamuél has also been referred to as Saint Anthony: whom helps us with finding peace, our careers, life path, & lost items.

[Holy Trumpet 6] Saint Raguel *"Friend of God"* is the Archangel of fairness and justice; he oversees all the other Archangels and Angels. Saint Raguel has also been known as "Zadkiel;" whom is often known for assisting Michael in battle, alongside Jophiél. Saint Raguel is the one whom disciplines Angels if they act with improper deeds. Saint Raguel maintains harmony and order amongst all that is living. He is the underdog, and represents the underdog; assisting with empowerment and respect. Allegedly Saint Raguel is also the Angel of Death, by assisting God to serve Judgment upon all life.

[Holy Trumpet 7] Saint Uriél *"God is light," "God's light," Fire of God"* is of the wisest of Thee Archangels because of his intellectual information, practical solutions, and creative insights; while he remains, subtle in demeanor. Saint Uriél is most known for informing Noah of the flood in which God had intended. He birthed the knowledge and practice of Alchemy from thin air, illuminates situations, and delivers prophetic information. Saint Uriél's knowledge and expertise includes: Divine Magic, problem solving, spiritual understanding, alchemy, Earth's weather, studies, and writings….. Saint Uriél controls the elements of Earth. Saint Uriél doesn't have a specific light of illumination, because he represents all energies of light…

The 2nd Realm consists of **Angels** whom are humans, in which repented, and were saved through Jesus Christ. Angels were those of the humans whom lived a life following and believing in Jesus Christ. Those of which whom understand we sin, for the mind is what creates sin; and it's because of such a restriction, which requires us to live a life of purity and repent for such sins. Angels consist of one of the larger Realms of Heaven; which ultimately, instigated the war. Angels were different amongst all the other Choirs of Angels too. Angels specifically, were given human life with the gift of Free Will.

However, it was because Adam and Eve ignored Fathers rules, which created sin. **Angels** have the option to become human, or humans to become Angels. No other Choirs of Angel can choose their own path; except, but a few named specifically; including, all Thee Archangels. Angels have a life of servitude and worship to the lord in the eternal life. Being granted eternity with Jesus Christ, Angels become reborn into their spiritual form; as Jesus transformed into, after His Ascension. Jesus Christ was chosen to be the first of the Angels; whom became human, to resurrect, and to show humans the truth of their existence and purpose. Angels are also the closest to the Realm of sins, which is the 1st realm of Angels. Angels being humans, bound by Free Will; are vulnerable to persuasion of Powers, from Thee Archangels or from Thee Darkdemons. Angels are known for being neutral, because they are Judged by their overall amount of sins in accordance with God's laws. Most Angels, never fully comprehend their choices. Their choices also average out a neutral bias. Even with the Crucifixion of Jesus Christ, Angels still don't fully comprehend their purpose in life or comprehend all he taught...

The 1st Realm of Heaven and lowest ranked Choir of Angels are the **Principalities.** They are most known for living with all deadly sins; overall, for the majority of their existence. They have grown hostile and hateful towards God and humans, because of the amount of sin in which they have absorbed. Their sole purpose for creation was to absorb the sins of existence and humanity; while protecting, all that God loves. In other words, the Principalities are spiritual orbs/wisps, whom can only be described as energy; unfortunately, bad energy. Principalities weren't always full of sin. In fact, they represent all matter and energy of life. Even with their hatred for God due to sin; nonetheless, they are ruled by Jesus Christ. When Lucifer rebelled and started the war against God; he stole the Principalities to build his Demon army, with their energy. For nearly 32 centuries, humanity has nearly failed to understand and appreciate God's Love. However, upon the 2nd Coming of Christ, all the Principalities will instantaneously revert back into positive energy. Without this Realm, without its existence of purpose; life, could not sustain itself, and would cause it to cease existence.

HELL: A place **opposite** to that of Heaven; ruled by a Rogue Angel, whom used to be God's best friend and Brother. Satan, designed Hell in the image of Earths sins…

The 9 Realms of Hell are all as beautiful and creative as the 9 Realms of Heaven. The only difference, is that Hell is all the horrific beauty in existence. The Realms are mostly a mystery, especially to Earth. For over a millennia, Hell has been a place most don't know about; except, for those from there. Its master goes by many names, and each Realm is as unique as those of Heaven. Everything of existence has a perfect equaled opposite; resulting, a negative balance. This balance, creates The Devils Darkness; which is, the opposite of God's Light. As I described each of the 9 realms in Heaven; think of each Realm of Hell, very similar in nature, but the opposite. Each of the Realms, lives with a high amount of Sins. Each Realm, consists of a strict army commanded by Lucifer. Hell serves one purpose: Lucifer's purpose, bound to him by the Judgment of God… Lucifer was once a Power of God, who turned Rogue, and betrayed all he ever knew. As there are seven Archangels, there are six Archdemons too. Archdemons dwell in the Realm of Minauros, they're special amongst the other Realms of Hell, and is also ruled by Satan's son; Mammon. The actual creatures, monsters, and demons that exist throughout these realms: are too fierce, horrific, and demonic to truly imagine. Thus, I will not describe them at all. I assure you, it's not a place you as a human want to be; EVER! Further more, humans can go to Hell and many do; but, not nearly enough to be half of how many demons that are in Hell. Humans only go to Hell, upon their death, and on Judgment Day. During the medium plane of existence; which is nothingness, they await their sentencing from God. In other words, the gates of Hell are currently sealed. Upon Judgment Day; the gates will be opened & resealed, once all evil is Judged. The 9 realms of Hell, which were also published in the *Dungeons and Dragons* game are listed below:

1. Tiamat, Lord of Avernus – Realm 1
2. Dispater, Lord of Dis – Realm 2
3. Mammon, Lord of Minauros – Realm 3
4. Belial, Lord of Phlegethos – Realm 4
5. Geryon, Lord of Stygia – Realm 5
6. Baalzebul, Lord of Malbolge – Realm 6
7. Baalzebul, Lord of Maladomini – Realm 7
8. Mephistopheles, Lord of Cania 8
9. Asmodeus – Lord of Nessus – Realm 9

Chapter 24: Section 10 – 10 Commandments of Judgment (24:10)

The 10 Commandments of Judgment, were created with existence of all life in Heaven. No matter which Realm, Galaxy, or Species the laws of God all apply to everything in which God created. Sometime during Moses' life, God had visited him, and explained to him the laws of God. God explained to Moses: Who and why he was created, and that humanity was meant to abide by these following laws…

- I am Thy Lord Thy God; Jesus Christ is the Son I give humanity, to rule over.
- Thou shalt have no other Gods, other than the Holy Father or Holy Mother of God.
- No graven images or likeness, because all representation of oneself is a mere copy.
- Not take thy Lord's name in vein; meaning aloud, whether privately or publicly.
- Remember Sabbath Day; every Sunday, which represents a day to rest and of thanks.
- Honor thy Father and thy Mother; as they have honored you.
- Thou shalt not steal; nor borrow, without returning.
- Thou shalt not bear false witness; even under oath.
- Thou shalt not commit adultery – one may remarry if they are divorced/widowed. Thou shall not covet anything – even if thy neighbor gives them to you.
- Thou shall not commit murder.

After God had given the laws to Moses, engraved upon stone; God told Moses to let the people know the law. As Moses prepared to hike back to the town, God finished by telling him "Complete what I request of thee and yee will be forgiven for thy sins." Moses didn't waste a seconds notice, after having been with God for hours on Mt. Sinai. As he delivered the laws to the Jews; he began to prepare for their voyage, escaping through the Red Sea. By delivering these laws, God tried to solve humanities flaw; which is Free Will. Free Will permits humanity to constantly evolve and change. As a result, the laws weren't enough to correct humanity from perishing by way of sin. God realized, he needed to create a permanent stage of evolution for humanity. This solution and stage of life was created through His only son, Jesus Christ. Jesus was born to explain the truth of existence to humanity; die by Crucifixion, which created a path to Heaven from Earth; and change history, by discovering the path of eternal life in multiple forms. Jesus Christ is the leader of Heaven, his Kingdom is Earth, and through him humans are eternal.

My entire life has been an extreme voyage of life's ultimate tests. These tests, were designed by God in order to prepare me for a day of days. This day, would require, 30 years of human existence to comprehend the very capacities of God's intellect… Through a human life, it takes the mind many years to understand your souls' purpose, or mission from God. Our souls, were created since the beginning of existence; our bodies, are a different story all together. Additionally, we as humans are part of God's extensive family and are designed with several basics. Our first basic is to live a life of faith; meaning, accept the best truth in your life because God guides us all. That truth is learned within our youth; but never comprehended, until we are mature adults, and I'm speaking of many topics. For some however, this maturity takes many decades to develop. Similar to me developing my understanding, of my own purpose, and life as a human as a son of God. Starting with, understanding that our lives co-exist in a fake reality. It's only through my hardship and spiritual awakening, throughout 2012; that I have been permitted and strategically prepared, to take leadership amongst our overall demeanors. This means, that I have grown mentally, physically, and spiritually to the point of miraculous evolution, beyond complete comprehension. This evolution, creates an existence of perplexed divinity in which reflects an opposite image of Earth; a positive image. Think of life on Earth in a similar nature as how a plant grows: Requiring sunlight/energy, water, and nutrients in order to create photosynthesis. Life for humans is very similar: Requiring food to survive, experience in life to comprehend our purposes, maturity, and self sacrifice to decide a life of Positive faith or Negative faith. Ultimately, we only have two paths in which we can pursue; each path is given a different codex of life, per individual, and each have a permanent result upon our expiration.

In this form, I am human, and I'm confined by the same parameters as you are. The only differences between us are our appearance, souls, minds, and destinies… However, my destiny requires more service of me, and requires me to one day lead The Realm of Eternal. Life on Earth is quite complex, compared to life in The Eternal Realm. The Earth has countries, hatred, social status, currency, sin, leaders, death, etc. Heaven however: Is a tranquil place, a never ending place, consistently bright for eternity, warm, happy, invigorating, humbly pleasant, magical, divine, spiritual, family orientated, community orientated; and is a place in which is ruled by faith, not by individuals...

EPILOGUE

I am thy Lord, thy God, and I have returned to reclaim my paradise. Reclaim this existence, for all those pure and righteous. I am Saint Michael Thee Archangel; reborn as a human, by the name of Michael Lee Edward Izzo. It has taken me 25 years of an enduring life, to comprehend my true purpose. With every new day, I continue to unfold all that God intends for me to fulfill. Most of what I must accomplish: requires several more years of discovery, learning, triumph, and gathering of righteous Angels. It is through my relentless behavior, in which I will succeed and be victorious over all evil. I vowed long ago, to never fail my Lord; while requesting, that he grant me with the strength, wisdom, and forgiveness to complete such unorthodox tasks. It is my destiny to rid evil from all of existence, for eternity. By doing so, I shall enslave all of Lucifer's followers within The Eternal Void.

As I have finally completed this very book, the book of God; I can begin my ministry once again... I have been forced to forget all I have come to know, love, enjoy, and foresee in my life; because all these things were preventing me, from fulfilling my Divine Oath. It wasn't until, I had found and lost a near replica of Mary, in a woman named Shaylin Jaquez; when I have lost my last bit of hope. Not hope in God, but hope in avoiding my destiny… This occurred because Lucifer attempted to use Shaylin against me, to destroy me, and prevent me from fulfilling my oath. As a result, I have decided to let her go; until, all evil is banished from all things in existence. It's through my selfless acts, I am now prepared to commence my ministry; rallying the 12 tribes of humanity; and summoning the end of days! My journey shall commence in the spring of 2014, with the publication of this very novel. I shall then, journey throughout Europe, the Mid-East, and other sections of the world. Upon my travels: I shall teach, heal, aid, and prepare all those worthy for the end of days! These end of days; shall only be the end, for all those Evil! If you're pure hearted, if you have repented, and if you praise Thy Lord Jesus Christ as your Savior; then, and only then, you shall be saved! Now say this with me... In thy Holy Lord's name, Jesus Christ, I pray; protect us from all Evil and deliver us from the temptations of the Devil, Amen! Follow me at **http://www.mizeryrecords.com**

Angelic Riddles

12 tribes, 12,000 souls each tribe; how many souls proclaimed to have survived? 144,000 destined for rapture, written over 10 centuries ago; however, many less humans alive then, so how many to be Rapture'd in the 21st century? 432,000 people will come to My aid, but how many are required to slay Satan?

The Lord will test us through thick and thin! The Lord will hurt us and then heal us; to teach us, what we have yet to learn. The Lord is merciful, but also vengeful. What is the ultimate test of human life?

It is alleged, I once had 12 apostles. It is argued, Mary Magdalene was not one of them. It is a fact: **Judas Iscariot** betrayed me for mere coins and committed suicide near after. It is an argued fact: I was married to Mary Magdalene. Whom is the thirteenth Apostle?

If there are 9 Realms of Heaven and 9 Realms of Hell; how many Realms are in-between?

7 Archangels; wield, 7 Angelic Weapons; equipped with, 7 alternate Powers, and each Angel has at least two wings; how many beasts do they create as one?

If it takes 2-lives and 2,000 years to create The-New-Heaven; how many years does it take to awaken from such a travesty? *Hint:* It is not the same age as Jesus…

Since Jesus Christ is our Lord and Saviour, whom is the direct Son of God; then, whom is **Michael Thee Archangel** and why is he equal to that of Jesus Christ?

All answers can be found on our website at **www.mizeryrecords.com/the2ndcoming**

Here are some other products you can purchase from Michael "MIZeRY" Izzo:

Title: 15 Years of My Life

Artist: MIZeRY

Distributor: *Island Def Jam Digital Distribution*

Record label: *MIZeRY ReCORDS*

Publishing: *Tunecore Publishing*

Release date: *MIZeRY ReCORDS* © May 17th, 2011

Photography by: Zack Meader

Art direction & design by: Michael "MIZeRY" Izzo

-For all availability and stores visit: www.mizeryrecords.com/home

Title: Til' Death Do Us Part

Artist: MIZeRY

Distributor: ***Island Def Jam Digital Distribution***

Record label: ***MIZeRY ReCORDS***

Publishing: ***Tunecore Publishing***

Release date: ***MIZeRY ReCORDS*** **© November 11th, 2011**

Photography by: Dayne Mahadeo

Art direction & design by: Michael "MIZeRY" Izzo

-For all availability and stores visit: www.mizeryrecords.com/home

-To purchase, any and all music albums, T-Shirts, Products, or Logos please visit our website at www.mizeryrecords.com/products

I want to thank you all for your patience, trust, and faithful surrender to God!

Lightning Source UK Ltd.
Milton Keynes UK
UKOW07n1521071217
314055UK00004B/90/P